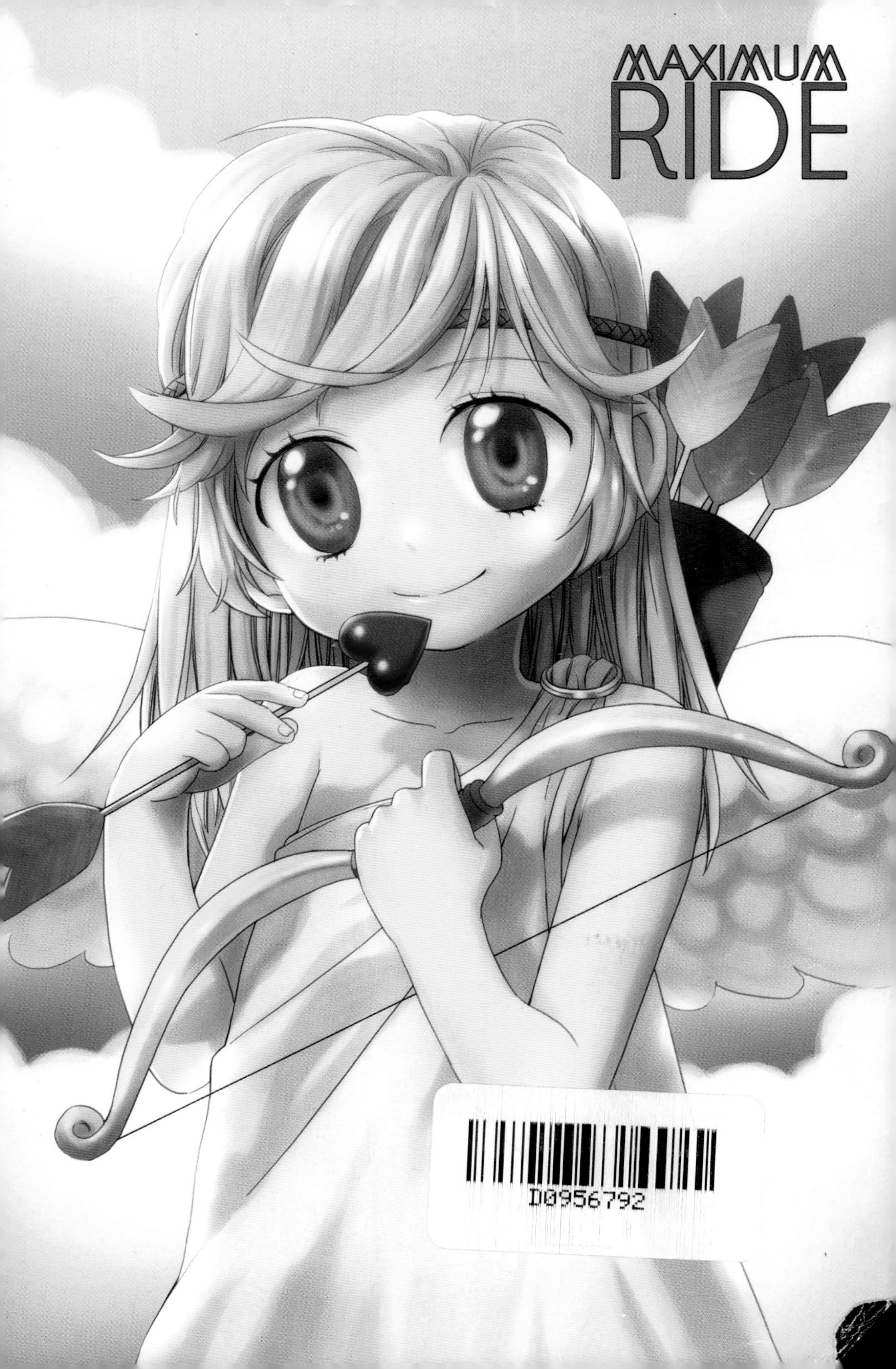
MAXIMUM
RIDE

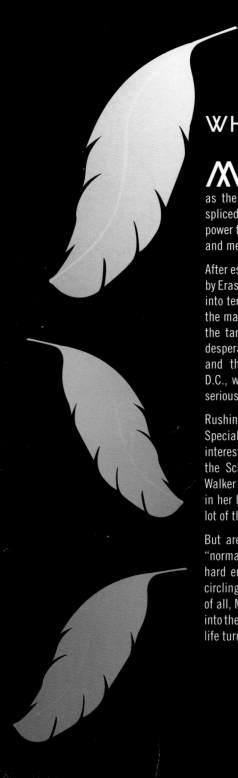

WHAT CAME BEFORE

Max and her flock are genetic experiments. Created by a mysterious lab known only as the "School," their genetic codes have been spliced with avian DNA, giving them wings and the power to soar. What they lack are homes, families, and memories of a real life.

After escaping from the School, the flock is hunted by Erasers, agents of the School who can transform into terrifying wolf creatures, and Jeb Batchelder, the man they once thought of as a father. Despite the targets on their backs, though, the flock is desperate to learn about their individual pasts, and their inquiries lead them to Washington, D.C., where the Erasers are waiting and Fang is seriously injured!

Rushing Fang to the hospital, the flock meets Special Agent Anne Walker of the FBI who's interested in learning everything they know about the School. In exchange for information, Agent Walker offers Max and her "siblings" a safe haven in her home — even going so far as to enroll the lot of them in a proper school!

But are Max and the others really cut out for a "normal" life? School crushes and jealousies are hard enough to deal with, but there are Erasers circling, a duplicate Max and, most concerning of all, Max keeps having visions of herself turning into the thing that she hates most! Is domesticated life turning the flock soft...?

CHARACTER INTRODUCTION

MAXIMUM RIDE

Max is the eldest member of the flock, and the responsibility of caring for her comrades has fallen to her since Jeb Batchelder's apparent death. Tough and uncompromising, she's willing to put everything on the line to protect her "family."

FANG

Only slightly younger than Max, Fang is one of the elder members of the flock. Cool and reliable, Fang is Max's rock. He may be the strongest of them all, but most of the time it is hard to figure out what is on his mind.

IGGY

Being blind doesn't mean that Iggy is helpless. He has not only an incredible sense of hearing, but also a particular knack (and fondness) for explosives.

NUDGE

Motormouth Nudge would probably spend most days at the mall if not for her pesky mutant-bird-girl-being-hunted-by-wolf-men problem.

GASMAN

The name pretty much says it all. The Gasman (or Gazzy) has the art of flatulence down to a science. He's also Angel's biological big brother.

ANGEL

The youngest member of the flock and Gazzy's little sister, Angel seems to have some peculiar abilities — mind reading for example.

ARI

Just seven years old, Ari is Jeb's son but was transformed into an Eraser. He appears to have a particular axe to grind with Max.

JEB BATCHELDER

The flock's former benefactor, Jeb was a scientist at the School before helping the flock to make their original escape.

MAXIMUM RIDE

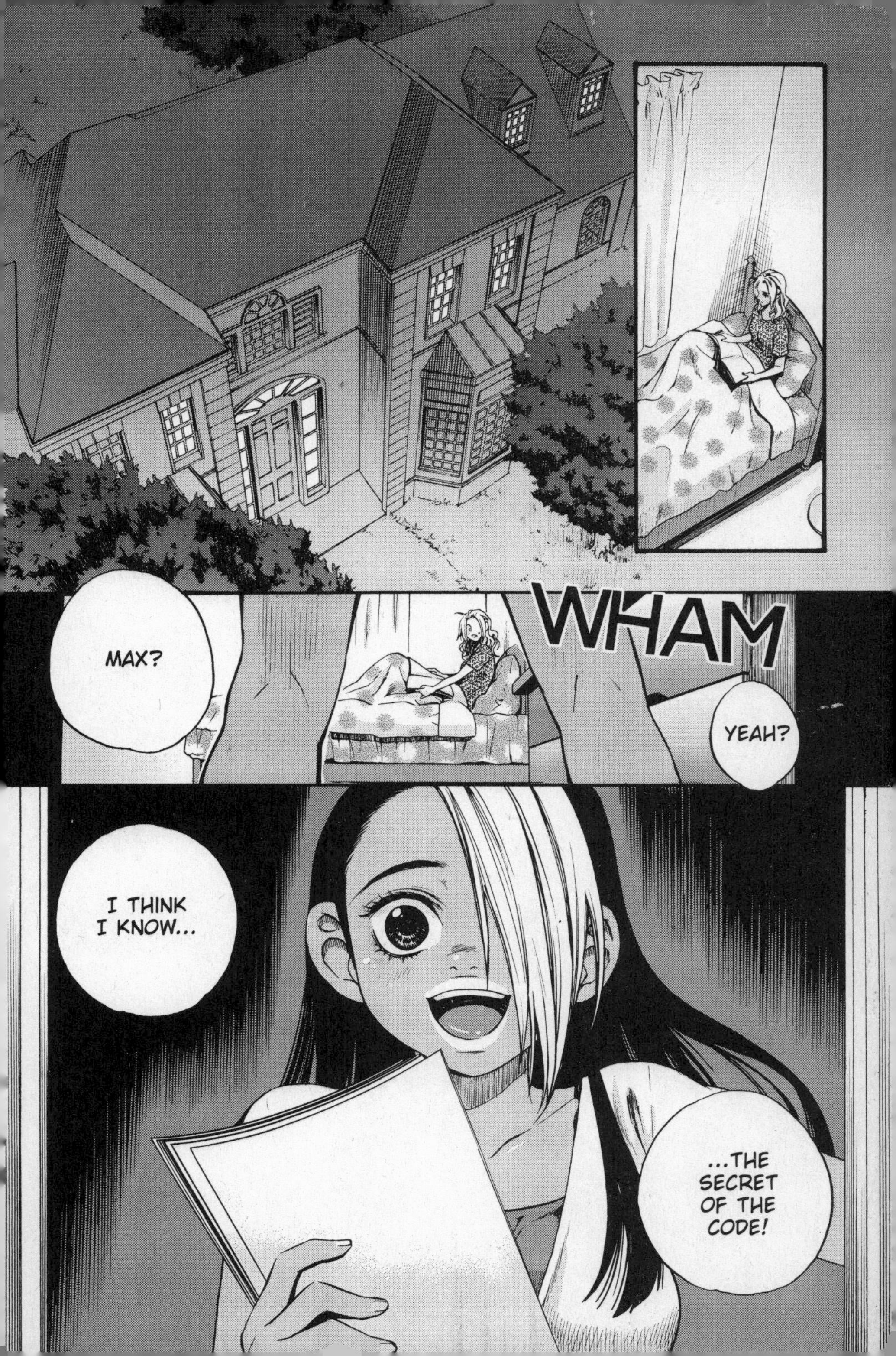
MAX?
WHAM
YEAH?
I THINK I KNOW...
...THE SECRET OF THE CODE!

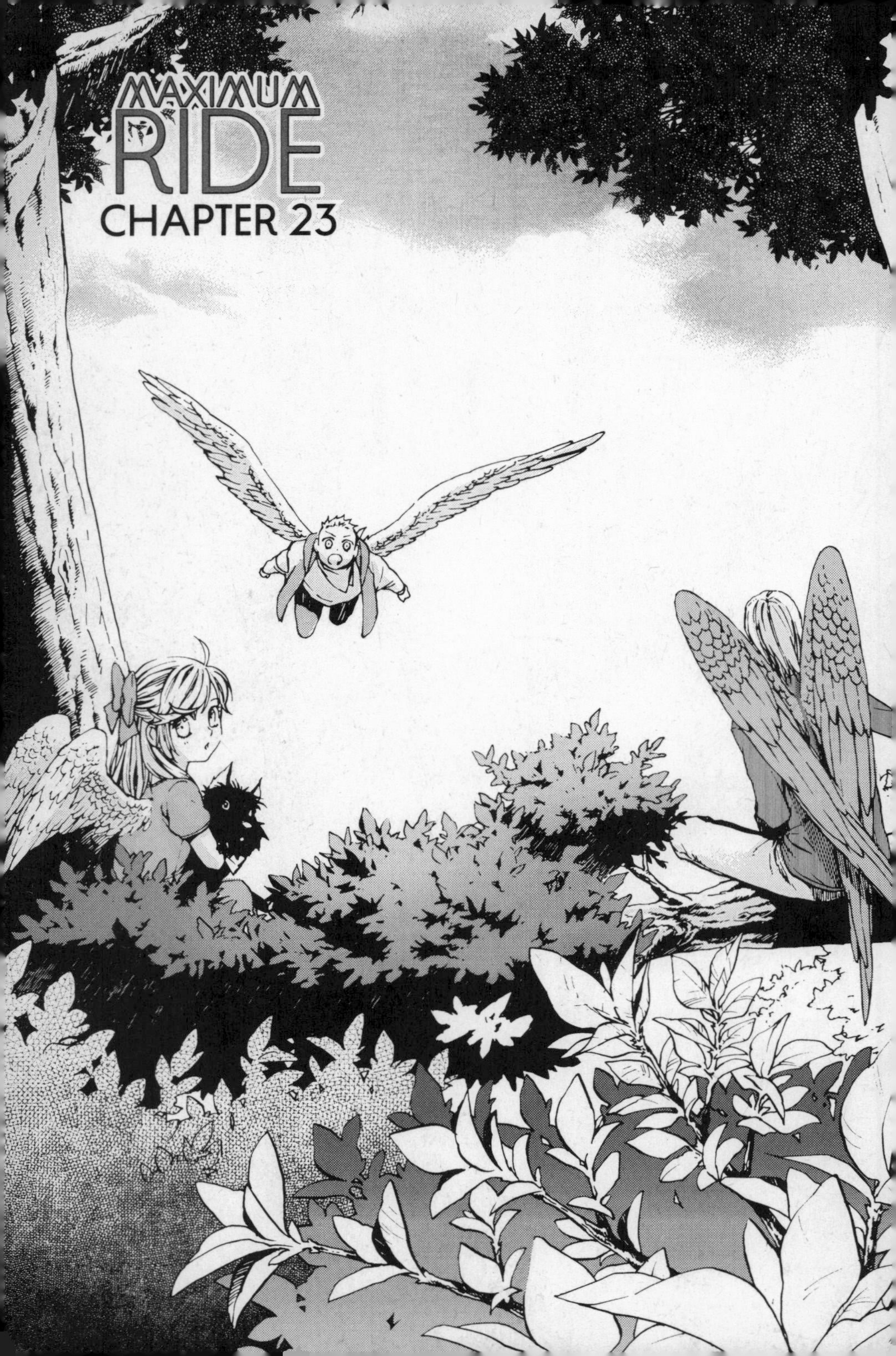
MAXIMUM RIDE
CHAPTER 23

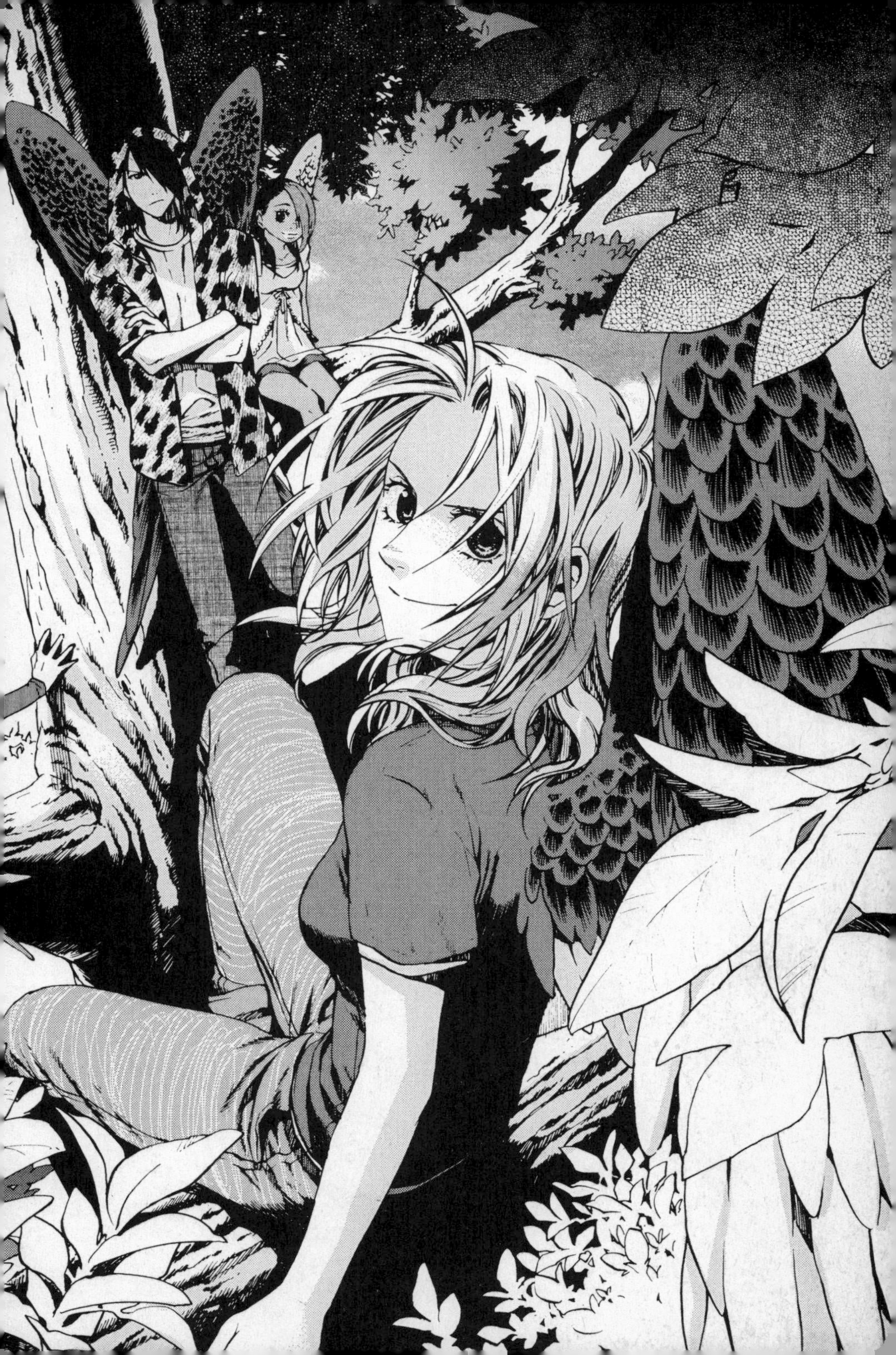

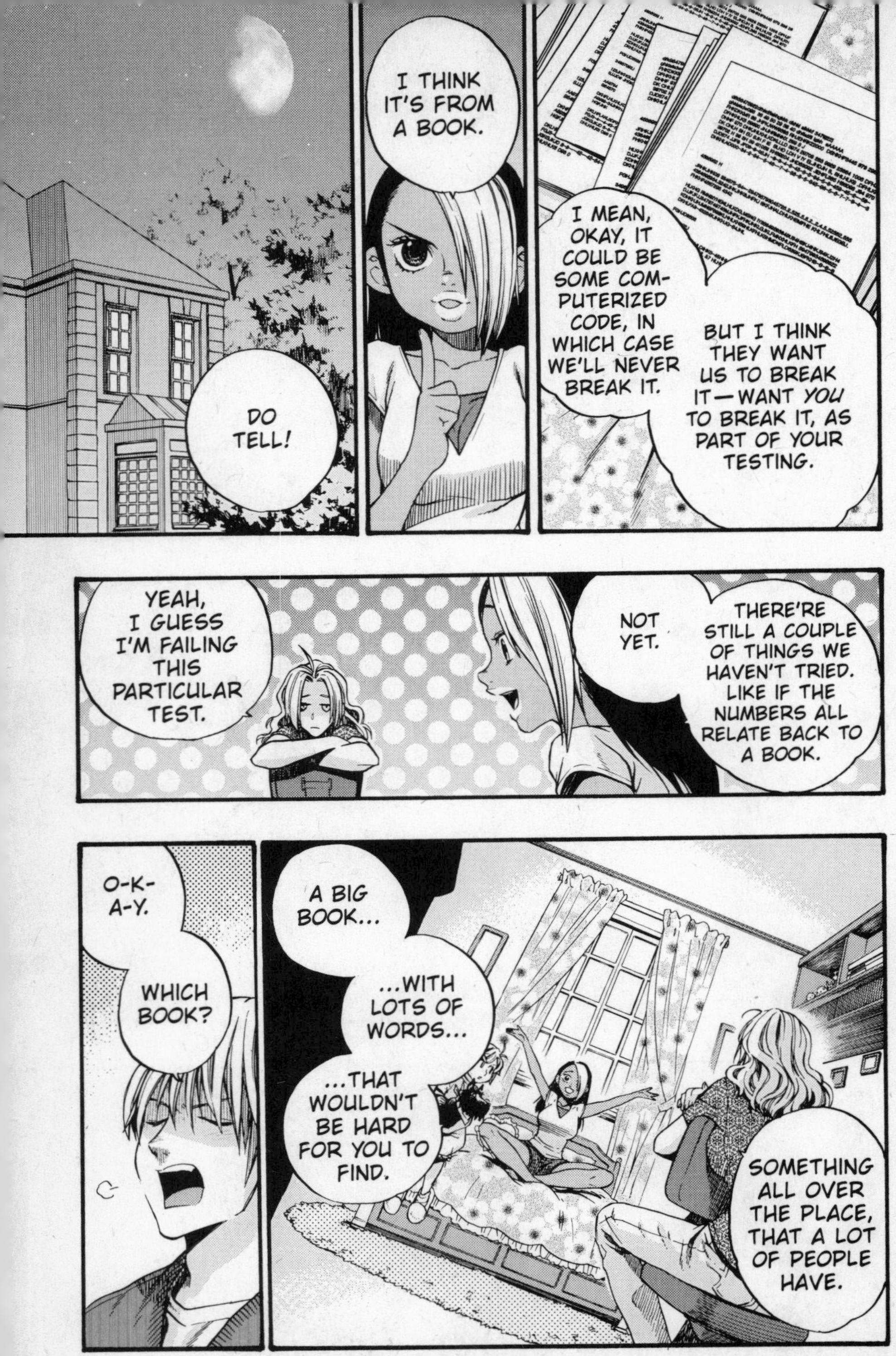
DO TELL!
I THINK IT'S FROM A BOOK.
I MEAN, OKAY, IT COULD BE SOME COM-PUTERIZED CODE, IN WHICH CASE WE'LL NEVER BREAK IT.
BUT I THINK THEY WANT US TO BREAK IT—WANT *YOU* TO BREAK IT, AS PART OF YOUR TESTING.
YEAH, I GUESS I'M FAILING THIS PARTICULAR TEST.
NOT YET.
THERE'RE STILL A COUPLE OF THINGS WE HAVEN'T TRIED. LIKE IF THE NUMBERS ALL RELATE BACK TO A BOOK.
O-K-A-Y.
WHICH BOOK?
A BIG BOOK...
...WITH LOTS OF WORDS...
...THAT WOULDN'T BE HARD FOR YOU TO FIND.
SOMETHING ALL OVER THE PLACE, THAT A LOT OF PEOPLE HAVE.

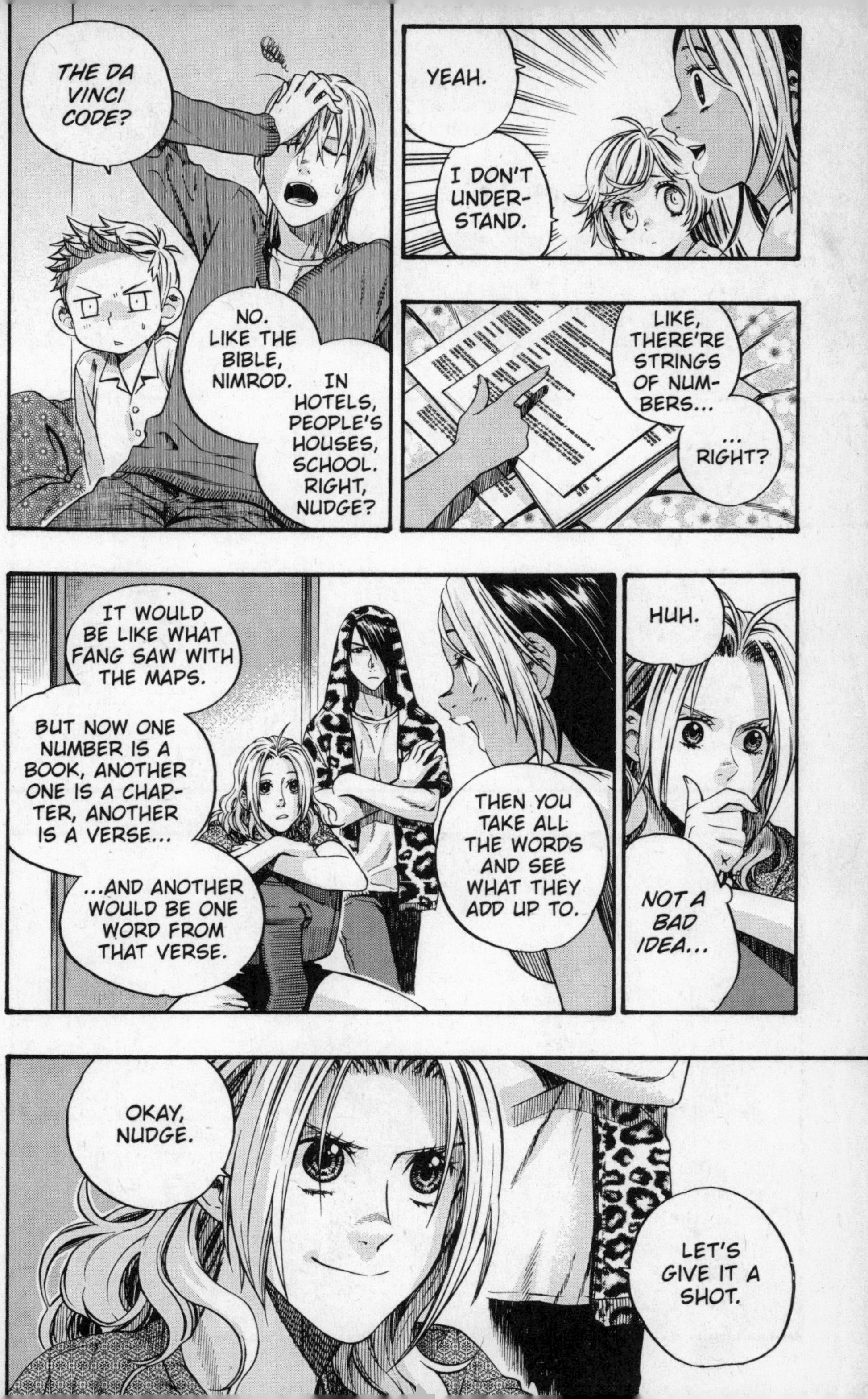
THE DA VINCI CODE?
NO. LIKE THE BIBLE, NIMROD.
IN HOTELS, PEOPLE'S HOUSES, SCHOOL. RIGHT, NUDGE?
YEAH.
I DON'T UNDER-STAND.
LIKE, THERE'RE STRINGS OF NUM-BERS...
... RIGHT?
IT WOULD BE LIKE WHAT FANG SAW WITH THE MAPS.
BUT NOW ONE NUMBER IS A BOOK, ANOTHER ONE IS A CHAP-TER, ANOTHER IS A VERSE...
...AND ANOTHER WOULD BE ONE WORD FROM THAT VERSE.
THEN YOU TAKE ALL THE WORDS AND SEE WHAT THEY ADD UP TO.
HUH.
NOT A BAD IDEA...
OKAY, NUDGE.
LET'S GIVE IT A SHOT.

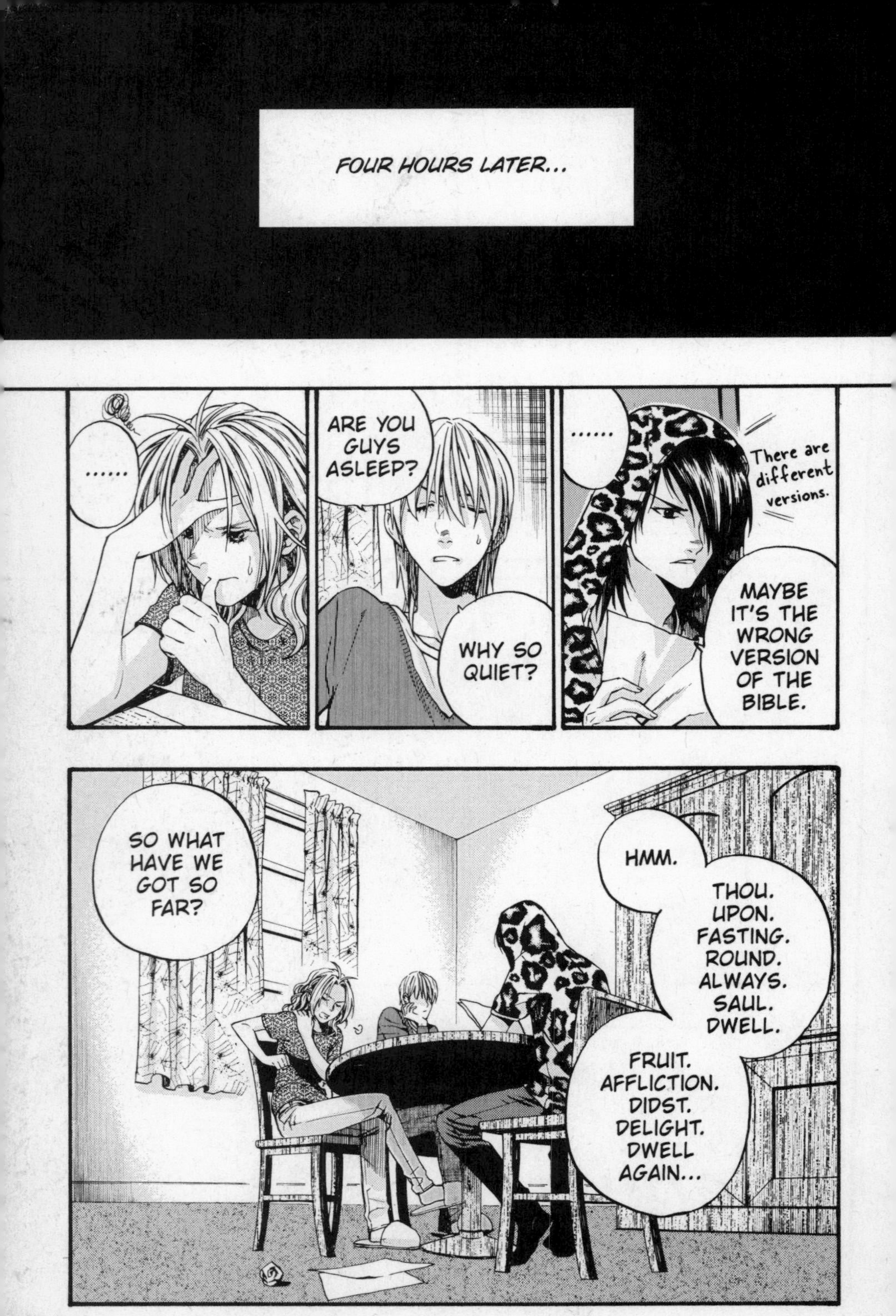
FOUR HOURS LATER...
......
ARE YOU GUYS ASLEEP?
WHY SO QUIET?
......
There are different versions.
MAYBE IT'S THE WRONG VERSION OF THE BIBLE.
SO WHAT HAVE WE GOT SO FAR?
HMM.
THOU. UPON. FASTING. ROUND. ALWAYS. SAUL. DWELL.
FRUIT. AFFLICTION. DIDST. DELIGHT. DWELL AGAIN...

NOTHING. NO PATTERN, NO MEANING.

THE BIBLE WAS A GREAT IDEA...

...BUT MAYBE WE'RE DOING IT WRONG.

......

SO I GUESS WE JUST KISS THE WORLD GOOD-BYE.

SO FUNNY.

YOU'RE QUITE THE WIT.

......

CRUNCH!!

THE LADIES LIKE IT.

...!!

PFFT.

@#$& $#%@#!

I'M BEAT. SEE YOU IN THE MORNING.

MAX

GOOD NIGHT!

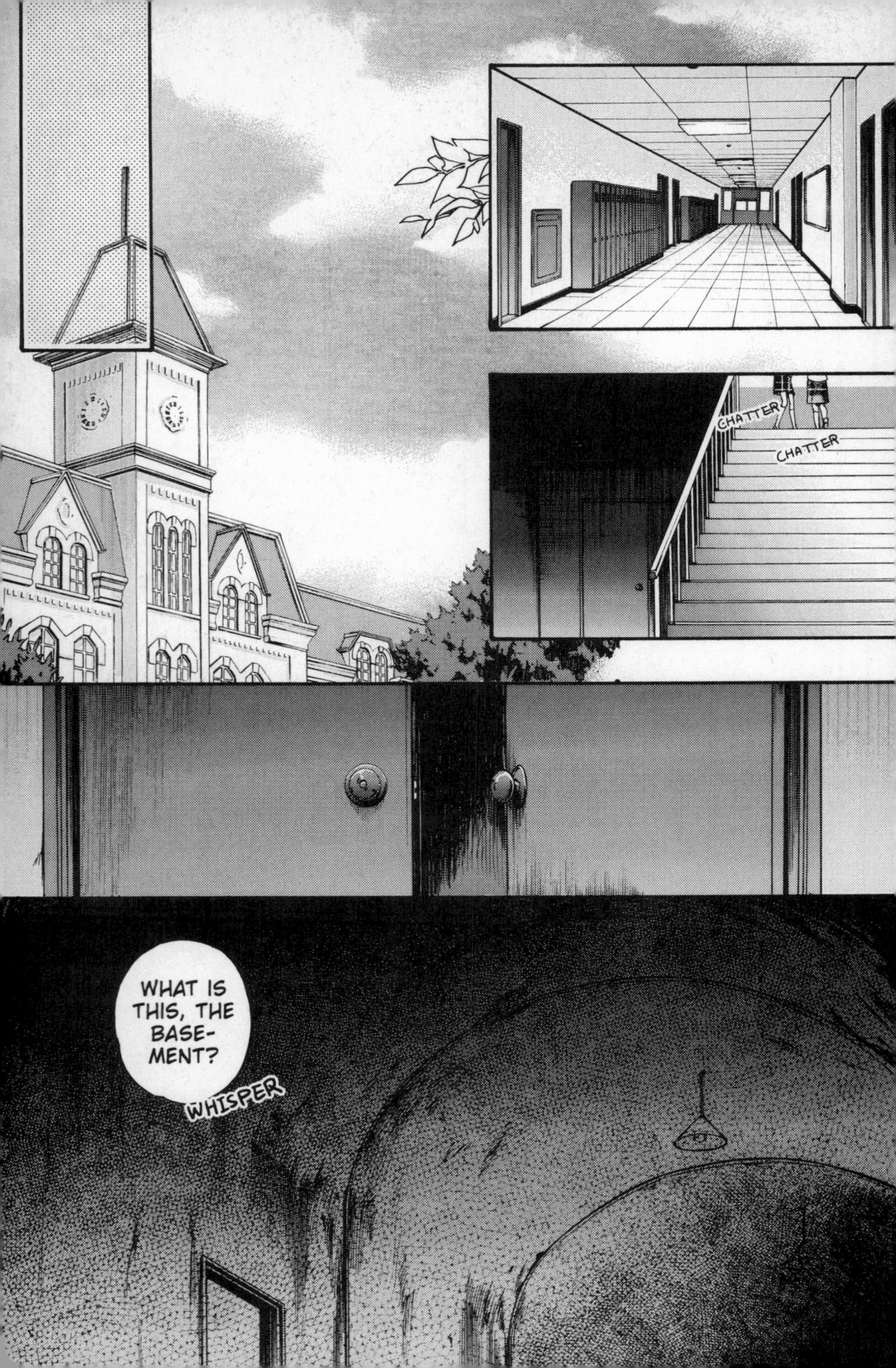
CHATTER
CHATTER
WHAT IS THIS, THE BASEMENT?
WHISPER

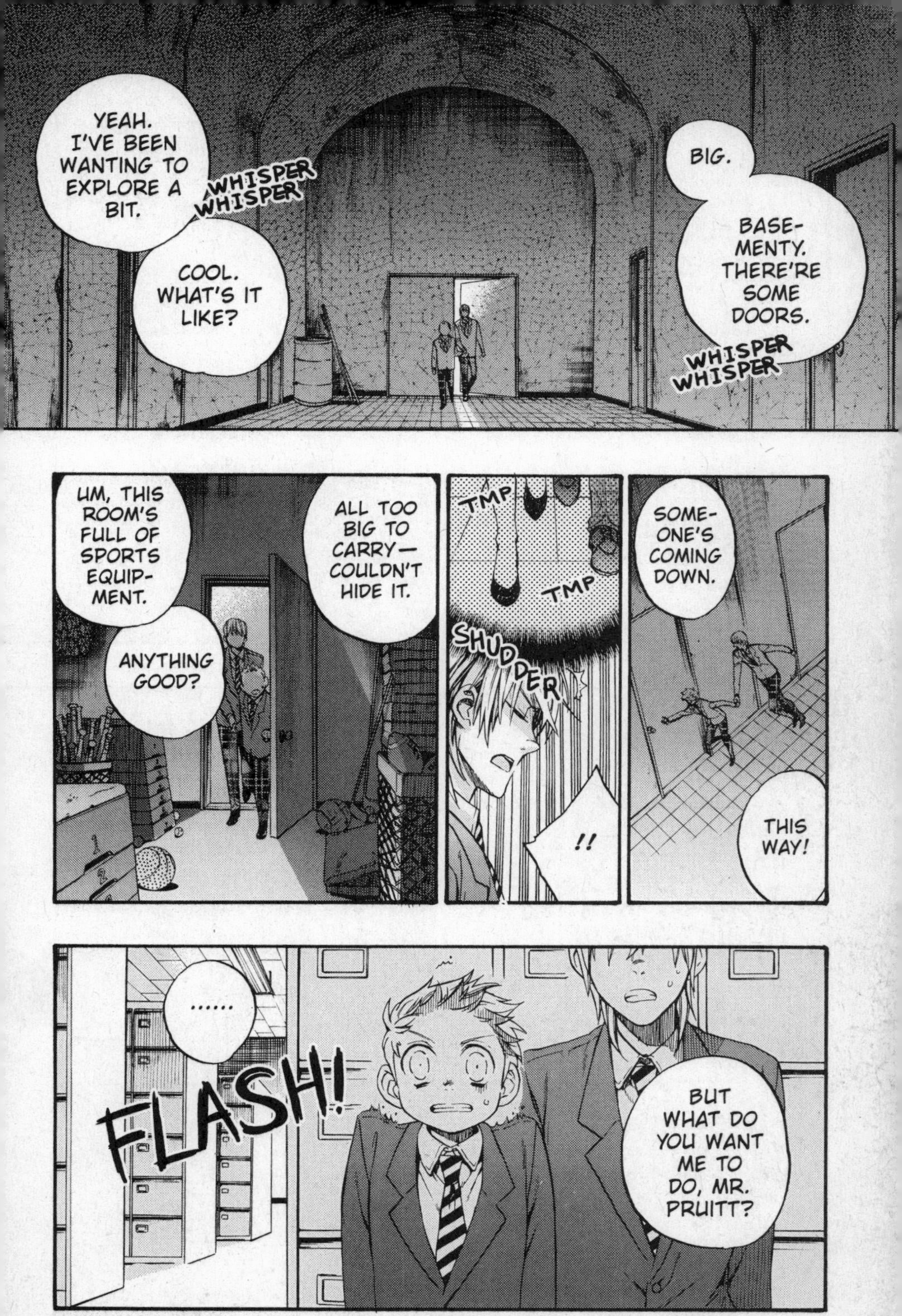
YEAH. I'VE BEEN WANTING TO EXPLORE A BIT.
WHISPER WHISPER
COOL. WHAT'S IT LIKE?
BIG.
BASE-MENTY. THERE'RE SOME DOORS.
WHISPER WHISPER
UM, THIS ROOM'S FULL OF SPORTS EQUIP-MENT.
ANYTHING GOOD?
ALL TOO BIG TO CARRY—COULDN'T HIDE IT.
TMP
TMP
SHUDDER
!!
SOME-ONE'S COMING DOWN.
THIS WAY!
......
FLASH!
BUT WHAT DO YOU WANT ME TO DO, MR. PRUITT?

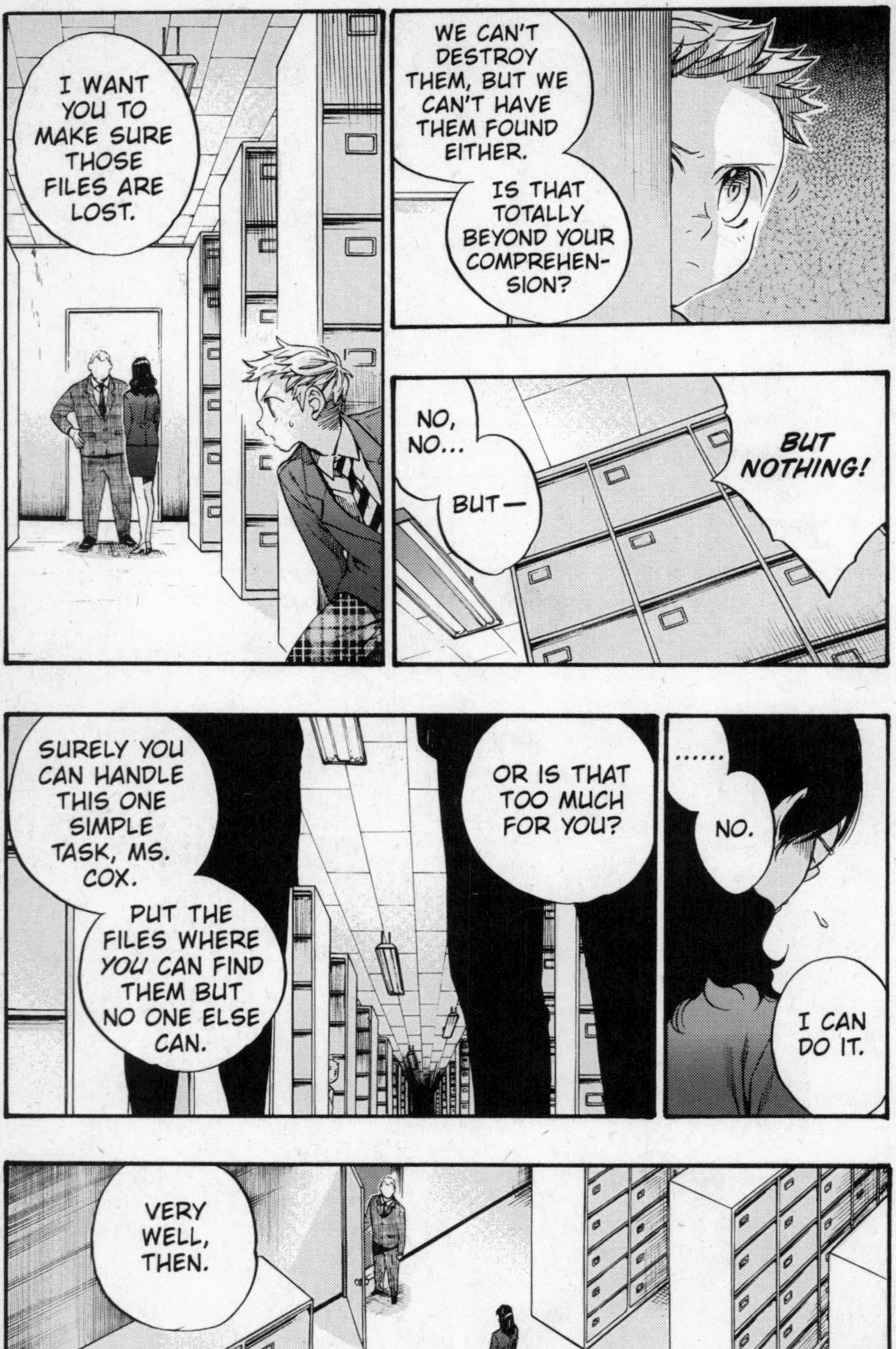
I WANT YOU TO MAKE SURE THOSE FILES ARE LOST.
WE CAN'T DESTROY THEM, BUT WE CAN'T HAVE THEM FOUND EITHER.
IS THAT TOTALLY BEYOND YOUR COMPREHENSION?
NO, NO...
BUT—
BUT NOTHING!
SURELY YOU CAN HANDLE THIS ONE SIMPLE TASK, MS. COX.
PUT THE FILES WHERE *YOU* CAN FIND THEM BUT NO ONE ELSE CAN.
OR IS THAT TOO MUCH FOR YOU?
......
NO.
I CAN DO IT.
VERY WELL, THEN.

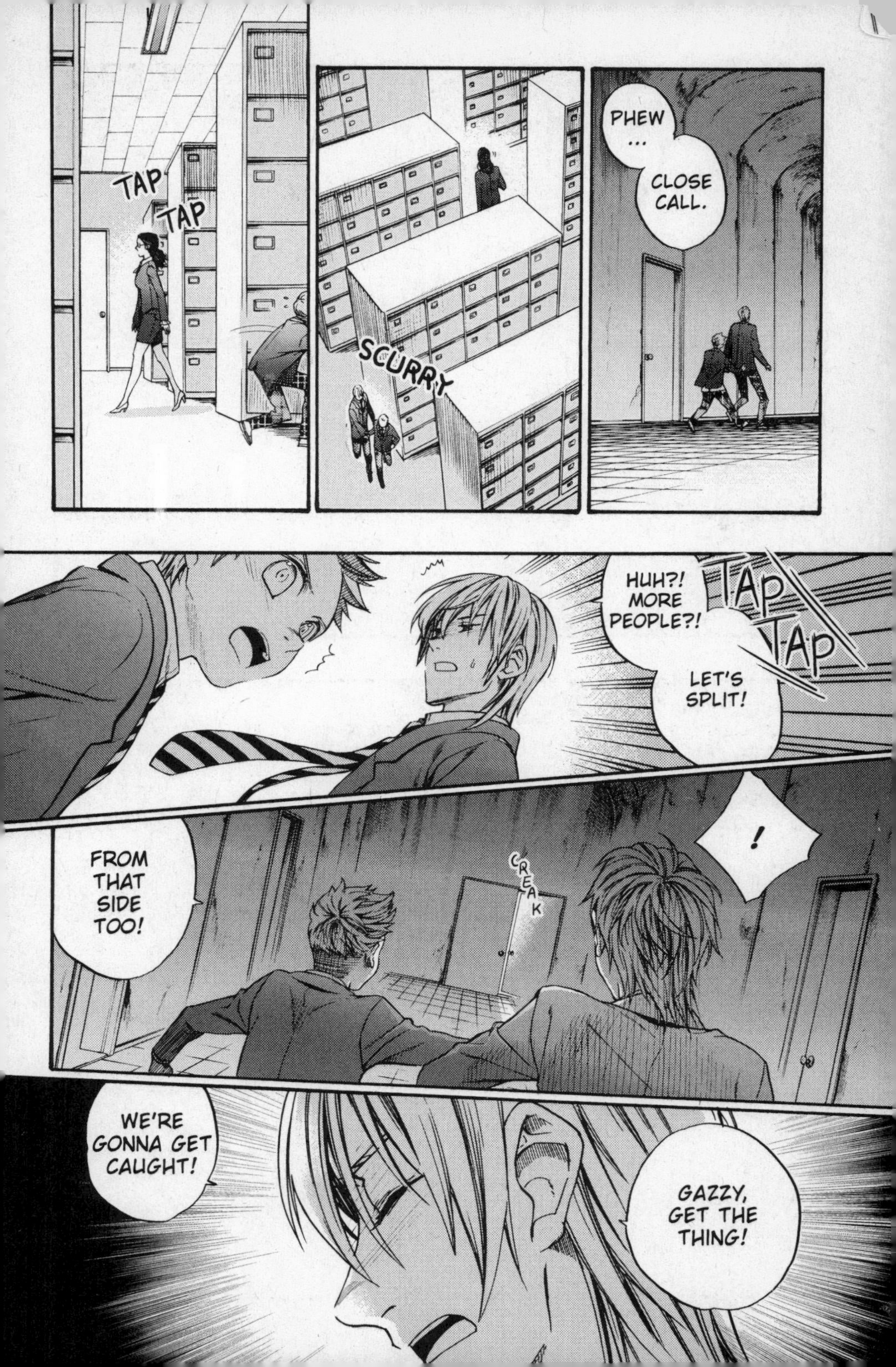
TAP
TAP
SCURRY
PHEW ...
CLOSE CALL.
HUH?! MORE PEOPLE?!
TAP TAP
LET'S SPLIT!
FROM THAT SIDE TOO!
CREAK
!
WE'RE GONNA GET CAUGHT!
GAZZY, GET THE THING!

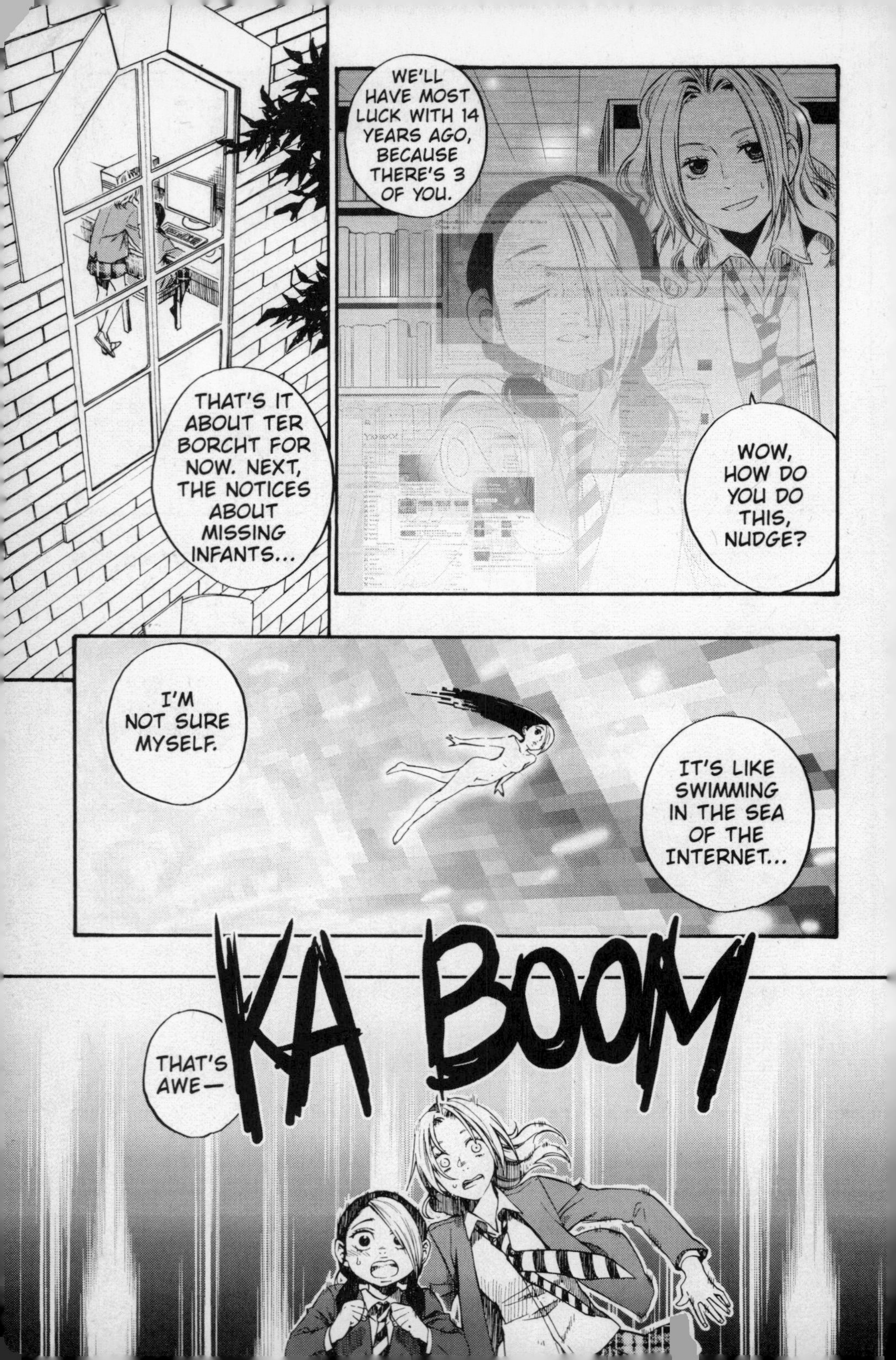
WE'LL HAVE MOST LUCK WITH 14 YEARS AGO, BECAUSE THERE'S 3 OF YOU.
THAT'S IT ABOUT TER BORCHT FOR NOW. NEXT, THE NOTICES ABOUT MISSING INFANTS...
WOW, HOW DO YOU DO THIS, NUDGE?
I'M NOT SURE MYSELF.
IT'S LIKE SWIMMING IN THE SEA OF THE INTERNET...
THAT'S AWE—
KA BOOM

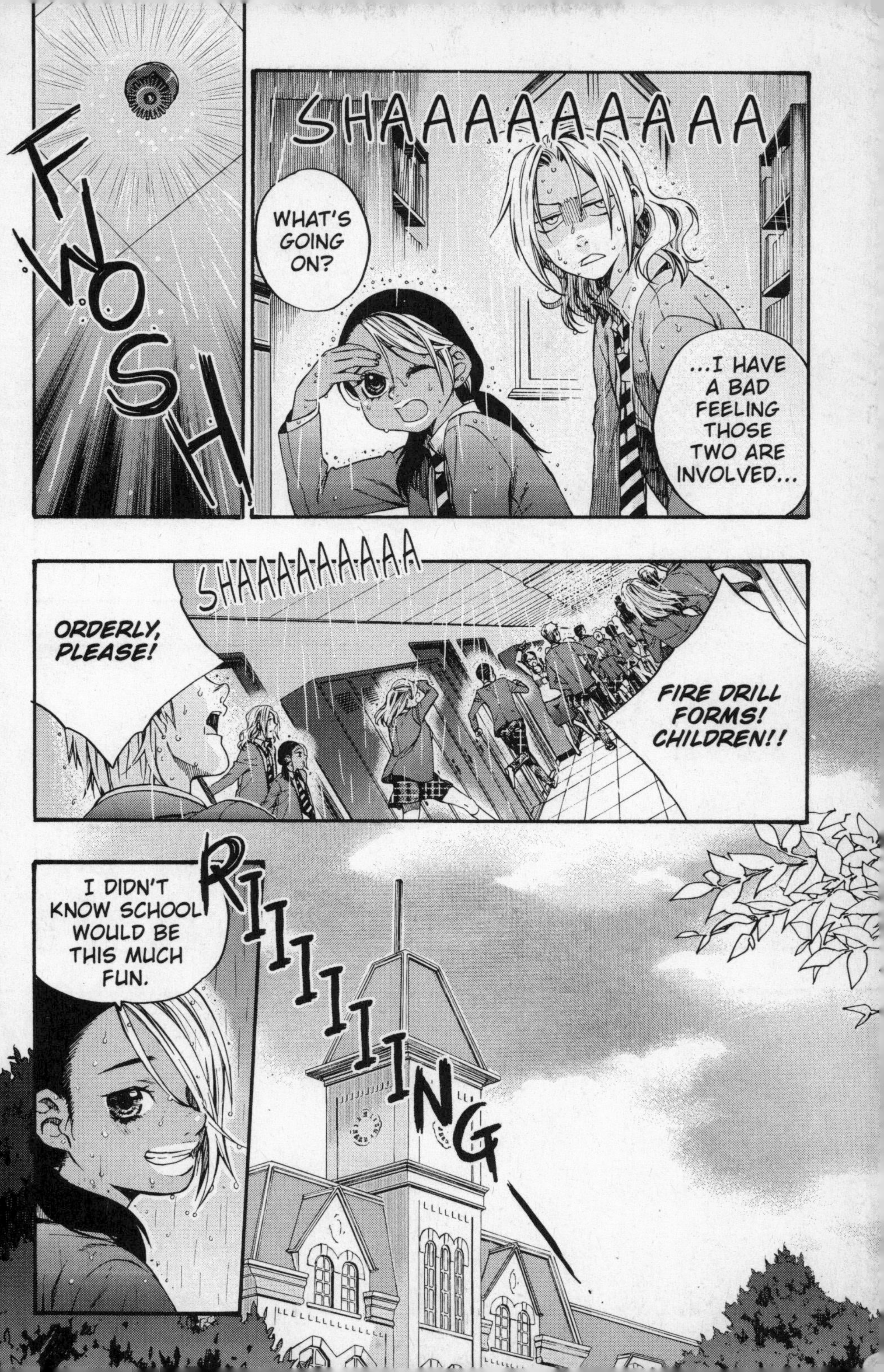
FWOSH
SHAAAAAAAAAA
WHAT'S GOING ON?
...I HAVE A BAD FEELING THOSE TWO ARE INVOLVED...
SHAAAAAAAAAA
ORDERLY, PLEASE!
FIRE DRILL FORMS! CHILDREN!!
I DIDN'T KNOW SCHOOL WOULD BE THIS MUCH FUN.
RIIIIING

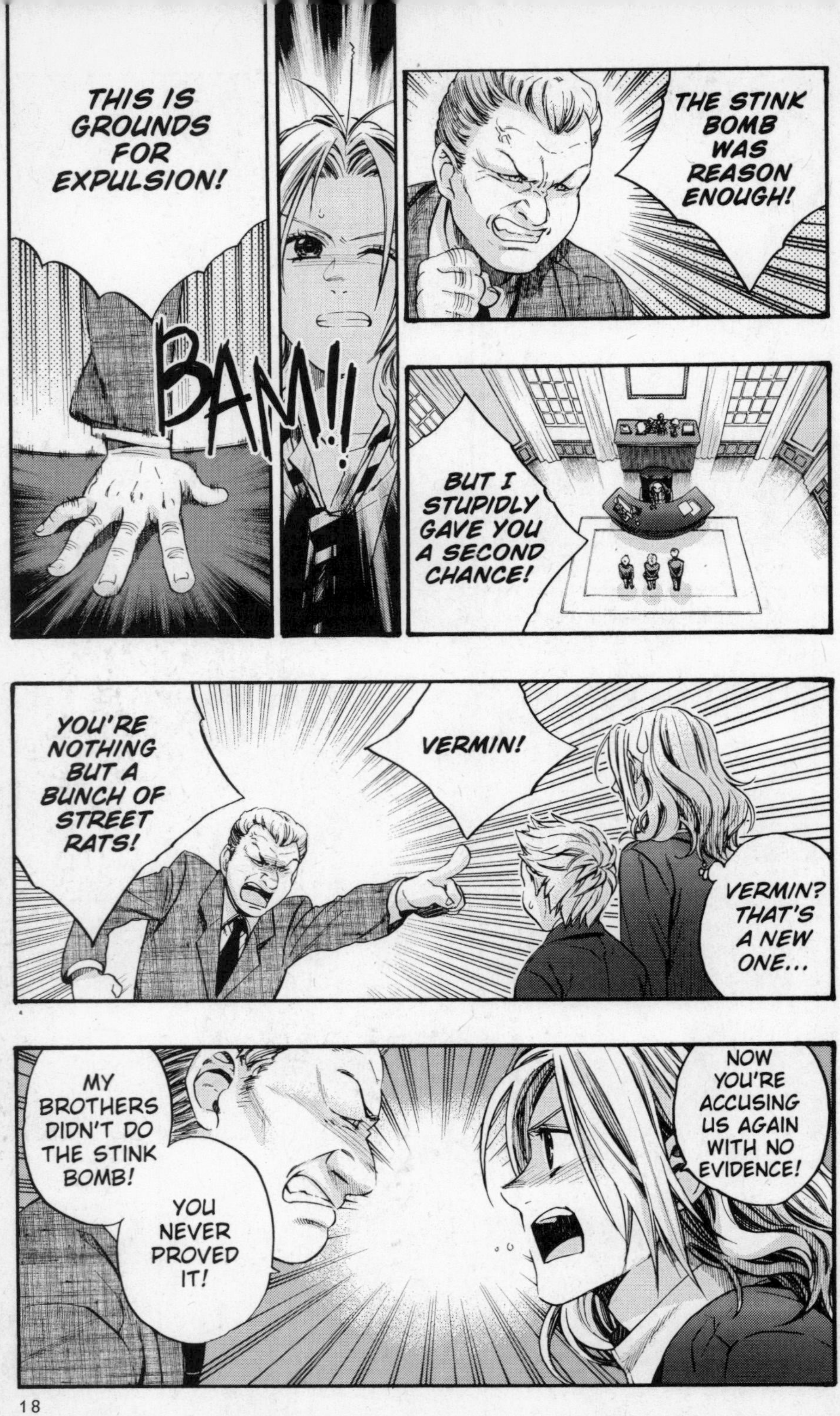
THIS IS GROUNDS FOR EXPULSION!
BAM!!
THE STINK BOMB WAS REASON ENOUGH!
BUT I STUPIDLY GAVE YOU A SECOND CHANCE!
YOU'RE NOTHING BUT A BUNCH OF STREET RATS!
VERMIN!
VERMIN? THAT'S A NEW ONE...
MY BROTHERS DIDN'T DO THE STINK BOMB!
YOU NEVER PROVED IT!
NOW YOU'RE ACCUSING US AGAIN WITH NO EVIDENCE!

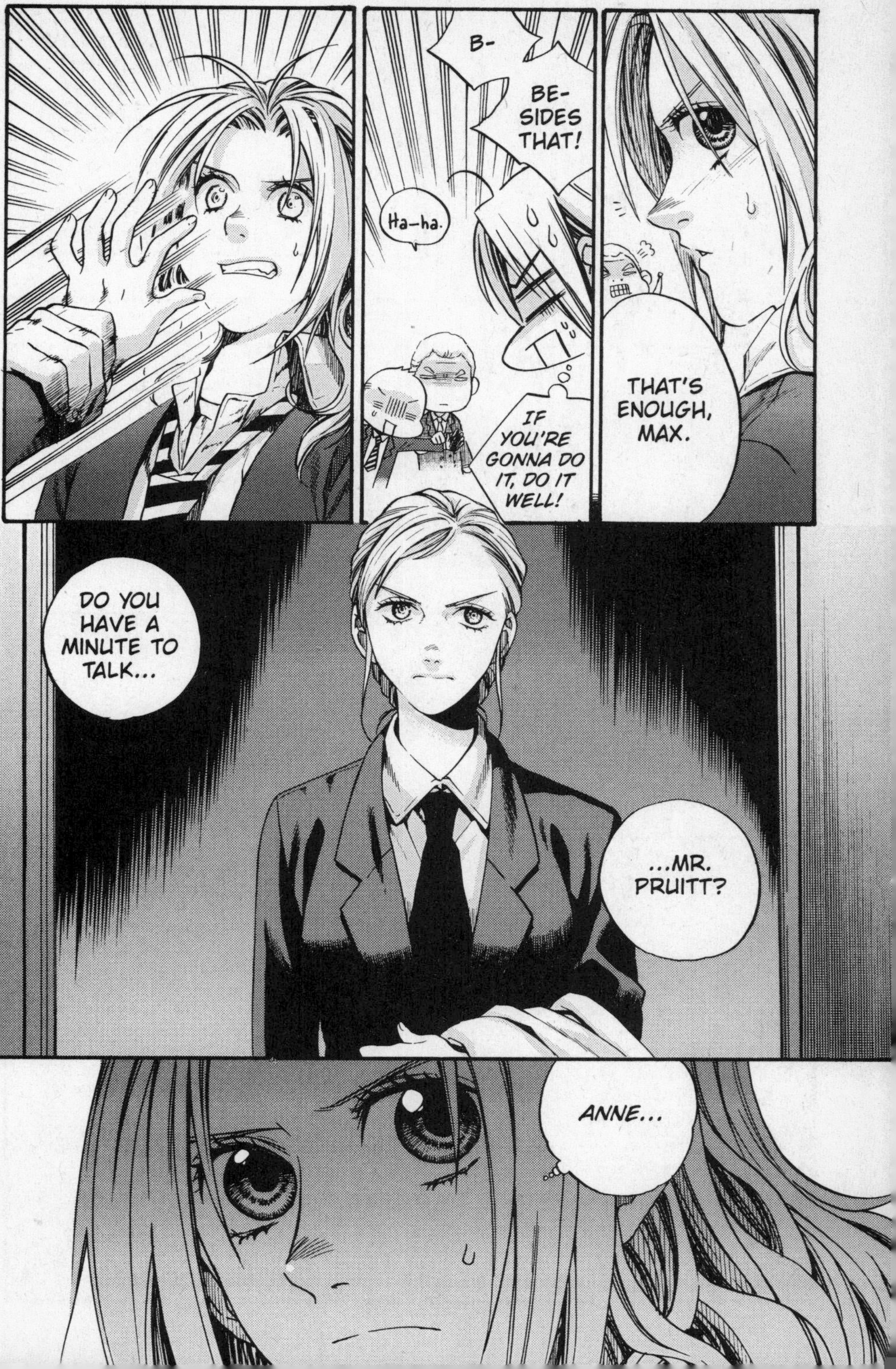
B-
BE-SIDES THAT!
Ha-ha.
IF YOU'RE GONNA DO IT, DO IT WELL!
THAT'S ENOUGH, MAX.
DO YOU HAVE A MINUTE TO TALK...
...MR. PRUITT?
ANNE...

SILENCE

THIS WAS YOUR BIG OPPORTUNITY, KIDS.

I'D HAD HIGHER HOPES...

I'M REALLY DISAPPOINTED WITH YOU.

YOU'RE ALL GROUNDED FOR NOW. NO TV, NO DESSERTS.

GO BACK TO YOUR ROOMS.

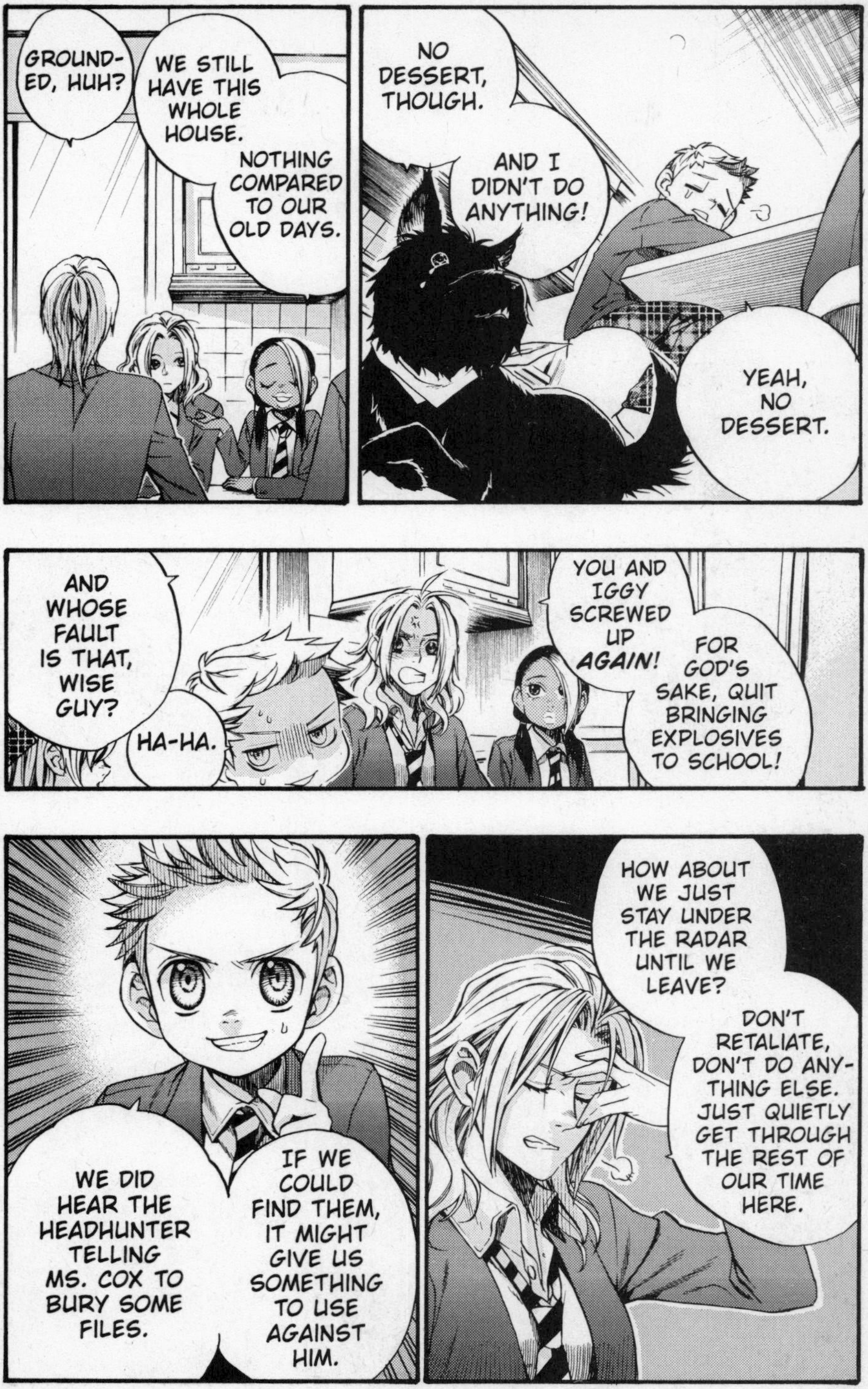
GROUND-ED, HUH?
WE STILL HAVE THIS WHOLE HOUSE.
NOTHING COMPARED TO OUR OLD DAYS.
NO DESSERT, THOUGH.
AND I DIDN'T DO ANYTHING!
YEAH, NO DESSERT.
AND WHOSE FAULT IS THAT, WISE GUY?
HA-HA.
YOU AND IGGY SCREWED UP *AGAIN*!
FOR GOD'S SAKE, QUIT BRINGING EXPLOSIVES TO SCHOOL!
WE DID HEAR THE HEADHUNTER TELLING MS. COX TO BURY SOME FILES.
IF WE COULD FIND THEM, IT MIGHT GIVE US SOMETHING TO USE AGAINST HIM.
HOW ABOUT WE JUST STAY UNDER THE RADAR UNTIL WE LEAVE?
DON'T RETALIATE, DON'T DO ANY-THING ELSE. JUST QUIETLY GET THROUGH THE REST OF OUR TIME HERE.

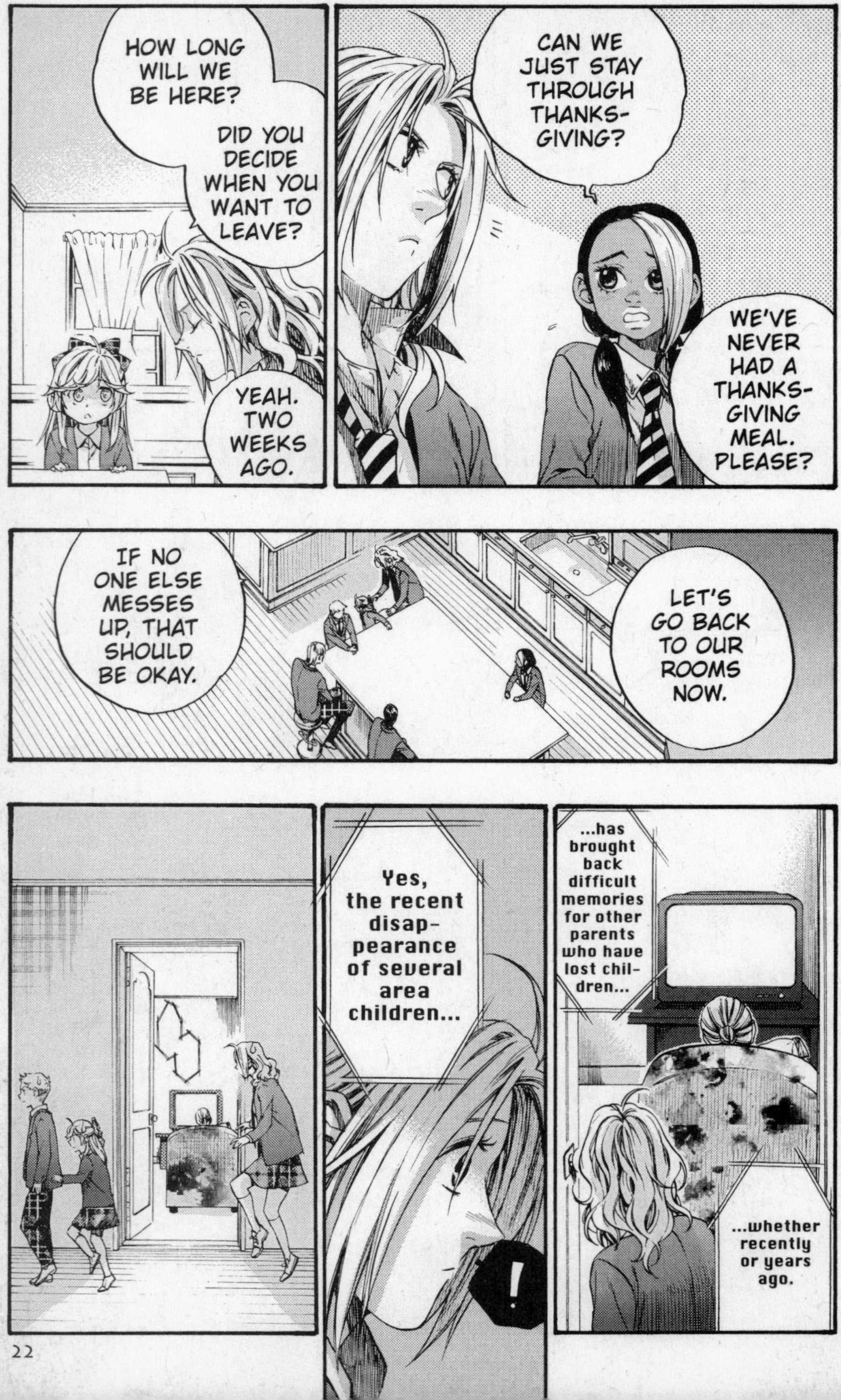
HOW LONG WILL WE BE HERE?
DID YOU DECIDE WHEN YOU WANT TO LEAVE?
YEAH. TWO WEEKS AGO.
CAN WE JUST STAY THROUGH THANKS-GIVING?
WE'VE NEVER HAD A THANKS-GIVING MEAL. PLEASE?
IF NO ONE ELSE MESSES UP, THAT SHOULD BE OKAY.
LET'S GO BACK TO OUR ROOMS NOW.
Yes, the recent disap-pearance of several area children...
!
...has brought back difficult memories for other parents who have lost chil-dren...
...whether recently or years ago.

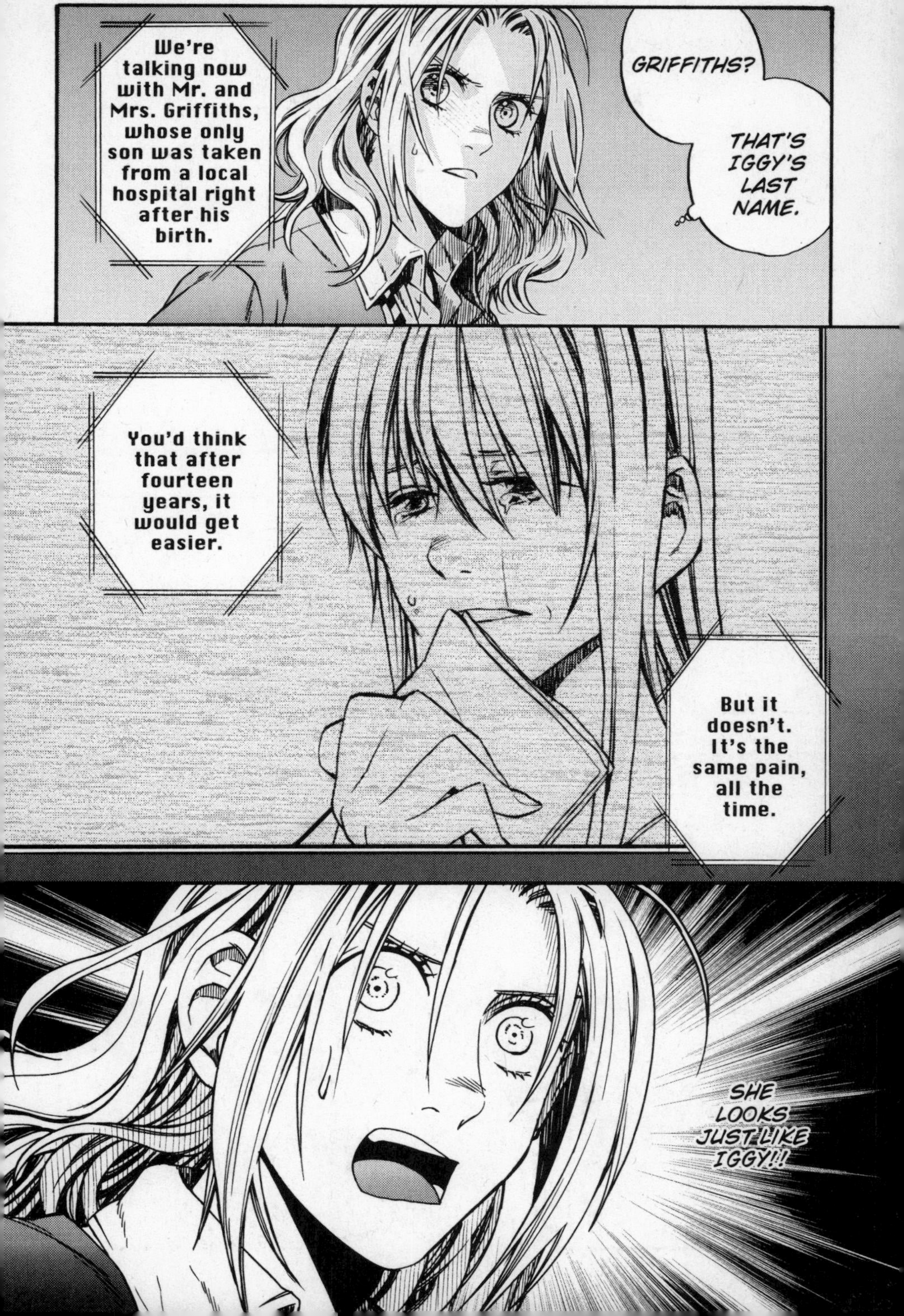
We're talking now with Mr. and Mrs. Griffiths, whose only son was taken from a local hospital right after his birth.
GRIFFITHS?
THAT'S IGGY'S LAST NAME.
You'd think that after fourteen years, it would get easier.
But it doesn't. It's the same pain, all the time.
SHE LOOKS JUST LIKE IGGY!!

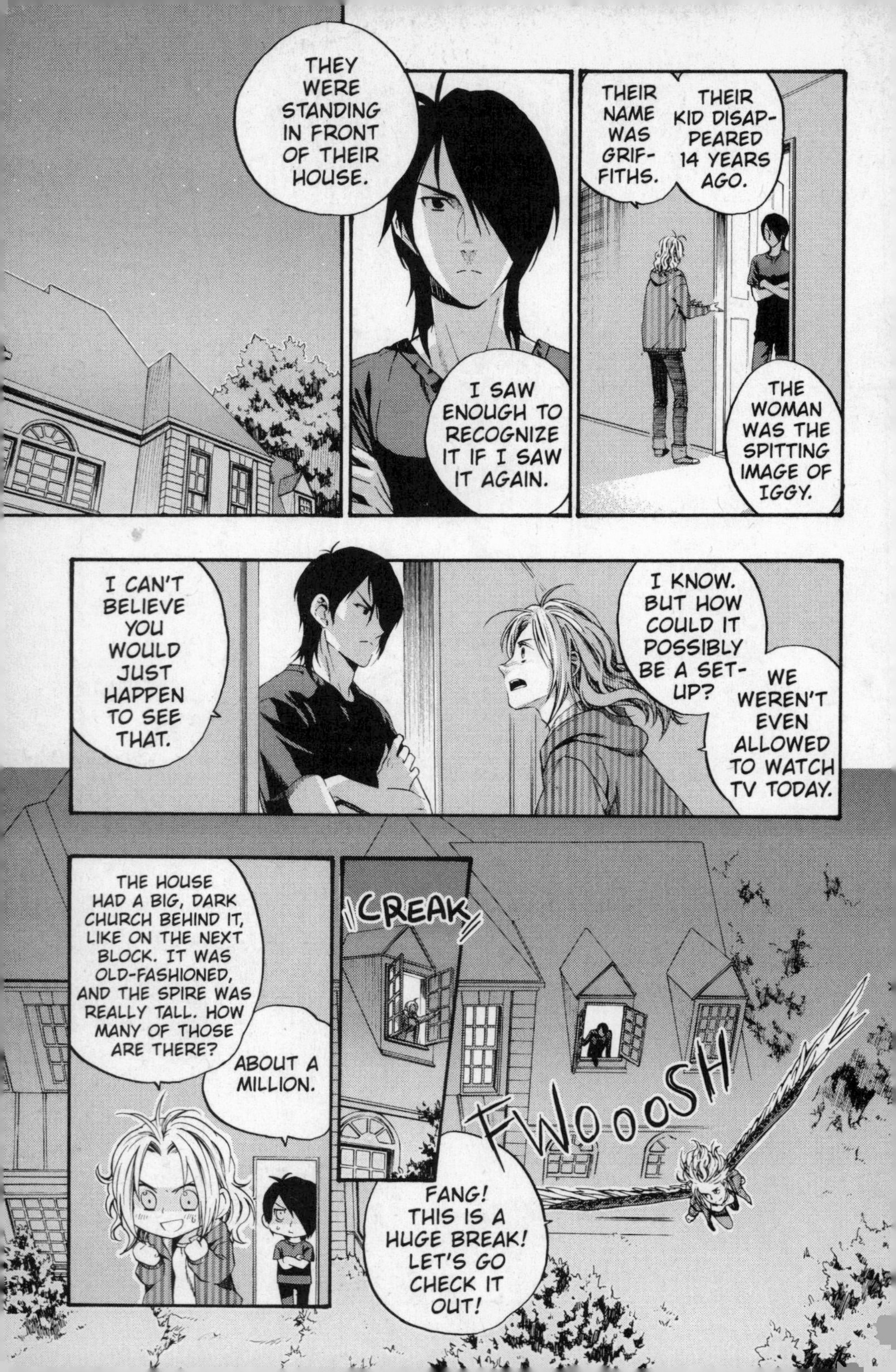
THEY WERE STANDING IN FRONT OF THEIR HOUSE.
I SAW ENOUGH TO RECOGNIZE IT IF I SAW IT AGAIN.
THEIR NAME WAS GRIF-FITHS.
THEIR KID DISAP-PEARED 14 YEARS AGO.
THE WOMAN WAS THE SPITTING IMAGE OF IGGY.
I CAN'T BELIEVE YOU WOULD JUST HAPPEN TO SEE THAT.
I KNOW. BUT HOW COULD IT POSSIBLY BE A SET-UP?
WE WEREN'T EVEN ALLOWED TO WATCH TV TODAY.
THE HOUSE HAD A BIG, DARK CHURCH BEHIND IT, LIKE ON THE NEXT BLOCK. IT WAS OLD-FASHIONED, AND THE SPIRE WAS REALLY TALL. HOW MANY OF THOSE ARE THERE?
ABOUT A MILLION.
CREAK
FWOOOSH
FANG! THIS IS A HUGE BREAK! LET'S GO CHECK IT OUT!

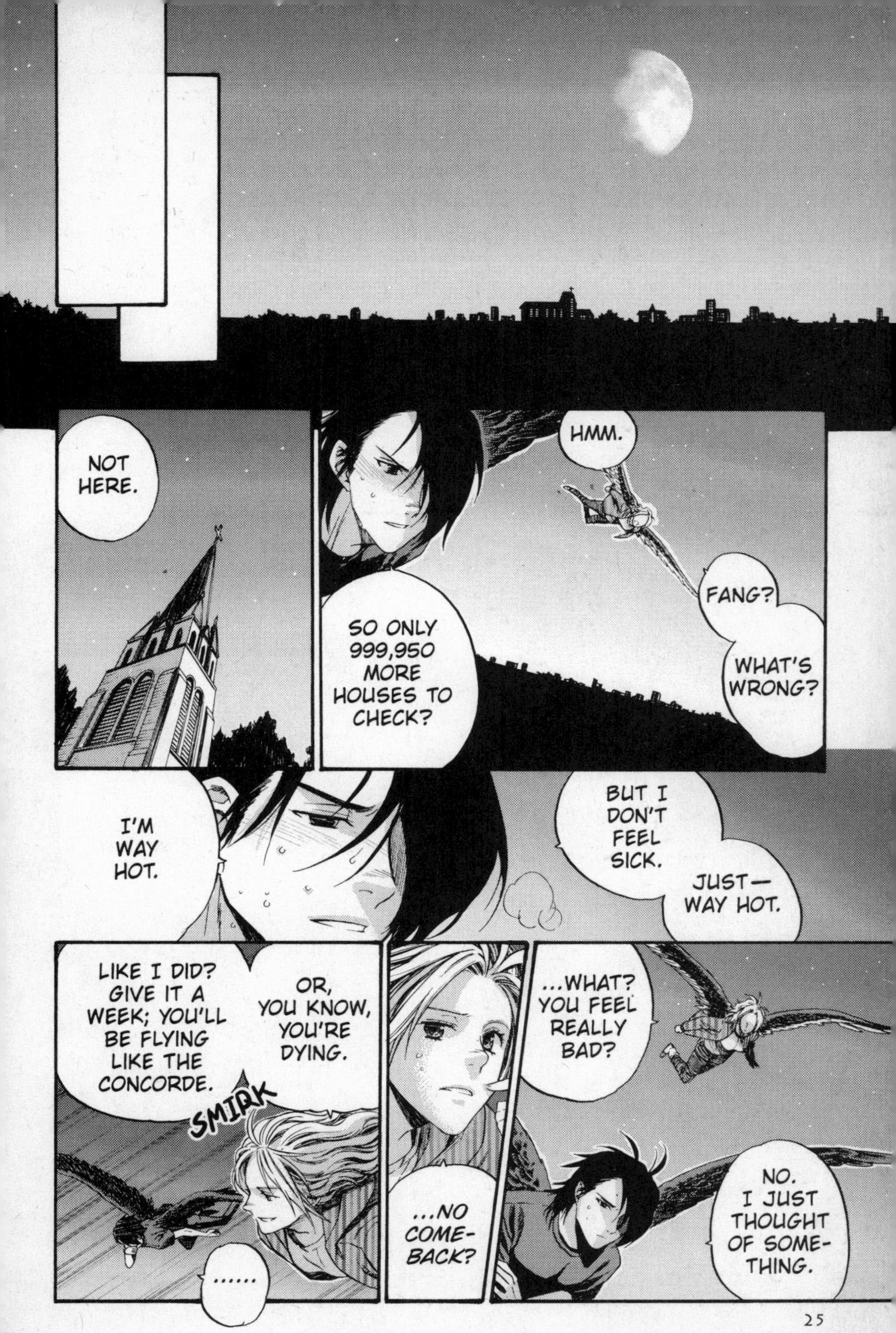
NOT HERE.
HMM.
SO ONLY 999,950 MORE HOUSES TO CHECK?
FANG?
WHAT'S WRONG?
I'M WAY HOT.
BUT I DON'T FEEL SICK.
JUST— WAY HOT.
LIKE I DID? GIVE IT A WEEK; YOU'LL BE FLYING LIKE THE CONCORDE.
OR, YOU KNOW, YOU'RE DYING.
SMIRK
......
...NO COME-BACK?
...WHAT? YOU FEEL REALLY BAD?
NO. I JUST THOUGHT OF SOME-THING.

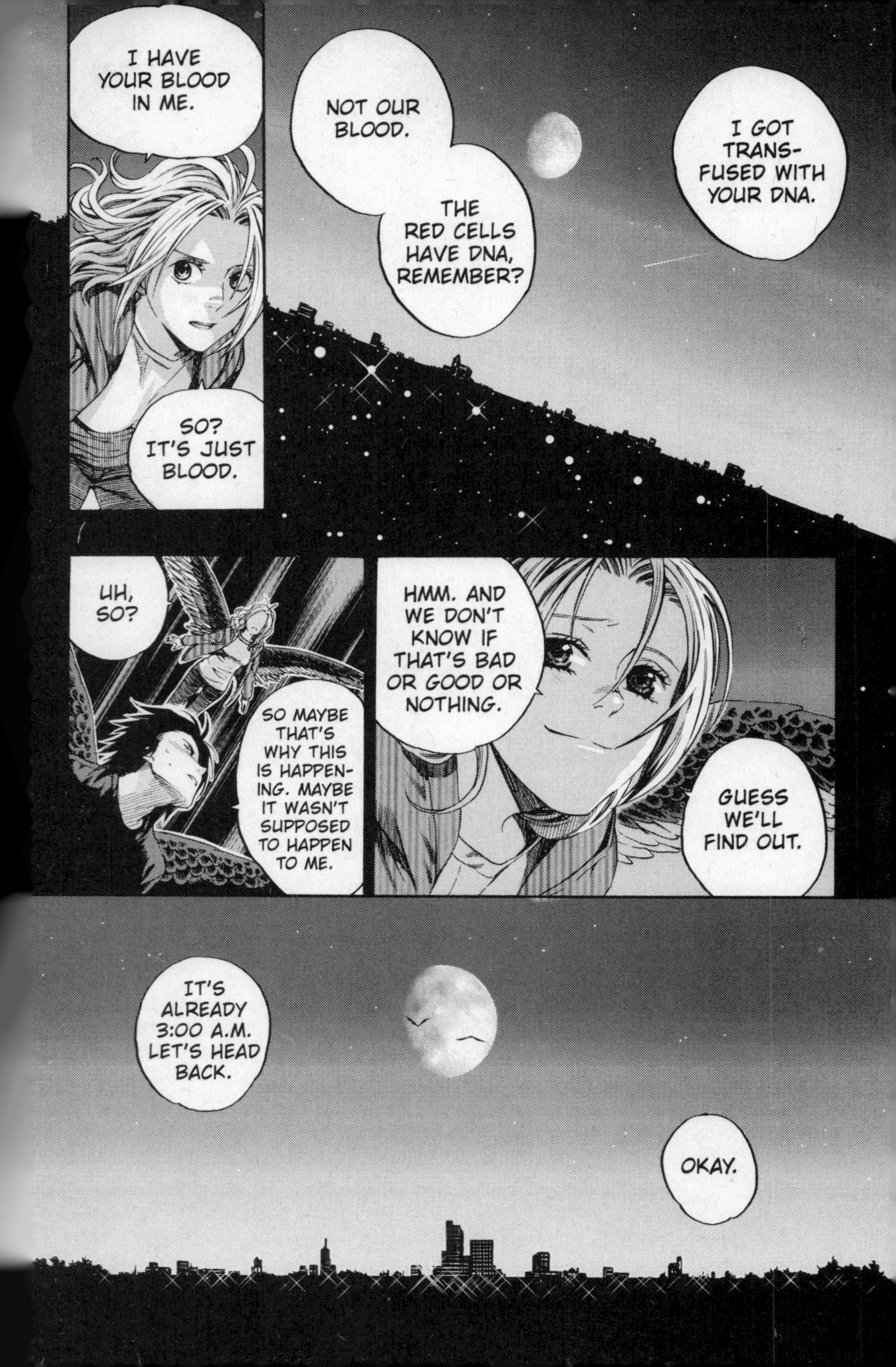
I HAVE YOUR BLOOD IN ME.
SO? IT'S JUST BLOOD.
NOT OUR BLOOD.
THE RED CELLS HAVE DNA, REMEMBER?
I GOT TRANS-FUSED WITH YOUR DNA.
UH, SO?
SO MAYBE THAT'S WHY THIS IS HAPPEN-ING. MAYBE IT WASN'T SUPPOSED TO HAPPEN TO ME.
HMM. AND WE DON'T KNOW IF THAT'S BAD OR GOOD OR NOTHING.
GUESS WE'LL FIND OUT.
IT'S ALREADY 3:00 A.M. LET'S HEAD BACK.
OKAY.

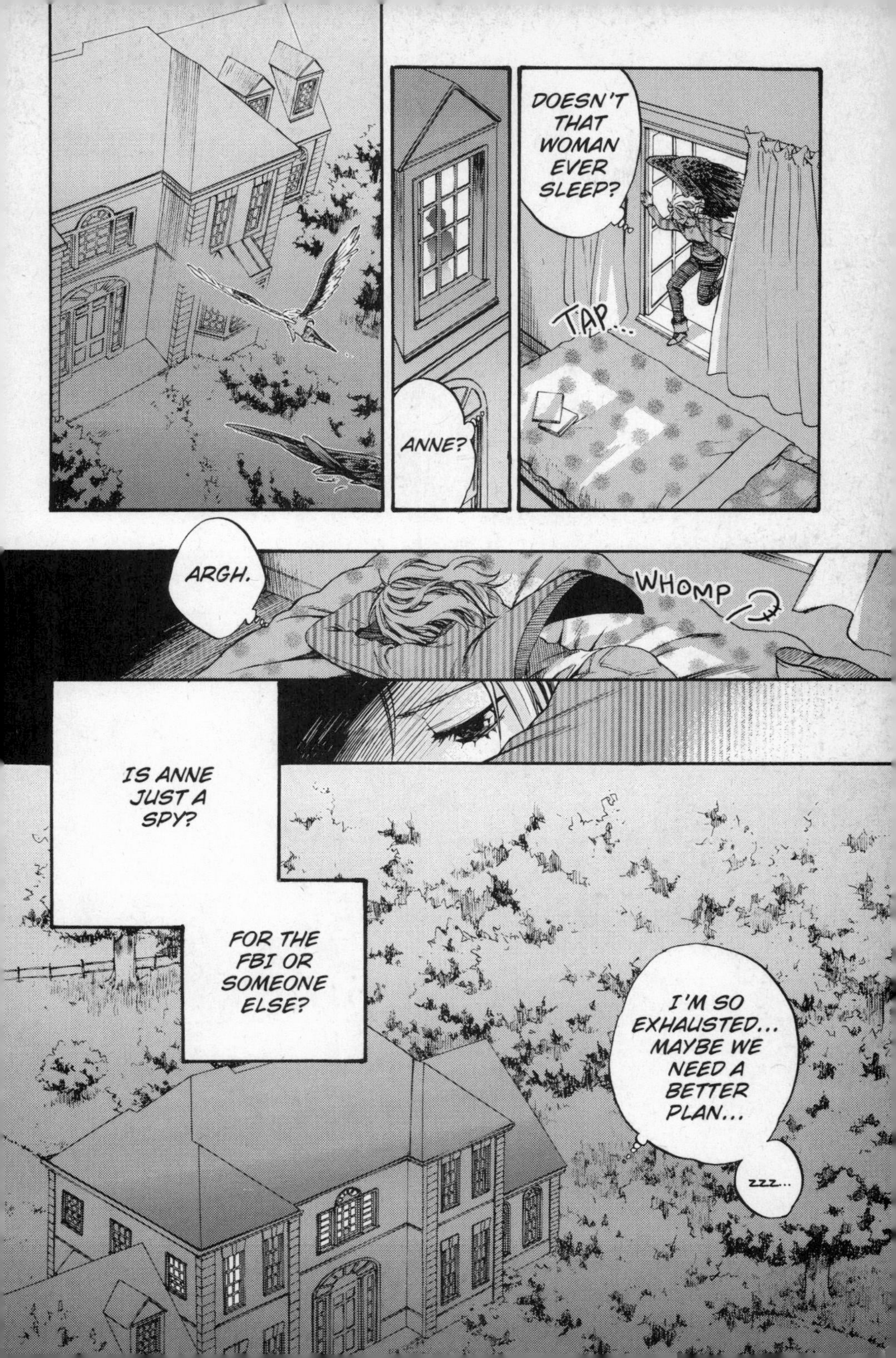
DOESN'T THAT WOMAN EVER SLEEP?
TAP...
ANNE?
ARGH.
WHOMP
IS ANNE JUST A SPY?
FOR THE FBI OR SOMEONE ELSE?
I'M SO EXHAUSTED... MAYBE WE NEED A BETTER PLAN...
zzz...

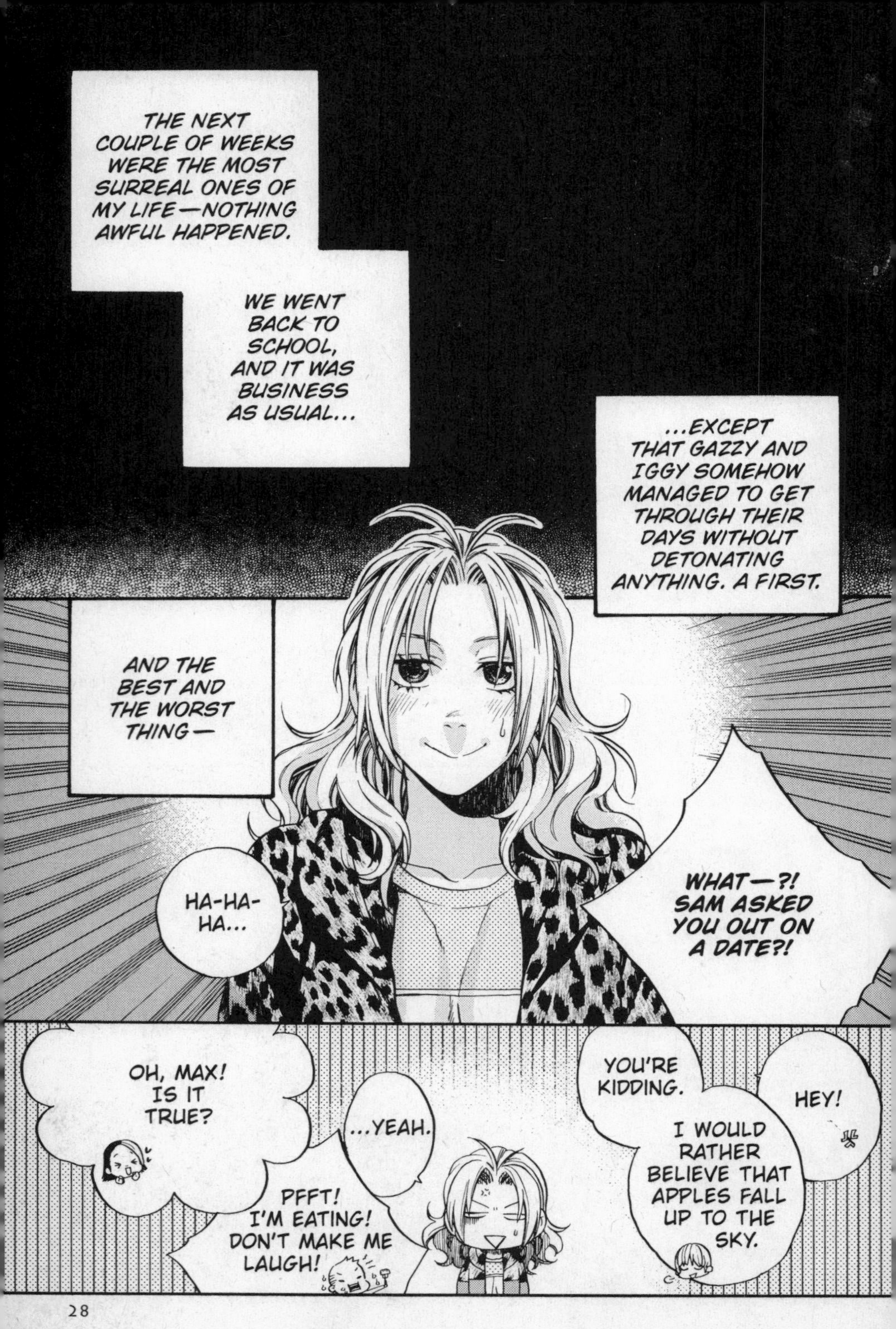
THE NEXT COUPLE OF WEEKS WERE THE MOST SURREAL ONES OF MY LIFE—NOTHING AWFUL HAPPENED.
WE WENT BACK TO SCHOOL, AND IT WAS BUSINESS AS USUAL...
...EXCEPT THAT GAZZY AND IGGY SOMEHOW MANAGED TO GET THROUGH THEIR DAYS WITHOUT DETONATING ANYTHING. A FIRST.
AND THE BEST AND THE WORST THING—
HA-HA-HA...
WHAT—?! SAM ASKED YOU OUT ON A DATE?!
OH, MAX! IS IT TRUE?
...YEAH.
PFFT! I'M EATING! DON'T MAKE ME LAUGH!
YOU'RE KIDDING.
I WOULD RATHER BELIEVE THAT APPLES FALL UP TO THE SKY.
HEY!

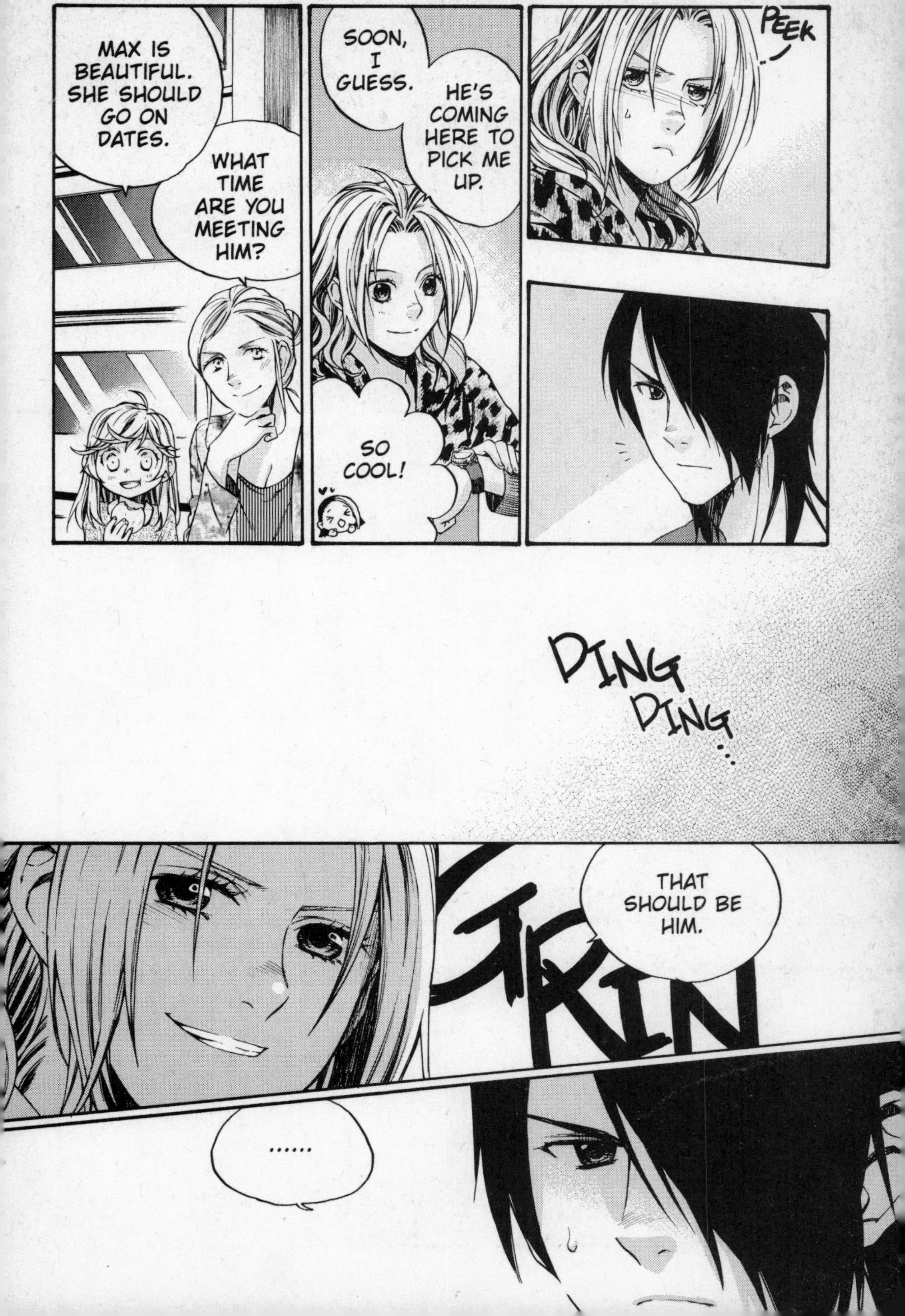
MAX IS BEAUTIFUL. SHE SHOULD GO ON DATES.
WHAT TIME ARE YOU MEETING HIM?
SOON, I GUESS.
HE'S COMING HERE TO PICK ME UP.
SO COOL!
PEEK
DING DING...
GRIN
THAT SHOULD BE HIM.
......

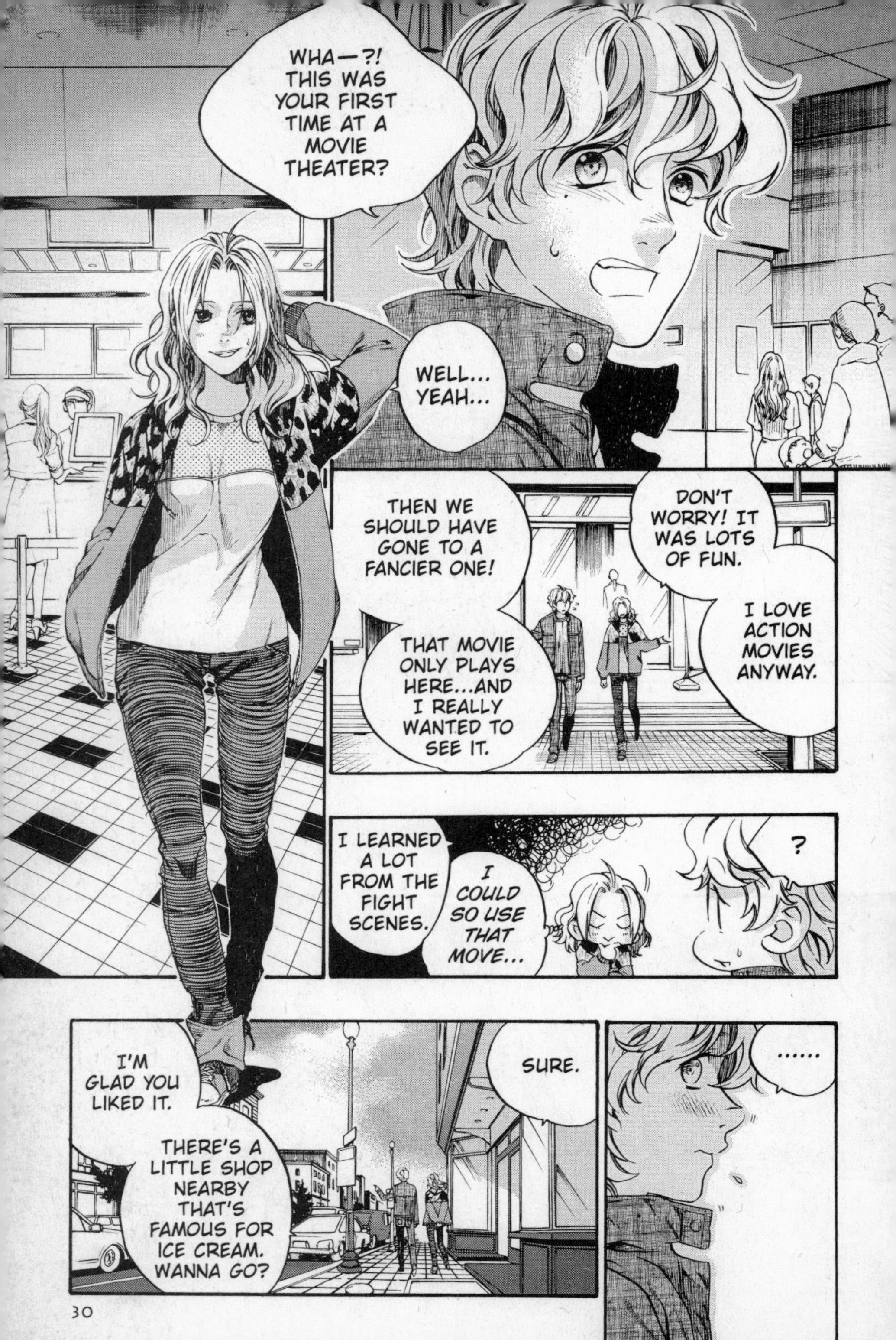
WHA—?! THIS WAS YOUR FIRST TIME AT A MOVIE THEATER?
WELL... YEAH...
THEN WE SHOULD HAVE GONE TO A FANCIER ONE!
THAT MOVIE ONLY PLAYS HERE...AND I REALLY WANTED TO SEE IT.
DON'T WORRY! IT WAS LOTS OF FUN.
I LOVE ACTION MOVIES ANYWAY.
I LEARNED A LOT FROM THE FIGHT SCENES.
I COULD SO USE THAT MOVE...
?
I'M GLAD YOU LIKED IT.
THERE'S A LITTLE SHOP NEARBY THAT'S FAMOUS FOR ICE CREAM. WANNA GO?
SURE.
......

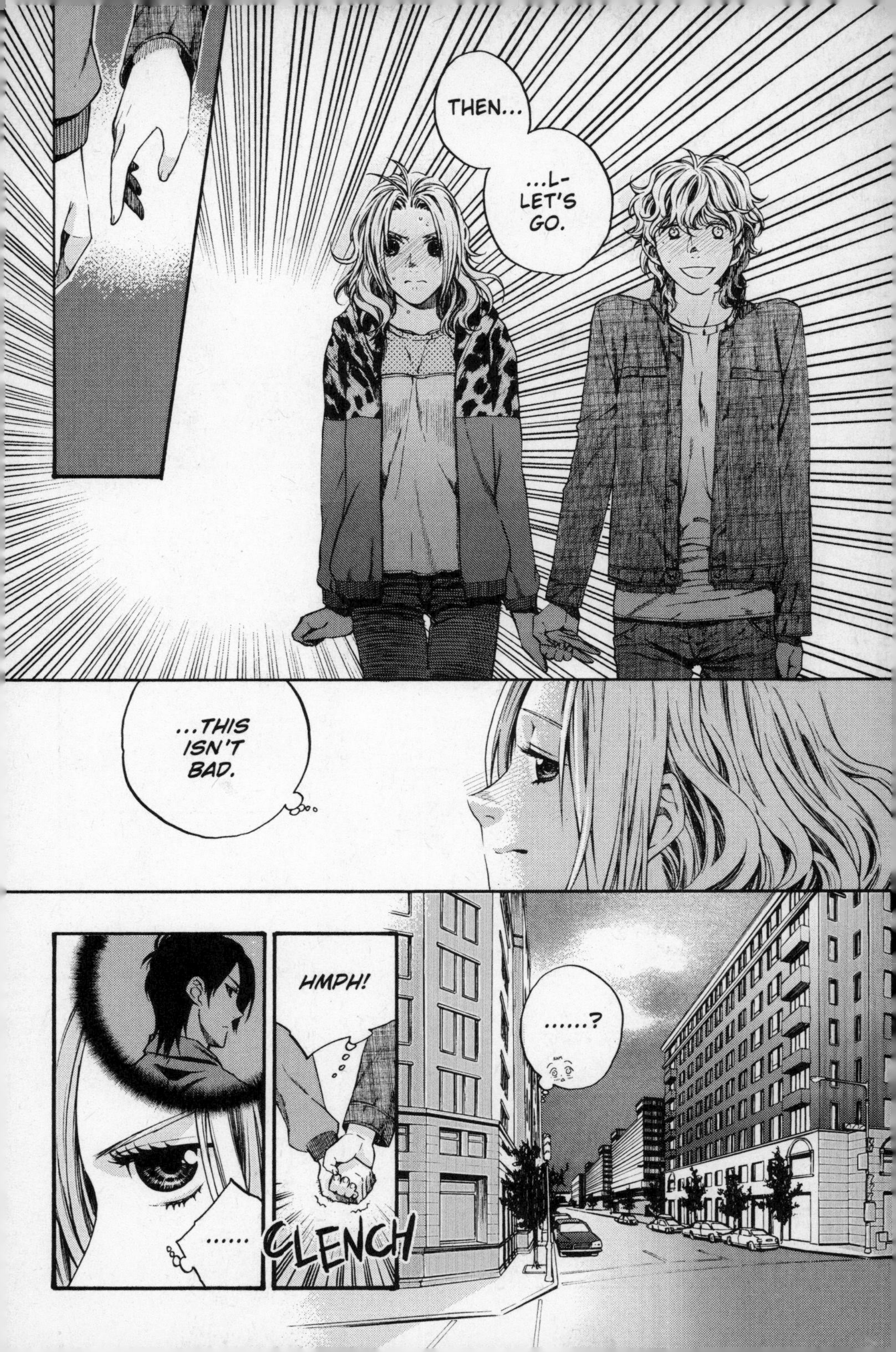
THEN...
...L-LET'S GO.
...THIS ISN'T BAD.
......
HMPH!
CLENCH
......?

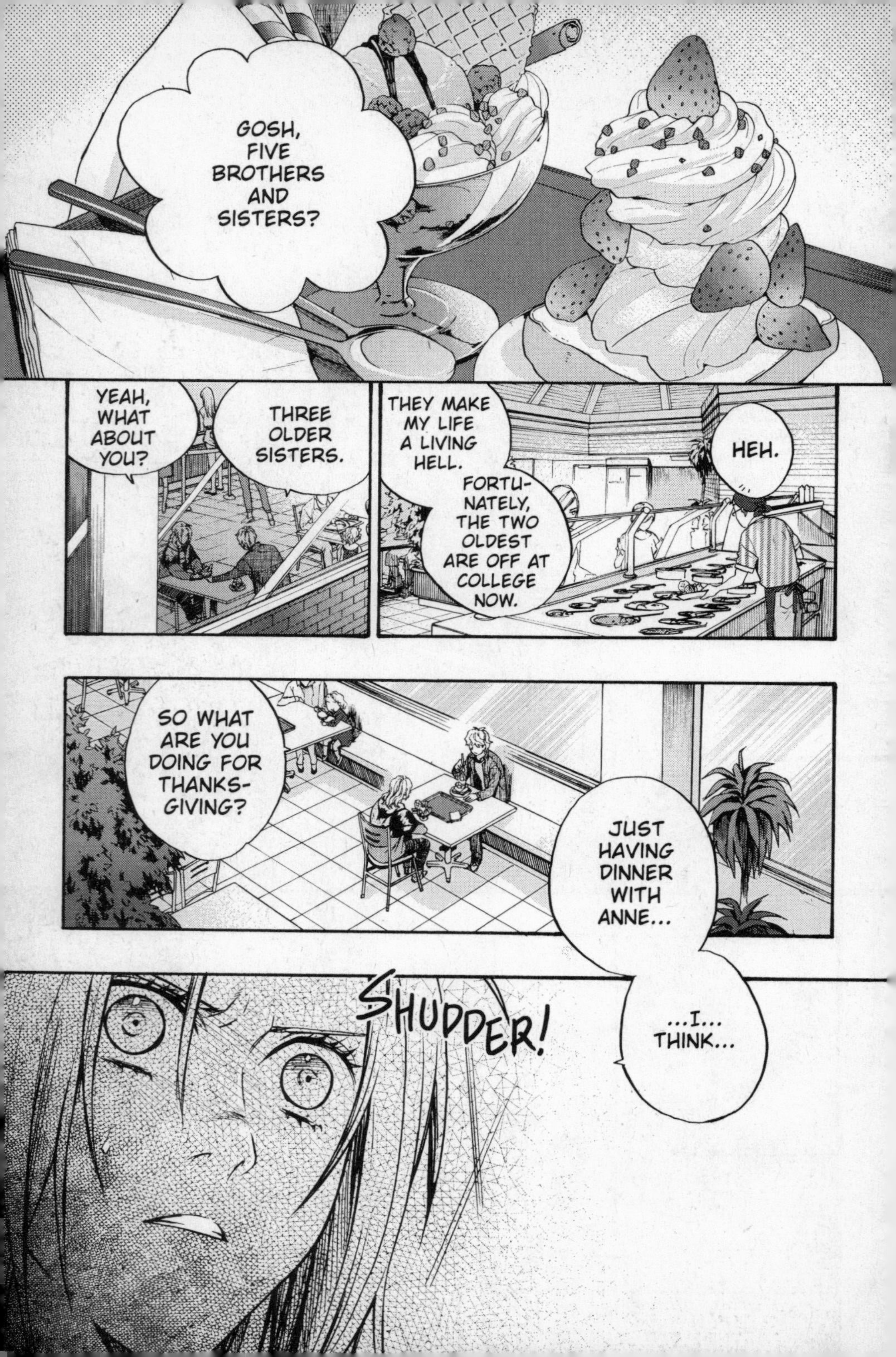
GOSH, FIVE BROTHERS AND SISTERS?
YEAH, WHAT ABOUT YOU?
THREE OLDER SISTERS.
THEY MAKE MY LIFE A LIVING HELL.
FORTUNATELY, THE TWO OLDEST ARE OFF AT COLLEGE NOW.
HEH.
SO WHAT ARE YOU DOING FOR THANKSGIVING?
JUST HAVING DINNER WITH ANNE...
SHUDDER!
...I... THINK...

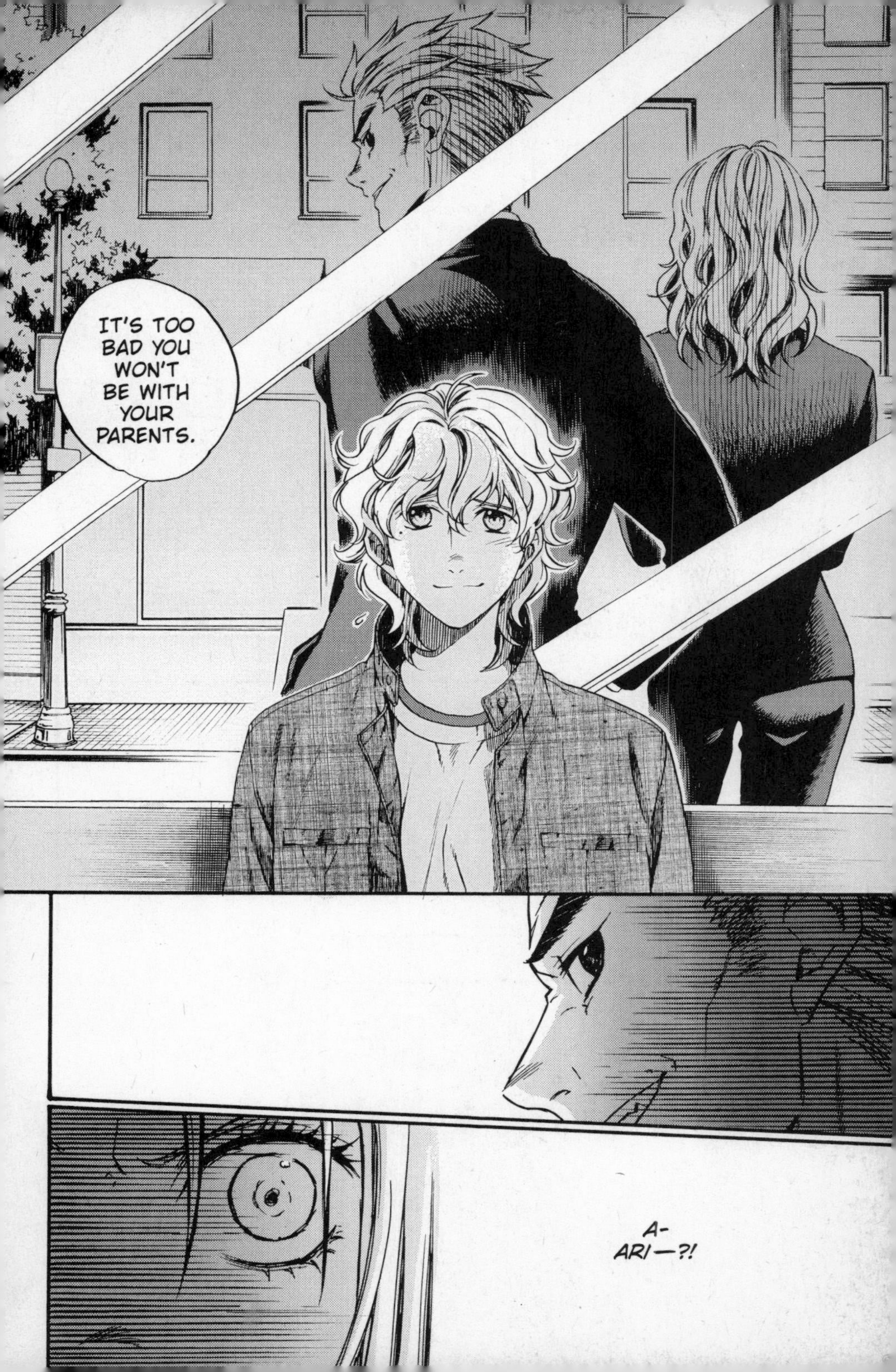
IT'S TOO BAD YOU WON'T BE WITH YOUR PARENTS.
A- ARI—?!

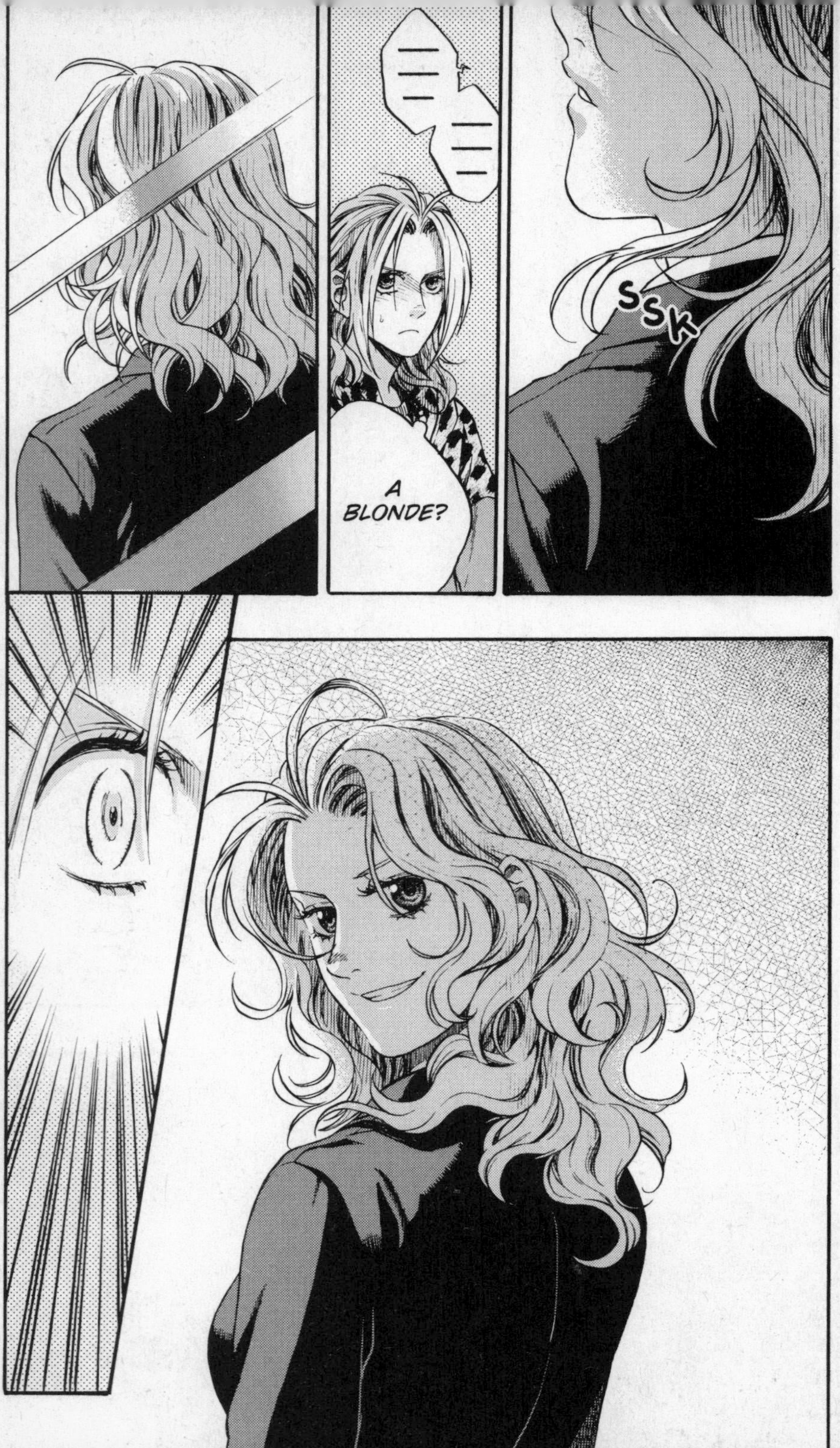
A BLONDE?
SSK

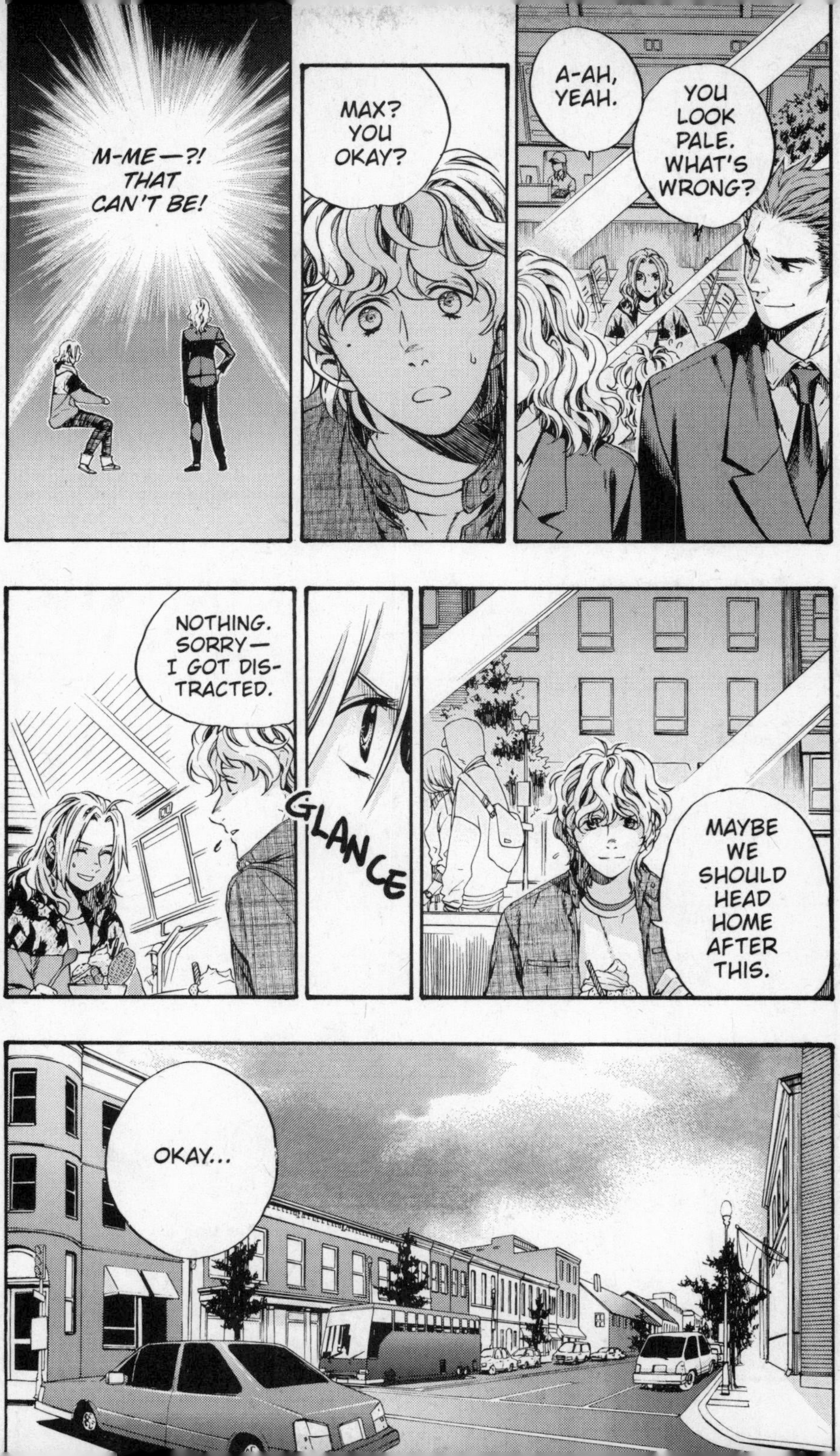
M-ME—?! THAT CAN'T BE!
MAX? YOU OKAY?
A-AH, YEAH.
YOU LOOK PALE. WHAT'S WRONG?
NOTHING. SORRY— I GOT DIS-TRACTED.
GLANCE
MAYBE WE SHOULD HEAD HOME AFTER THIS.
OKAY...

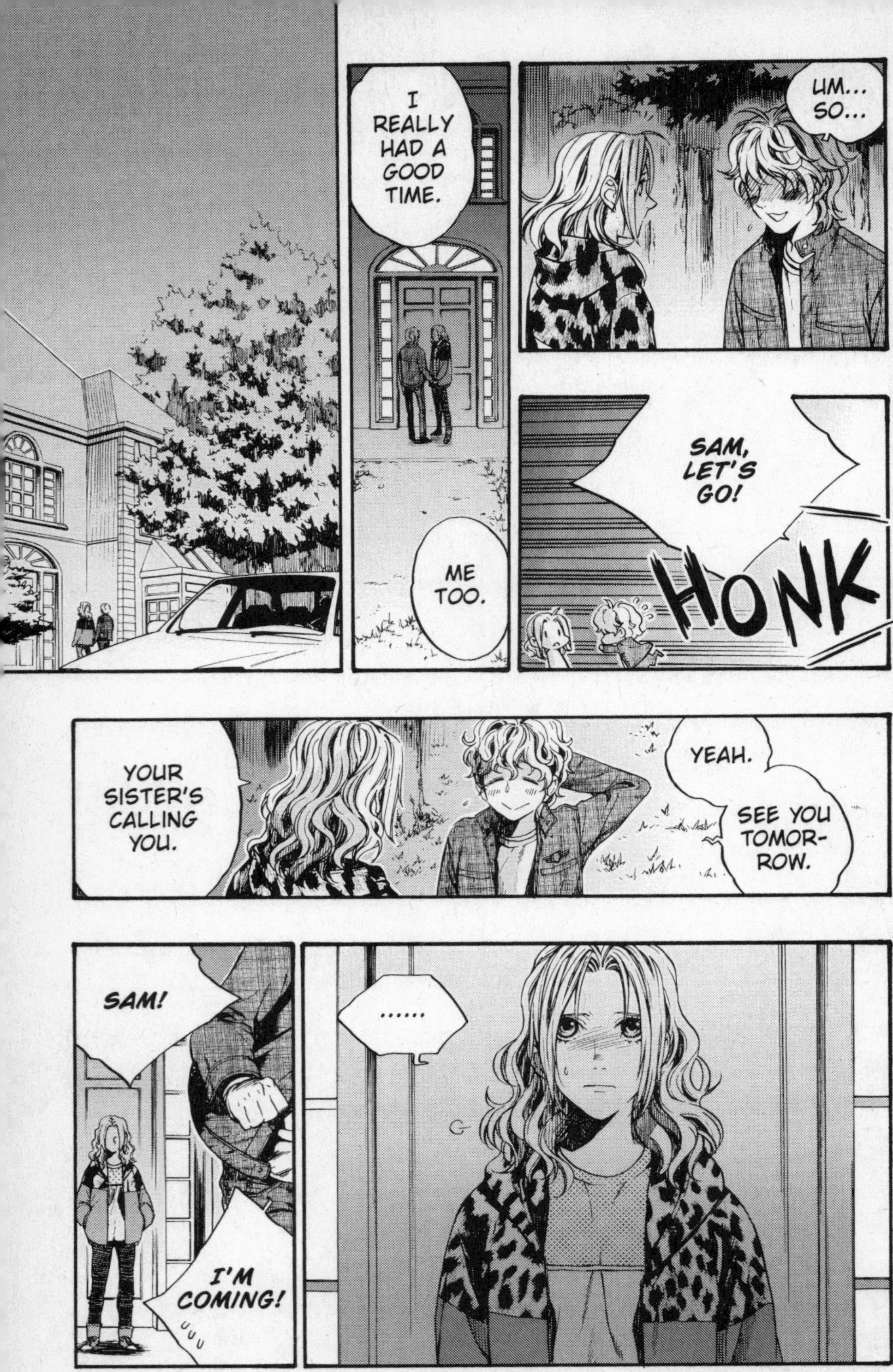
I REALLY HAD A GOOD TIME.
ME TOO.
UM... SO...
SAM, LET'S GO!
HONK
YOUR SISTER'S CALLING YOU.
YEAH.
SEE YOU TOMORROW.
SAM!
I'M COMING!
......

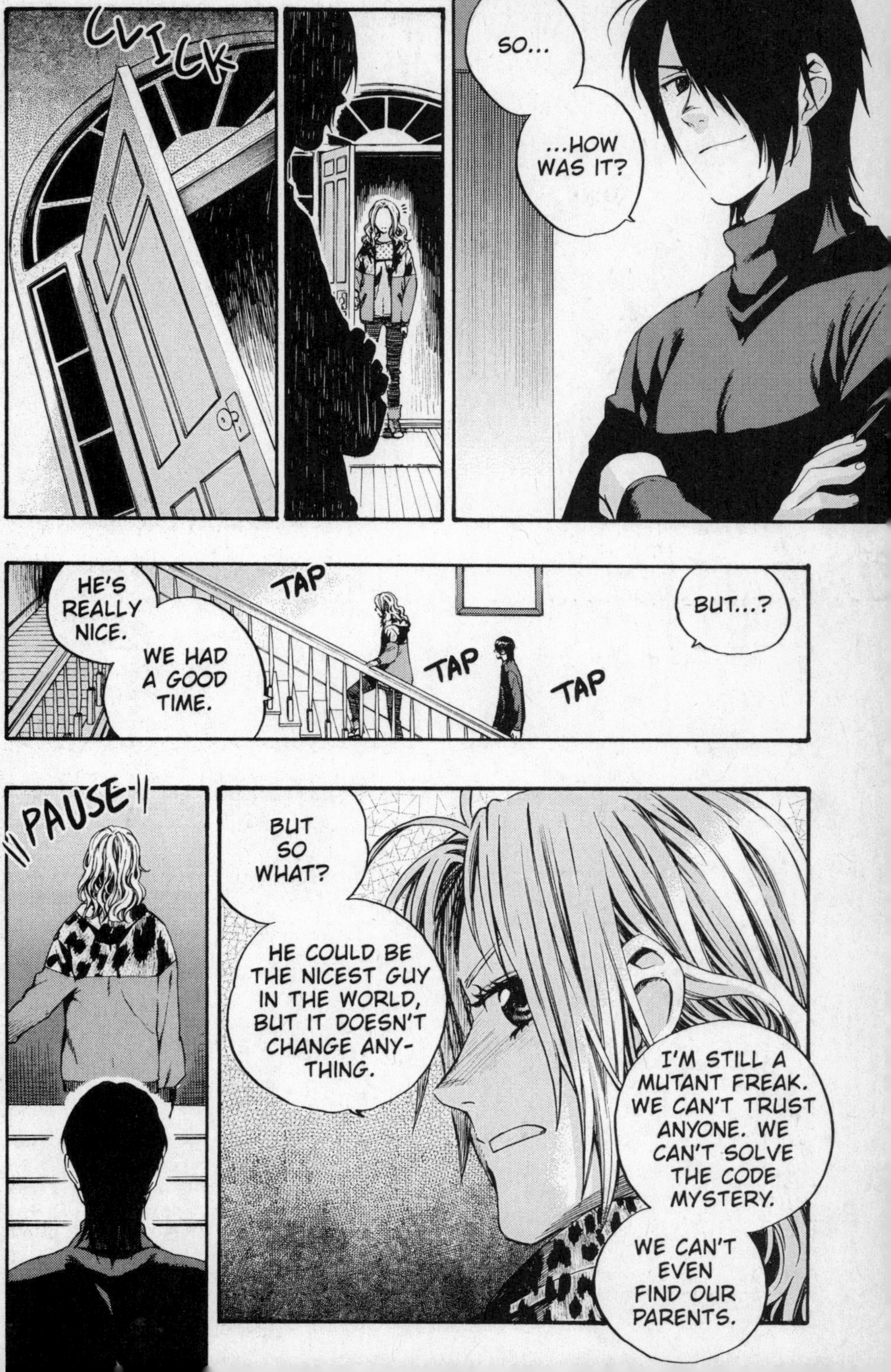
CLICK
SO...
...HOW WAS IT?
HE'S REALLY NICE.
WE HAD A GOOD TIME.
TAP
TAP
TAP
BUT...?
PAUSE
BUT SO WHAT?
HE COULD BE THE NICEST GUY IN THE WORLD, BUT IT DOESN'T CHANGE ANY-THING.
I'M STILL A MUTANT FREAK. WE CAN'T TRUST ANYONE. WE CAN'T SOLVE THE CODE MYSTERY.
WE CAN'T EVEN FIND OUR PARENTS.

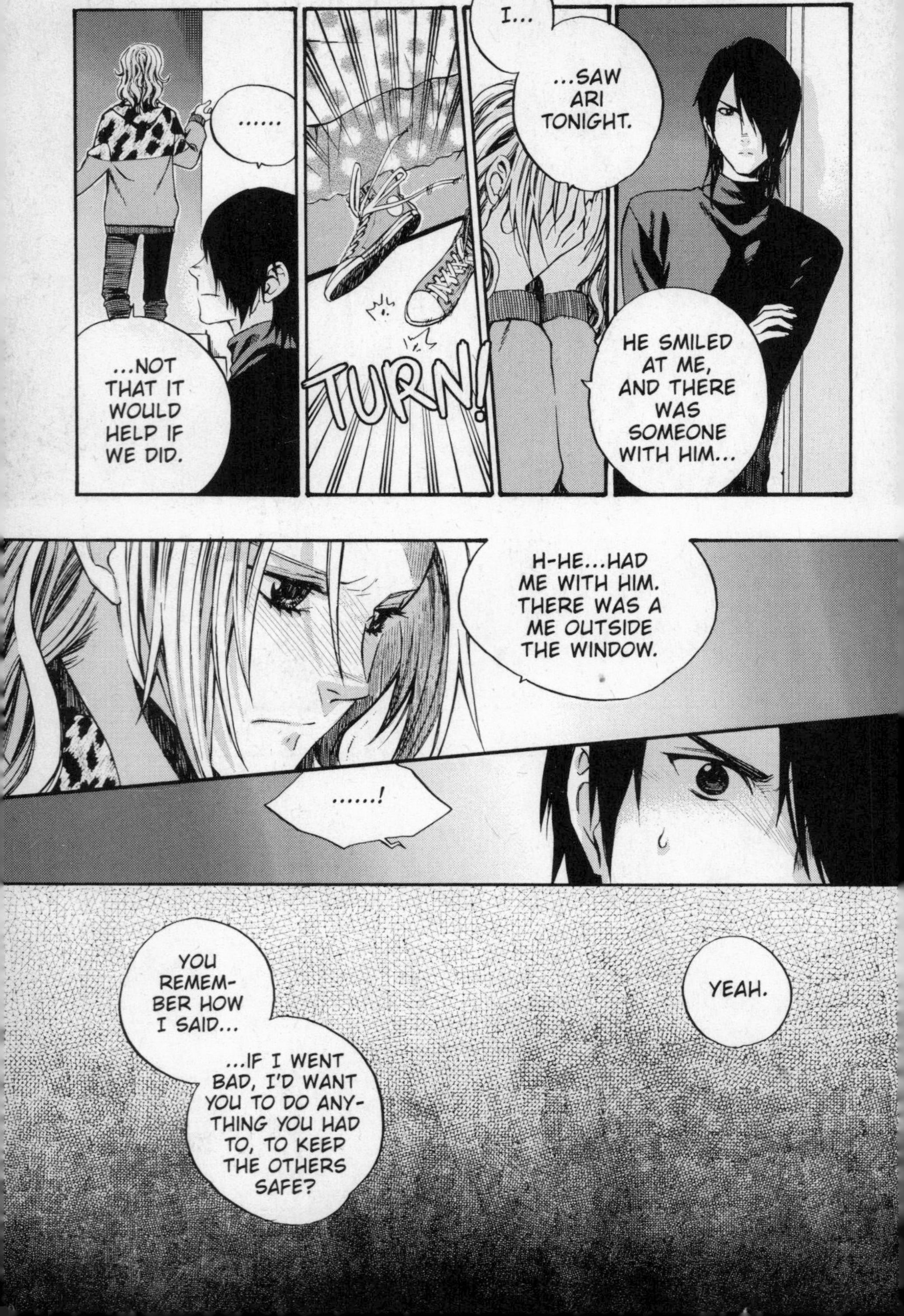
......
...NOT THAT IT WOULD HELP IF WE DID.
TURN!
I...
...SAW ARI TONIGHT.
HE SMILED AT ME, AND THERE WAS SOMEONE WITH HIM...
H-HE...HAD ME WITH HIM. THERE WAS A ME OUTSIDE THE WINDOW.
......!
YOU REMEMBER HOW I SAID...
...IF I WENT BAD, I'D WANT YOU TO DO ANYTHING YOU HAD TO, TO KEEP THE OTHERS SAFE?
YEAH.

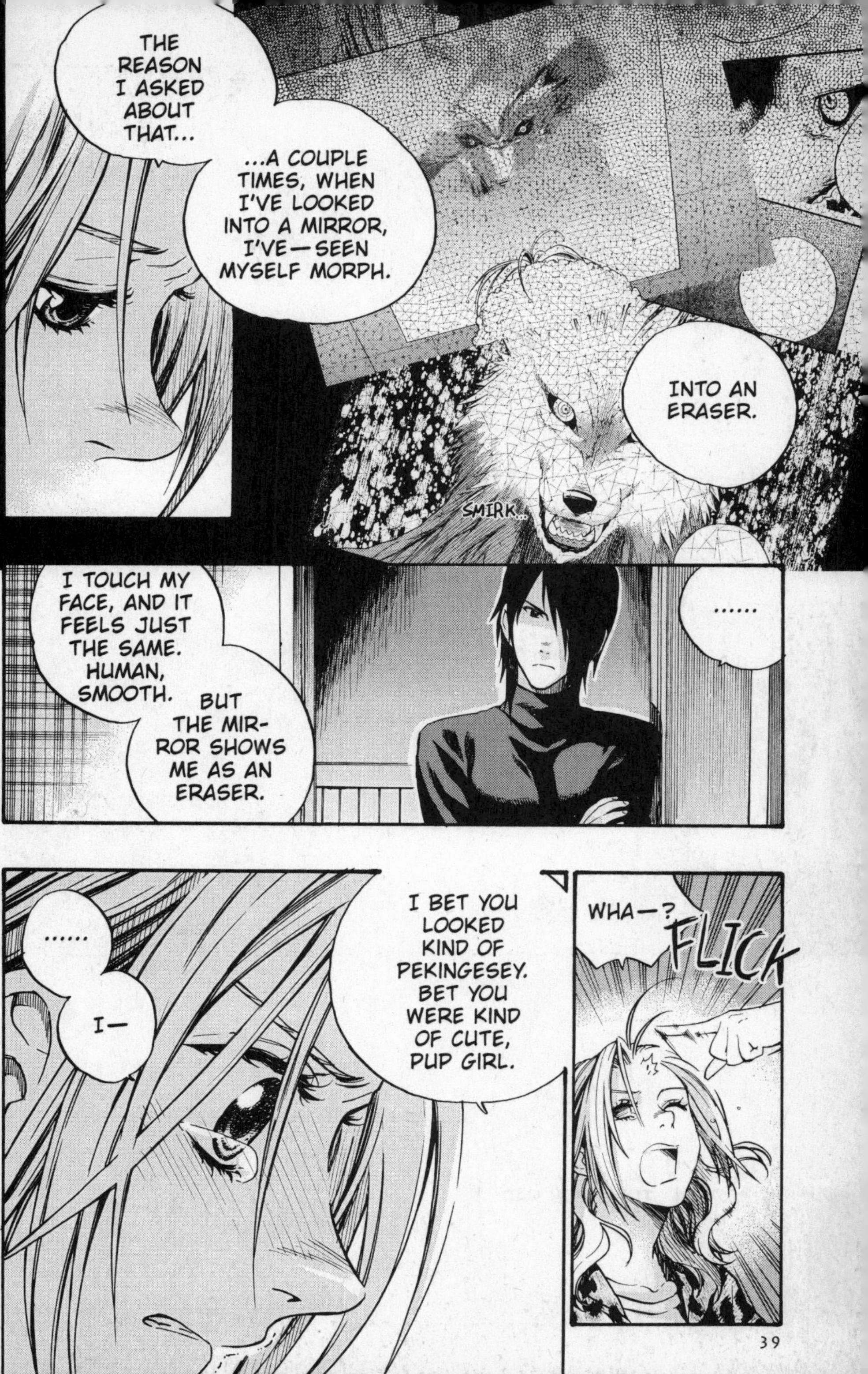
THE REASON I ASKED ABOUT THAT...
...A COUPLE TIMES, WHEN I'VE LOOKED INTO A MIRROR, I'VE—SEEN MYSELF MORPH.
INTO AN ERASER.
SMIRK...
I TOUCH MY FACE, AND IT FEELS JUST THE SAME. HUMAN, SMOOTH.
BUT THE MIRROR SHOWS ME AS AN ERASER.
......
......
I—
I BET YOU LOOKED KIND OF PEKINGESEY. BET YOU WERE KIND OF CUTE, PUP GIRL.
WHA—?
FLICK

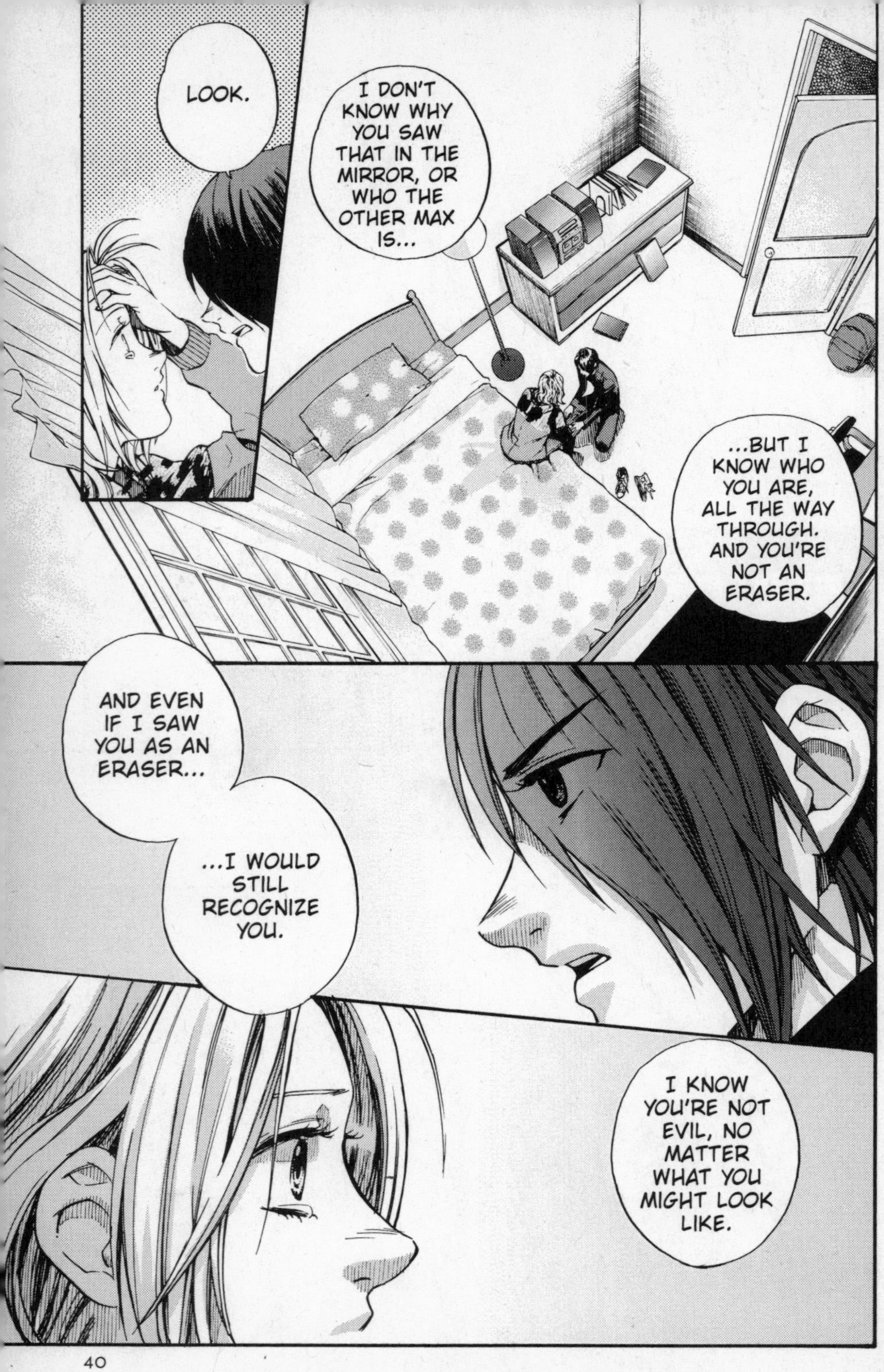
LOOK.
I DON'T KNOW WHY YOU SAW THAT IN THE MIRROR, OR WHO THE OTHER MAX IS...
...BUT I KNOW WHO YOU ARE, ALL THE WAY THROUGH. AND YOU'RE NOT AN ERASER.
AND EVEN IF I SAW YOU AS AN ERASER...
...I WOULD STILL RECOGNIZE YOU.
I KNOW YOU'RE NOT EVIL, NO MATTER WHAT YOU MIGHT LOOK LIKE.

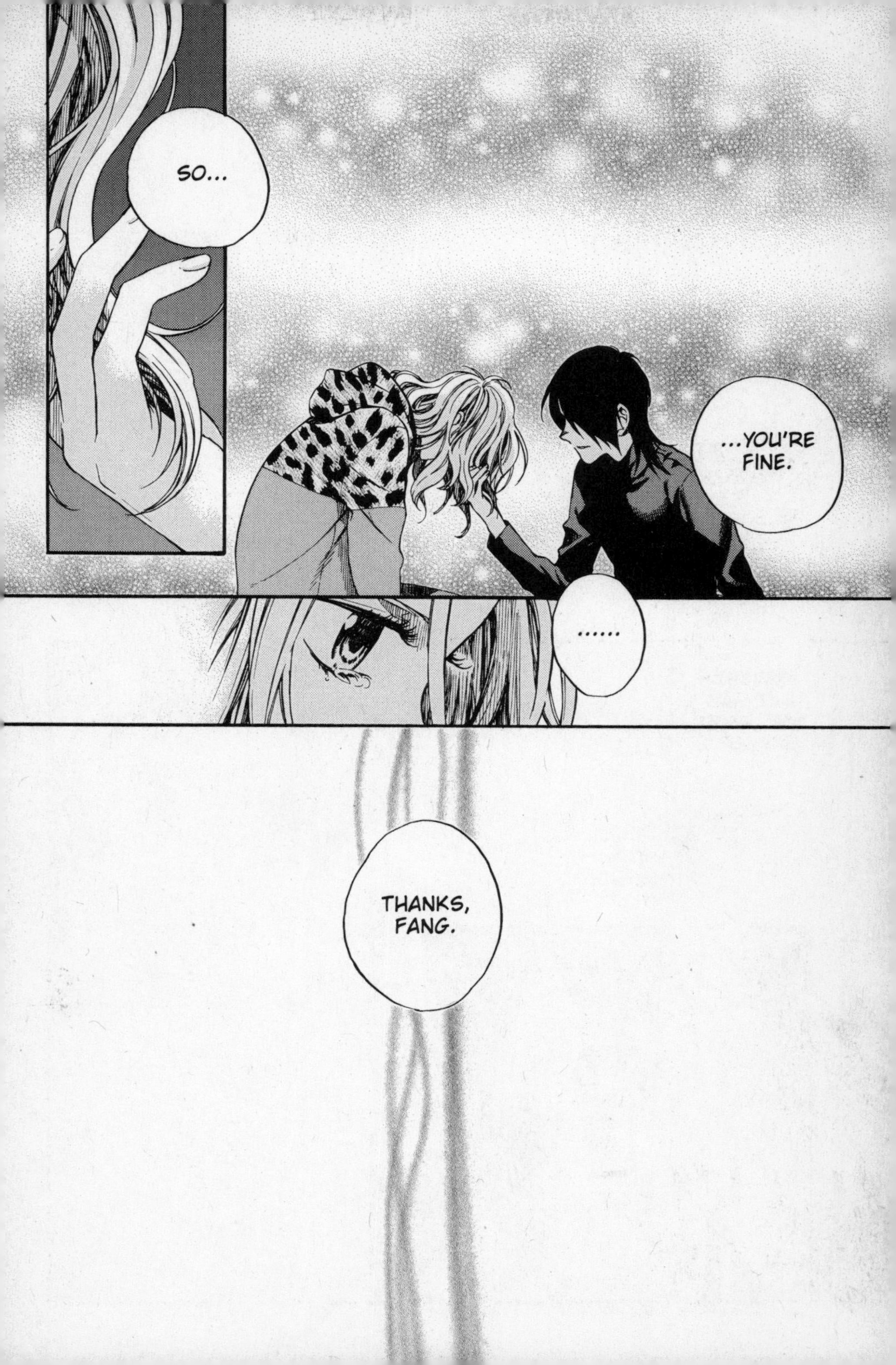
SO...
...YOU'RE FINE.
......
THANKS, FANG.

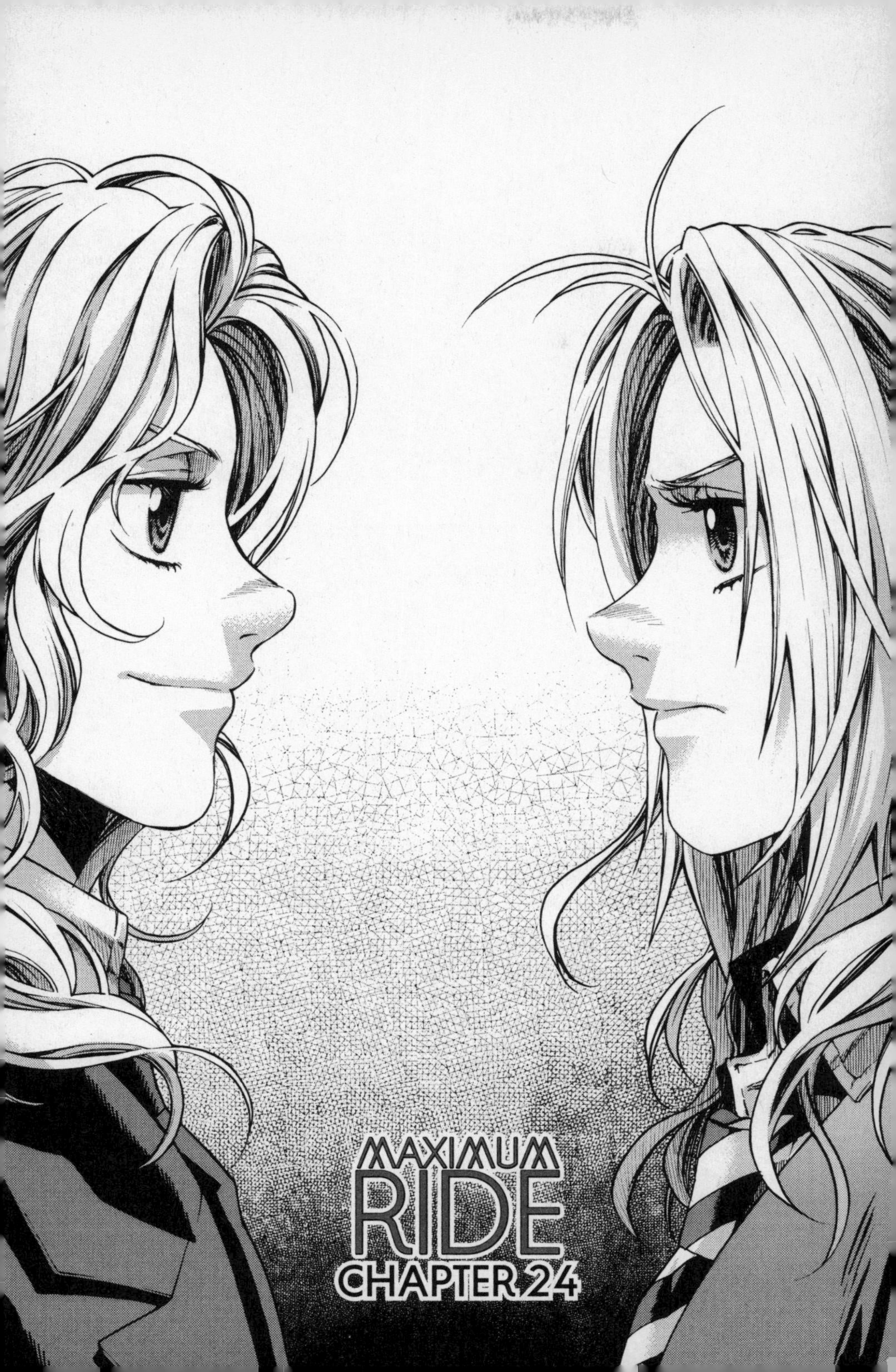
MAXIMUM
RIDE
CHAPTER 24

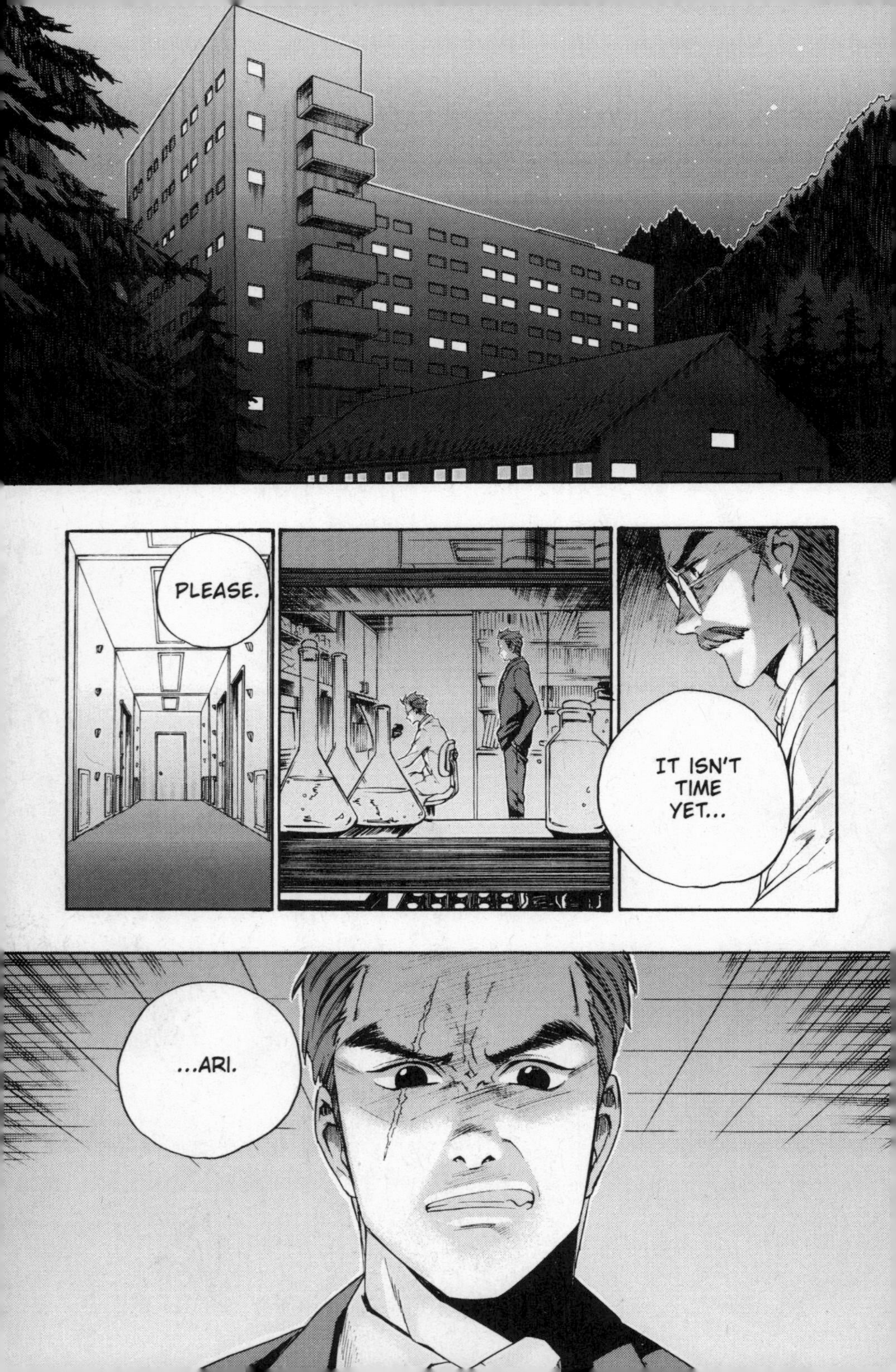
PLEASE.
IT ISN'T TIME YET...
...ARI.

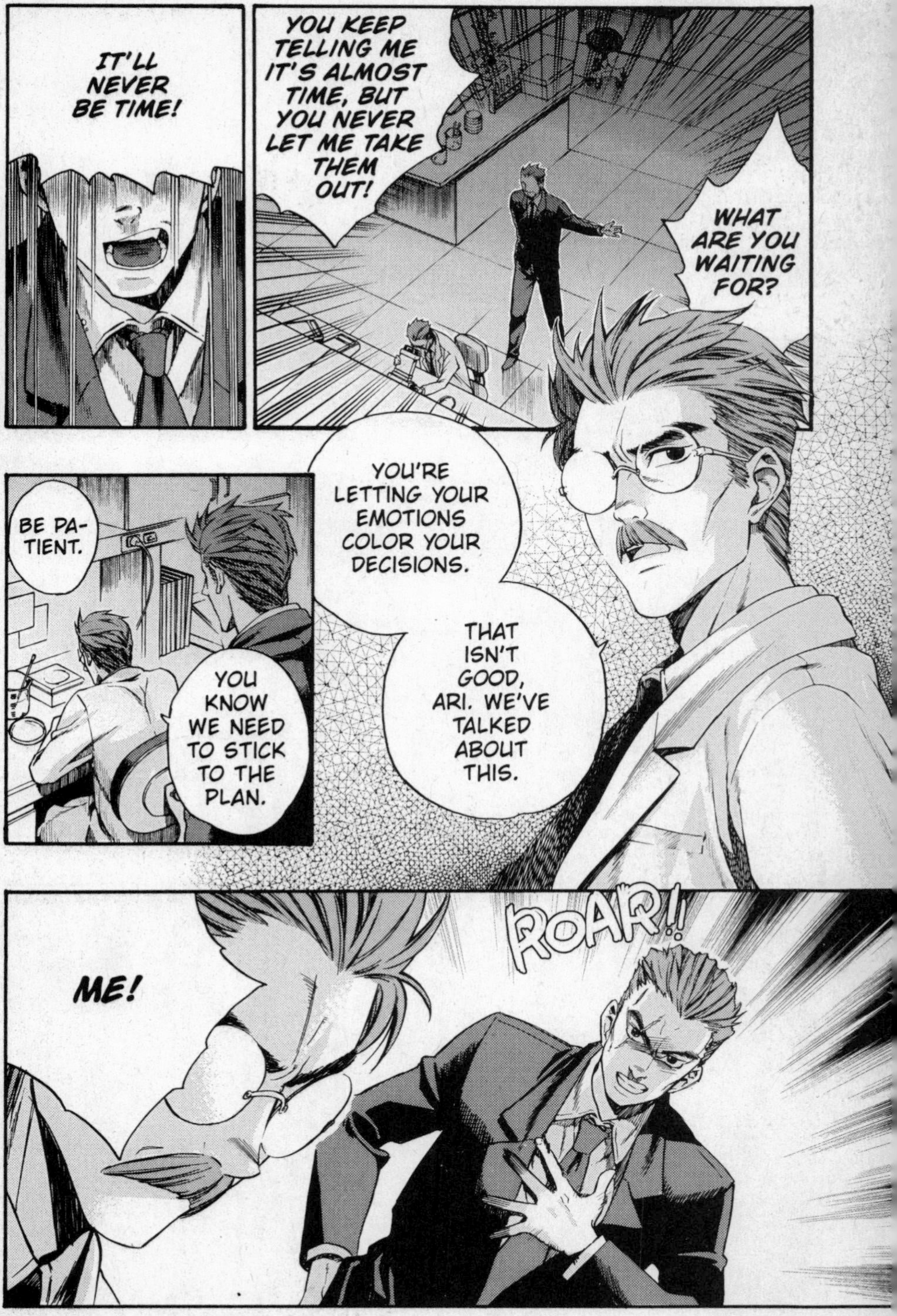
IT'LL NEVER BE TIME!
YOU KEEP TELLING ME IT'S ALMOST TIME, BUT YOU NEVER LET ME TAKE THEM OUT!
WHAT ARE YOU WAITING FOR?
BE PA- TIENT.
YOU KNOW WE NEED TO STICK TO THE PLAN.
YOU'RE LETTING YOUR EMOTIONS COLOR YOUR DECISIONS.
THAT ISN'T GOOD, ARI. WE'VE TALKED ABOUT THIS.
ME!
ROAR!!

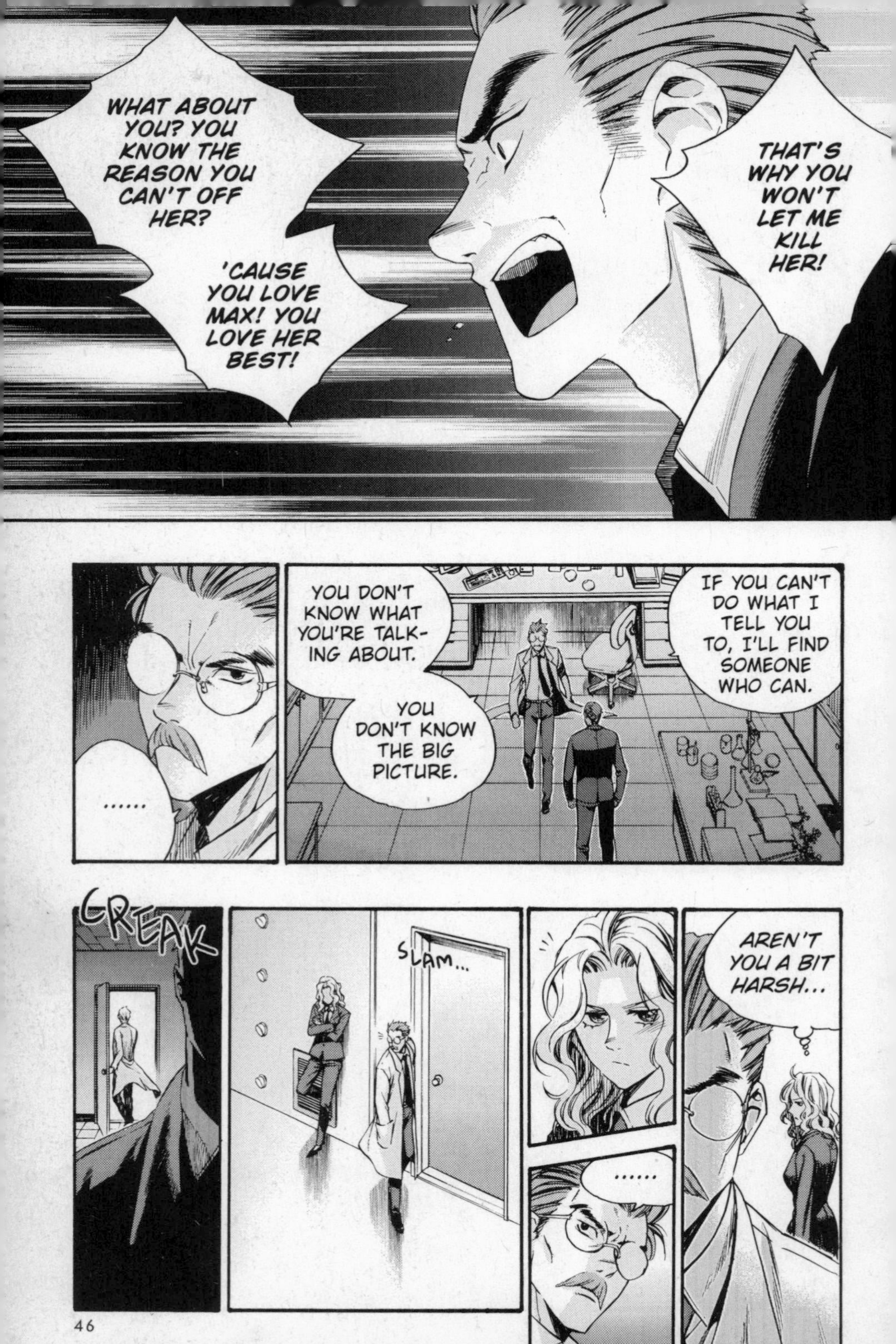
WHAT ABOUT YOU? YOU KNOW THE REASON YOU CAN'T OFF HER?
'CAUSE YOU LOVE MAX! YOU LOVE HER BEST!
THAT'S WHY YOU WON'T LET ME KILL HER!
......
YOU DON'T KNOW WHAT YOU'RE TALK-ING ABOUT.
YOU DON'T KNOW THE BIG PICTURE.
IF YOU CAN'T DO WHAT I TELL YOU TO, I'LL FIND SOMEONE WHO CAN.
CREAK
SLAM...
AREN'T YOU A BIT HARSH...
......

HIS COLD EYES... CAN'T HE JUST ONCE...

...SHOW THE SAME LOVE AND ADMIRATION...

...FOR ME AS HE DOES FOR MAX?

GRIT...

CAN'T YOU, FATHER?

WHAM

AAARGHH!!

AAARGH!!

DAMN!!!!

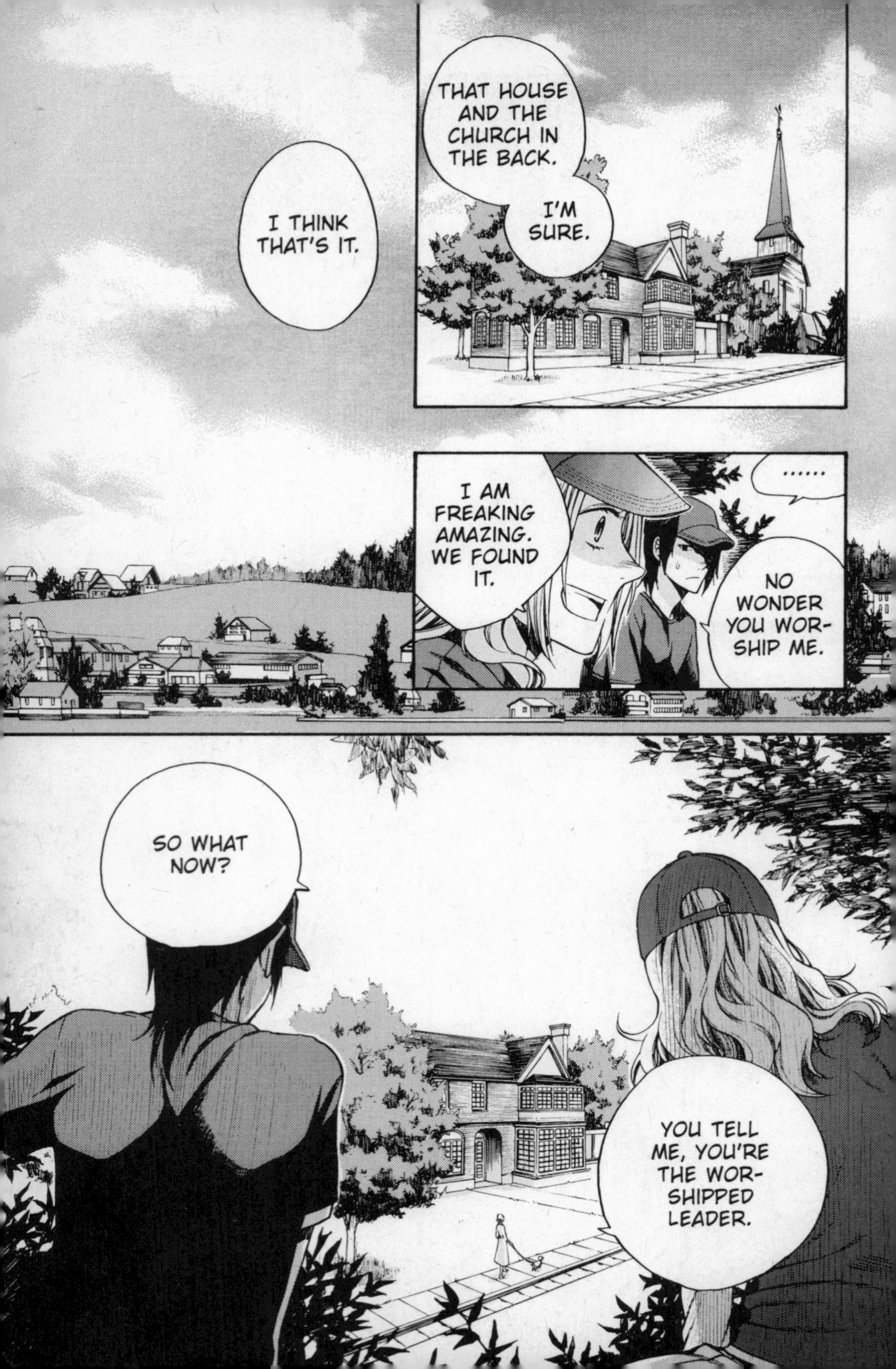

THAT HOUSE AND THE CHURCH IN THE BACK.
I'M SURE.
I THINK THAT'S IT.
......
I AM FREAKING AMAZING. WE FOUND IT.
NO WONDER YOU WOR-SHIP ME.
SO WHAT NOW?
YOU TELL ME, YOU'RE THE WOR-SHIPPED LEADER.

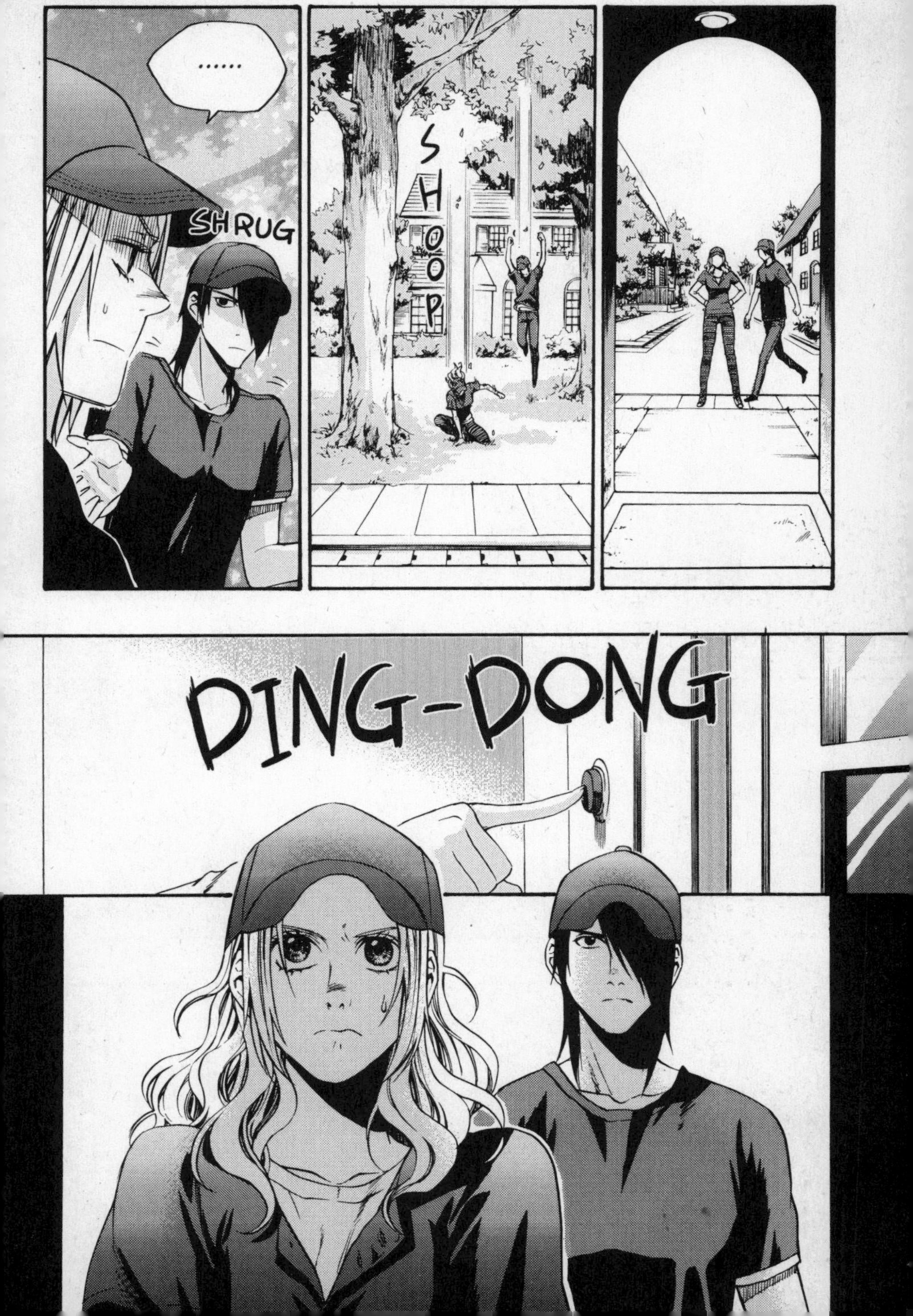

......
SHRUG
SHOOP
DING-DONG

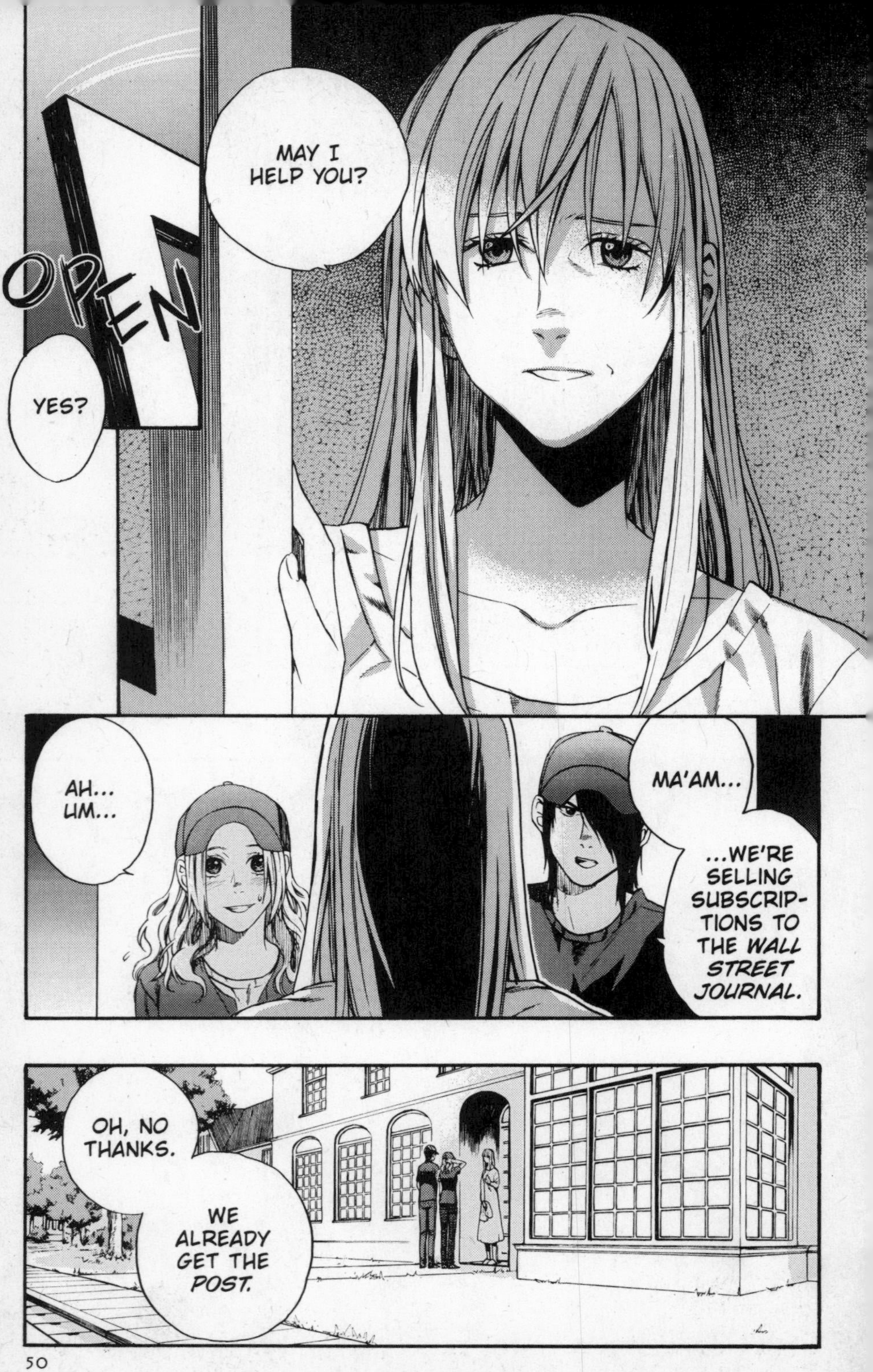
OPEN
YES?
MAY I HELP YOU?
AH... UM...
MA'AM...
...WE'RE SELLING SUBSCRIPTIONS TO THE *WALL STREET JOURNAL*.
OH, NO THANKS.
WE ALREADY GET THE *POST*.

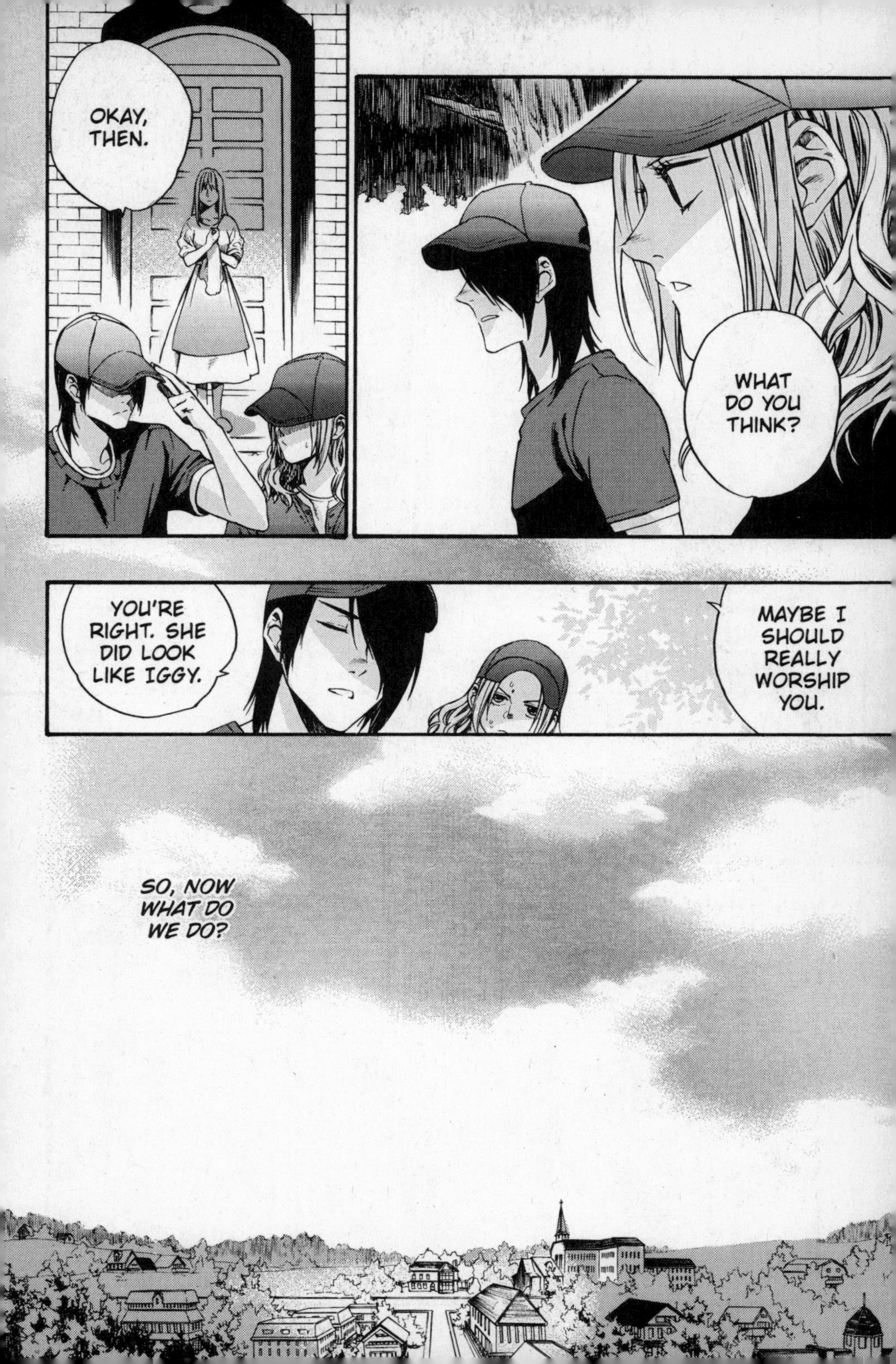
OKAY, THEN.
WHAT DO YOU THINK?
YOU'RE RIGHT. SHE DID LOOK LIKE IGGY.
MAYBE I SHOULD REALLY WORSHIP YOU.
SO, NOW WHAT DO WE DO?

STILL SMELLS KIND OF LIKE EXPLOSIVES.

CREAK

YEAH.

I LIKE THAT SMELL.

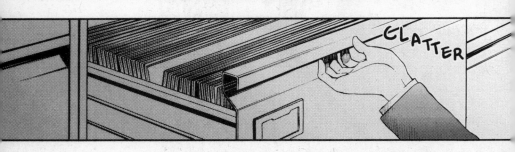

CLATTER

SHE PUT THOSE FILES SOMEPLACE TOWARD THE FRONT OF THE ROOM.

OKAY.

ON THE RIGHT SIDE. IS THERE A METAL CABINET?

THEY'RE ALL METAL.

I DON'T EVEN KNOW WHAT I'M LOOKING FOR.

ALL THE FILES LOOK ALIKE.

BUT WHY IS THE HEADHUNTER SAVING THEM?

OH, MAKES SENSE. LET'S SHOW THESE TO MAX.

DID HE RUN THE NUTHOUSE? MAYBE HE WAS A PATIENT AND HE KILLED ALL THE OTHERS AND OPENED THIS SCHOOL.

OKAY. WE BETTER BE HEADING BACK.

?!

BUMP

THAT'S FUNNY.

Off limits

THERE'S A DOOR HERE I NEVER NOTICED.

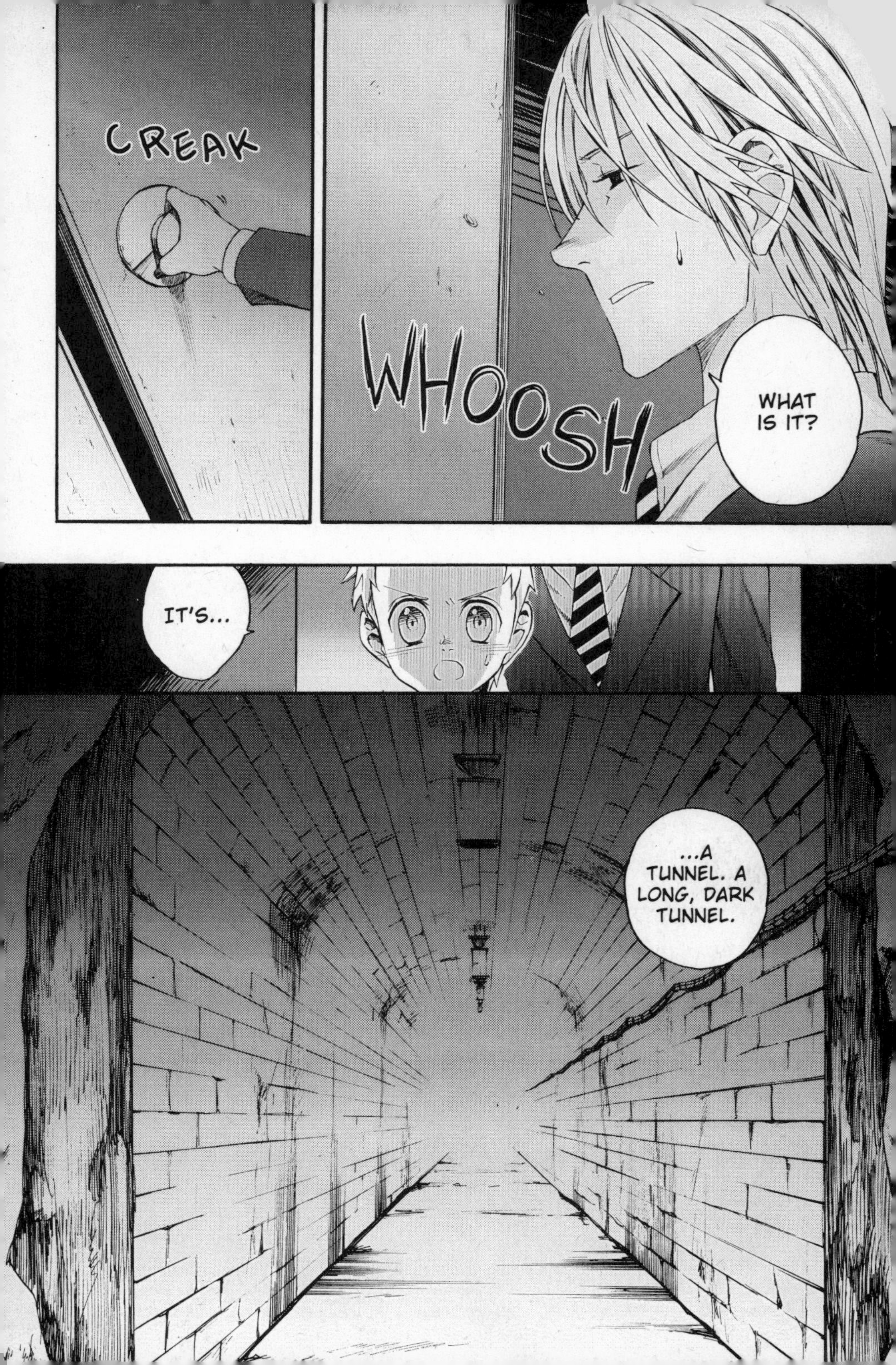
CREAK
WHOOSH
WHAT IS IT?
IT'S...
...A TUNNEL. A LONG, DARK TUNNEL.

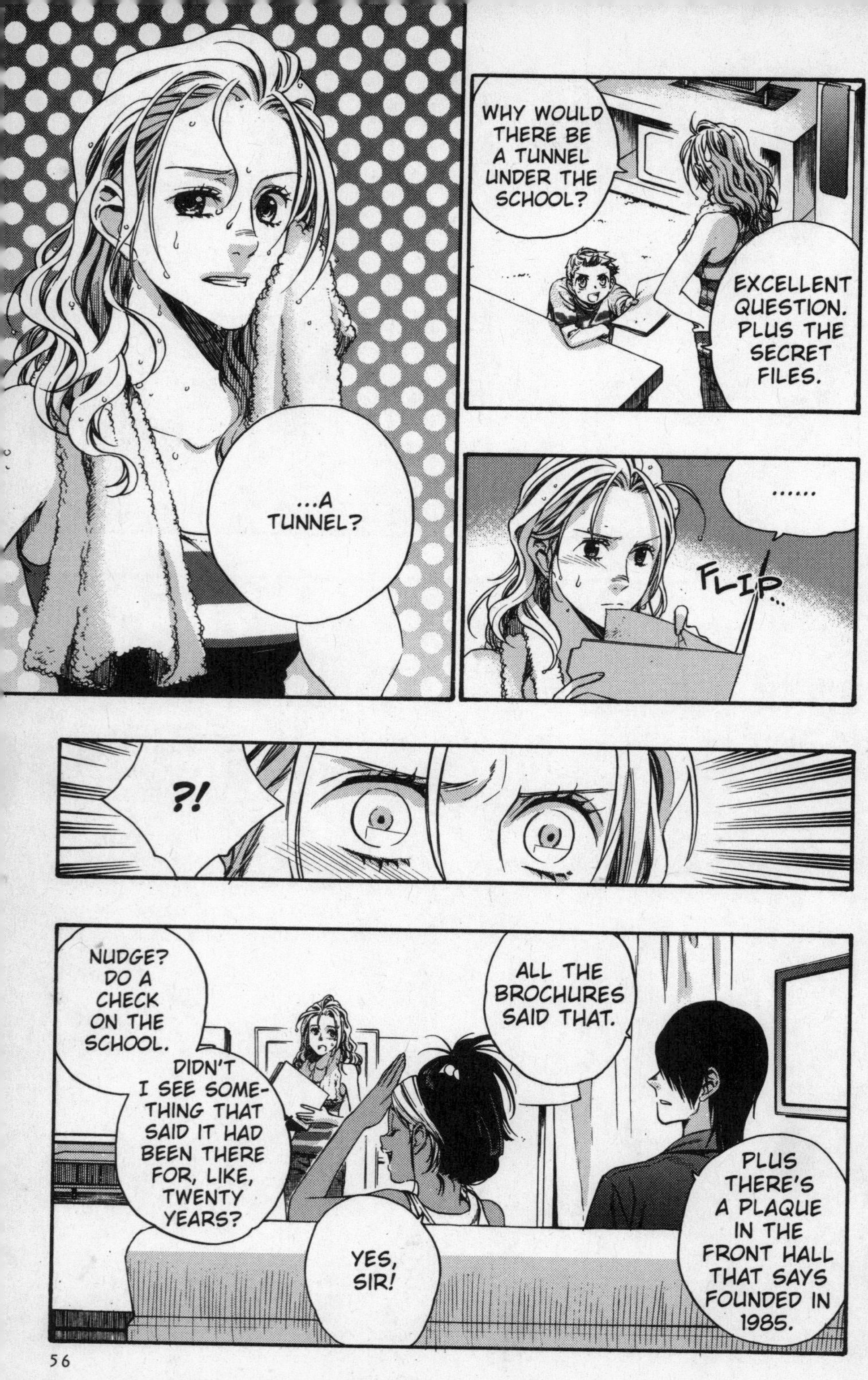

...A TUNNEL?
WHY WOULD THERE BE A TUNNEL UNDER THE SCHOOL?
EXCELLENT QUESTION. PLUS THE SECRET FILES.
......
FLIP...
?!
NUDGE? DO A CHECK ON THE SCHOOL.
DIDN'T I SEE SOME-THING THAT SAID IT HAD BEEN THERE FOR, LIKE, TWENTY YEARS?
ALL THE BROCHURES SAID THAT.
YES, SIR!
PLUS THERE'S A PLAQUE IN THE FRONT HALL THAT SAYS FOUNDED IN 1985.

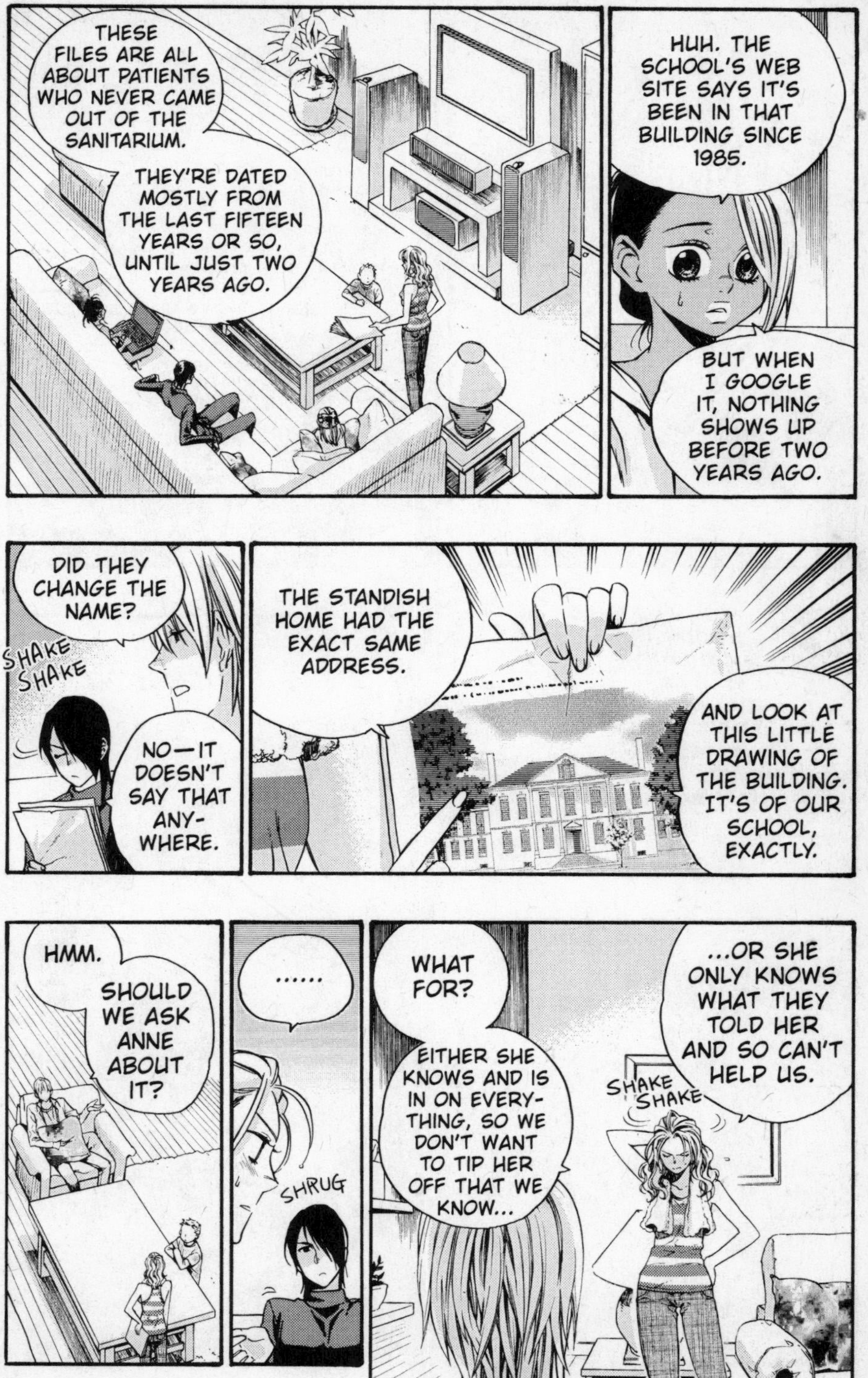
THESE FILES ARE ALL ABOUT PATIENTS WHO NEVER CAME OUT OF THE SANITARIUM.
THEY'RE DATED MOSTLY FROM THE LAST FIFTEEN YEARS OR SO, UNTIL JUST TWO YEARS AGO.
HUH. THE SCHOOL'S WEB SITE SAYS IT'S BEEN IN THAT BUILDING SINCE 1985.
BUT WHEN I GOOGLE IT, NOTHING SHOWS UP BEFORE TWO YEARS AGO.
DID THEY CHANGE THE NAME?
SHAKE SHAKE
NO—IT DOESN'T SAY THAT ANY-WHERE.
THE STANDISH HOME HAD THE EXACT SAME ADDRESS.
AND LOOK AT THIS LITTLE DRAWING OF THE BUILDING. IT'S OF OUR SCHOOL, EXACTLY.
HMM.
SHOULD WE ASK ANNE ABOUT IT?
......
SHRUG
WHAT FOR?
EITHER SHE KNOWS AND IS IN ON EVERY-THING, SO WE DON'T WANT TO TIP HER OFF THAT WE KNOW...
...OR SHE ONLY KNOWS WHAT THEY TOLD HER AND SO CAN'T HELP US.
SHAKE SHAKE

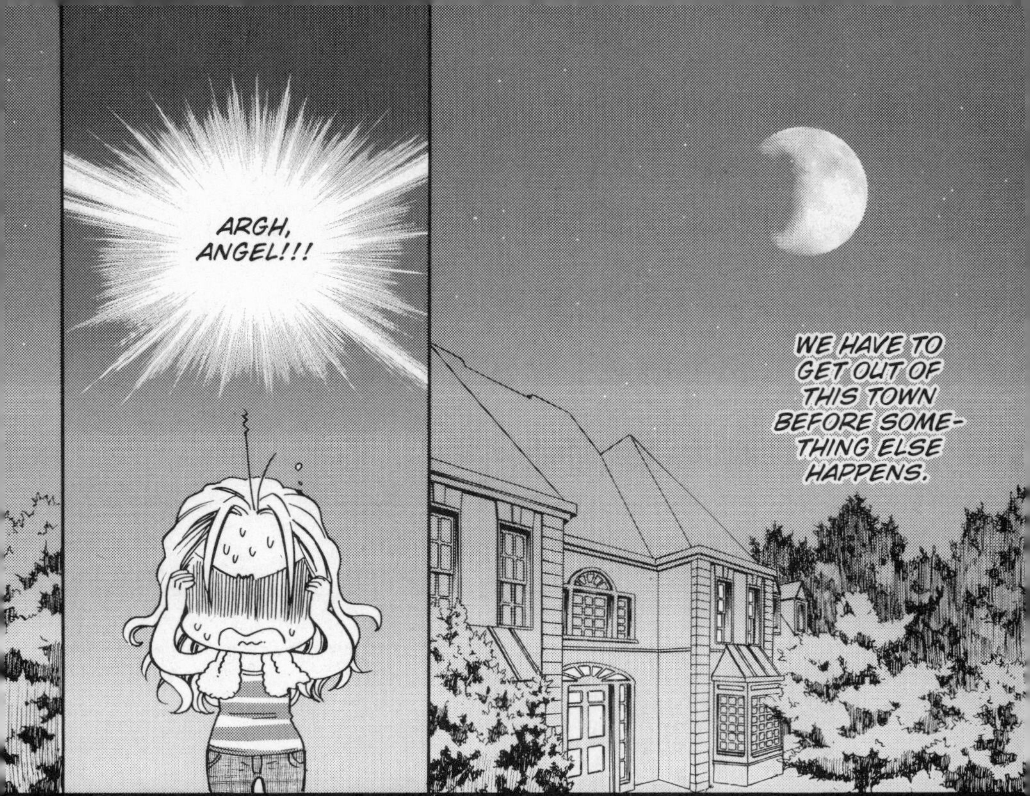
ARGH, ANGEL!!!
WE HAVE TO GET OUT OF THIS TOWN BEFORE SOME-THING ELSE HAPPENS.

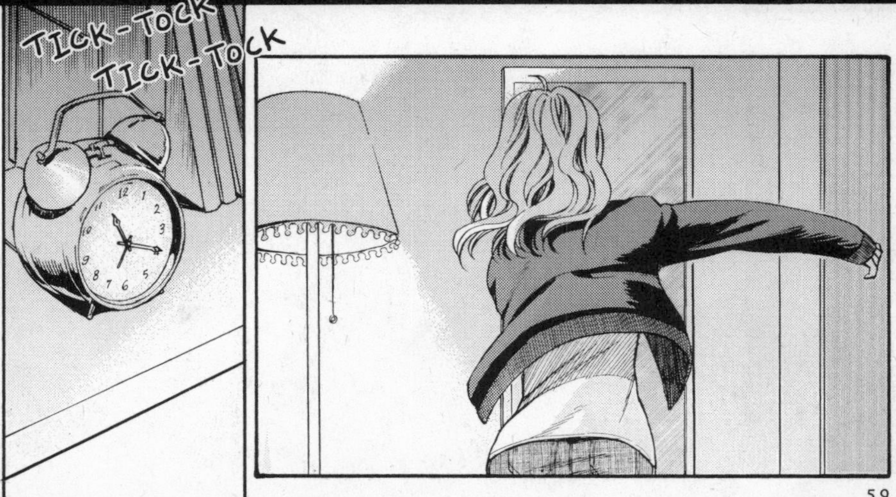
TICK-TOCK
TICK-TOCK

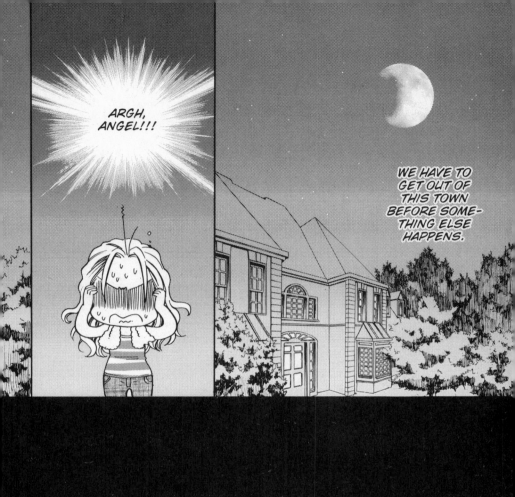

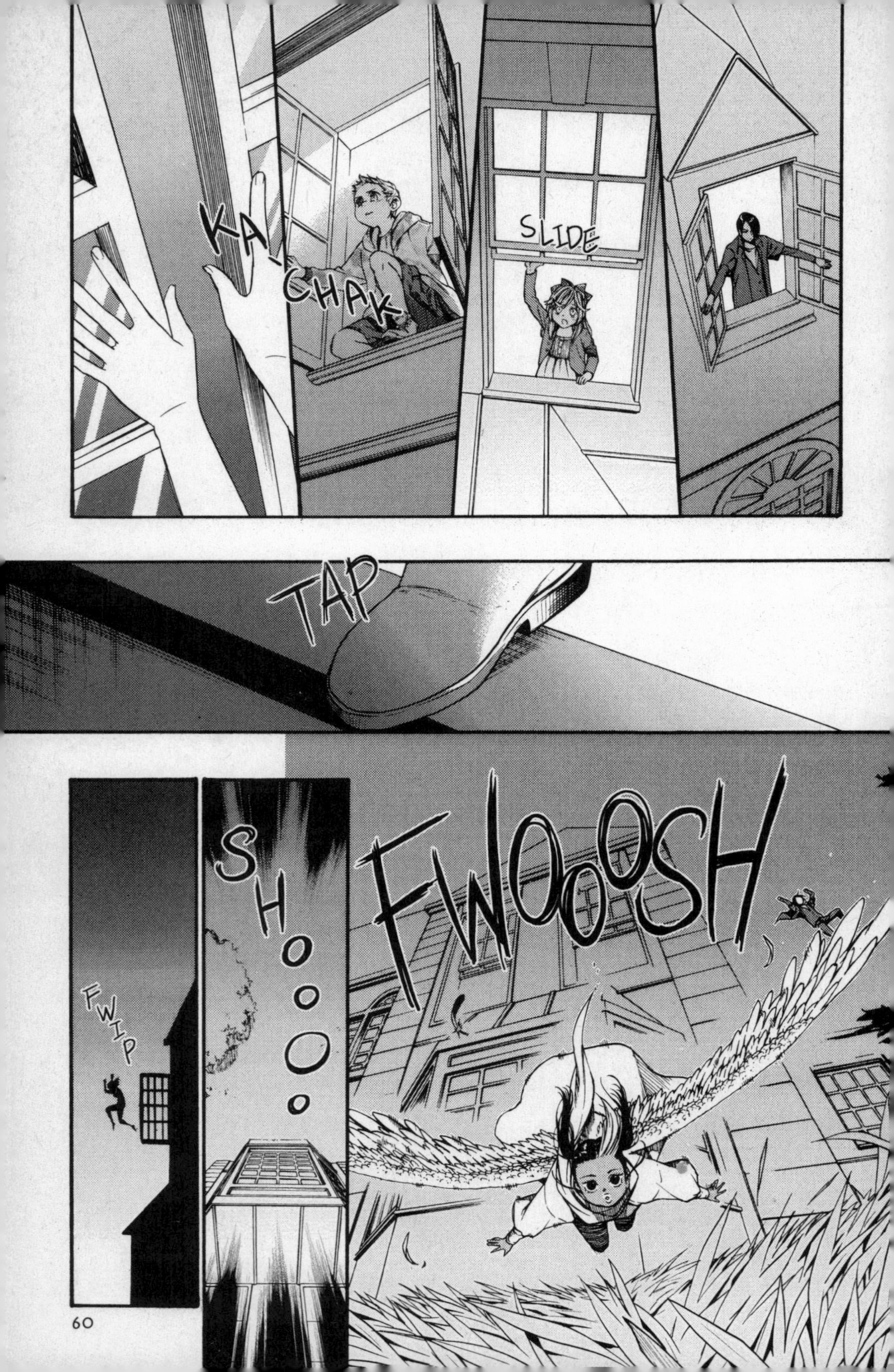
KA-CHAK
SLIDE
TAP
FWIP
SHOOOOO
FWOOOSH

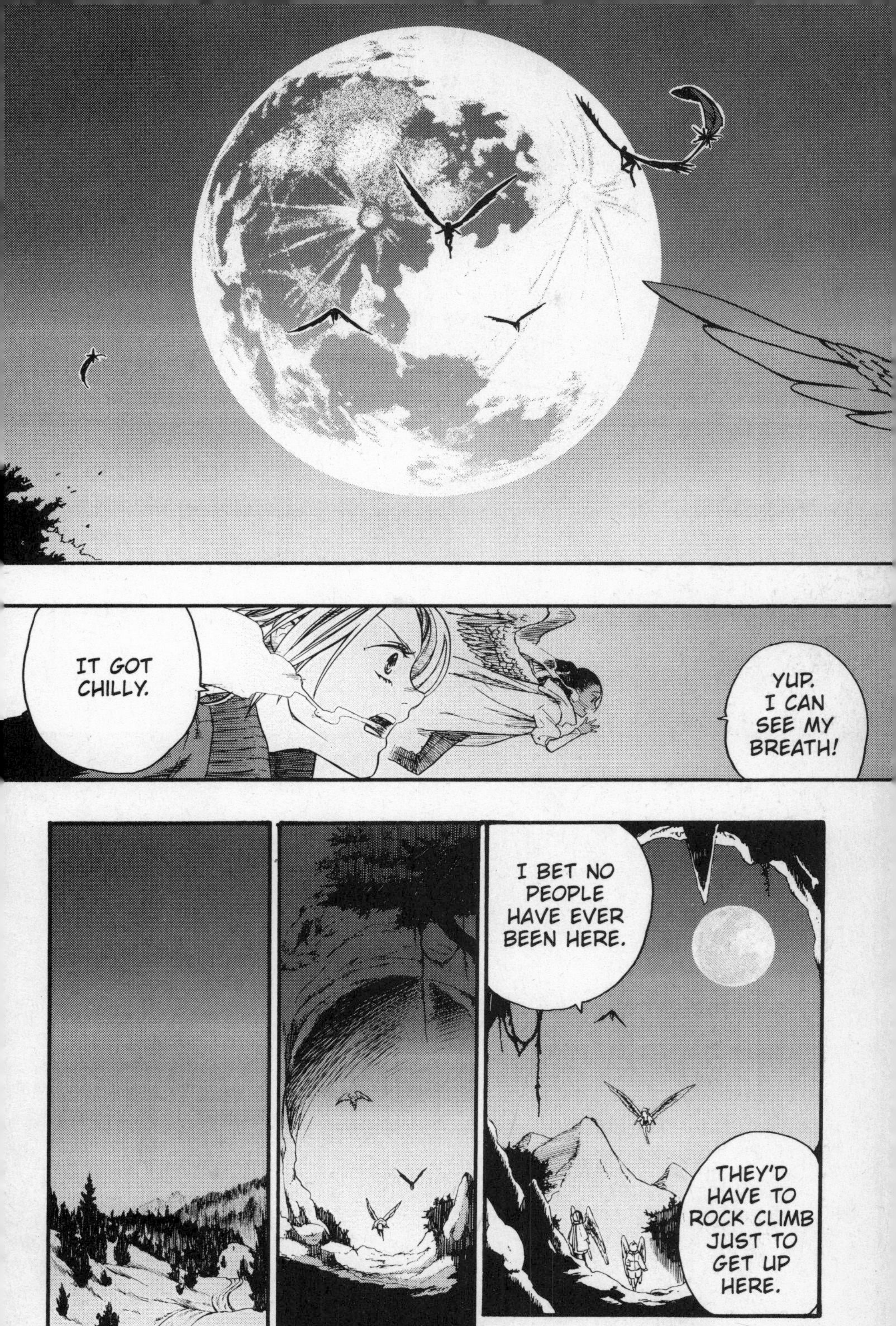
IT GOT CHILLY.
YUP. I CAN SEE MY BREATH!
I BET NO PEOPLE HAVE EVER BEEN HERE.
THEY'D HAVE TO ROCK CLIMB JUST TO GET UP HERE.

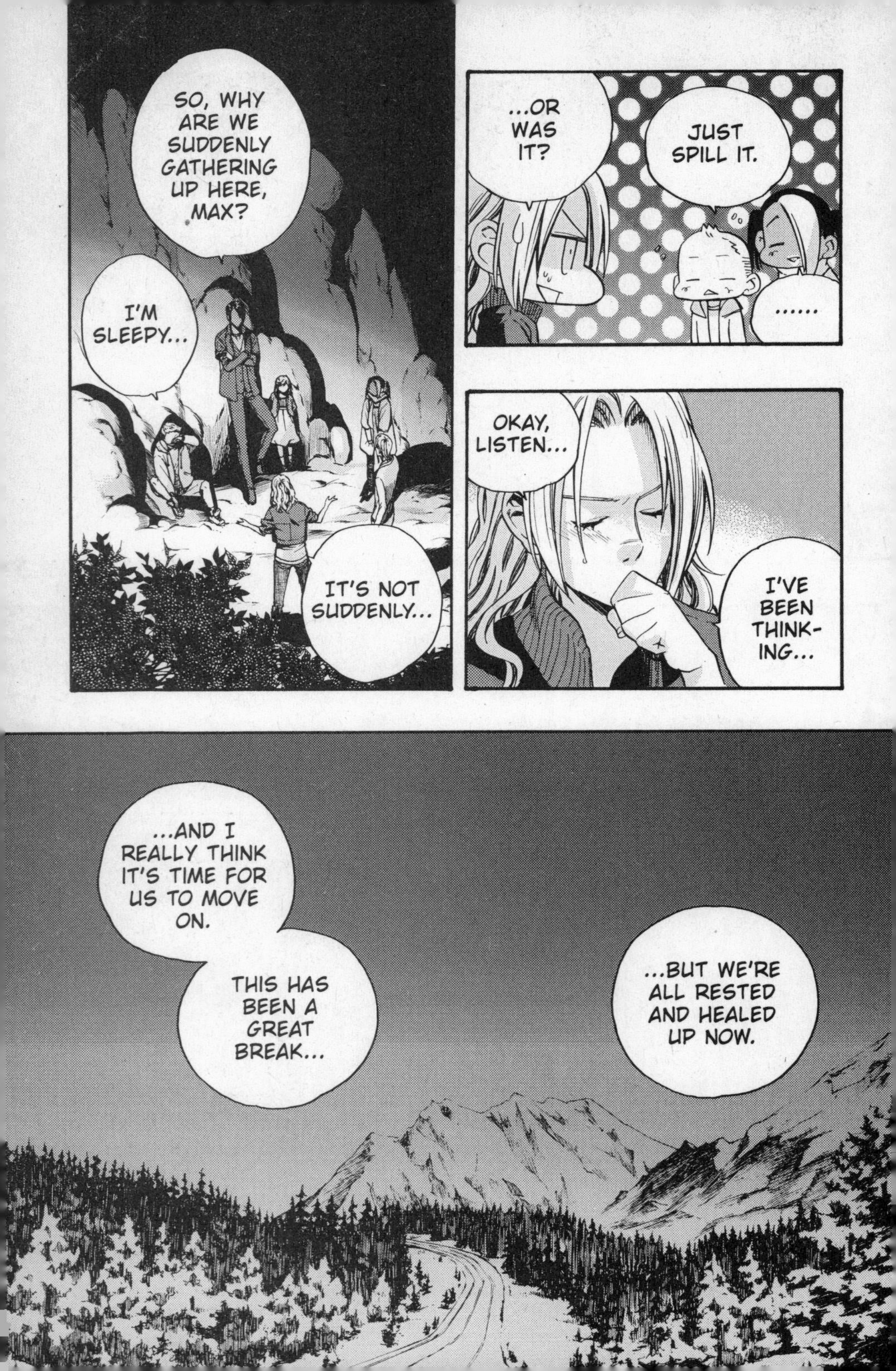
SO, WHY ARE WE SUDDENLY GATHERING UP HERE, MAX?
I'M SLEEPY...
IT'S NOT SUDDENLY...
...OR WAS IT?
JUST SPILL IT.
......
OKAY, LISTEN...
I'VE BEEN THINKING...
...AND I REALLY THINK IT'S TIME FOR US TO MOVE ON.
THIS HAS BEEN A GREAT BREAK...
...BUT WE'RE ALL RESTED AND HEALED UP NOW.

......

SO IT'S TIME WE DISAPPEAR AGAIN.

I MEAN... ARI KNOWS WE'RE CLOSE BY.

HE ATTACKED US ON OUR WAY HOME—HE PROBABLY HAS CAMERAS TRAINED ON ANNE'S HOUSE.

THE HEAD-HUNTER HAS IT IN FOR US.

NOW THE WEIRD FILES FROM THE SCHOOL...

...THE MYSTERY TUNNEL—IT'S ALL ADDING UP TO AN UGLY PICTURE.

NOT TO MENTION WHAT ANGEL MIGHT BE DOING TO THE LEADER OF THE FREE WORLD.

STARE

Heh-heh.

?

HMMM.

WE SHOULD CLEAR OUT OF HERE BEFORE ALL THIS STUFF STARTS HITTING THE FAN.

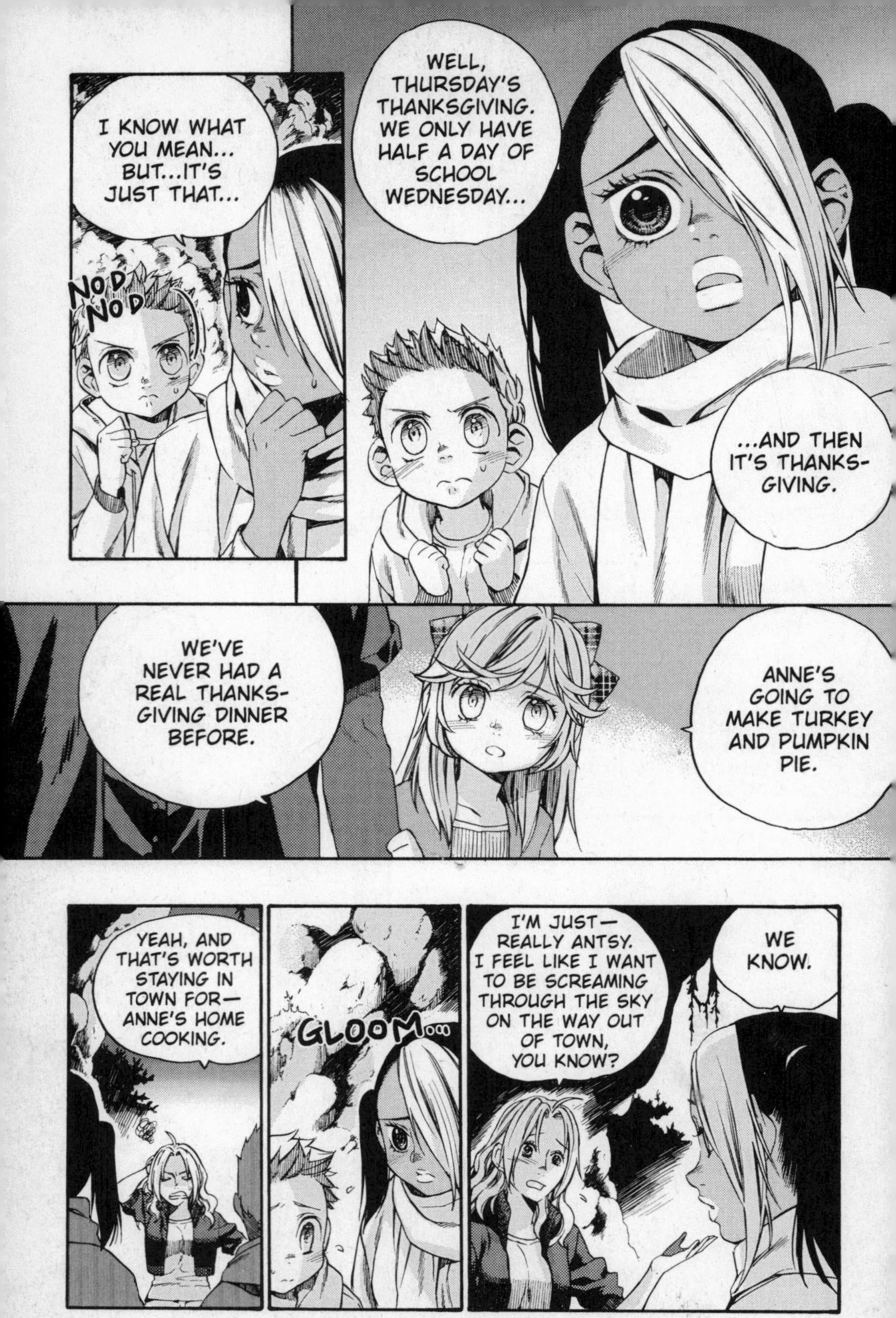

I KNOW WHAT YOU MEAN... BUT...IT'S JUST THAT...
NOD NOD
WELL, THURSDAY'S THANKSGIVING. WE ONLY HAVE HALF A DAY OF SCHOOL WEDNESDAY...
...AND THEN IT'S THANKS-GIVING.
WE'VE NEVER HAD A REAL THANKS-GIVING DINNER BEFORE.
ANNE'S GOING TO MAKE TURKEY AND PUMPKIN PIE.
YEAH, AND THAT'S WORTH STAYING IN TOWN FOR— ANNE'S HOME COOKING.
GLOOM...
I'M JUST— REALLY ANTSY. I FEEL LIKE I WANT TO BE SCREAMING THROUGH THE SKY ON THE WAY OUT OF TOWN, YOU KNOW?
WE KNOW.

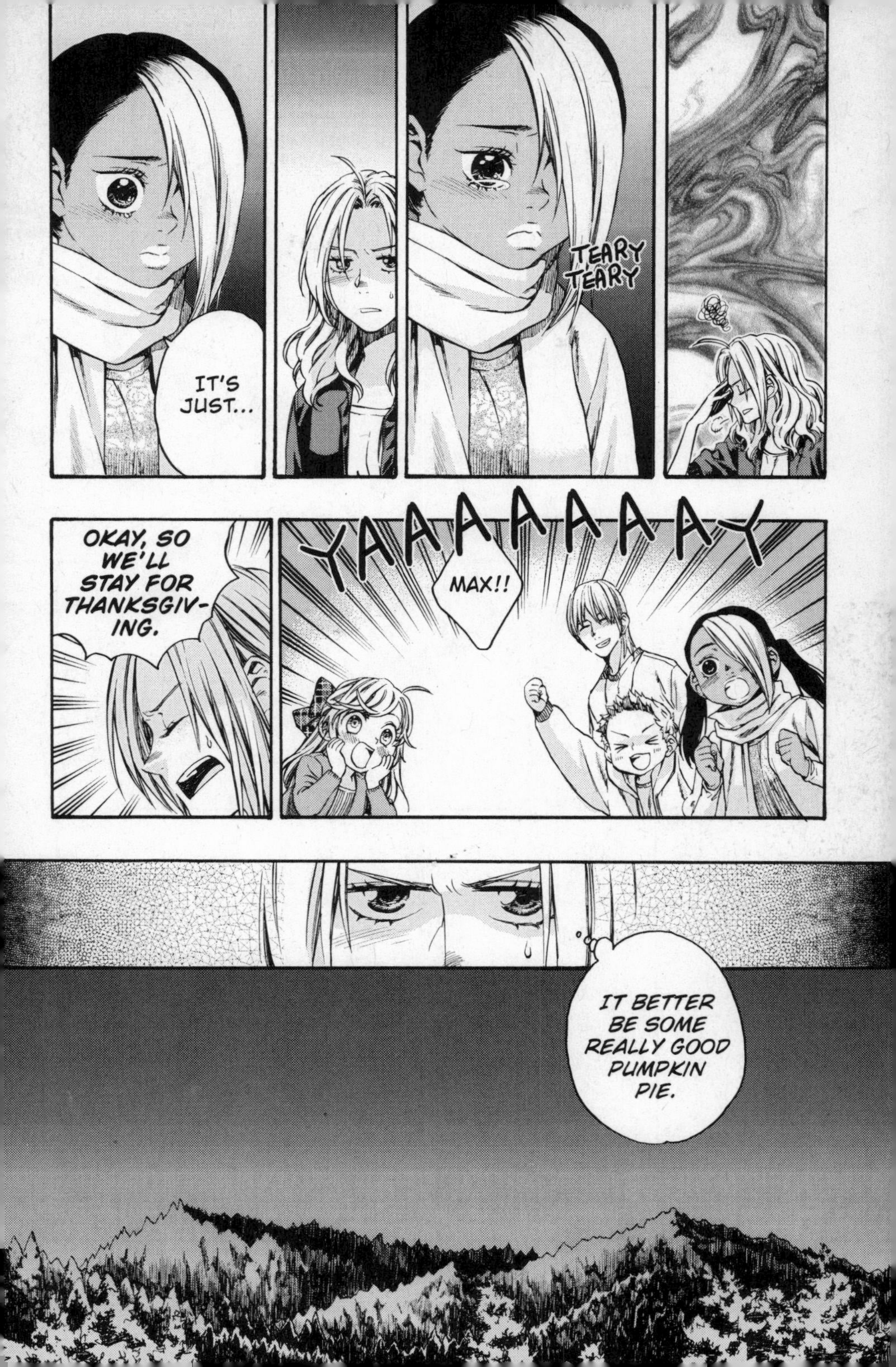
IT'S JUST...
TEARY TEARY
OKAY, SO WE'LL STAY FOR THANKSGIV-ING.
YAAAAAAAY
MAX!!
IT BETTER BE SOME REALLY GOOD PUMPKIN PIE.

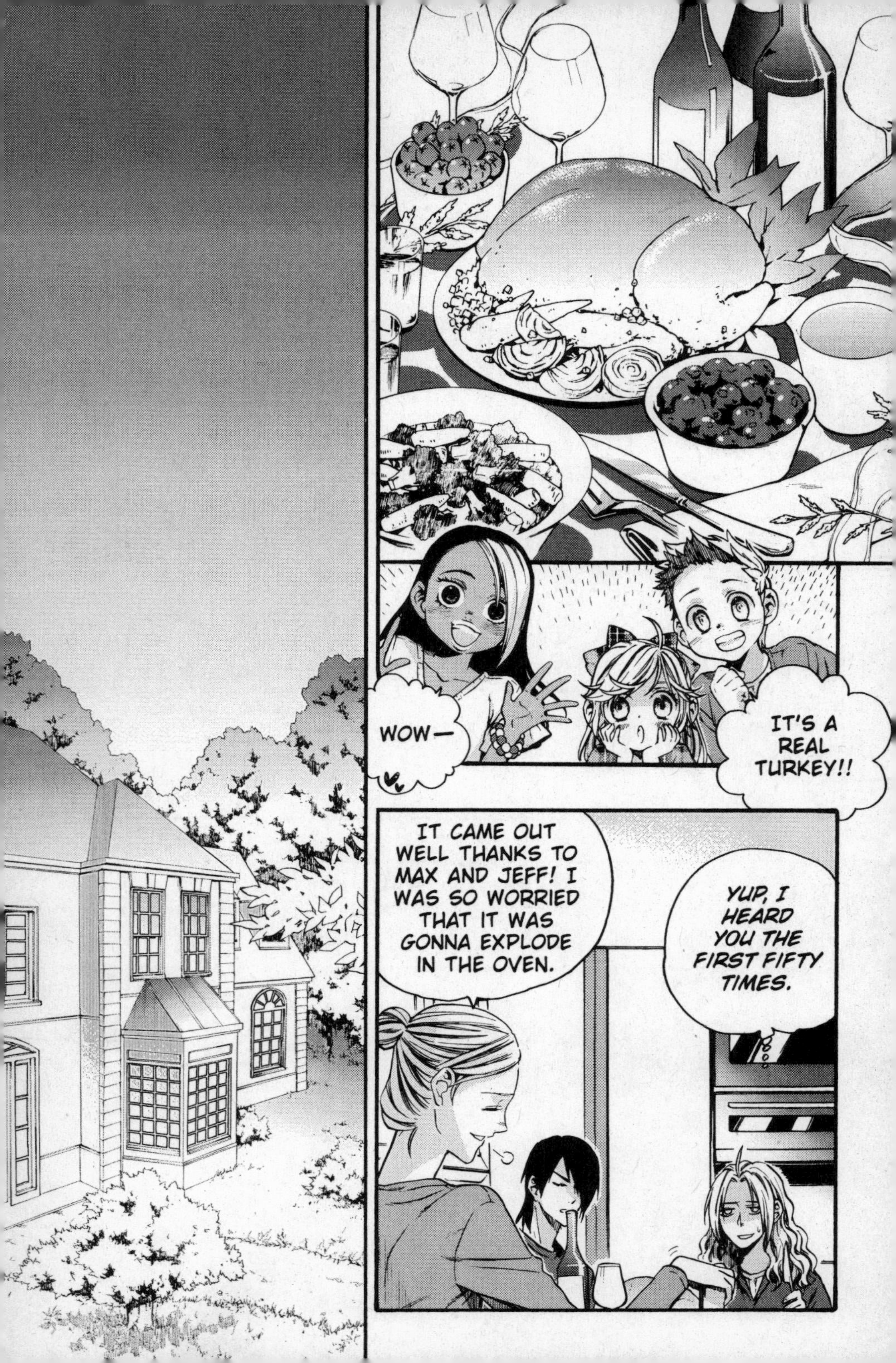
WOW—
IT'S A REAL TURKEY!!
IT CAME OUT WELL THANKS TO MAX AND JEFF! I WAS SO WORRIED THAT IT WAS GONNA EXPLODE IN THE OVEN.
YUP, I HEARD YOU THE FIRST FIFTY TIMES.

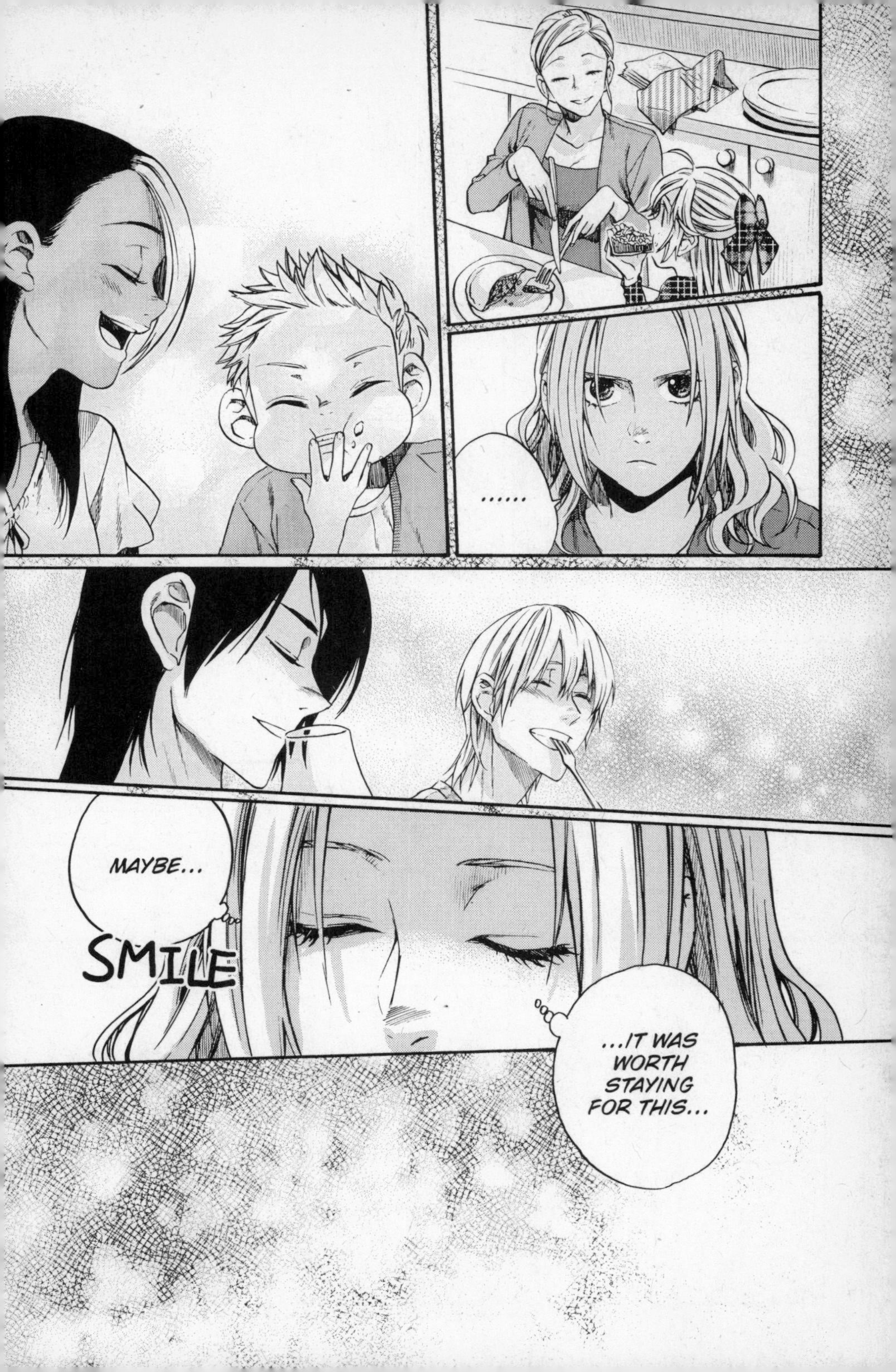
......
MAYBE...
SMILE
...IT WAS WORTH STAYING FOR THIS...

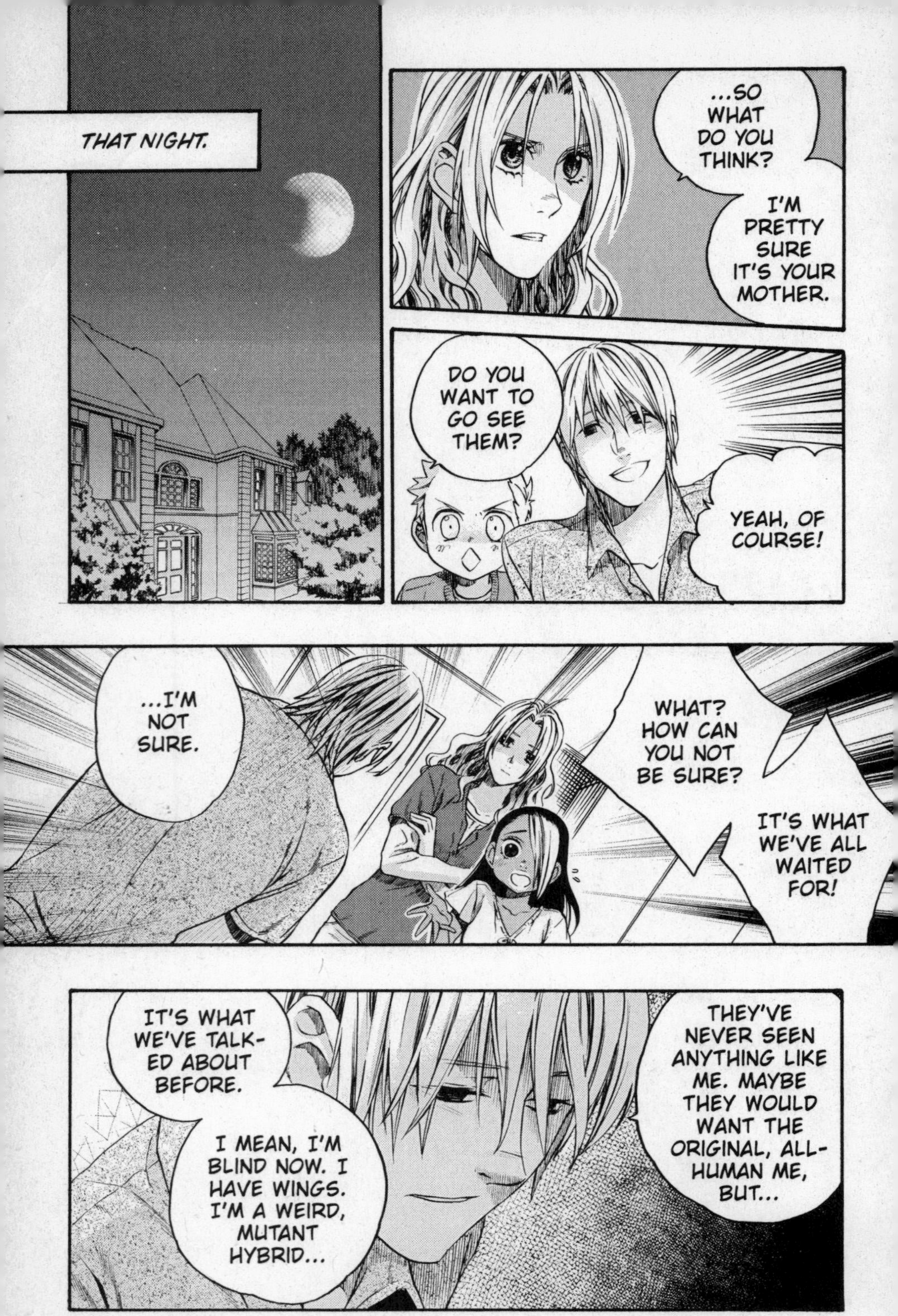
THAT NIGHT.
...SO WHAT DO YOU THINK?
I'M PRETTY SURE IT'S YOUR MOTHER.
DO YOU WANT TO GO SEE THEM?
YEAH, OF COURSE!
...I'M NOT SURE.
WHAT? HOW CAN YOU NOT BE SURE?
IT'S WHAT WE'VE ALL WAITED FOR!
IT'S WHAT WE'VE TALK-ED ABOUT BEFORE.
I MEAN, I'M BLIND NOW. I HAVE WINGS. I'M A WEIRD, MUTANT HYBRID...
THEY'VE NEVER SEEN ANYTHING LIKE ME. MAYBE THEY WOULD WANT THE ORIGINAL, ALL-HUMAN ME, BUT...

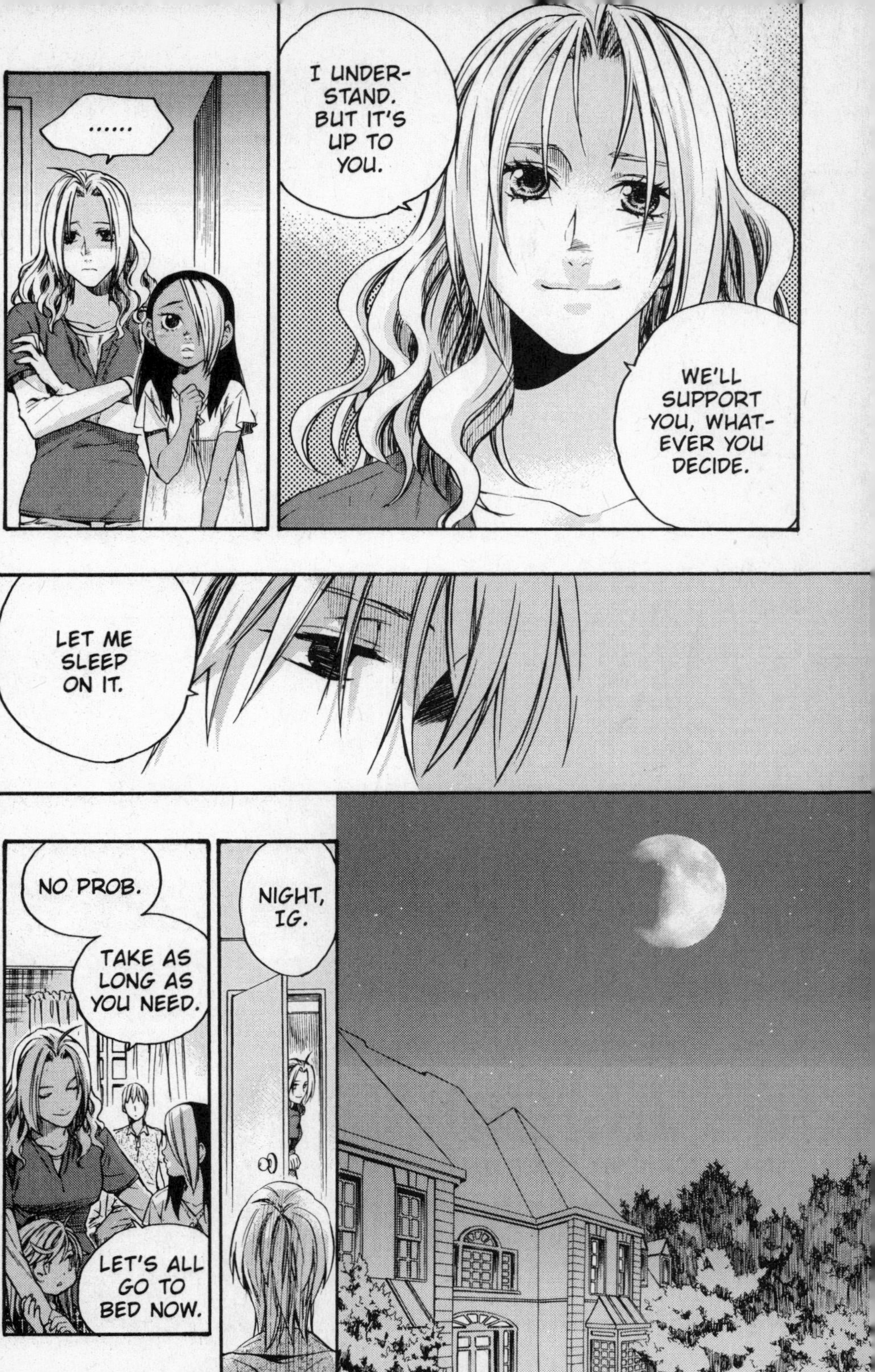
......
I UNDER-STAND. BUT IT'S UP TO YOU.
WE'LL SUPPORT YOU, WHAT-EVER YOU DECIDE.
LET ME SLEEP ON IT.
NO PROB.
TAKE AS LONG AS YOU NEED.
LET'S ALL GO TO BED NOW.
NIGHT, IG.

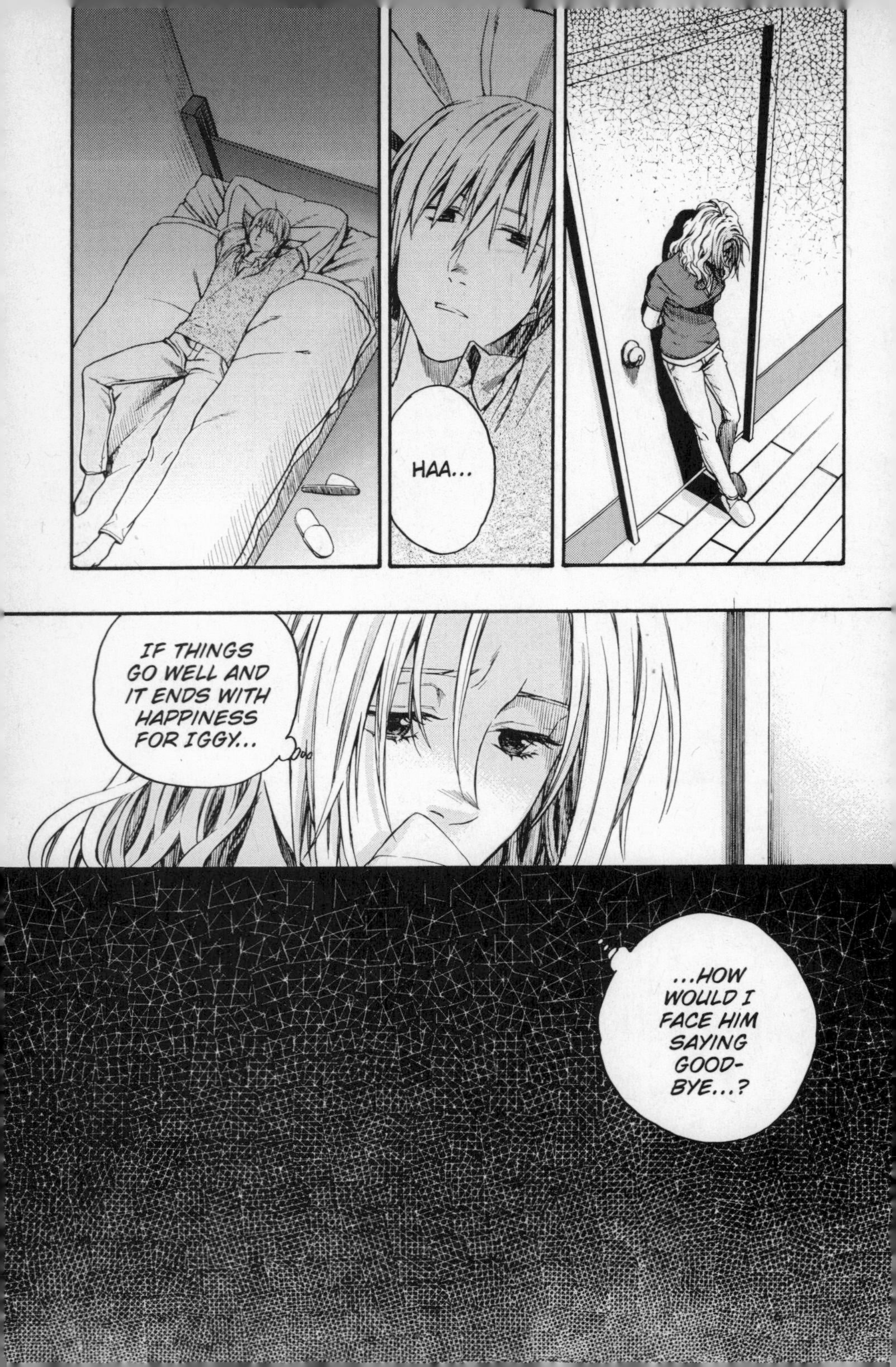
HAA...
IF THINGS GO WELL AND IT ENDS WITH HAPPINESS FOR IGGY...
...HOW WOULD I FACE HIM SAYING GOOD-BYE...?

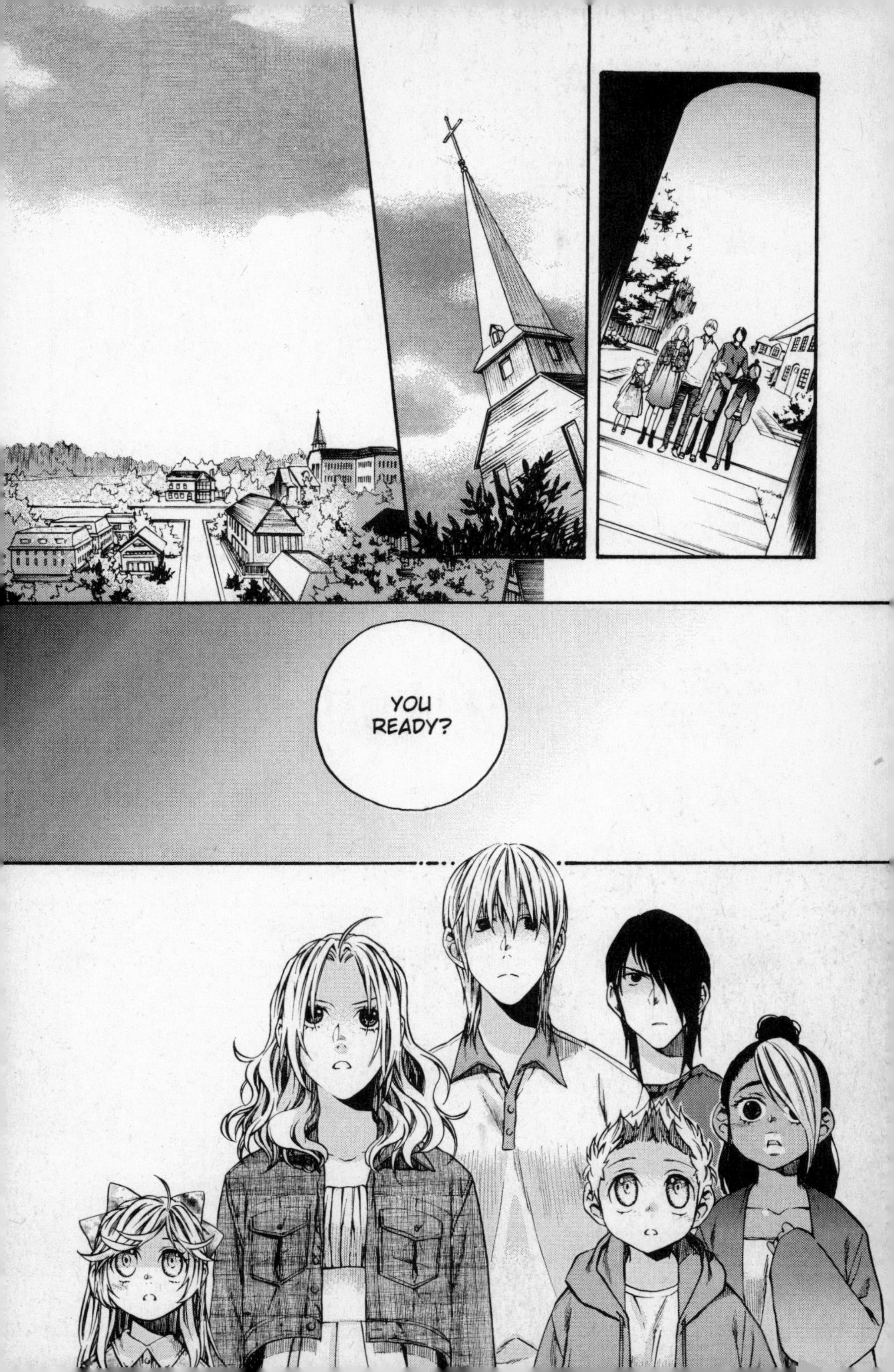
YOU READY?

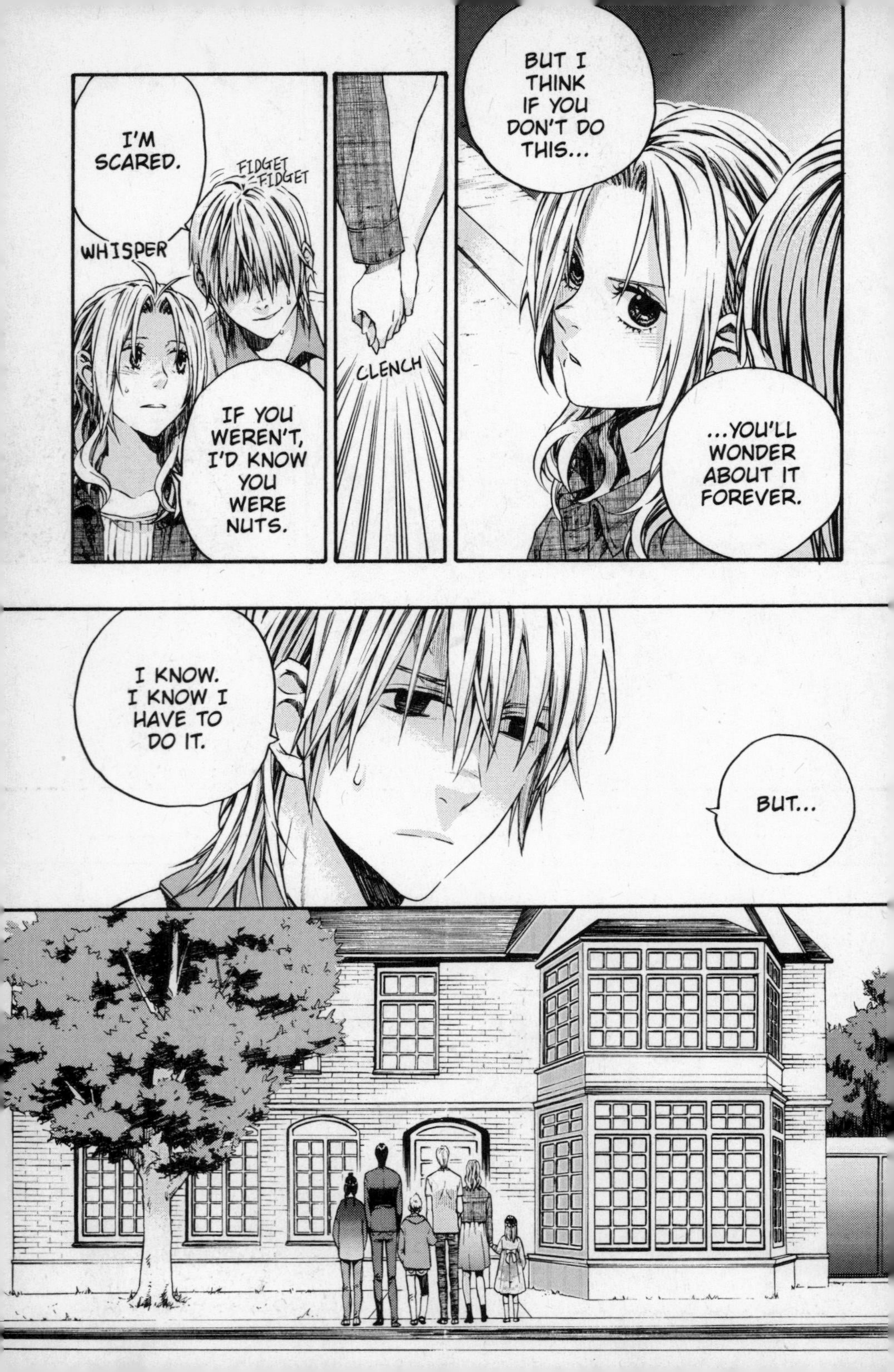
I'M SCARED.
FIDGET FIDGET
WHISPER
IF YOU WEREN'T, I'D KNOW YOU WERE NUTS.
CLENCH
BUT I THINK IF YOU DON'T DO THIS...
...YOU'LL WONDER ABOUT IT FOREVER.
I KNOW. I KNOW I HAVE TO DO IT.
BUT...

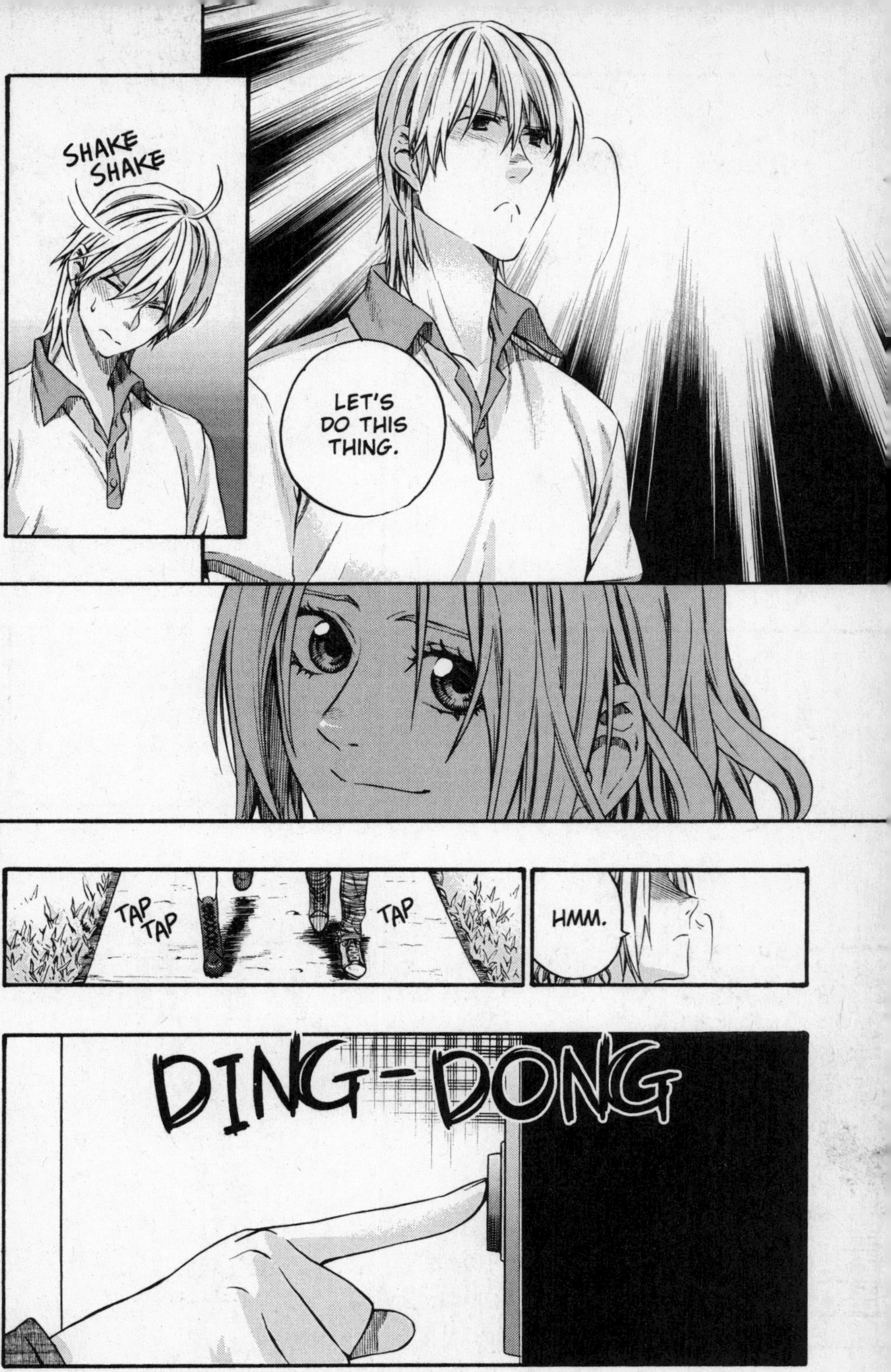
SHAKE SHAKE
LET'S DO THIS THING.
TAP TAP
TAP
HMM.
DING-DONG

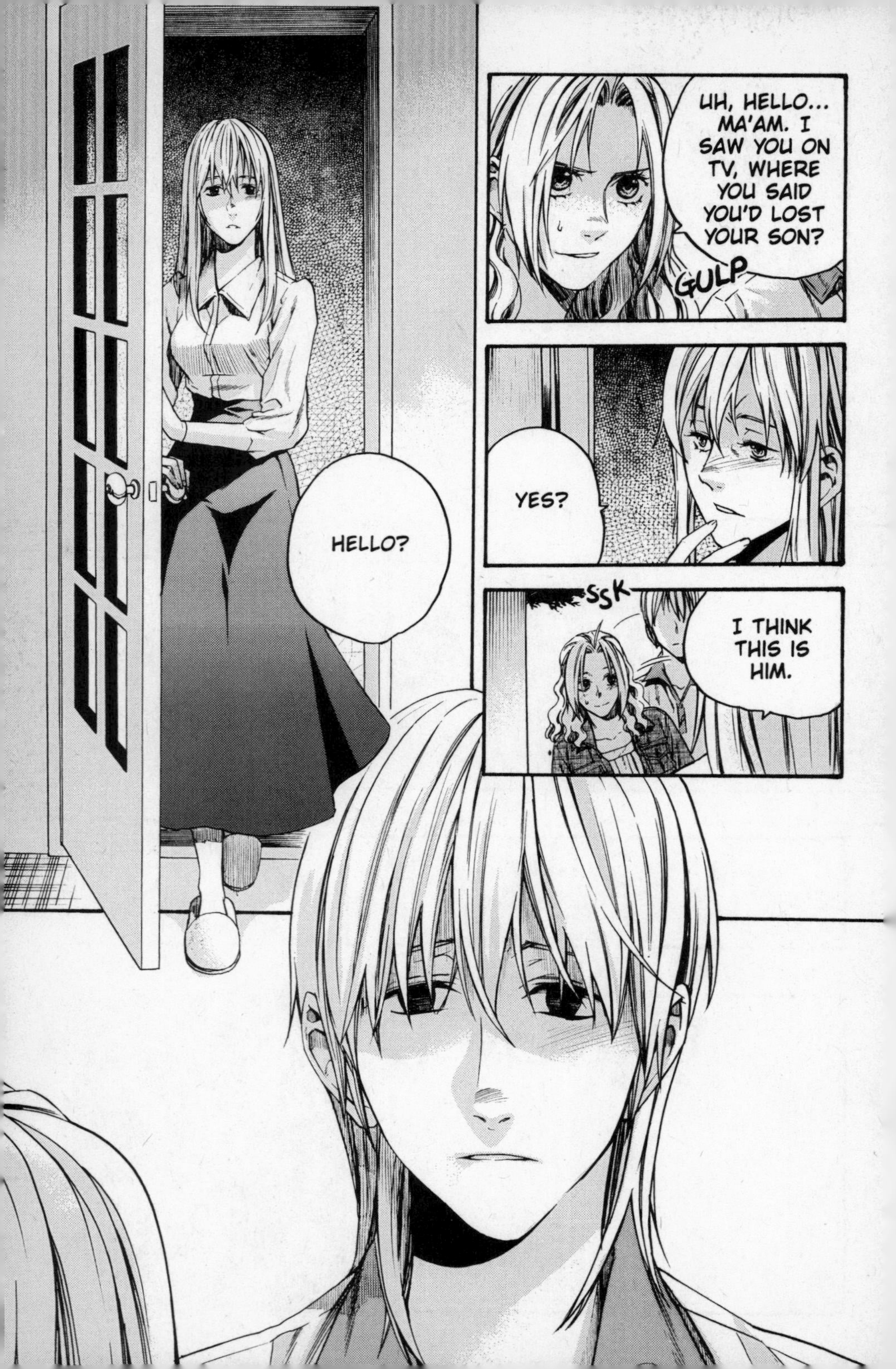
HELLO?
UH, HELLO... MA'AM. I SAW YOU ON TV, WHERE YOU SAID YOU'D LOST YOUR SON?
GULP
YES?
SSK
I THINK THIS IS HIM.

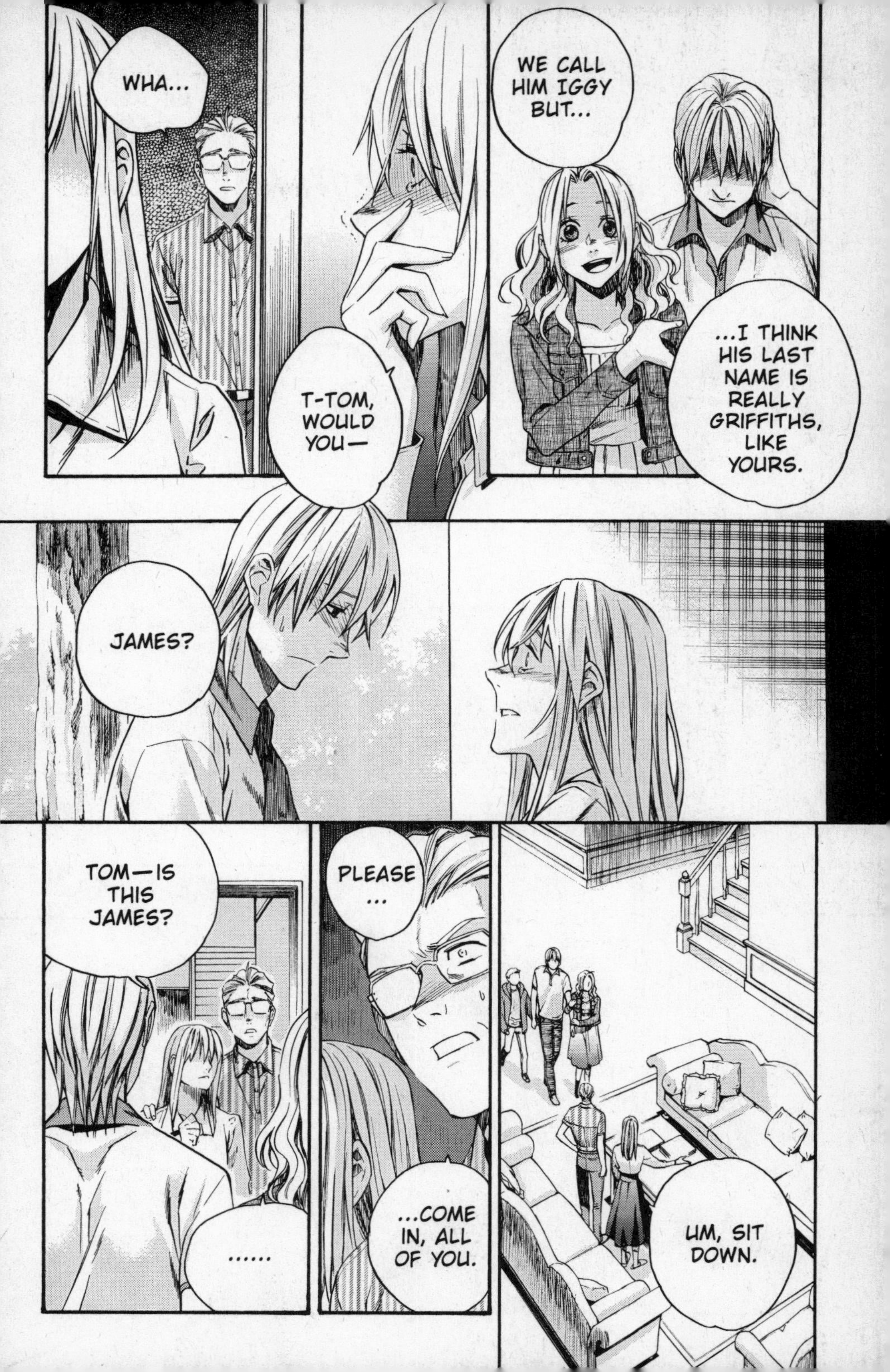
WE CALL HIM IGGY BUT...
...I THINK HIS LAST NAME IS REALLY GRIFFITHS, LIKE YOURS.
T-TOM, WOULD YOU—
WHA...
JAMES?
UM, SIT DOWN.
PLEASE ...
...COME IN, ALL OF YOU.
TOM—IS THIS JAMES?
......

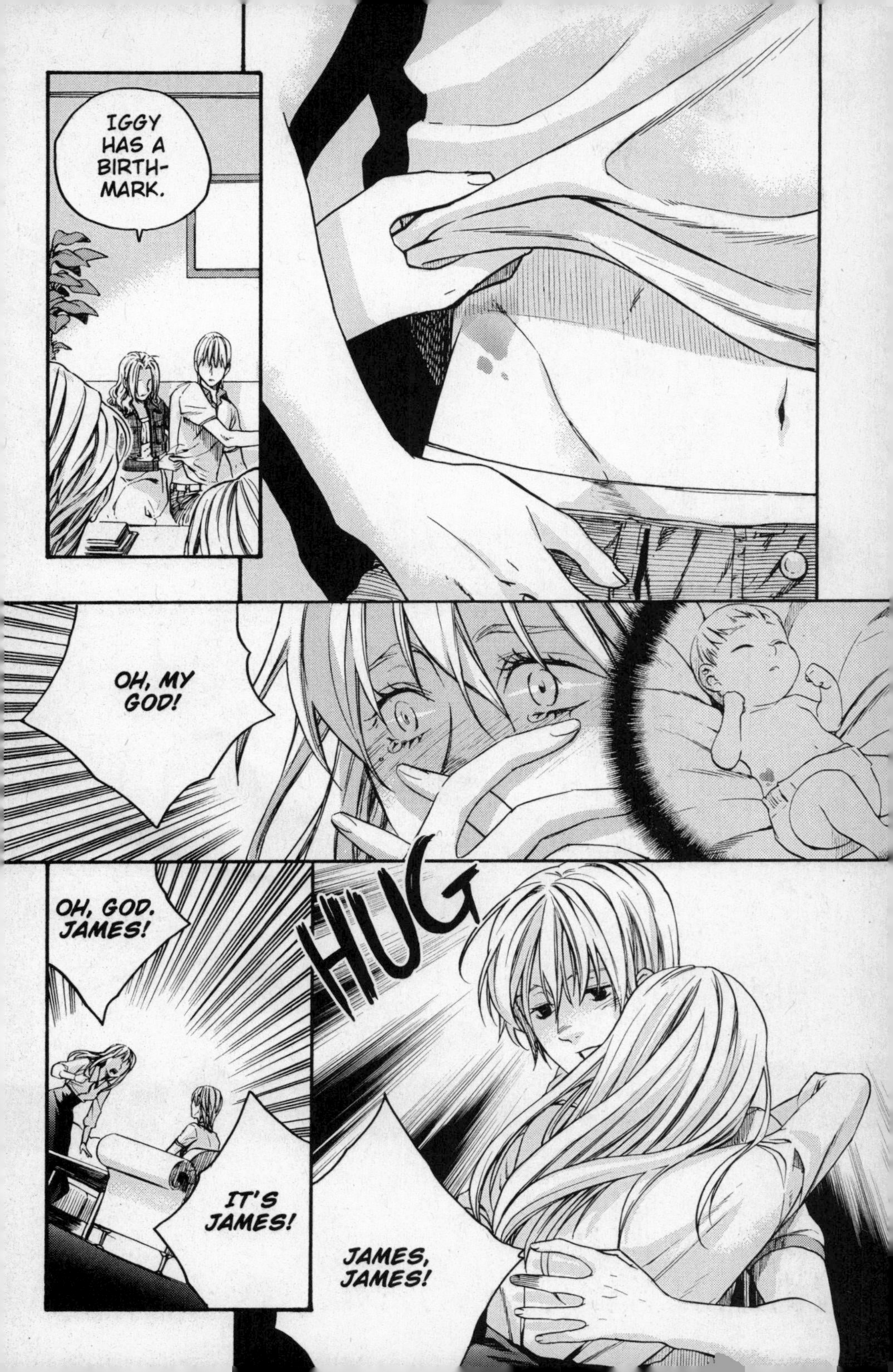
IGGY HAS A BIRTH-MARK.
OH, MY GOD!
OH, GOD. JAMES!
HUG
IT'S JAMES!
JAMES, JAMES!

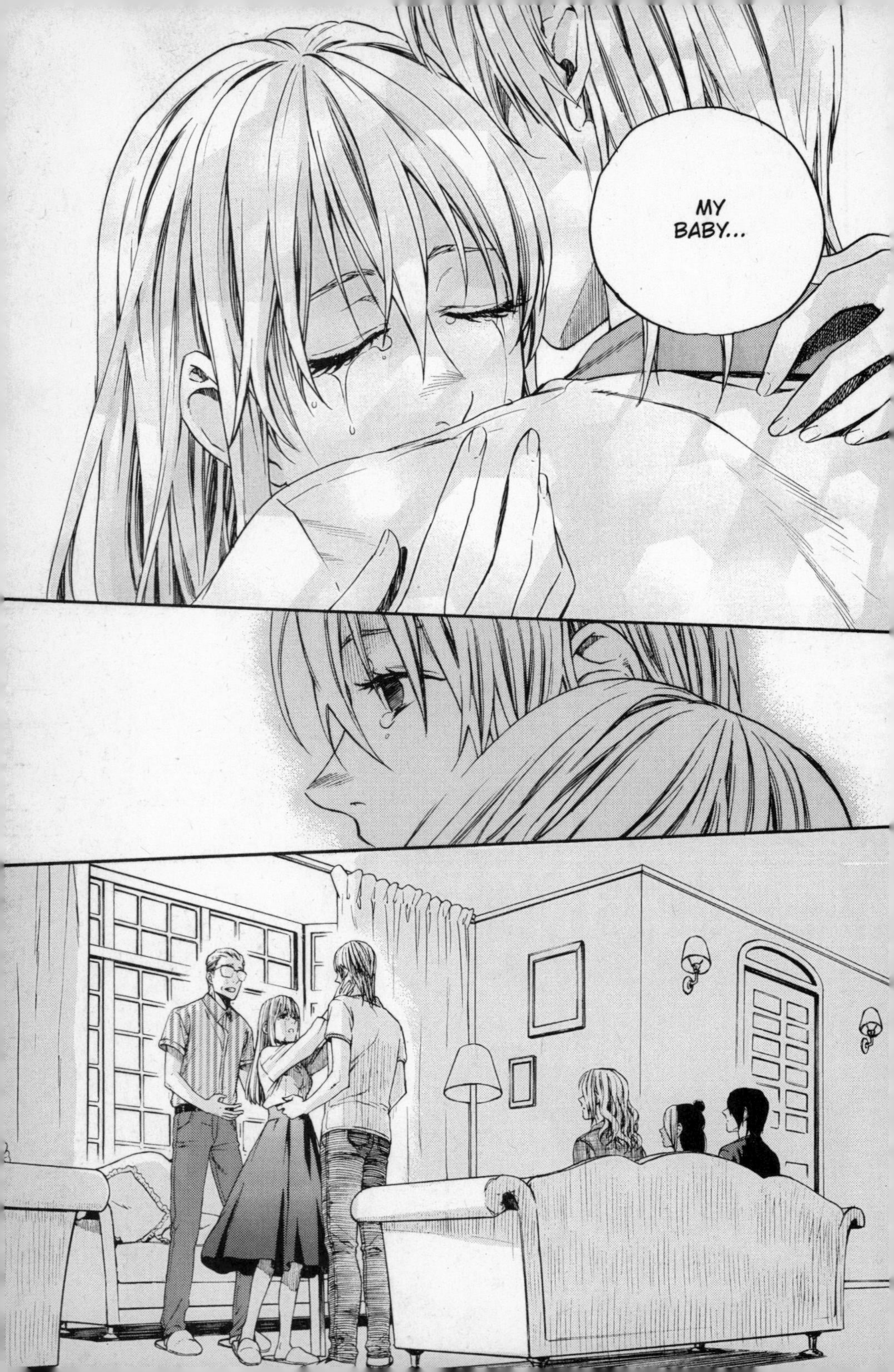
MY BABY...

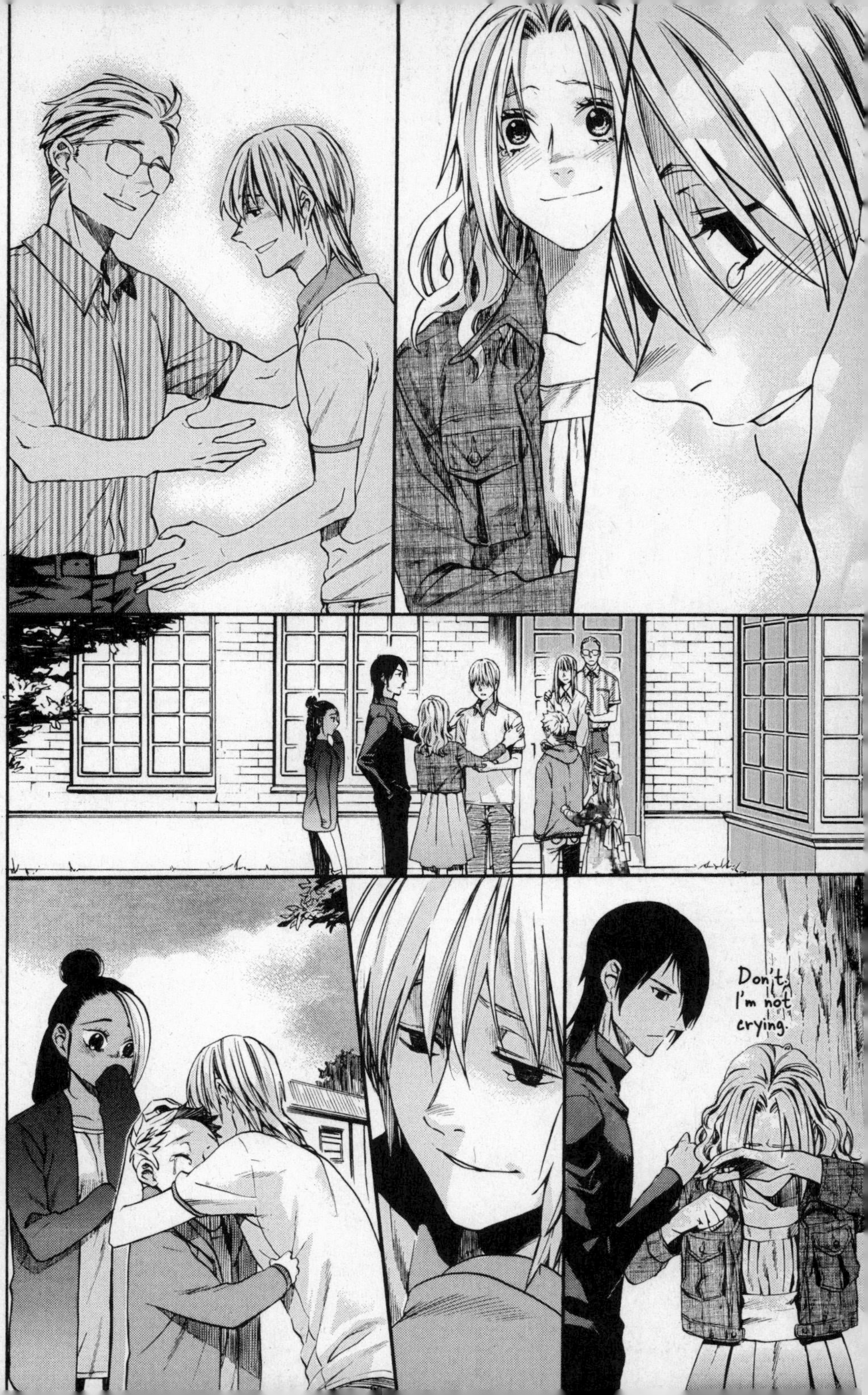
Don't. I'm not crying.

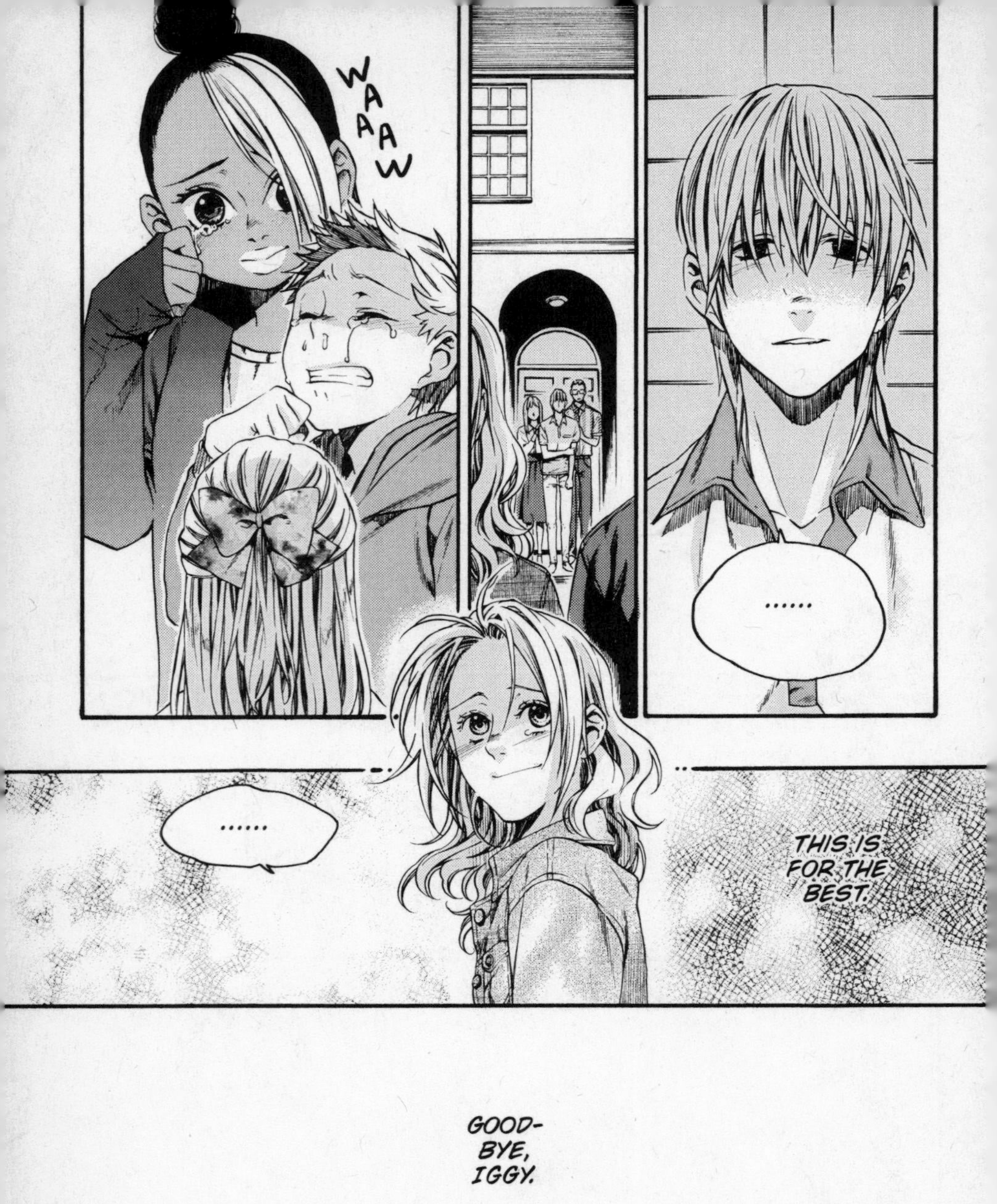
WAAAW
......
......
THIS IS FOR THE BEST.
GOOD-BYE, IGGY.

MAXIMUM
RIDE

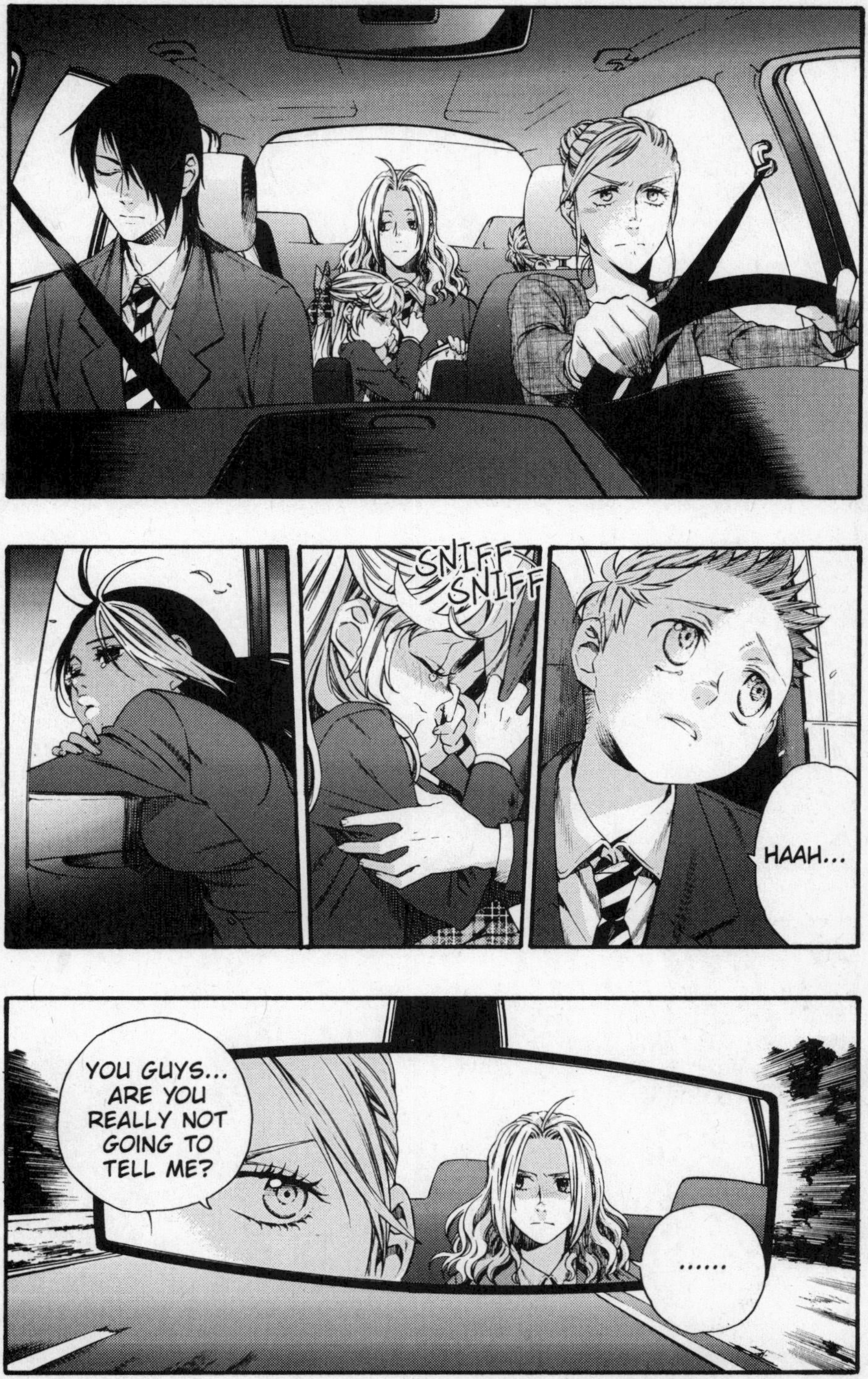
SNIFF SNIFF
HAAH...
YOU GUYS... ARE YOU REALLY NOT GOING TO TELL ME?
......

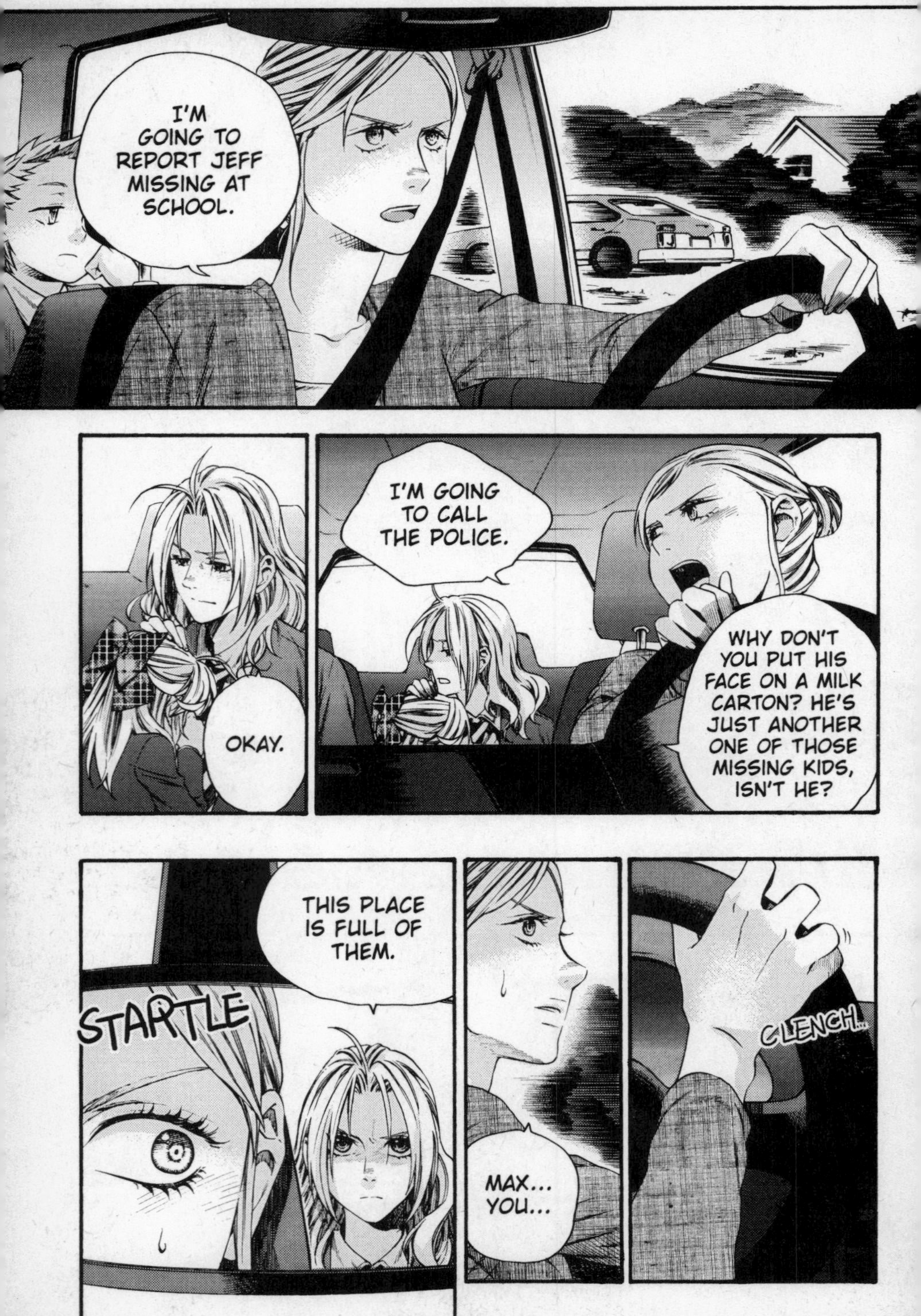
I'M GOING TO REPORT JEFF MISSING AT SCHOOL.
OKAY.
I'M GOING TO CALL THE POLICE.
WHY DON'T YOU PUT HIS FACE ON A MILK CARTON? HE'S JUST ANOTHER ONE OF THOSE MISSING KIDS, ISN'T HE?
THIS PLACE IS FULL OF THEM.
STARTLE
MAX... YOU...
CLENCH...

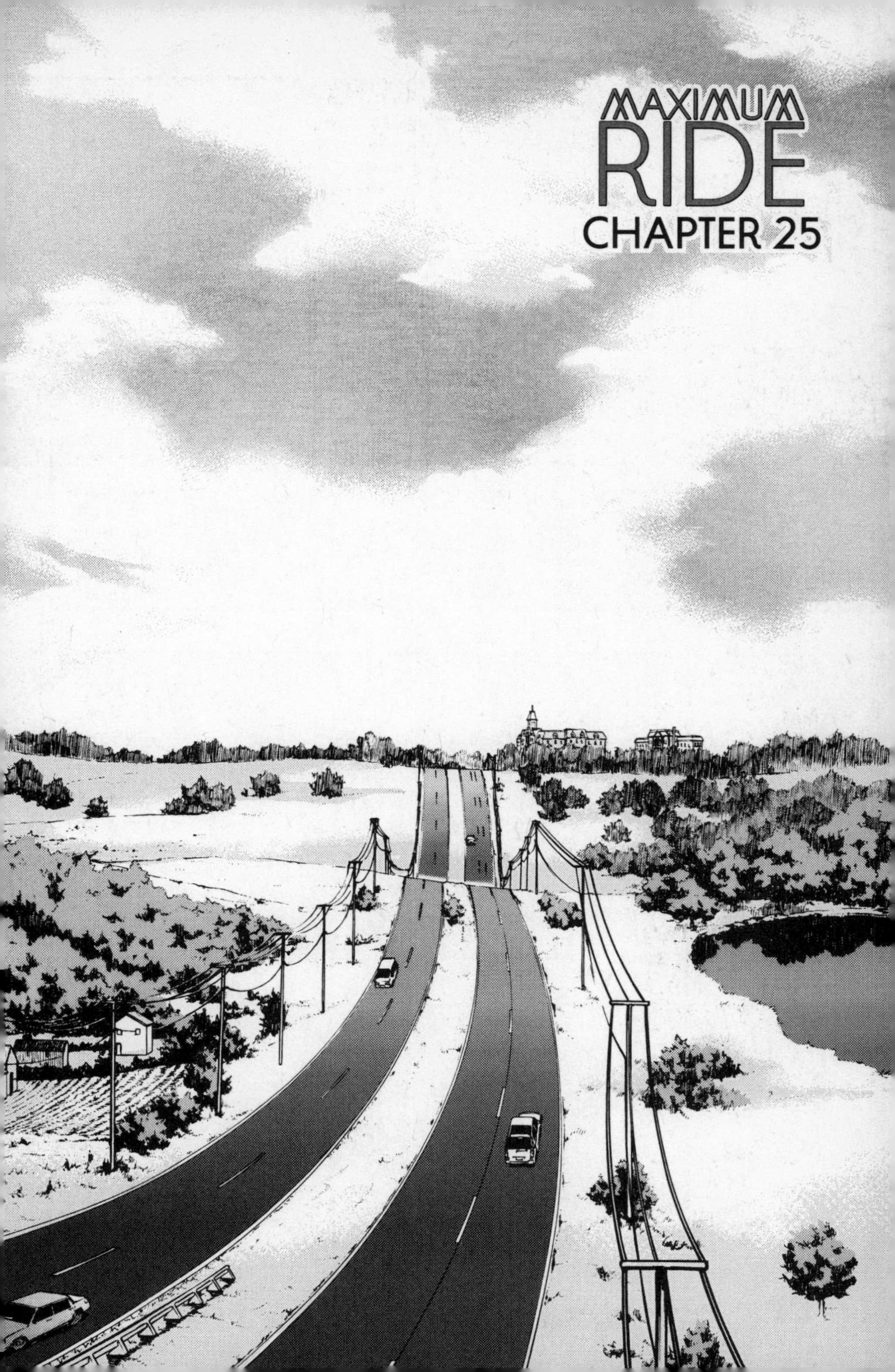
MAXIMUM RIDE
CHAPTER 25

...and make sure to always be quiet in the cafeteria...

...so I don't have to repeat myself every time!

And I have one more announcement.

YAWN.

One of our students has gone missing— Jeff Walker.

I'm sure you all know whom I'm talking about.

We're calling in a special detective unit.

But if any of you have seen him, or know anything, or have any information whatsoever, come forward now.

If we later find out that you did know something and did not come forward, it will be very bad for you.

Bear that in mind.

Dismissed.

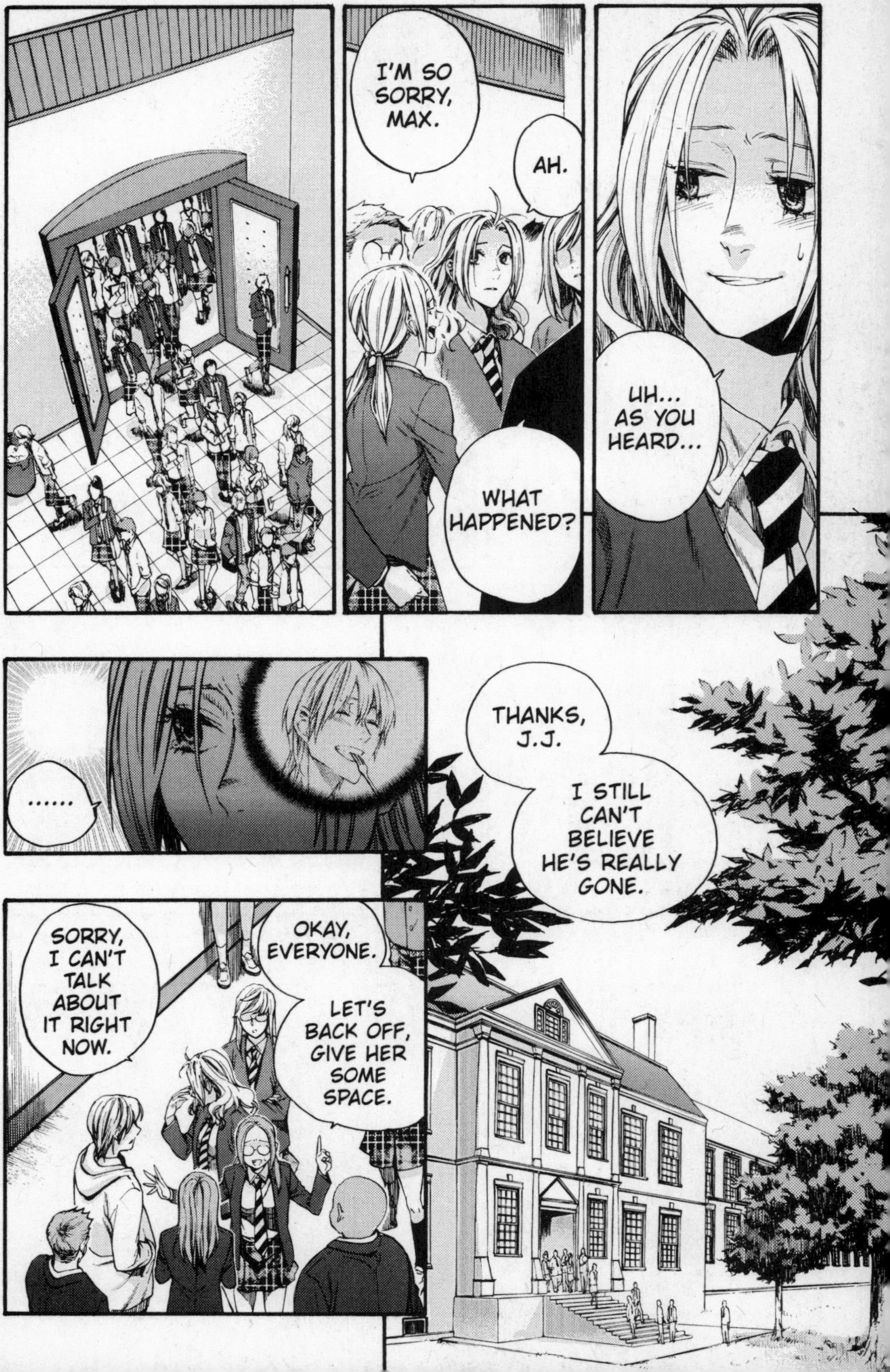
I'M SO SORRY, MAX.
AH.
WHAT HAPPENED?
UH... AS YOU HEARD...
......
THANKS, J.J.
I STILL CAN'T BELIEVE HE'S REALLY GONE.
SORRY, I CAN'T TALK ABOUT IT RIGHT NOW.
OKAY, EVERYONE.
LET'S BACK OFF, GIVE HER SOME SPACE.

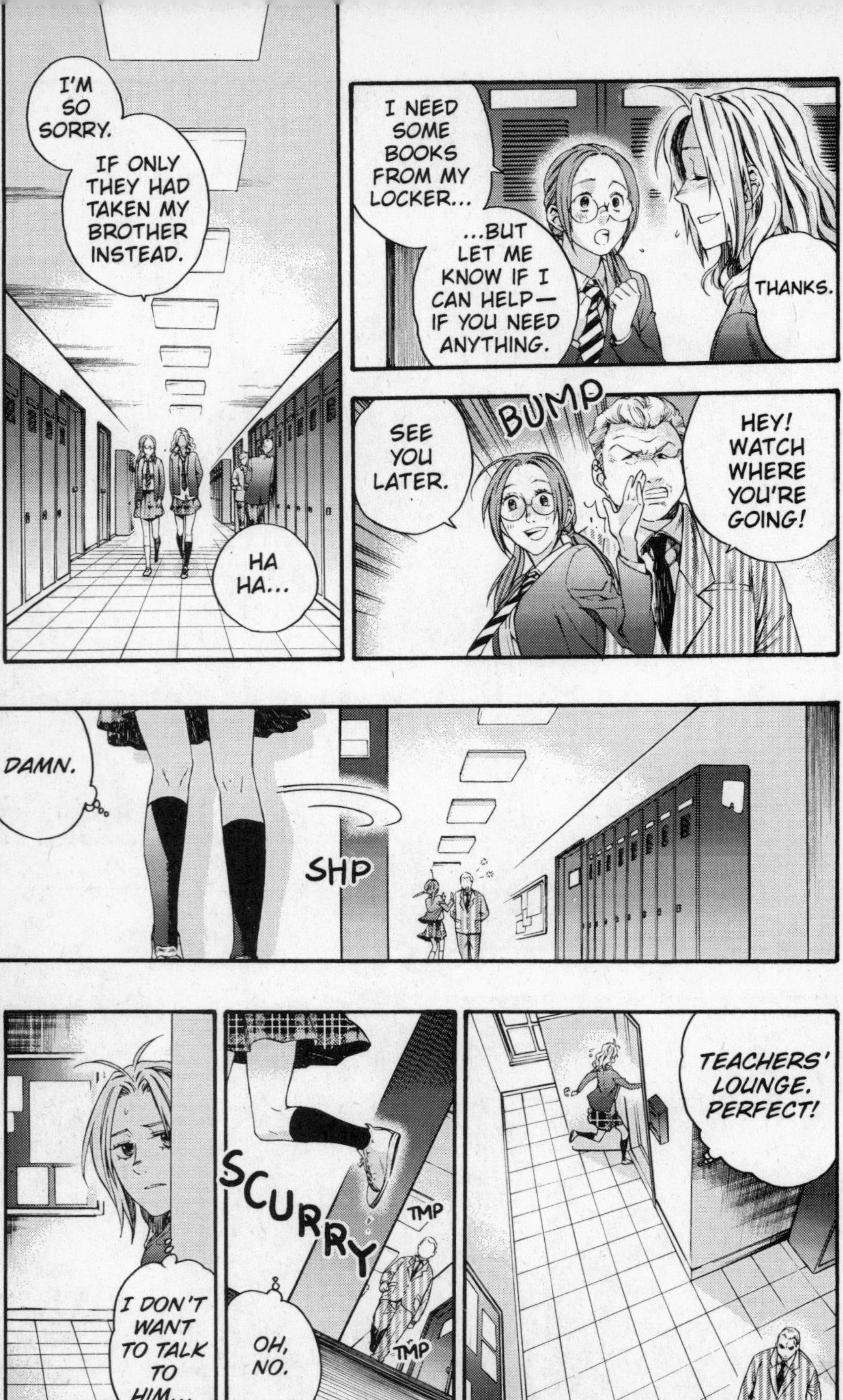
I'M SO SORRY.
IF ONLY THEY HAD TAKEN MY BROTHER INSTEAD.
HA HA...
I NEED SOME BOOKS FROM MY LOCKER...
...BUT LET ME KNOW IF I CAN HELP— IF YOU NEED ANYTHING.
THANKS.
SEE YOU LATER.
BUMP
HEY! WATCH WHERE YOU'RE GOING!
DAMN.
SHP
I DON'T WANT TO TALK TO HIM...
SCURRY
TMP
OH, NO.
TMP
TEACHERS' LOUNGE. PERFECT!

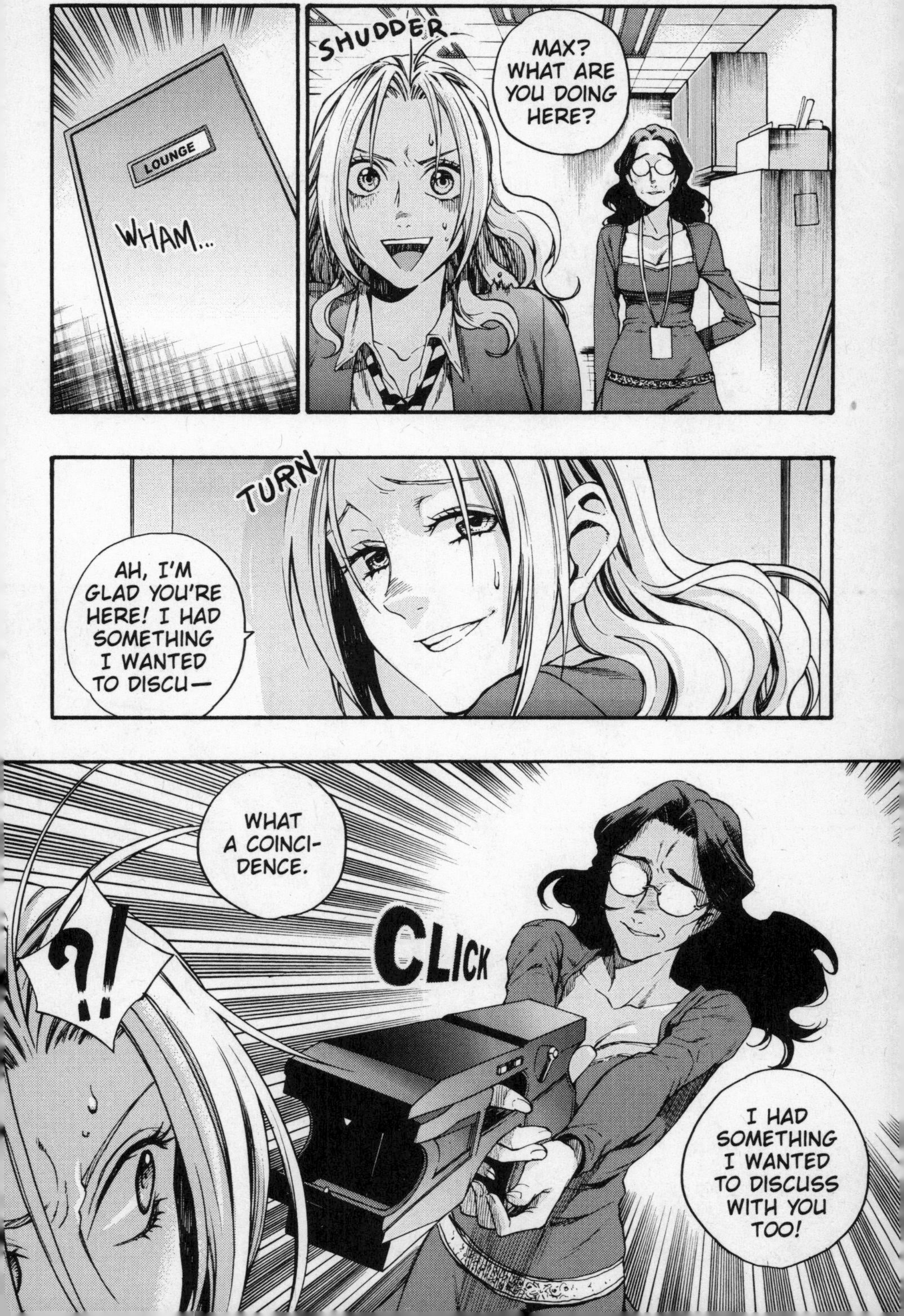
LOUNGE
WHAM...
SHUDDER
MAX? WHAT ARE YOU DOING HERE?
TURN
AH, I'M GLAD YOU'RE HERE! I HAD SOMETHING I WANTED TO DISCU—
WHAT A COINCI-DENCE.
?!
CLICK
I HAD SOMETHING I WANTED TO DISCUSS WITH YOU TOO!

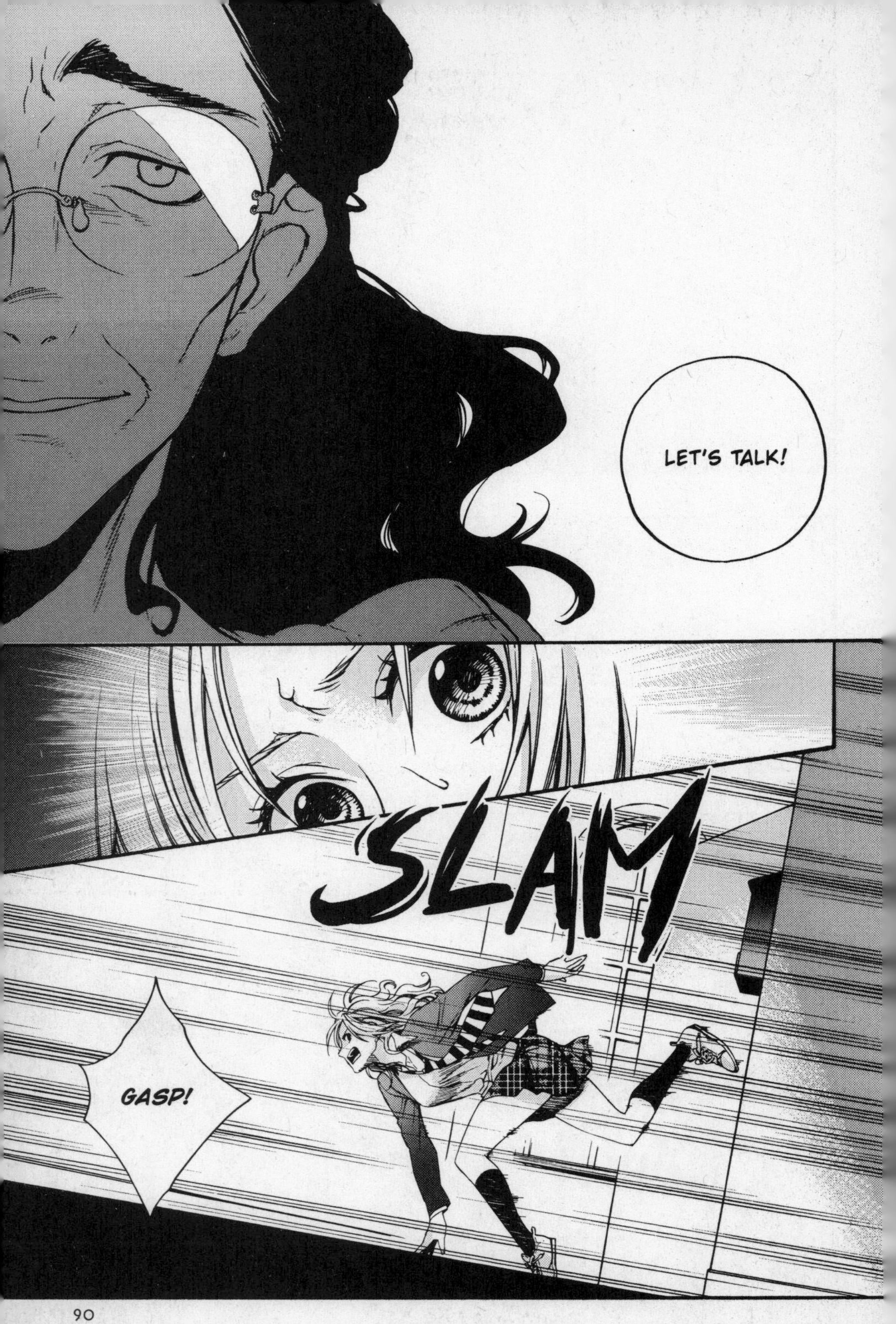
LET'S TALK!
SLAM
GASP!

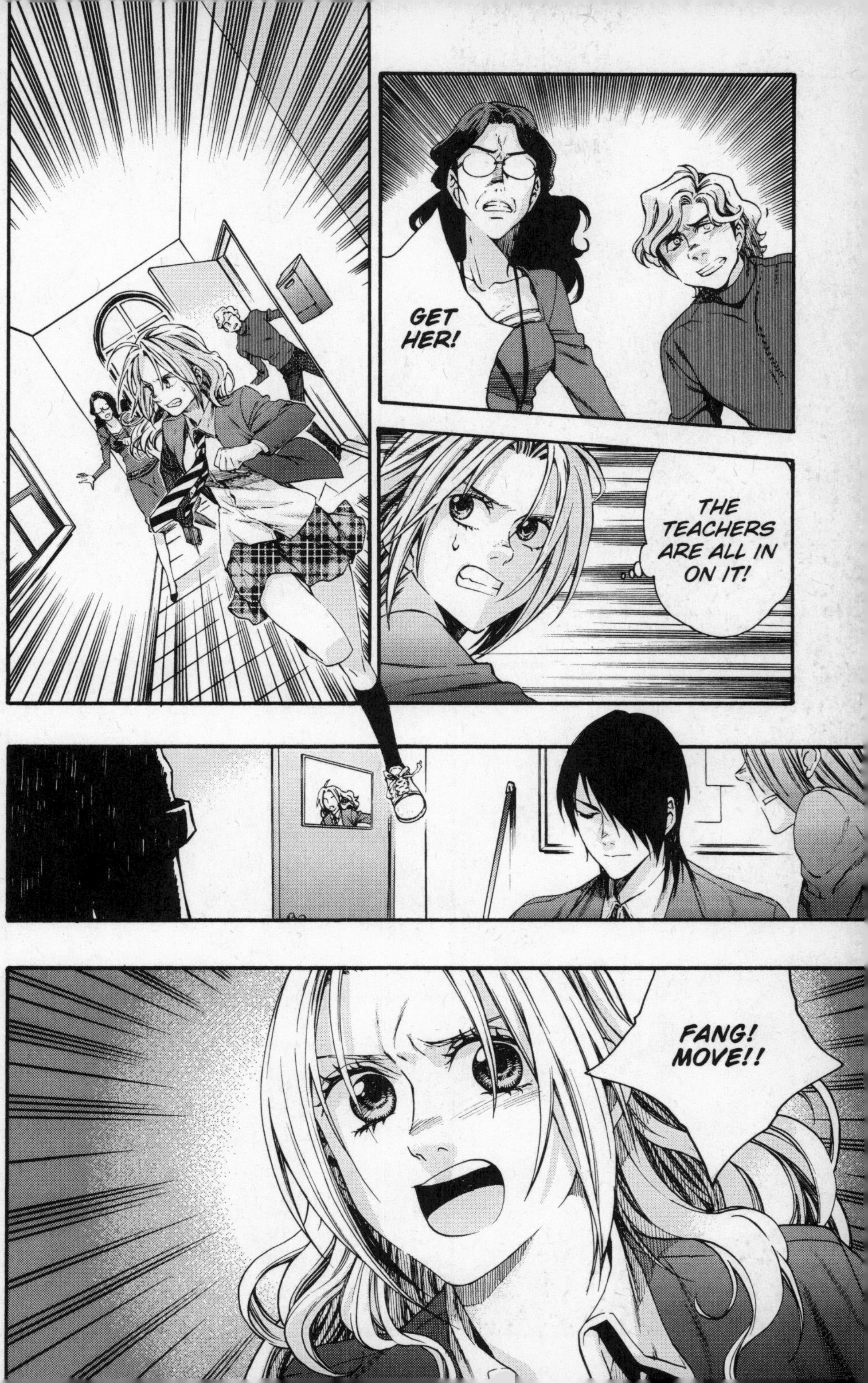
GET HER!
THE TEACHERS ARE ALL IN ON IT!
FANG! MOVE!!

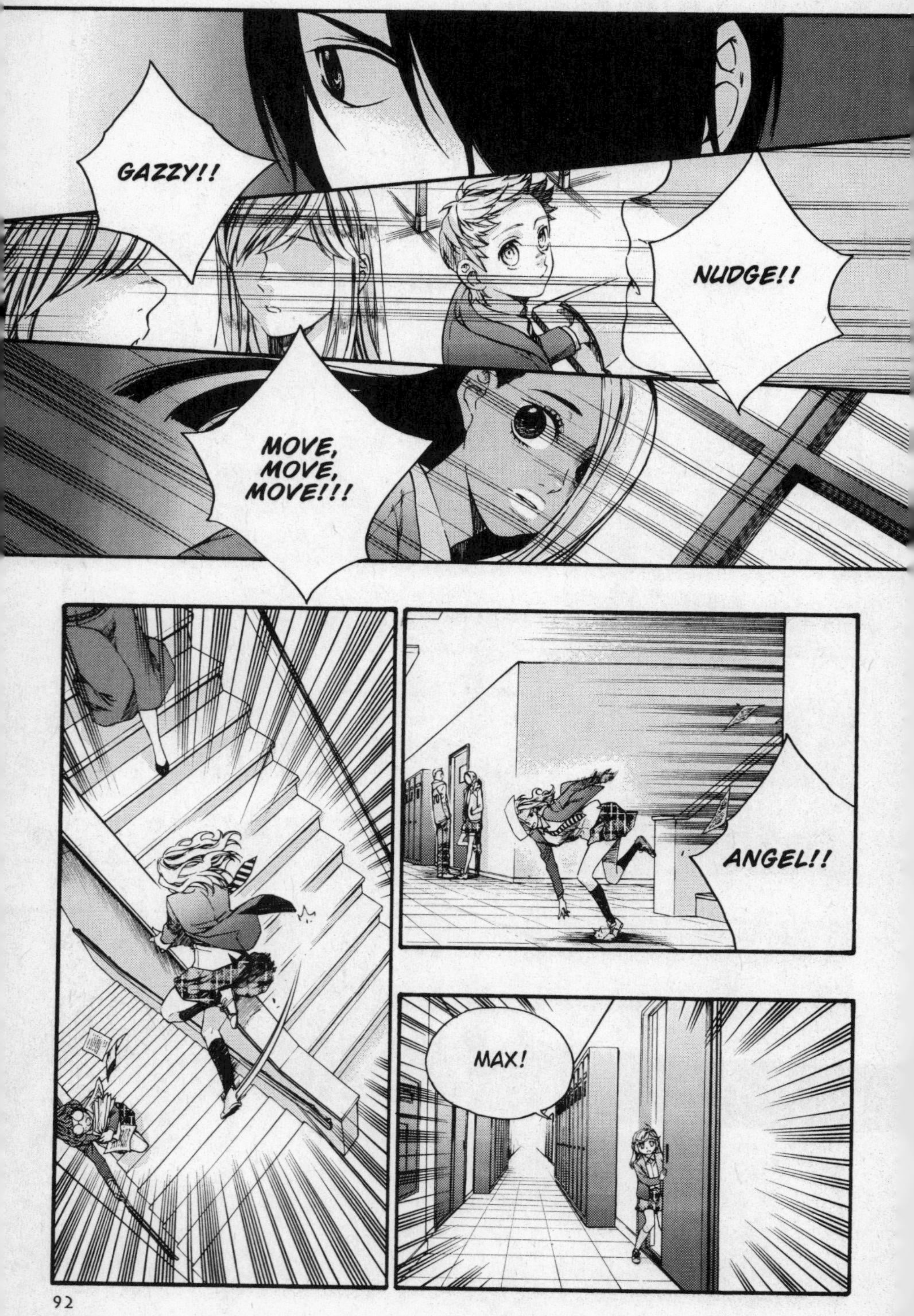
GAZZY!!
NUDGE!!
MOVE, MOVE, MOVE!!!
ANGEL!!
MAX!

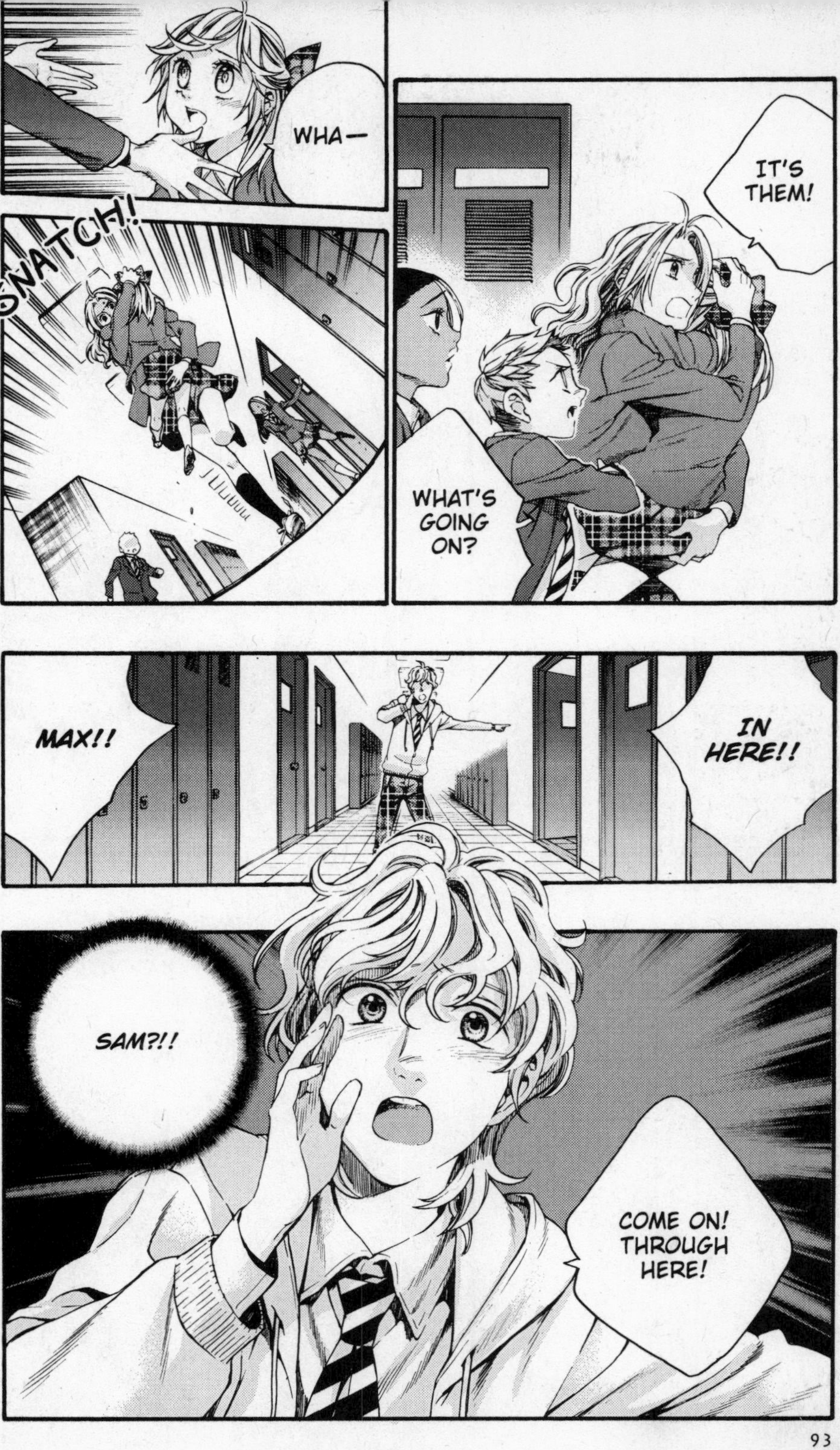
WHA—
SNATCH!
IT'S THEM!
WHAT'S GOING ON?
MAX!!
IN HERE!!
SAM?!!
COME ON! THROUGH HERE!

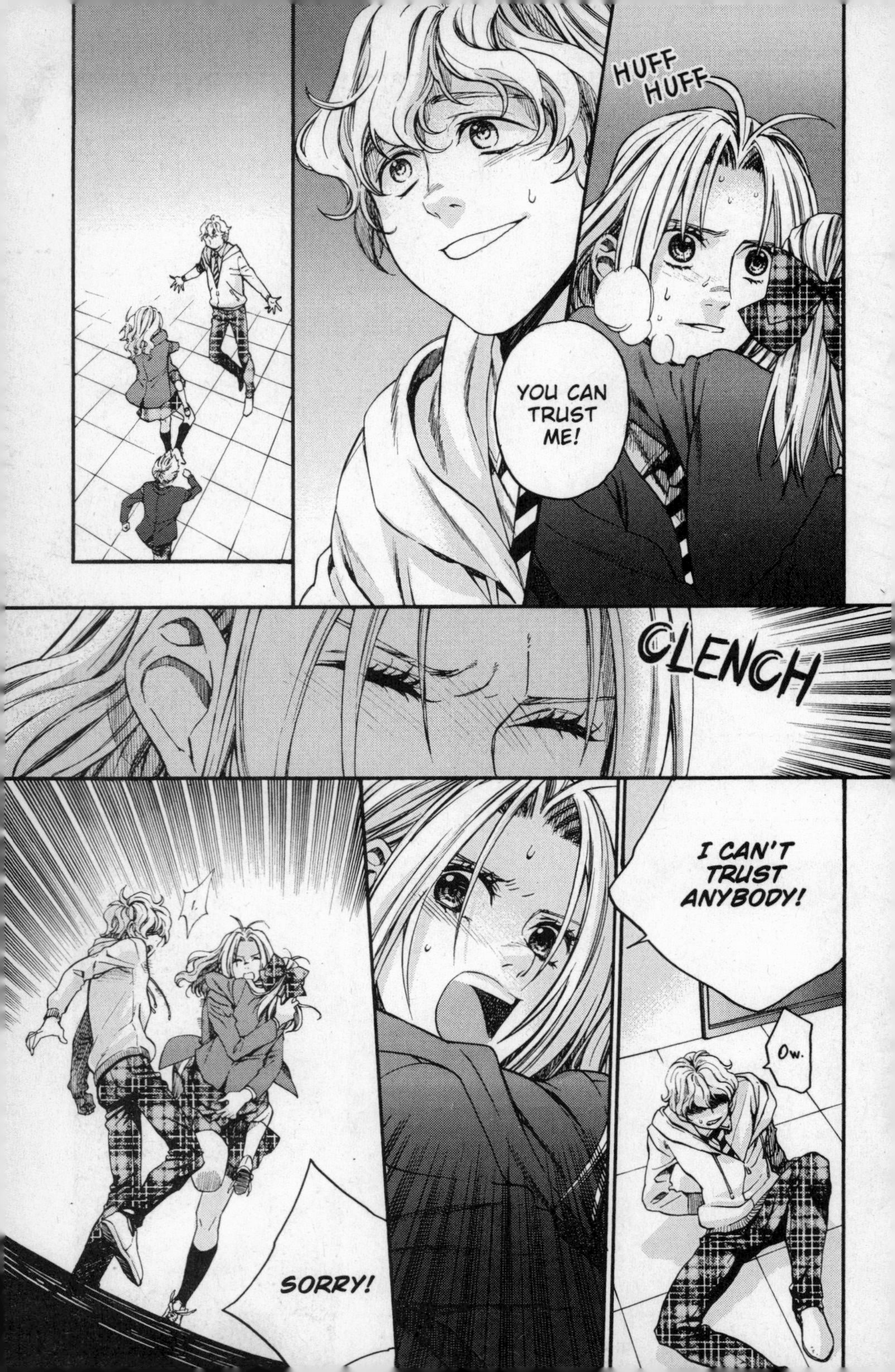
HUFF HUFF
YOU CAN TRUST ME!
CLENCH
!
SORRY!
I CAN'T TRUST ANYBODY!
Ow.

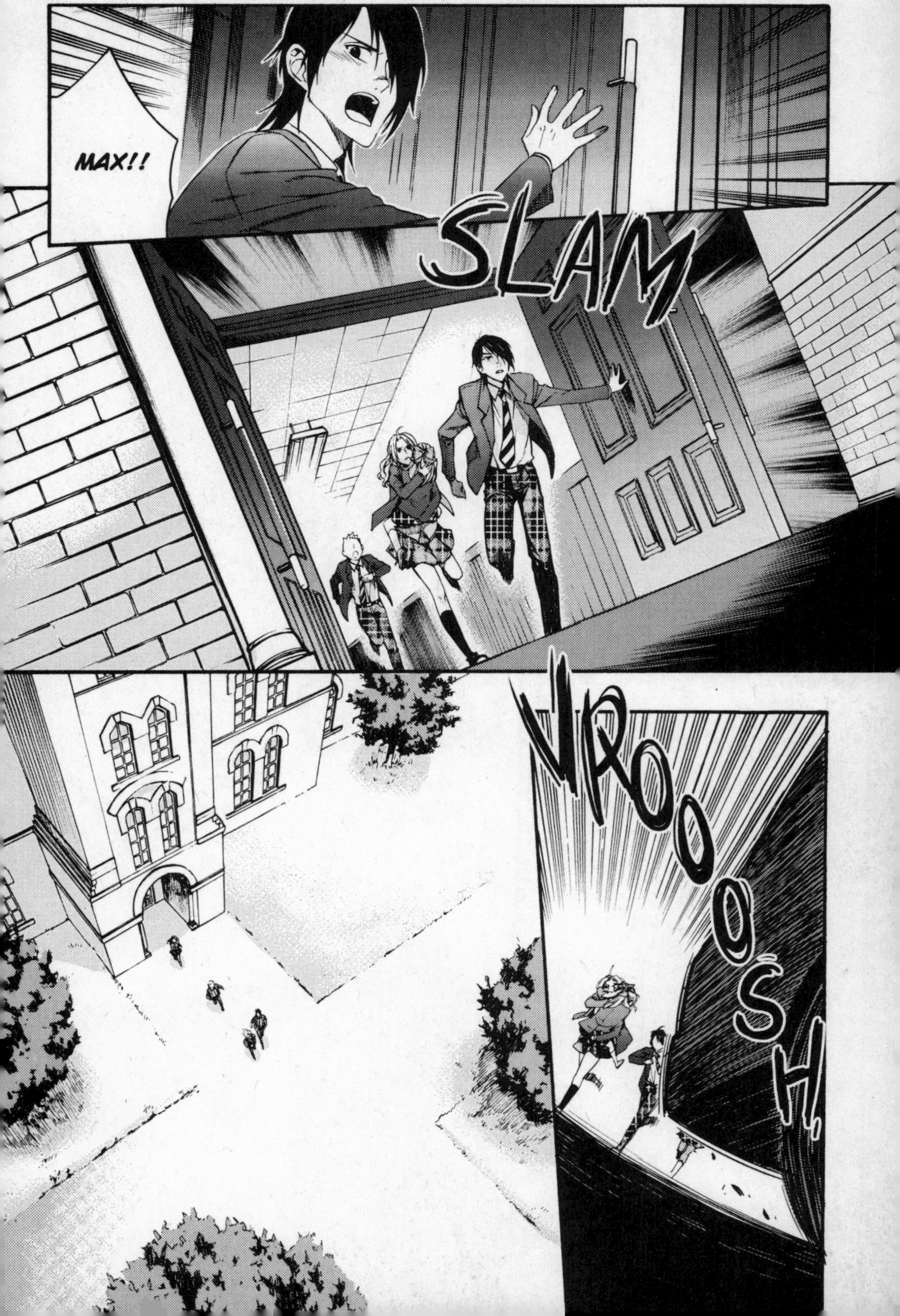
MAX!!
SLAM
VROOOOSH

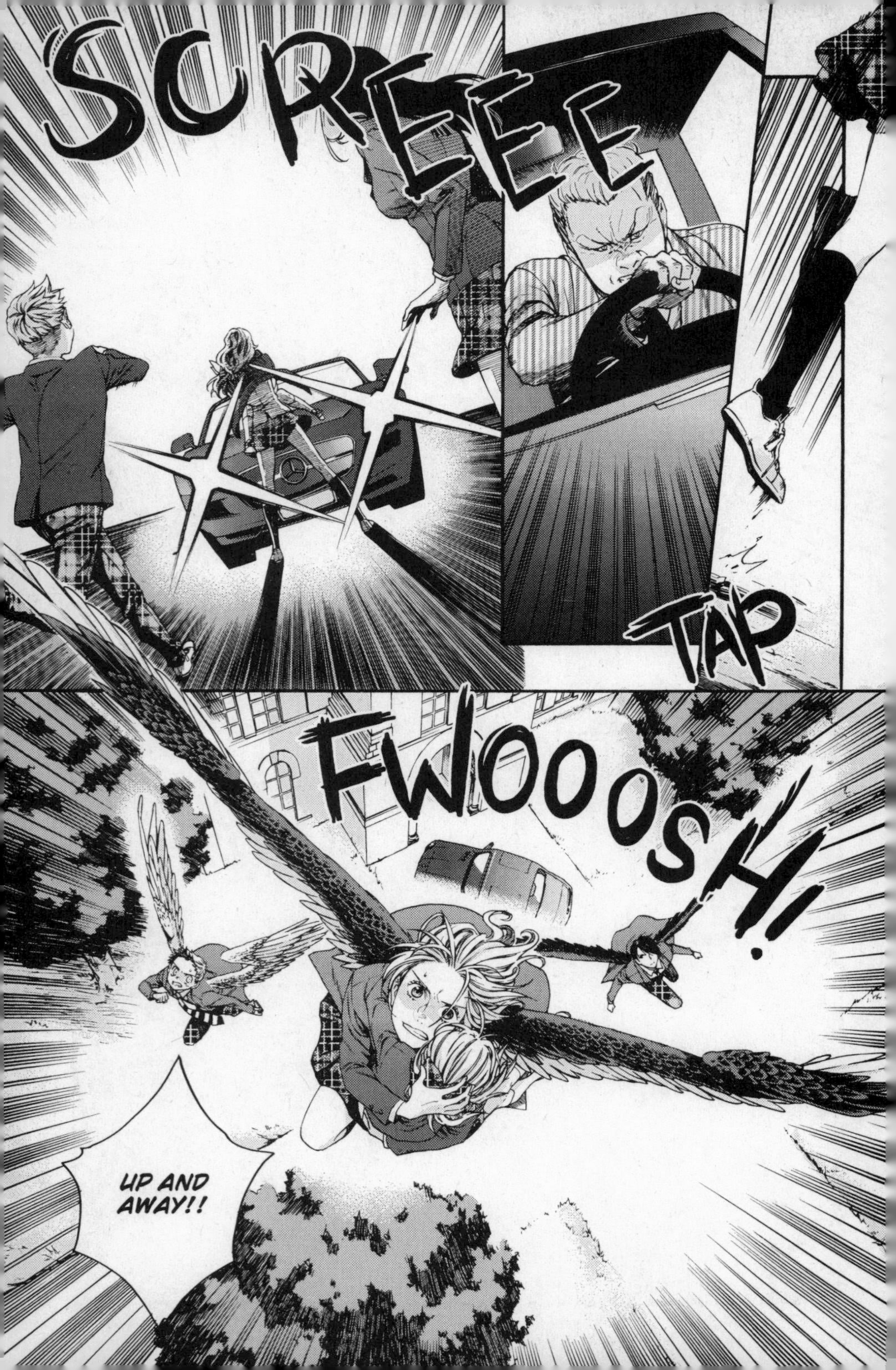
SCREEEE
TAP
FWOOOSH!!
UP AND AWAY!!

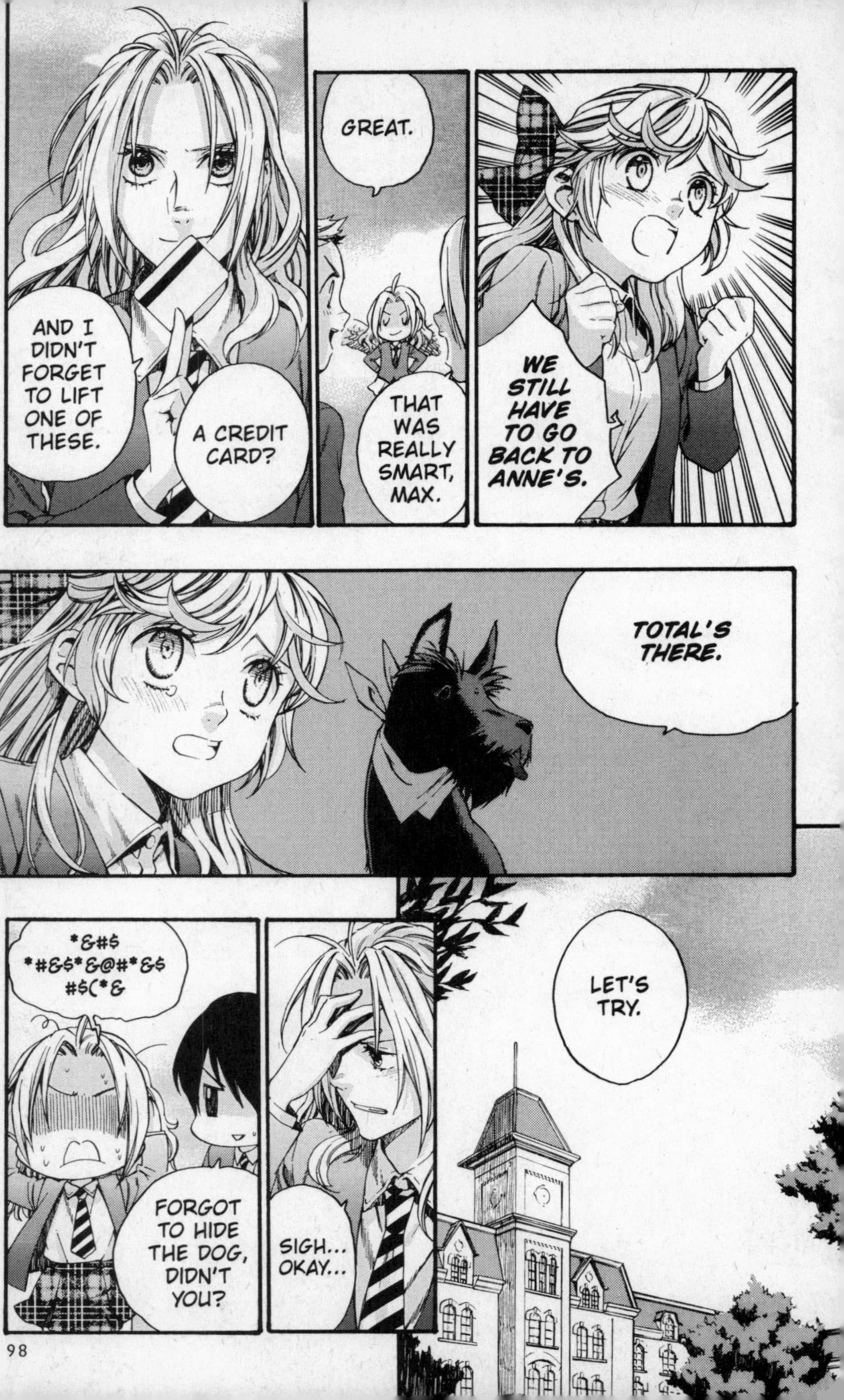
AND I DIDN'T FORGET TO LIFT ONE OF THESE.
A CREDIT CARD?
GREAT.
THAT WAS REALLY SMART, MAX.
WE STILL HAVE TO GO BACK TO ANNE'S.
TOTAL'S THERE.
*&#$ *#&$*&@#*&$ #$(*&
FORGOT TO HIDE THE DOG, DIDN'T YOU?
SIGH... OKAY...
LET'S TRY.

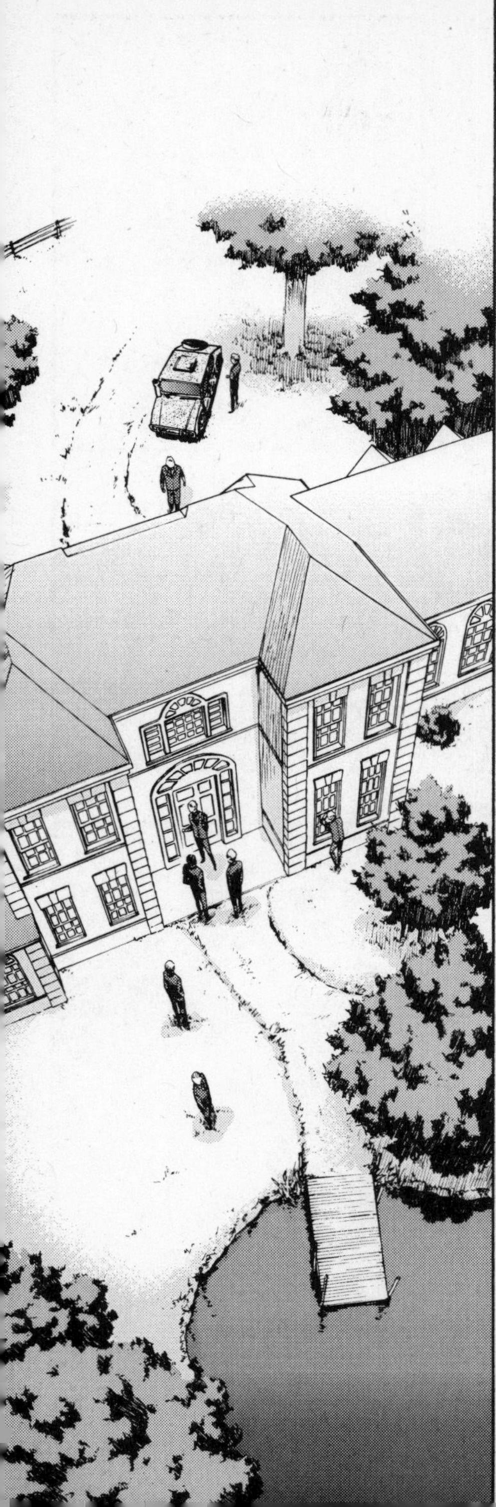

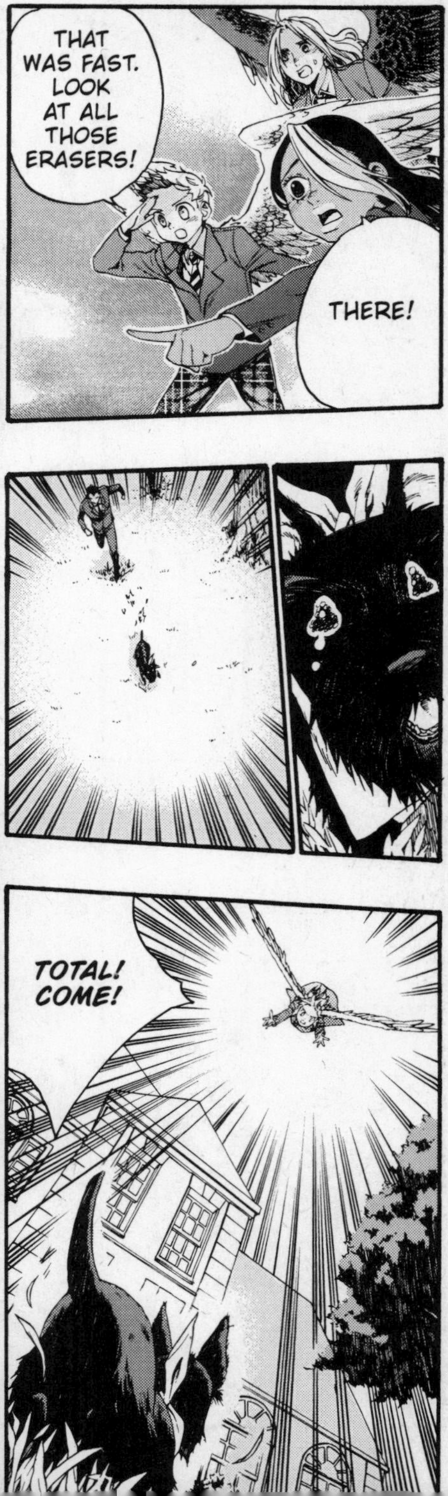
THAT WAS FAST. LOOK AT ALL THOSE ERASERS!
THERE!
TOTAL! COME!

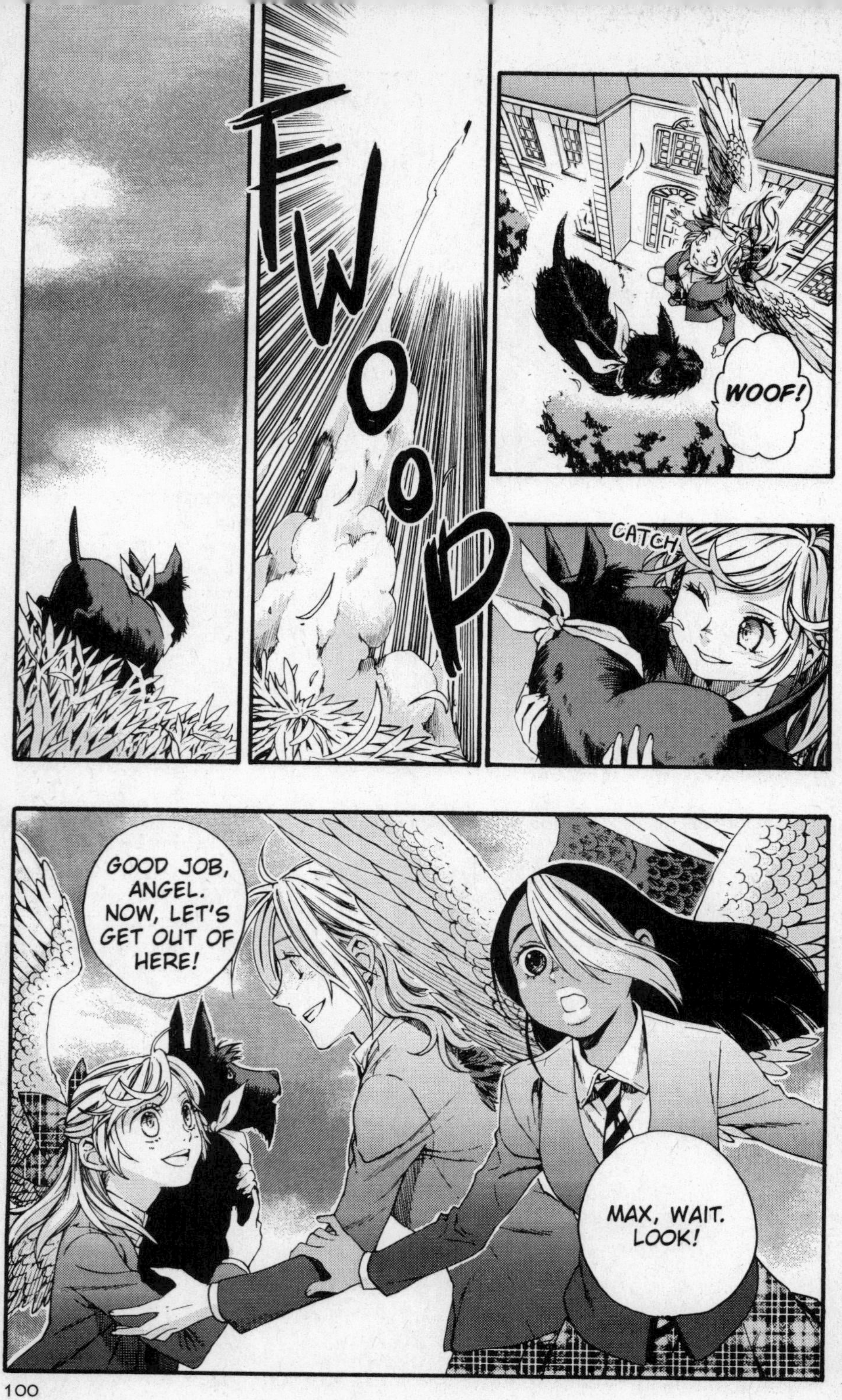
FWOOP
WOOF!
CATCH
GOOD JOB, ANGEL. NOW, LET'S GET OUT OF HERE!
MAX, WAIT. LOOK!

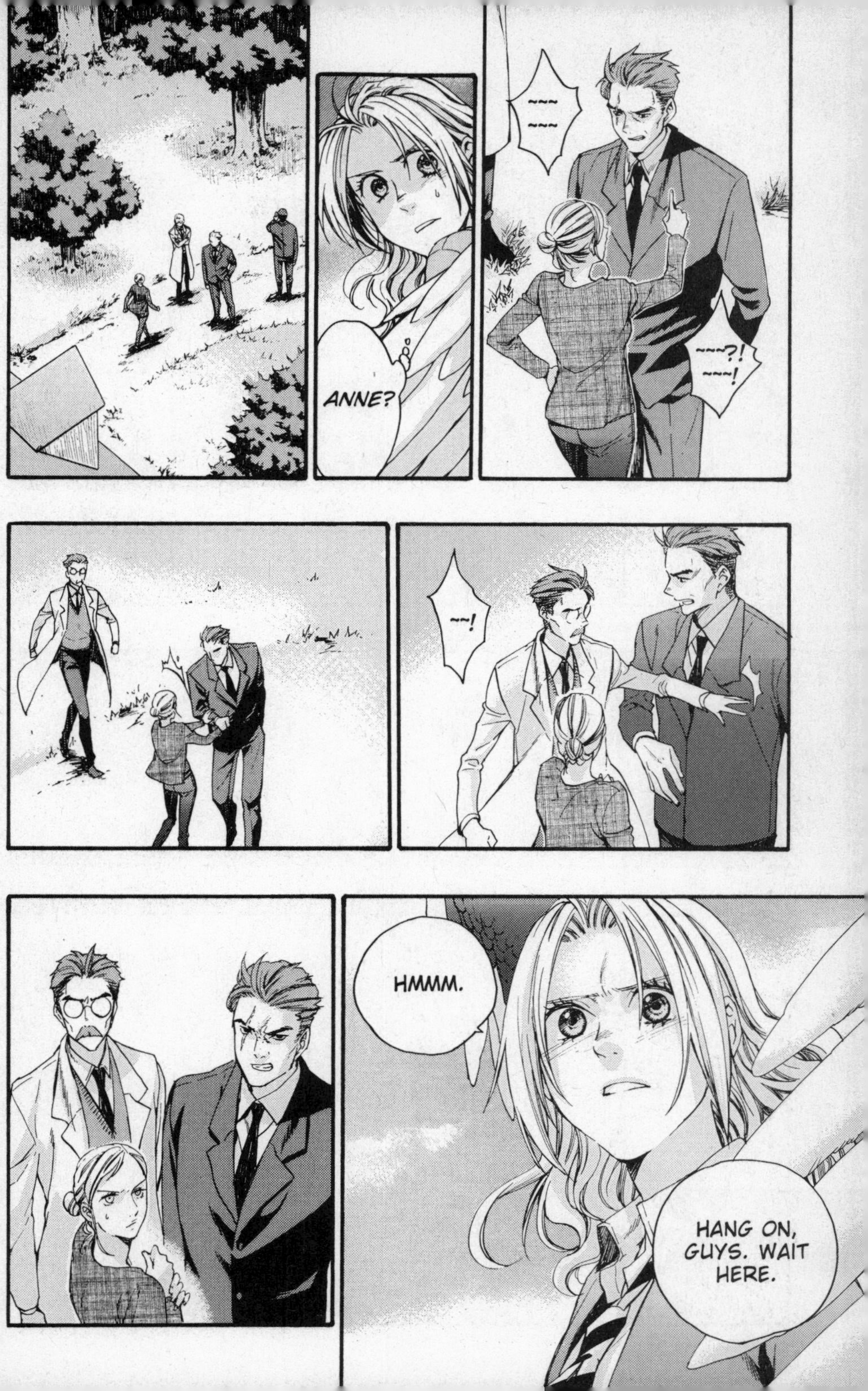
ANNE?
~~~
~~~
~~~?!
~~~!
~~!
HMMM.
HANG ON, GUYS. WAIT HERE.

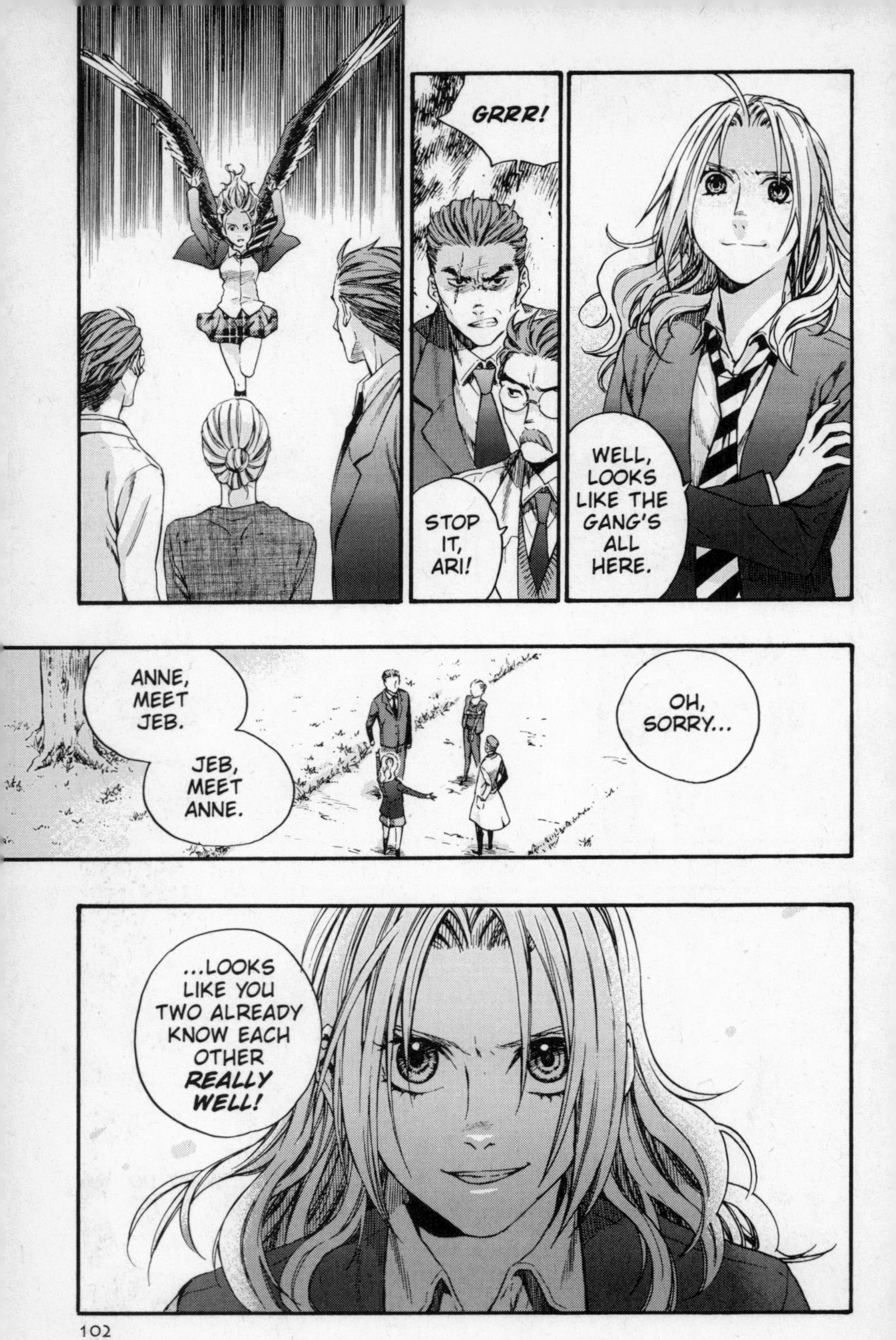
GRRR!
STOP IT, ARI!
WELL, LOOKS LIKE THE GANG'S ALL HERE.
ANNE, MEET JEB.
JEB, MEET ANNE.
OH, SORRY...
...LOOKS LIKE YOU TWO ALREADY KNOW EACH OTHER *REALLY WELL!*

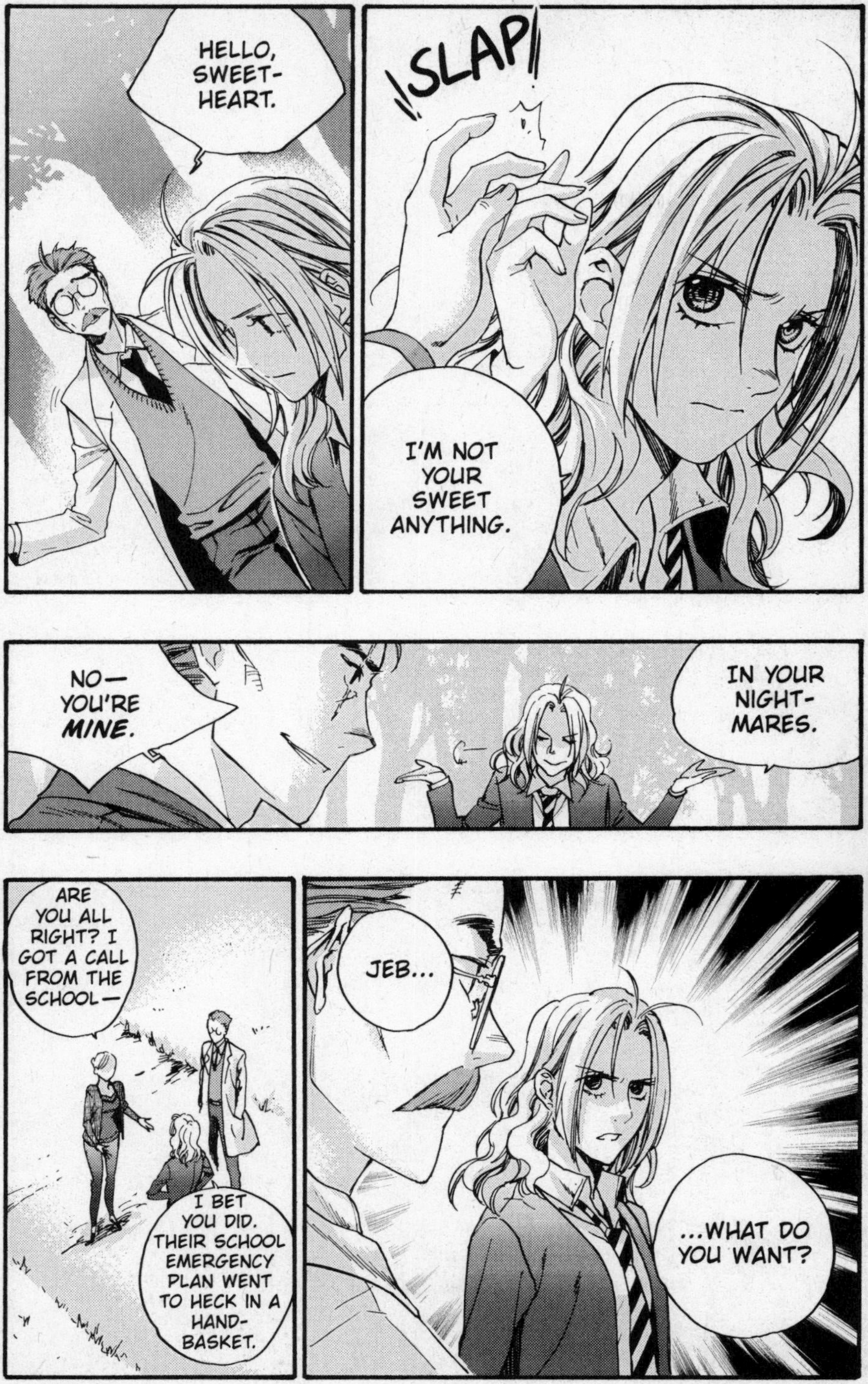

HELLO, SWEET-HEART.
SLAP
I'M NOT YOUR SWEET ANYTHING.
NO— YOU'RE *MINE*.
IN YOUR NIGHT-MARES.
ARE YOU ALL RIGHT? I GOT A CALL FROM THE SCHOOL—
I BET YOU DID. THEIR SCHOOL EMERGENCY PLAN WENT TO HECK IN A HAND-BASKET.
JEB...
...WHAT DO YOU WANT?

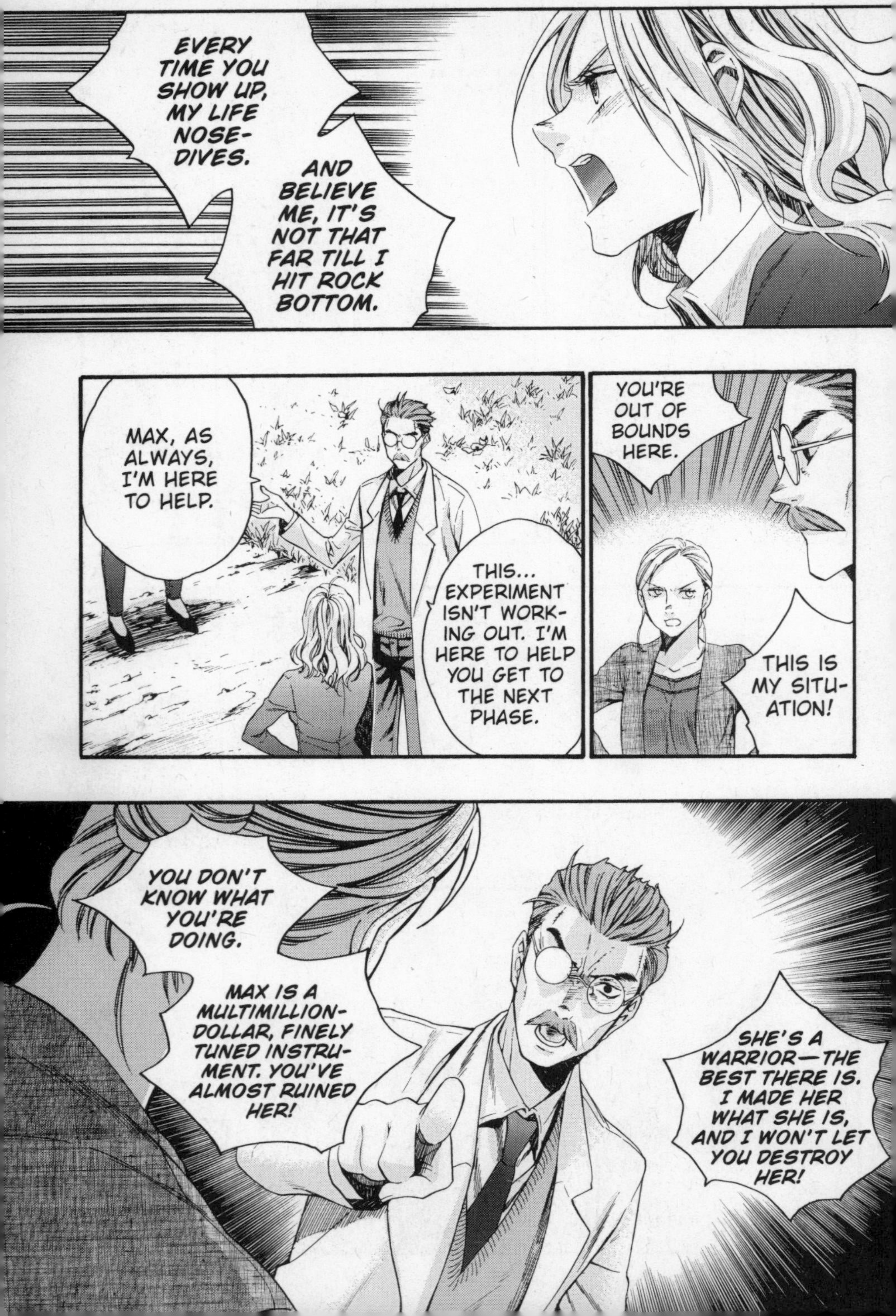
EVERY TIME YOU SHOW UP, MY LIFE NOSE-DIVES.
AND BELIEVE ME, IT'S NOT THAT FAR TILL I HIT ROCK BOTTOM.
MAX, AS ALWAYS, I'M HERE TO HELP.
THIS... EXPERIMENT ISN'T WORKING OUT. I'M HERE TO HELP YOU GET TO THE NEXT PHASE.
YOU'RE OUT OF BOUNDS HERE.
THIS IS MY SITUATION!
YOU DON'T KNOW WHAT YOU'RE DOING.
MAX IS A MULTIMILLION-DOLLAR, FINELY TUNED INSTRUMENT. YOU'VE ALMOST RUINED HER!
SHE'S A WARRIOR—THE BEST THERE IS. I MADE HER WHAT SHE IS, AND I WON'T LET YOU DESTROY HER!

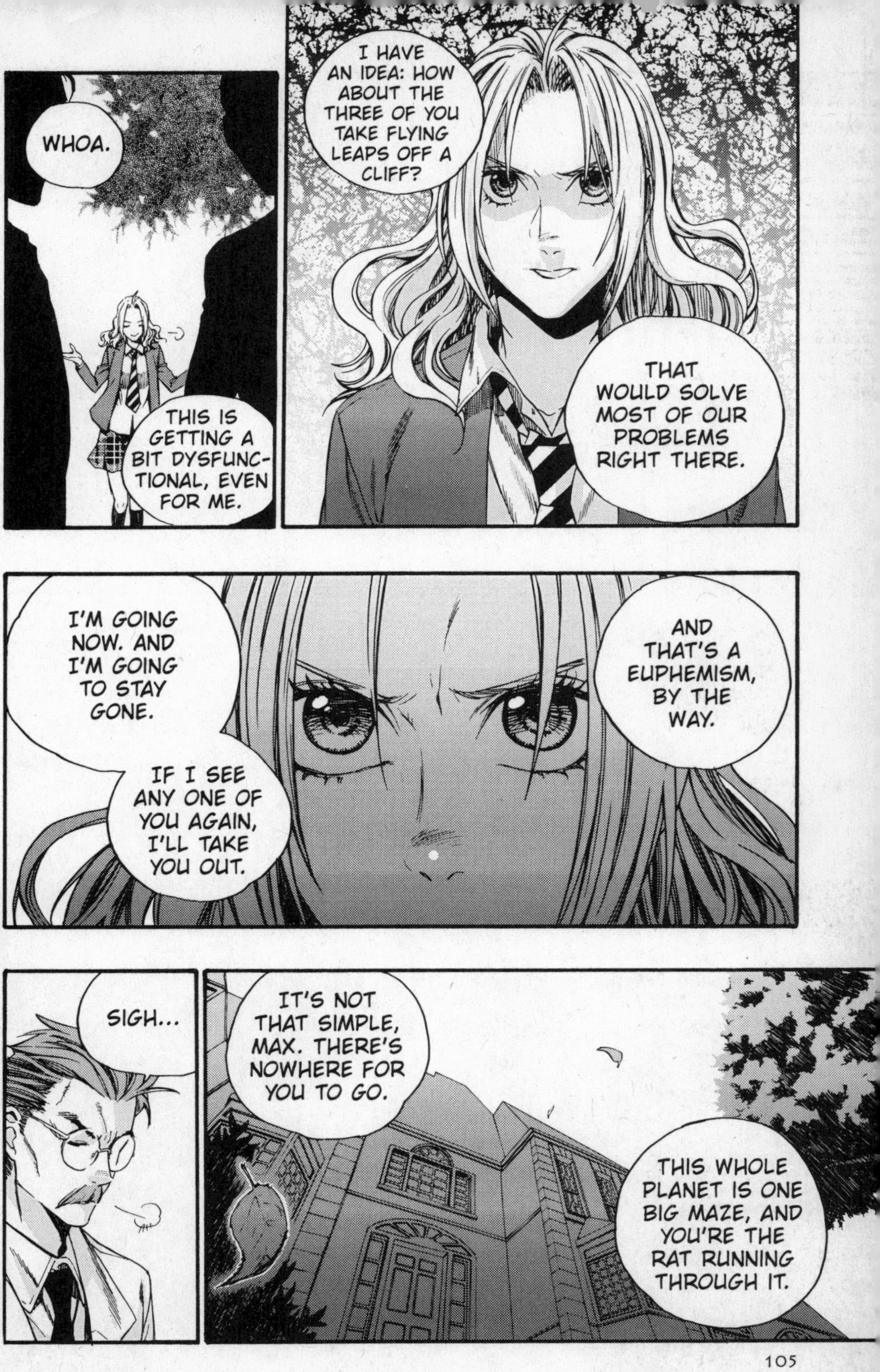
WHOA.
THIS IS GETTING A BIT DYSFUNCTIONAL, EVEN FOR ME.
I HAVE AN IDEA: HOW ABOUT THE THREE OF YOU TAKE FLYING LEAPS OFF A CLIFF?
THAT WOULD SOLVE MOST OF OUR PROBLEMS RIGHT THERE.
I'M GOING NOW. AND I'M GOING TO STAY GONE.
IF I SEE ANY ONE OF YOU AGAIN, I'LL TAKE YOU OUT.
AND THAT'S A EUPHEMISM, BY THE WAY.
SIGH...
IT'S NOT THAT SIMPLE, MAX. THERE'S NOWHERE FOR YOU TO GO.
THIS WHOLE PLANET IS ONE BIG MAZE, AND YOU'RE THE RAT RUNNING THROUGH IT.

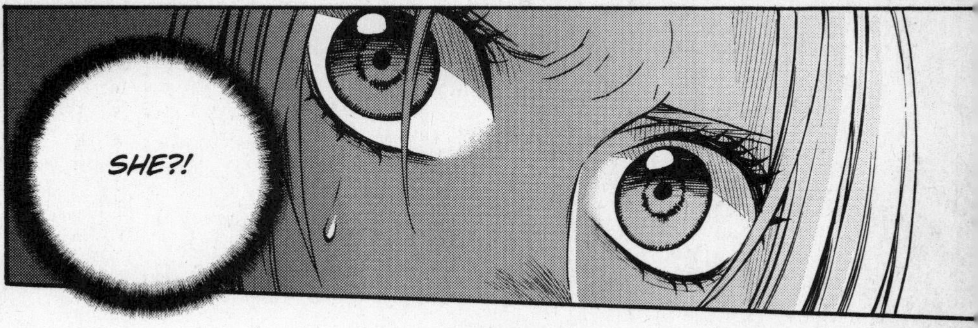
SHE?!

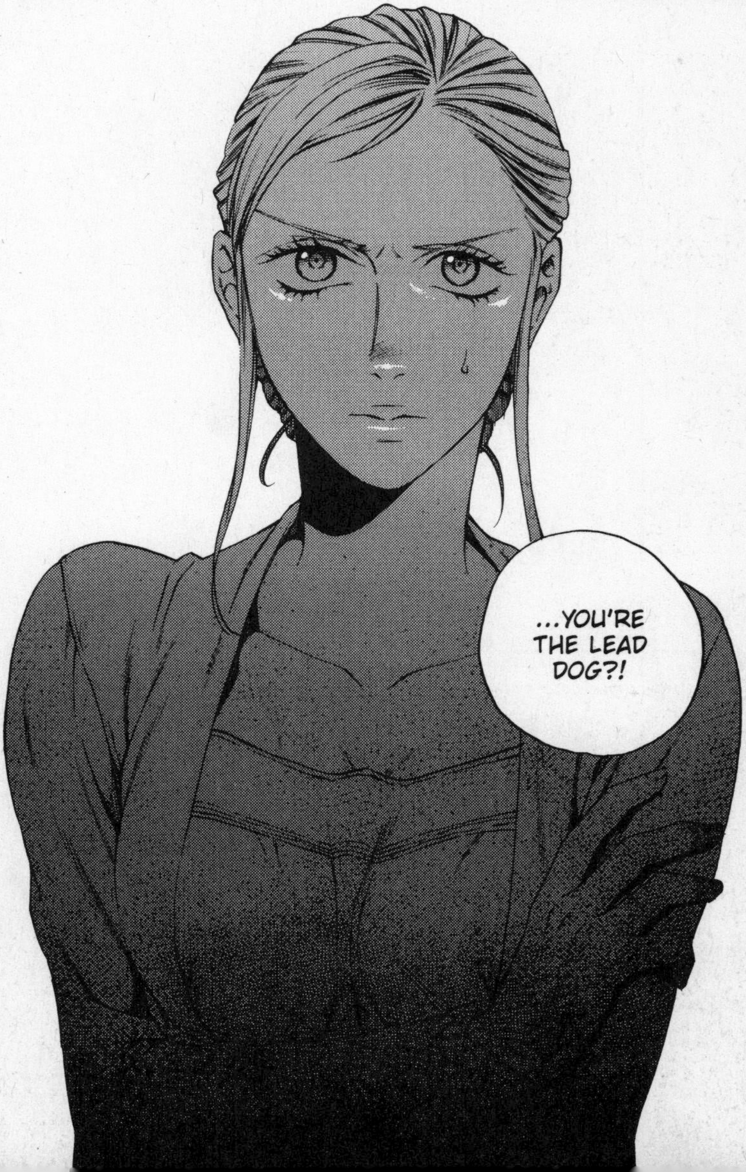
...YOU'RE THE LEAD DOG?!

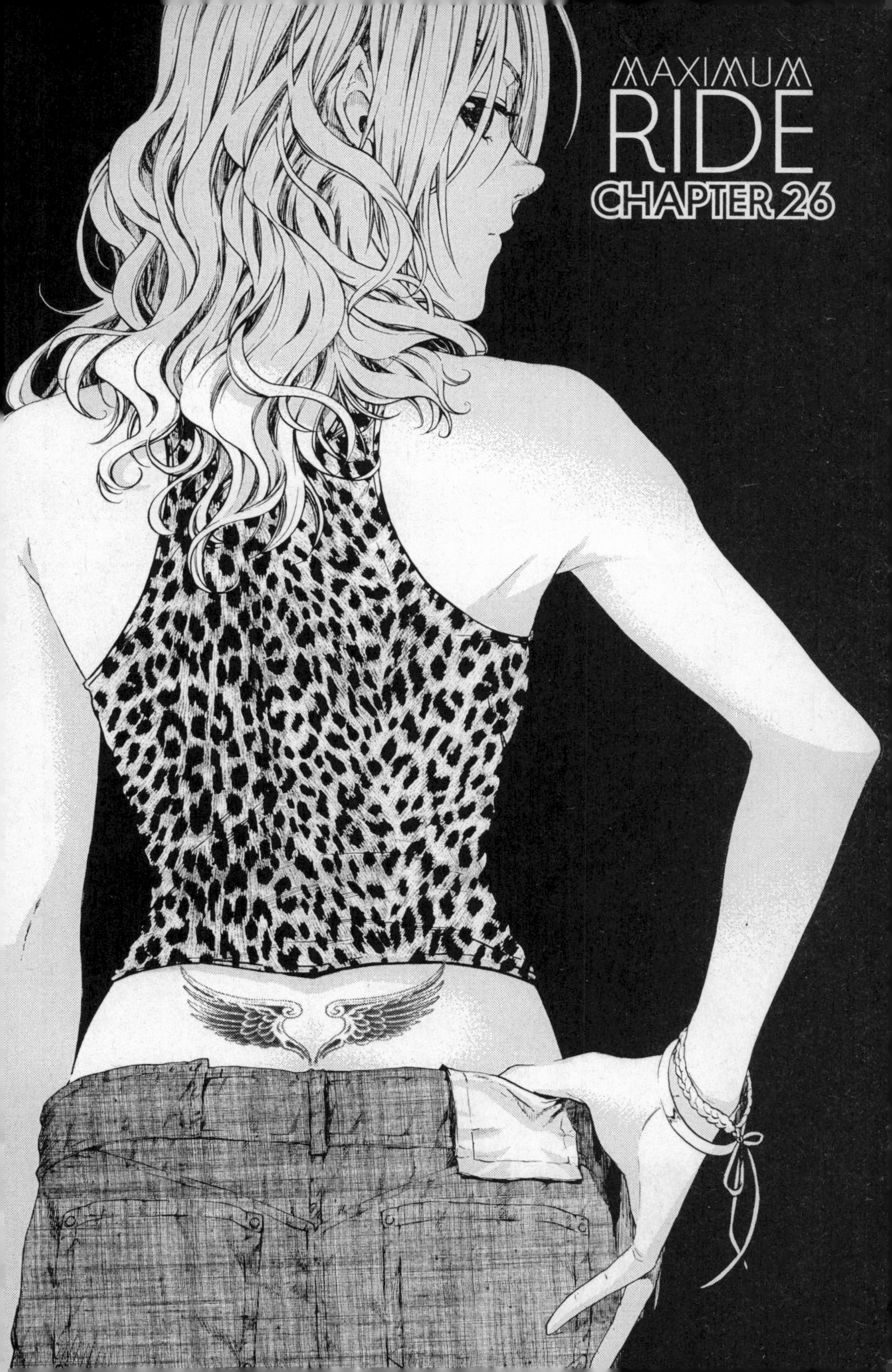
MAXIMUM
RIDE
CHAPTER 26

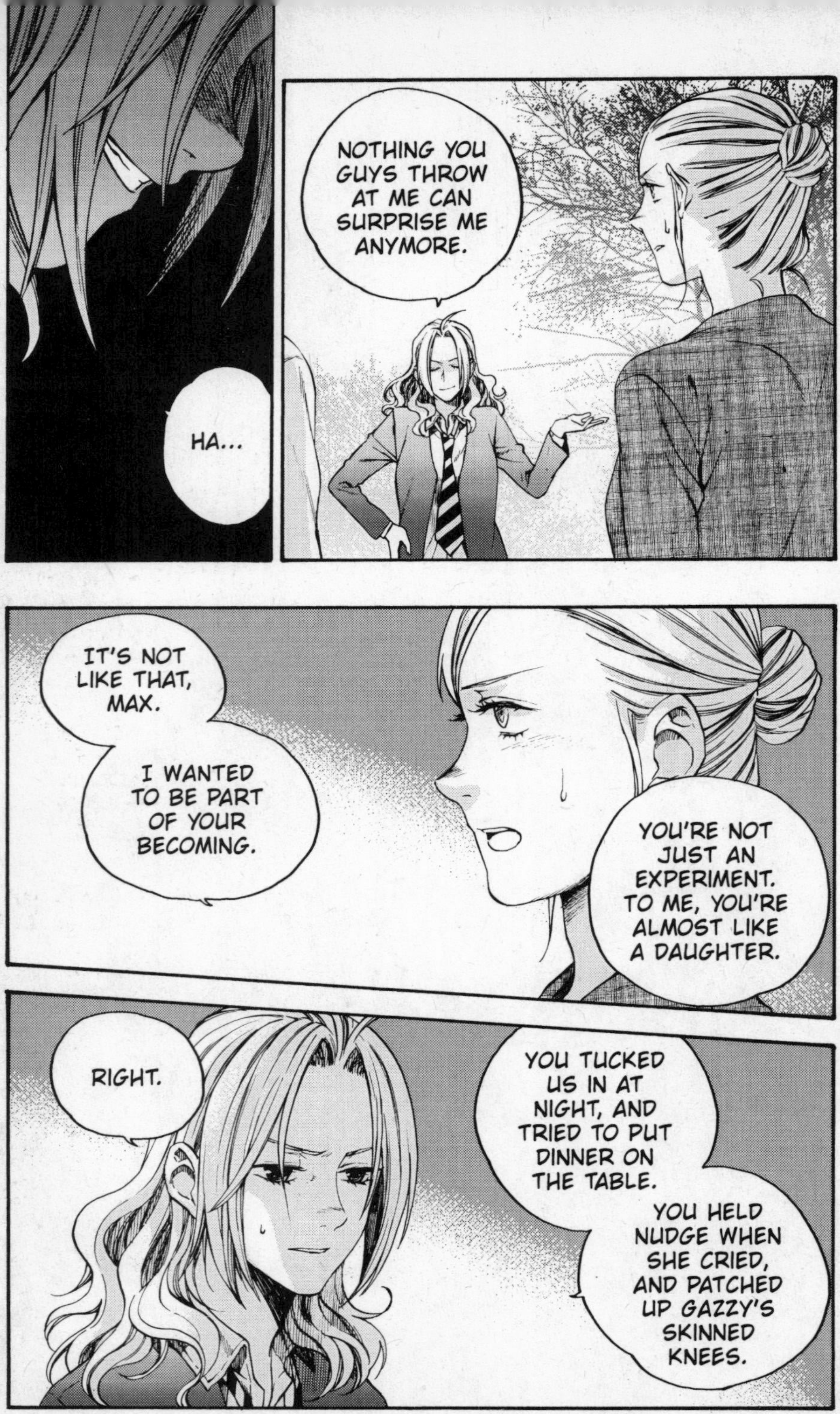
HA...
NOTHING YOU GUYS THROW AT ME CAN SURPRISE ME ANYMORE.
IT'S NOT LIKE THAT, MAX.
I WANTED TO BE PART OF YOUR BECOMING.
YOU'RE NOT JUST AN EXPERIMENT. TO ME, YOU'RE ALMOST LIKE A DAUGHTER.
RIGHT.
YOU TUCKED US IN AT NIGHT, AND TRIED TO PUT DINNER ON THE TABLE.
YOU HELD NUDGE WHEN SHE CRIED, AND PATCHED UP GAZZY'S SKINNED KNEES.

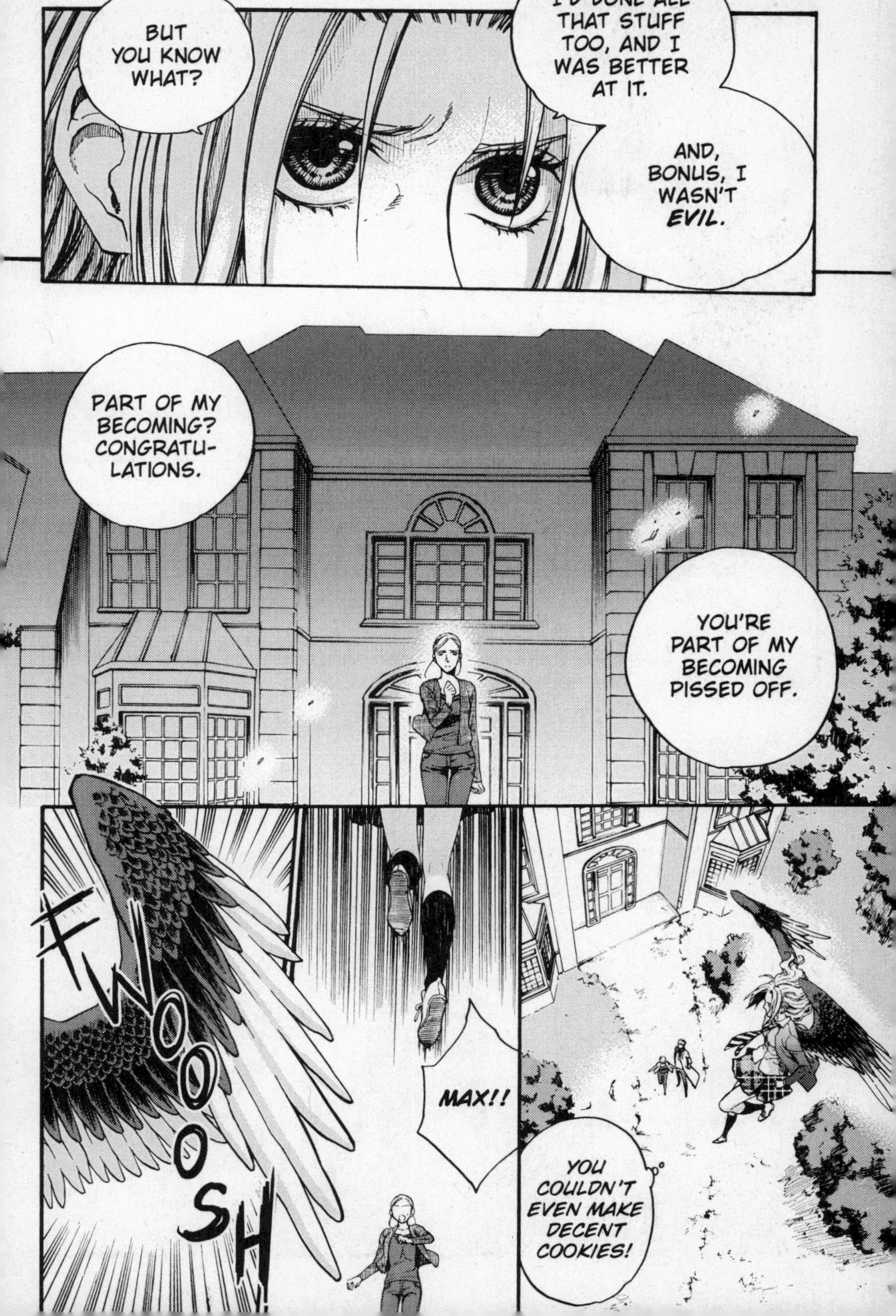

BUT YOU KNOW WHAT?
I'D DONE ALL THAT STUFF TOO, AND I WAS BETTER AT IT.
AND, BONUS, I WASN'T *EVIL*.
PART OF MY BECOMING? CONGRATU-LATIONS.
YOU'RE PART OF MY BECOMING PISSED OFF.
FWOOOSH
MAX!!
YOU COULDN'T EVEN MAKE DECENT COOKIES!

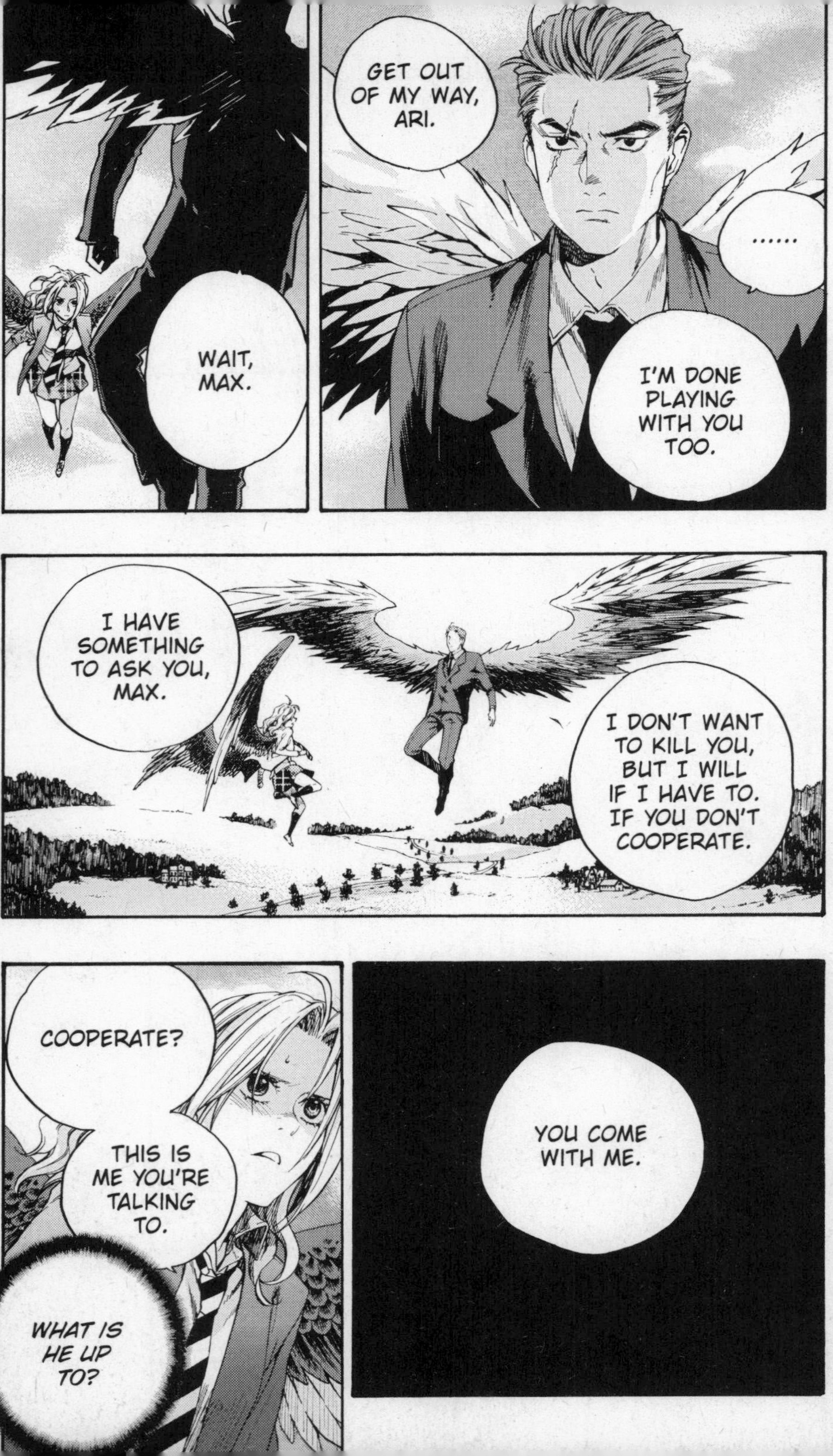
WAIT, MAX.
GET OUT OF MY WAY, ARI.
......
I'M DONE PLAYING WITH YOU TOO.
I HAVE SOMETHING TO ASK YOU, MAX.
I DON'T WANT TO KILL YOU, BUT I WILL IF I HAVE TO. IF YOU DON'T COOPERATE.
COOPERATE?
THIS IS ME YOU'RE TALKING TO.
WHAT IS HE UP TO?
YOU COME WITH ME.

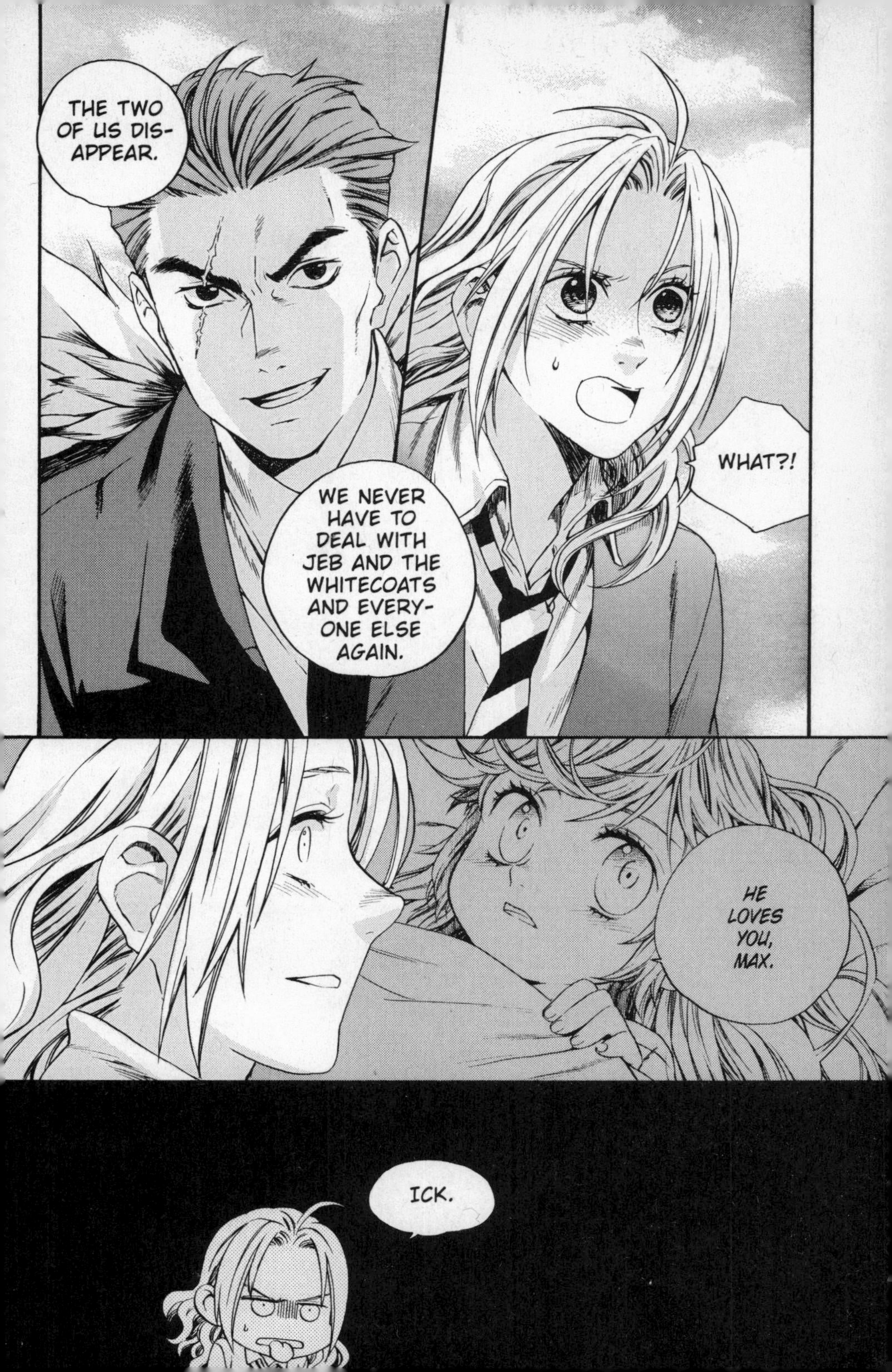
THE TWO OF US DIS-APPEAR.
WE NEVER HAVE TO DEAL WITH JEB AND THE WHITECOATS AND EVERY-ONE ELSE AGAIN.
WHAT?!
HE LOVES YOU, MAX.
ICK.

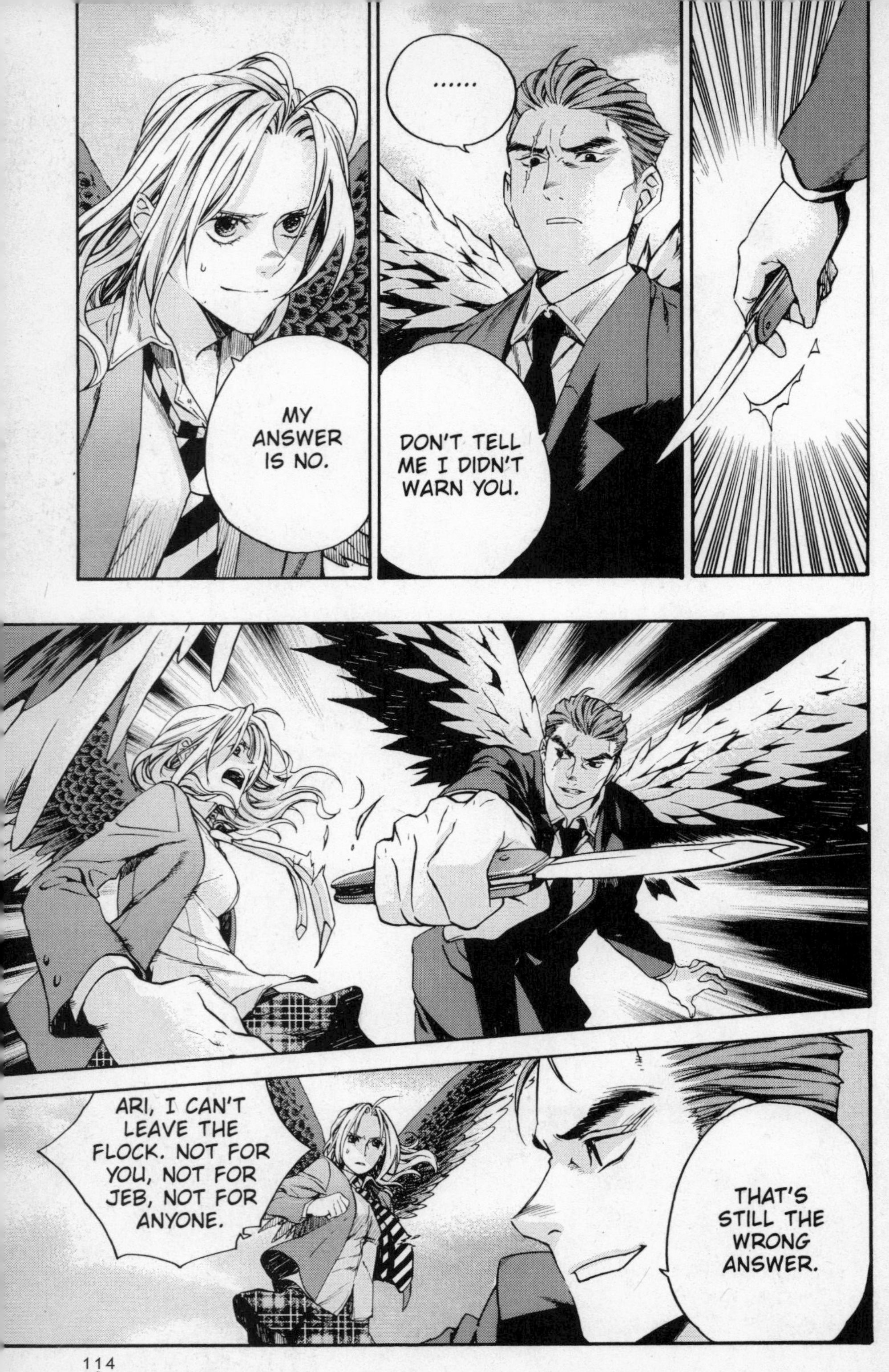
MY ANSWER IS NO.
......
DON'T TELL ME I DIDN'T WARN YOU.
ARI, I CAN'T LEAVE THE FLOCK. NOT FOR YOU, NOT FOR JEB, NOT FOR ANYONE.
THAT'S STILL THE WRONG ANSWER.

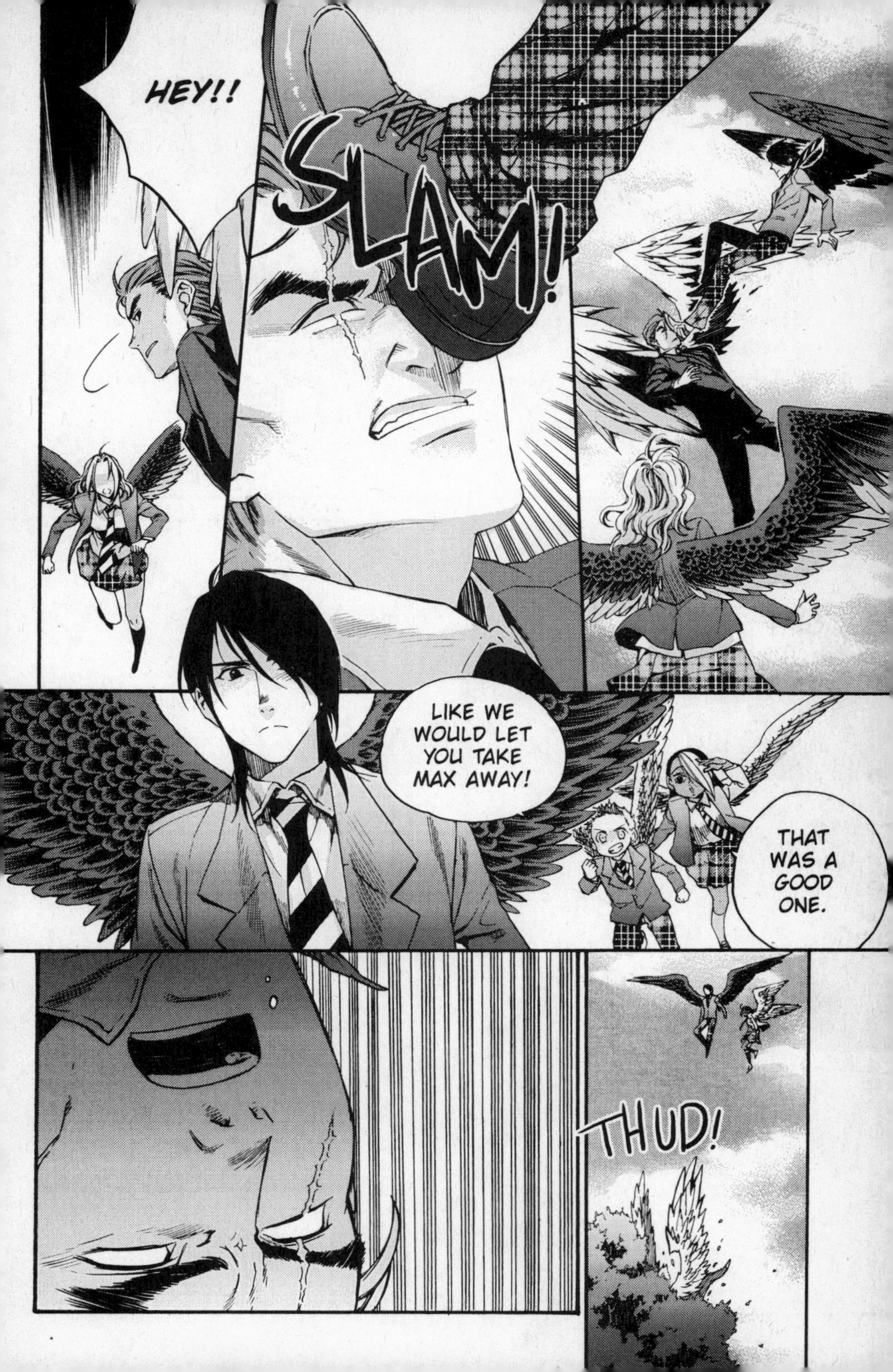
HEY!!
SLAM!
LIKE WE WOULD LET YOU TAKE MAX AWAY!
THAT WAS A GOOD ONE.
THUD!

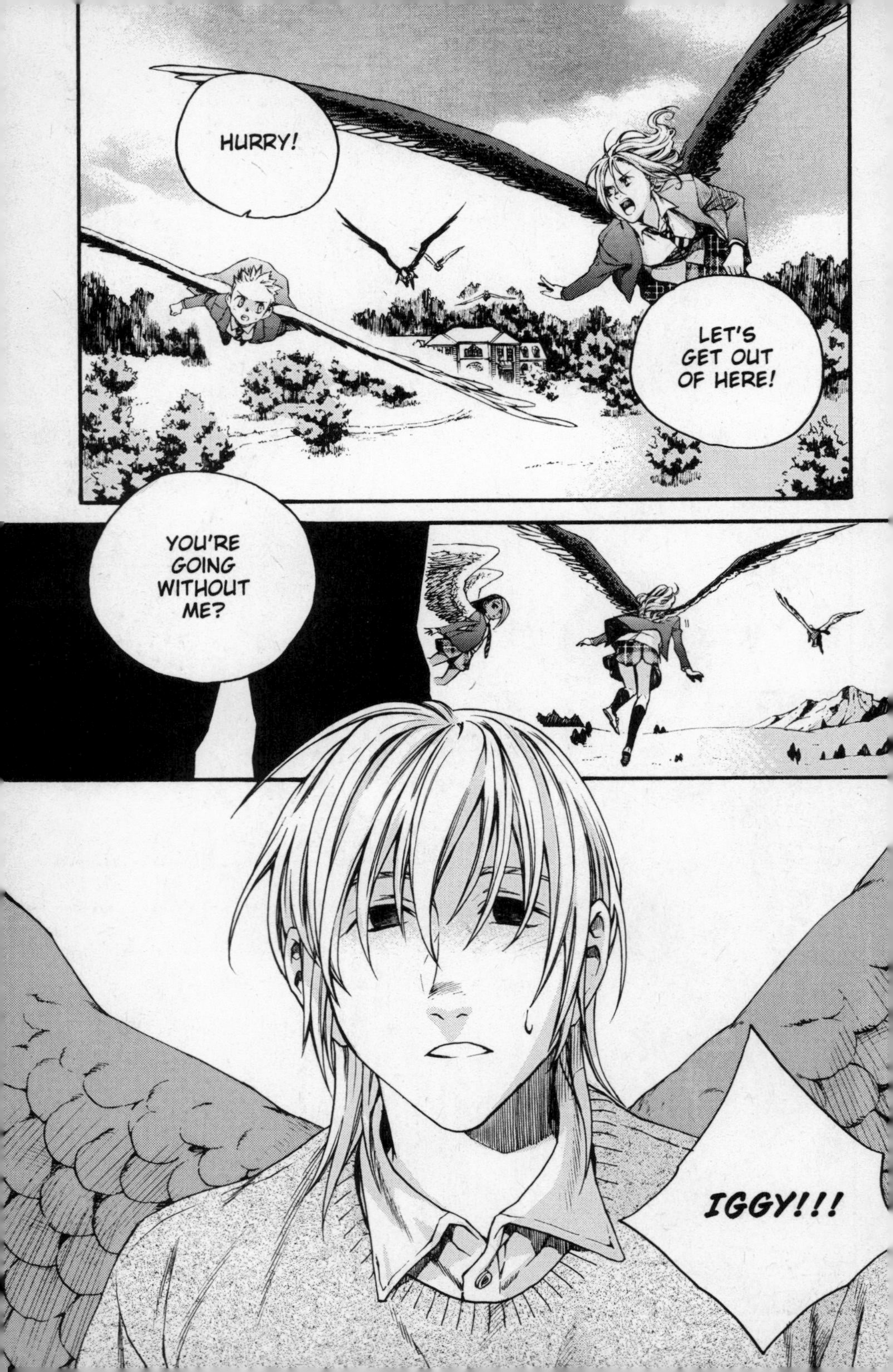
HURRY!
LET'S GET OUT OF HERE!
YOU'RE GOING WITHOUT ME?
IGGY!!!

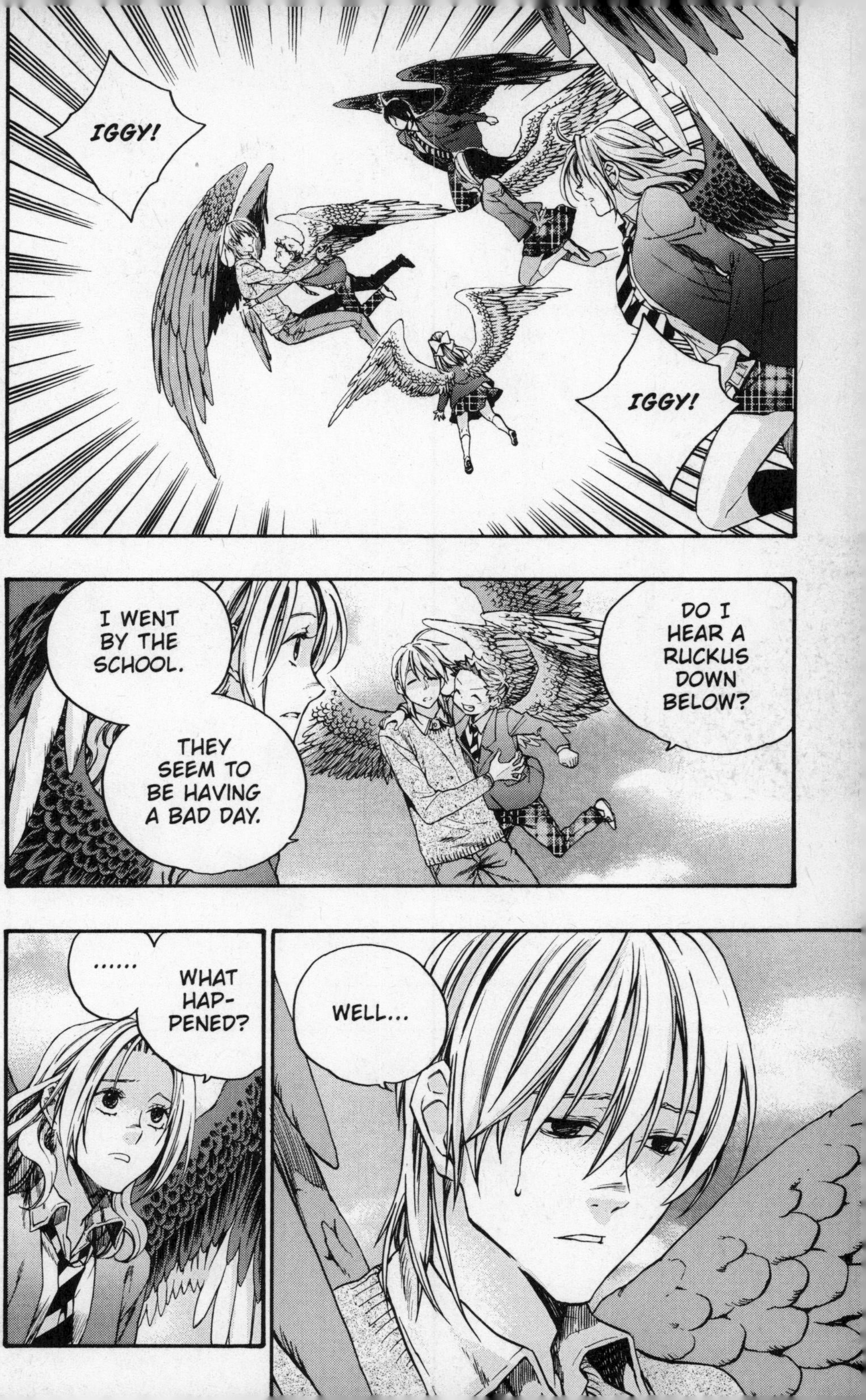
IGGY!
IGGY!
I WENT BY THE SCHOOL.
THEY SEEM TO BE HAVING A BAD DAY.
DO I HEAR A RUCKUS DOWN BELOW?
...... WHAT HAP-PENED?
WELL...

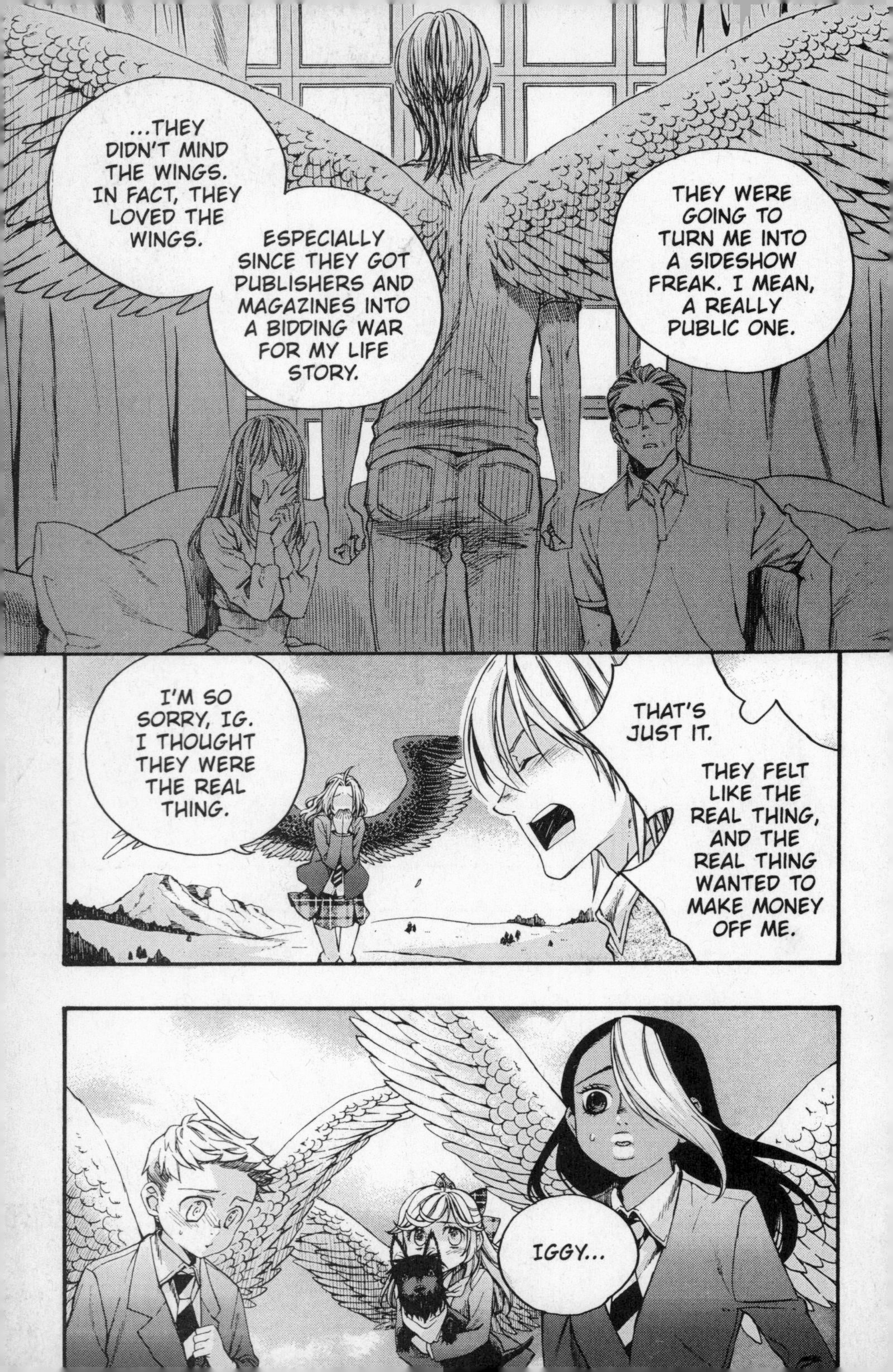
...THEY DIDN'T MIND THE WINGS. IN FACT, THEY LOVED THE WINGS.
ESPECIALLY SINCE THEY GOT PUBLISHERS AND MAGAZINES INTO A BIDDING WAR FOR MY LIFE STORY.
THEY WERE GOING TO TURN ME INTO A SIDESHOW FREAK. I MEAN, A REALLY PUBLIC ONE.
I'M SO SORRY, IG. I THOUGHT THEY WERE THE REAL THING.
THAT'S JUST IT.
THEY FELT LIKE THE REAL THING, AND THE REAL THING WANTED TO MAKE MONEY OFF ME.
IGGY...

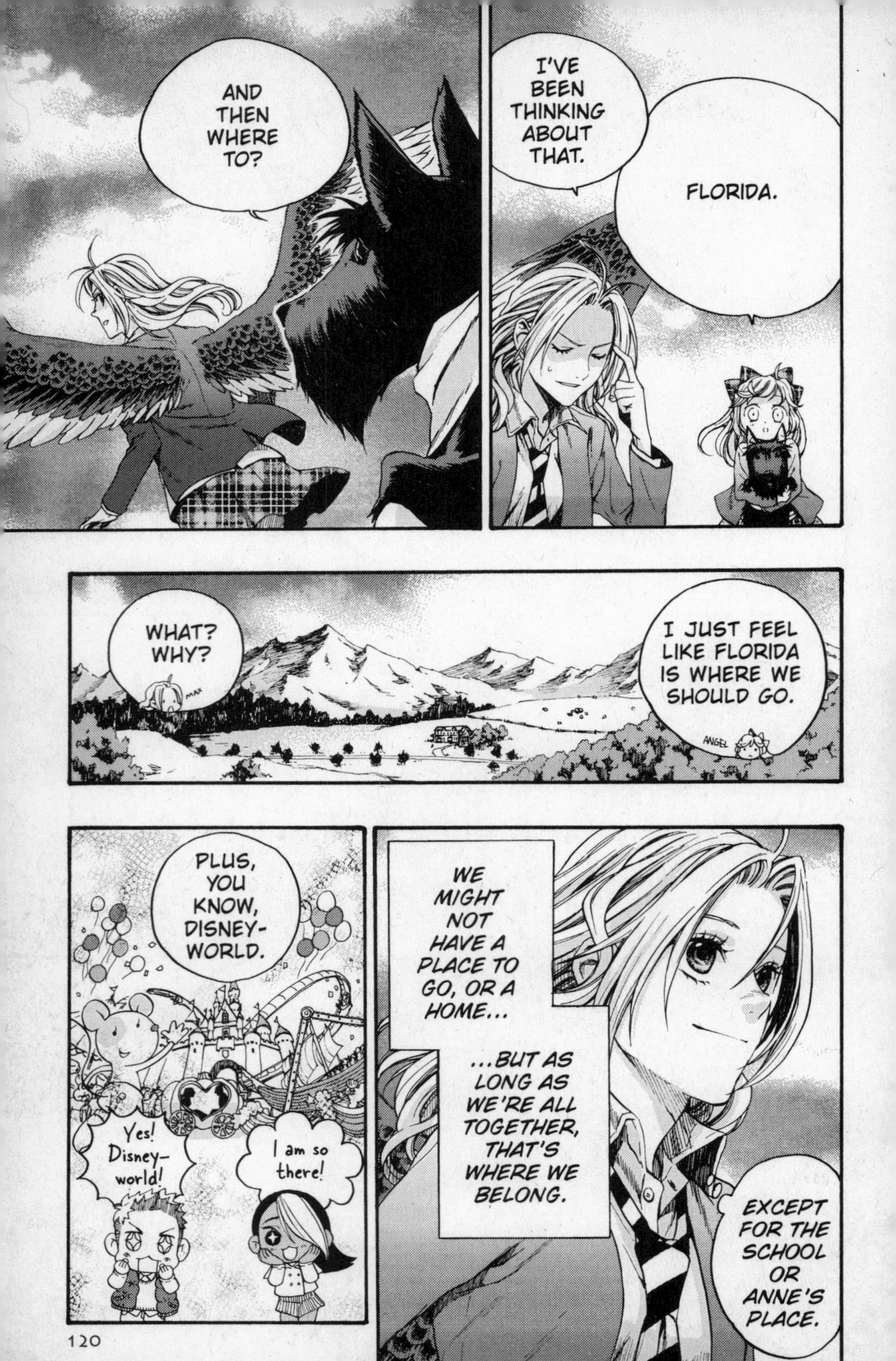
AND THEN WHERE TO?
I'VE BEEN THINKING ABOUT THAT.
FLORIDA.
WHAT? WHY?
MAX
I JUST FEEL LIKE FLORIDA IS WHERE WE SHOULD GO.
ANGEL
PLUS, YOU KNOW, DISNEY-WORLD.
Yes! Disney-world!
I am so there!
WE MIGHT NOT HAVE A PLACE TO GO, OR A HOME...
...BUT AS LONG AS WE'RE ALL TOGETHER, THAT'S WHERE WE BELONG.
EXCEPT FOR THE SCHOOL OR ANNE'S PLACE.

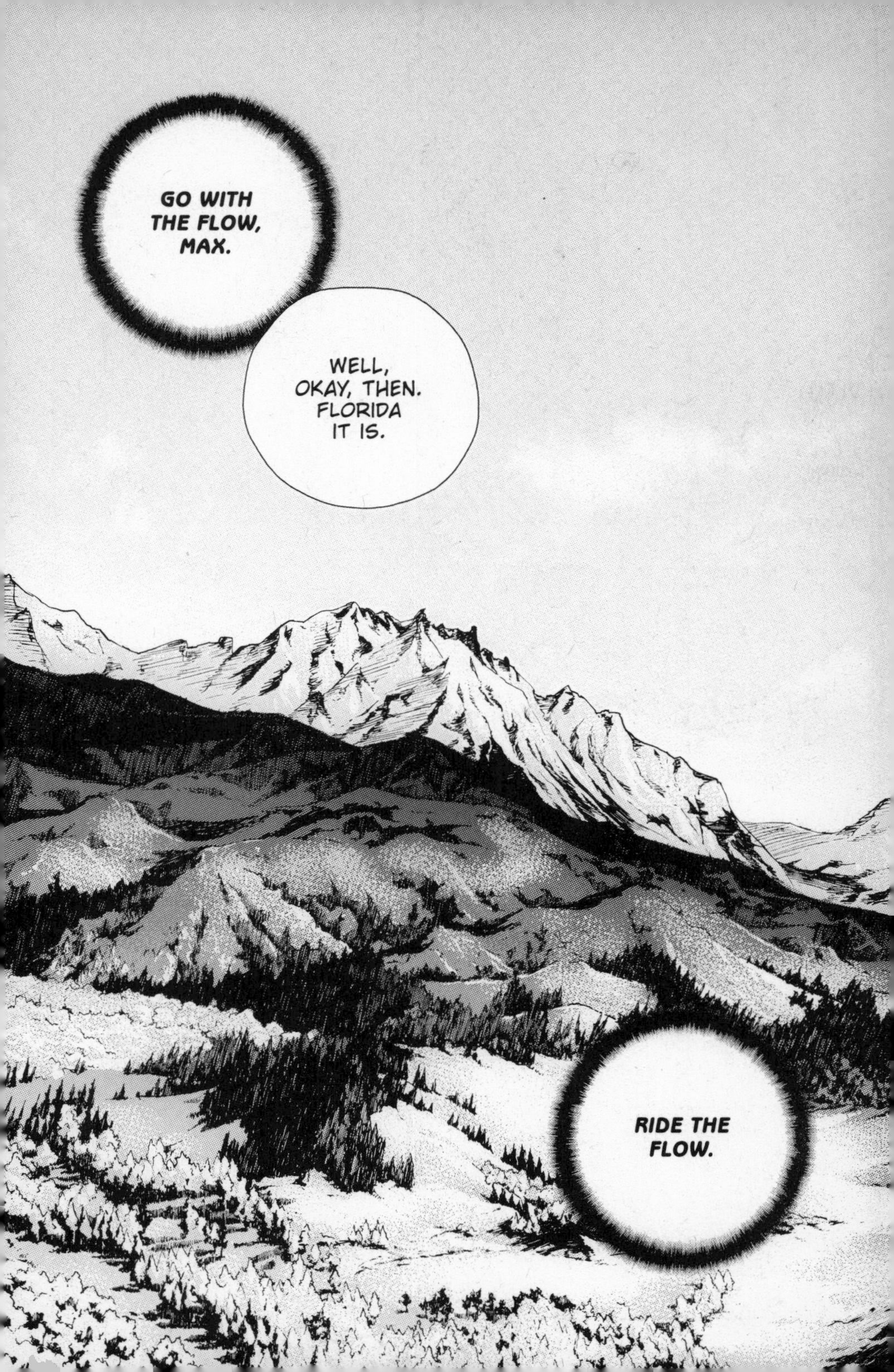
GO WITH THE FLOW, MAX.
WELL, OKAY, THEN. FLORIDA IT IS.
RIDE THE FLOW.

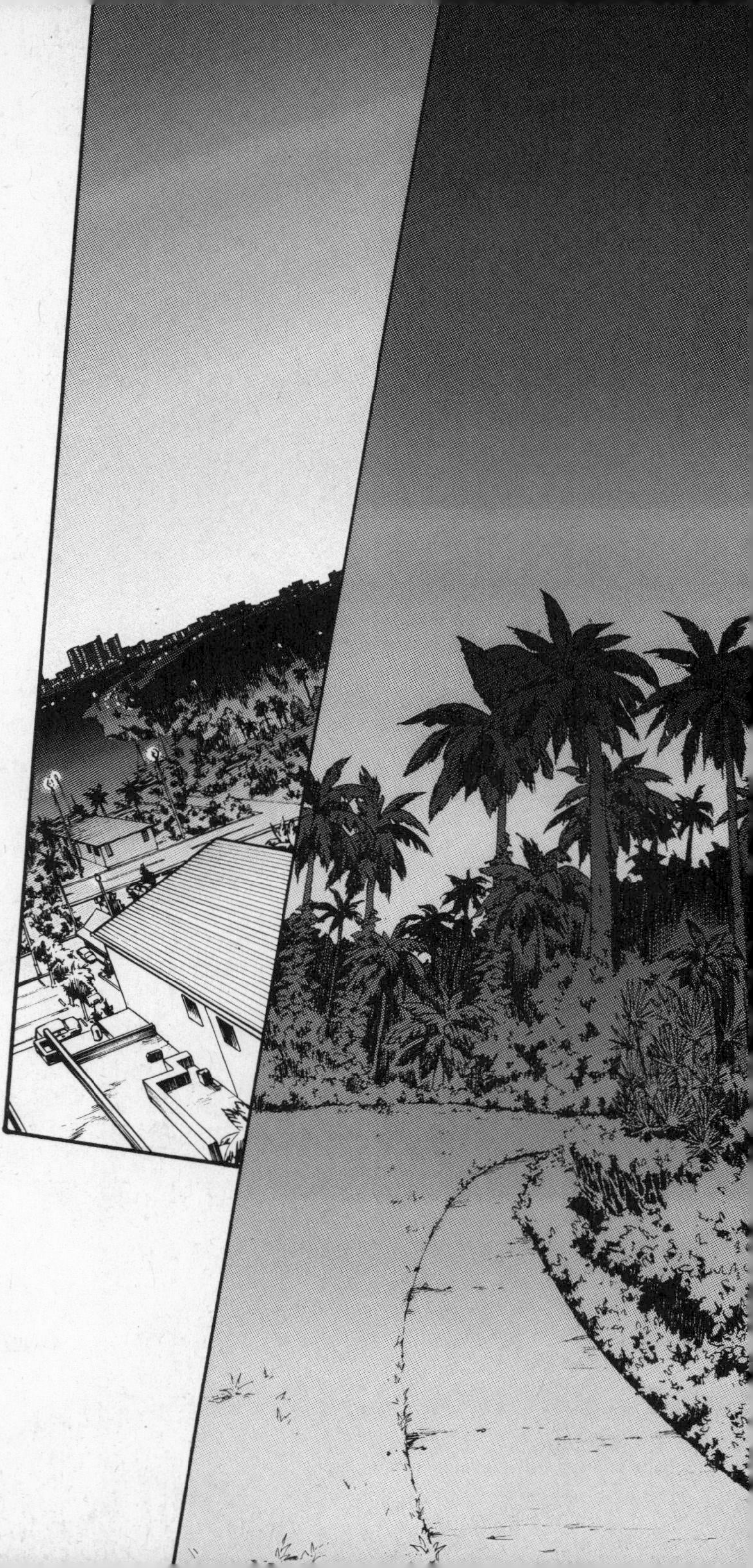

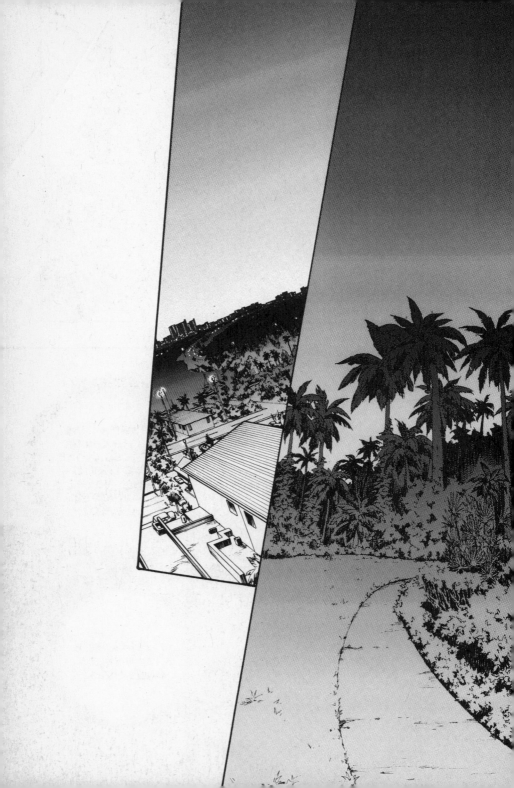

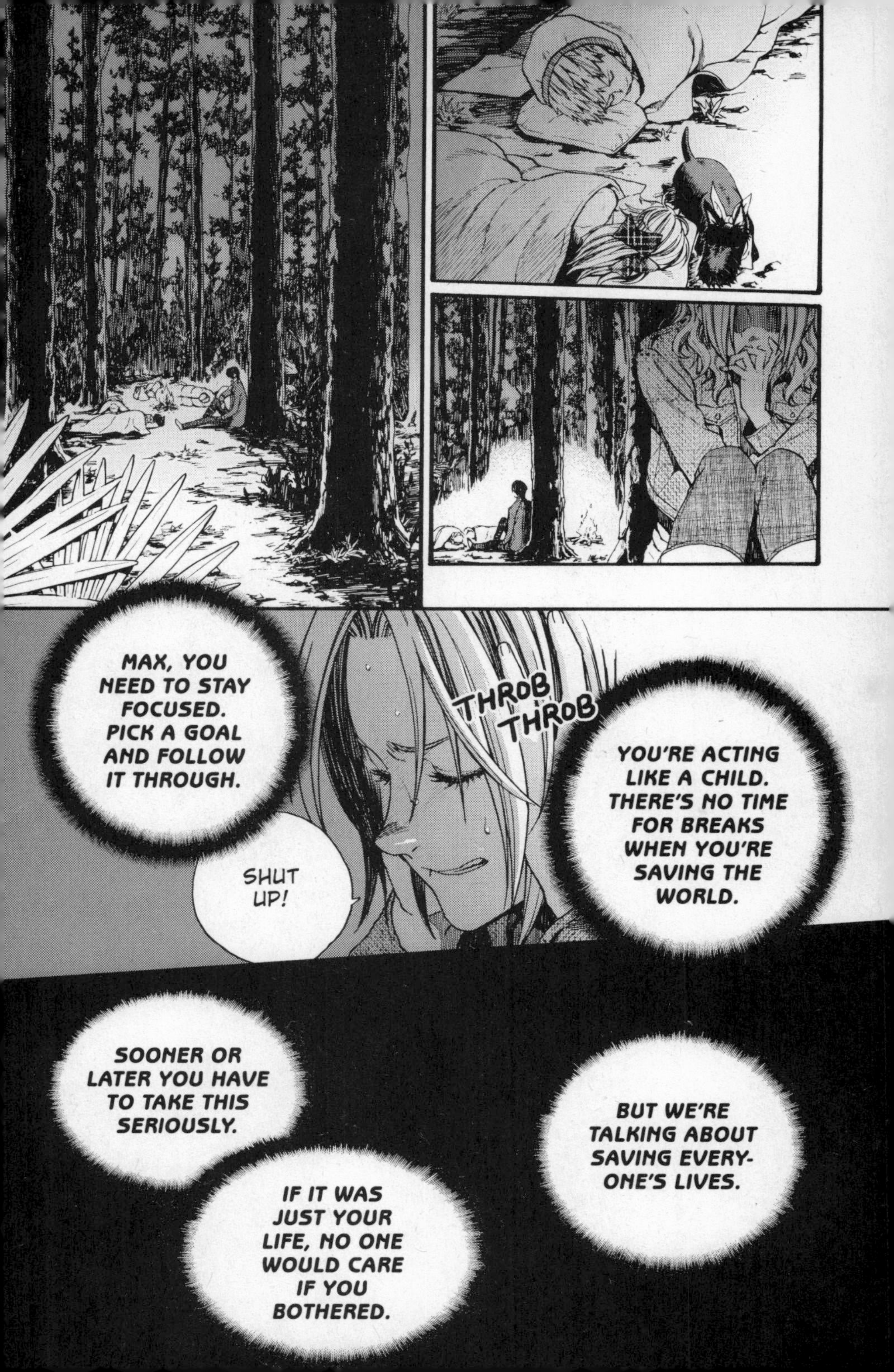
MAX, YOU NEED TO STAY FOCUSED. PICK A GOAL AND FOLLOW IT THROUGH.
THROB THROB
SHUT UP!
YOU'RE ACTING LIKE A CHILD. THERE'S NO TIME FOR BREAKS WHEN YOU'RE SAVING THE WORLD.
SOONER OR LATER YOU HAVE TO TAKE THIS SERIOUSLY.
IF IT WAS JUST YOUR LIFE, NO ONE WOULD CARE IF YOU BOTHERED.
BUT WE'RE TALKING ABOUT SAVING EVERY-ONE'S LIVES.

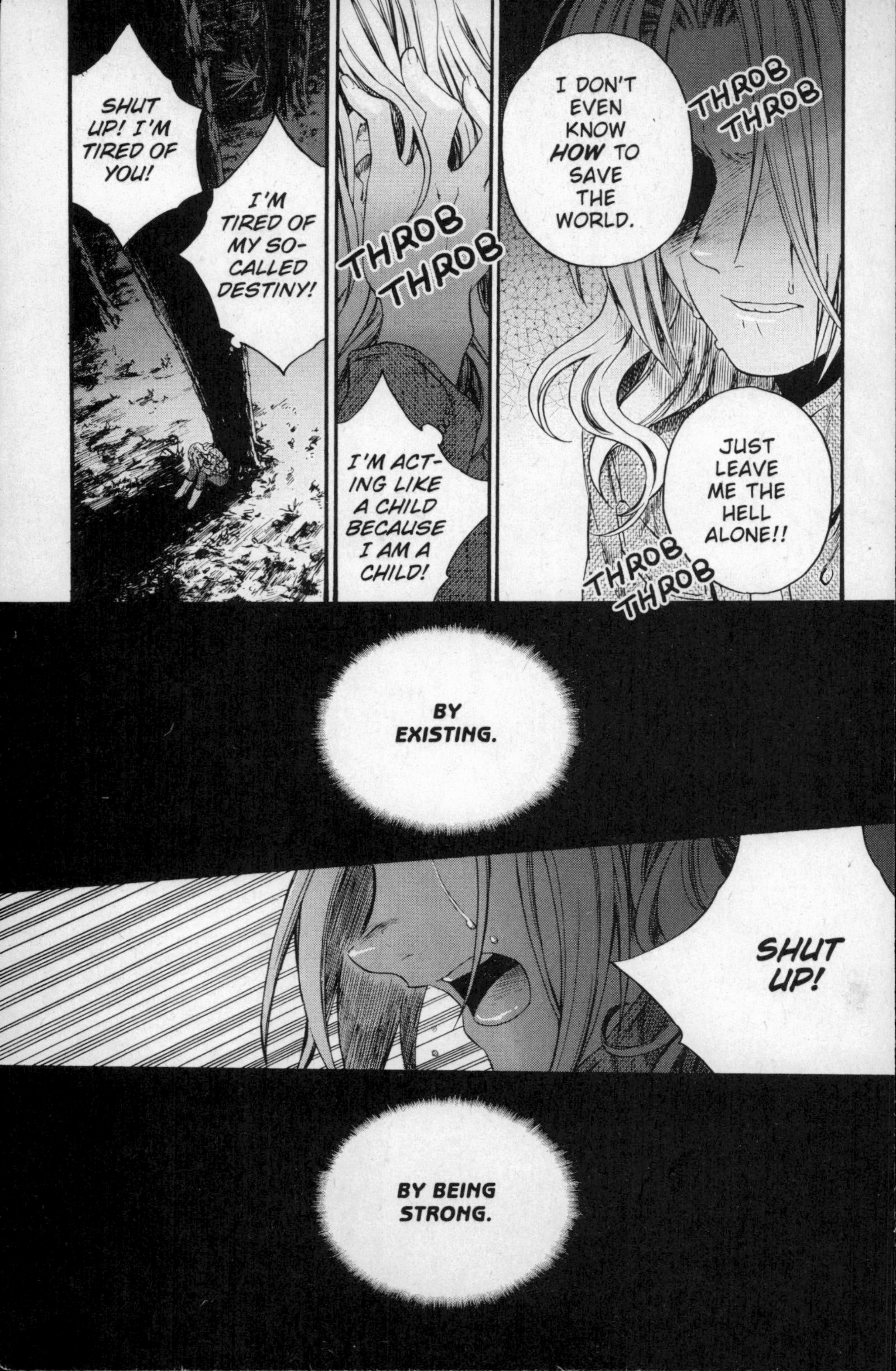
SHUT UP! I'M TIRED OF YOU!
I'M TIRED OF MY SO-CALLED DESTINY!
THROB THROB
I'M ACT-ING LIKE A CHILD BECAUSE I AM A CHILD!
I DON'T EVEN KNOW *HOW* TO SAVE THE WORLD.
THROB THROB
JUST LEAVE ME THE HELL ALONE!!
THROB THROB
BY EXISTING.
SHUT UP!
BY BEING STRONG.

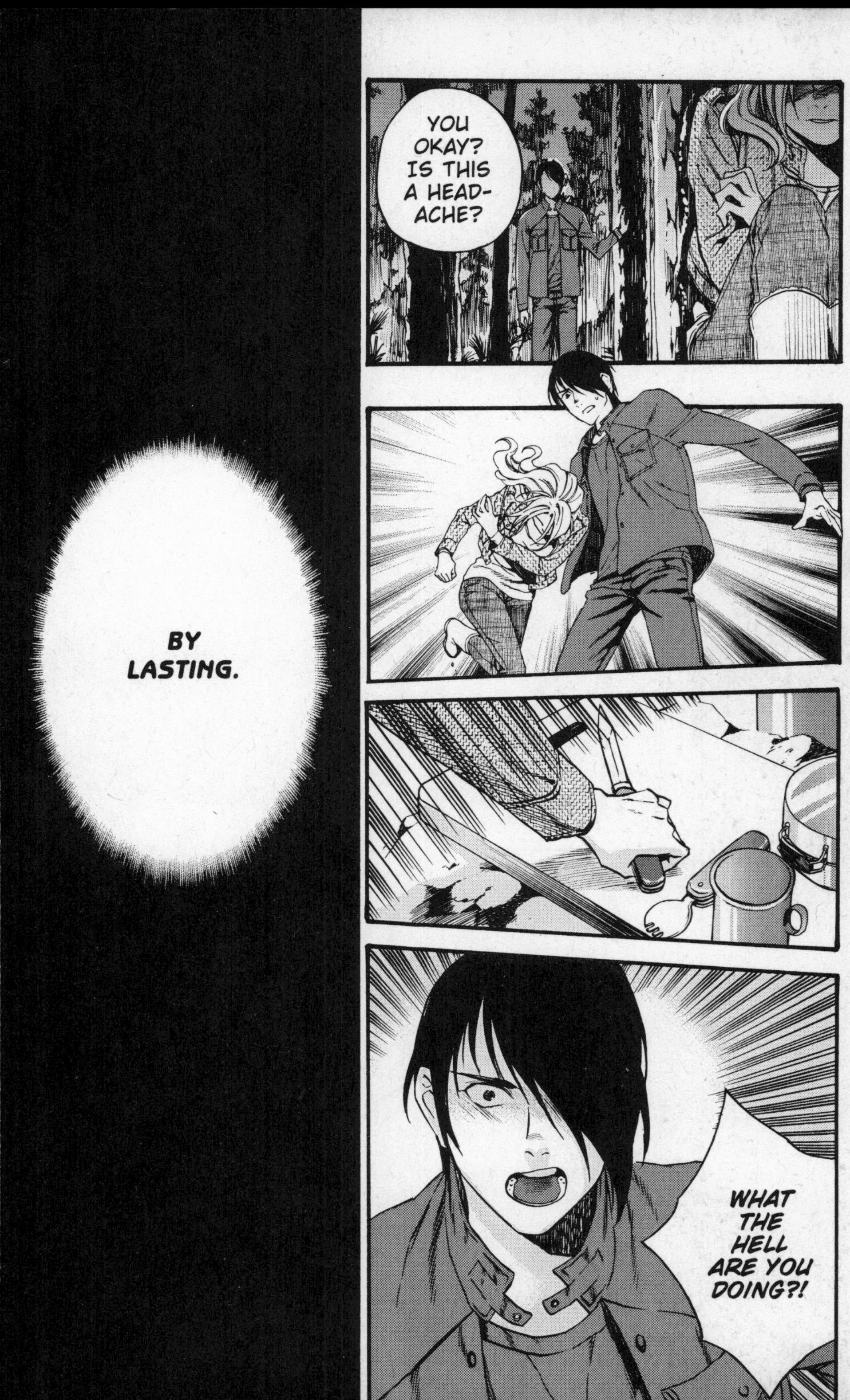
BY LASTING.
YOU OKAY? IS THIS A HEAD-ACHE?
WHAT THE HELL ARE YOU DOING?!

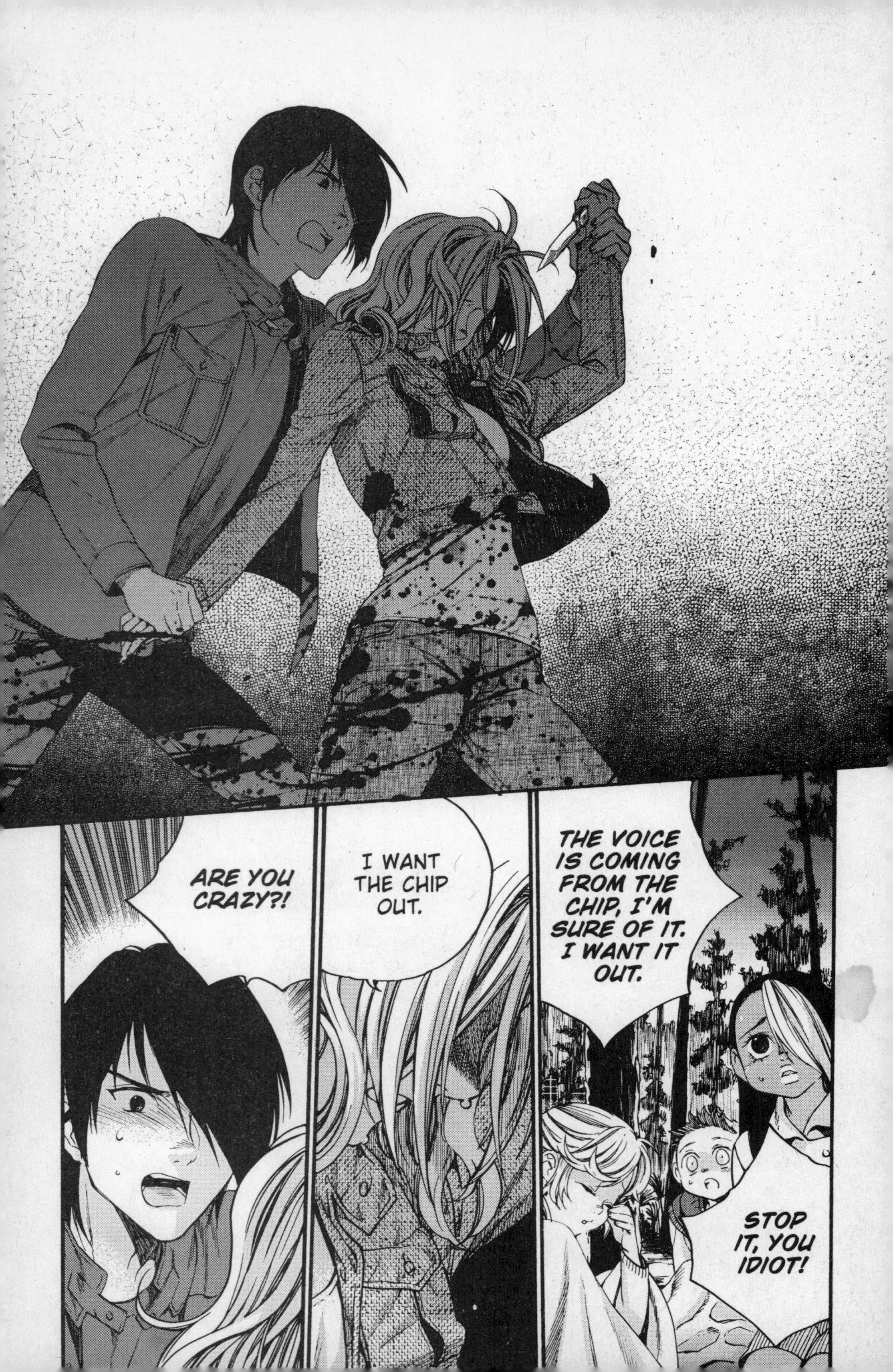
ARE YOU CRAZY?!
I WANT THE CHIP OUT.
THE VOICE IS COMING FROM THE CHIP, I'M SURE OF IT. I WANT IT OUT.
STOP IT, YOU IDIOT!

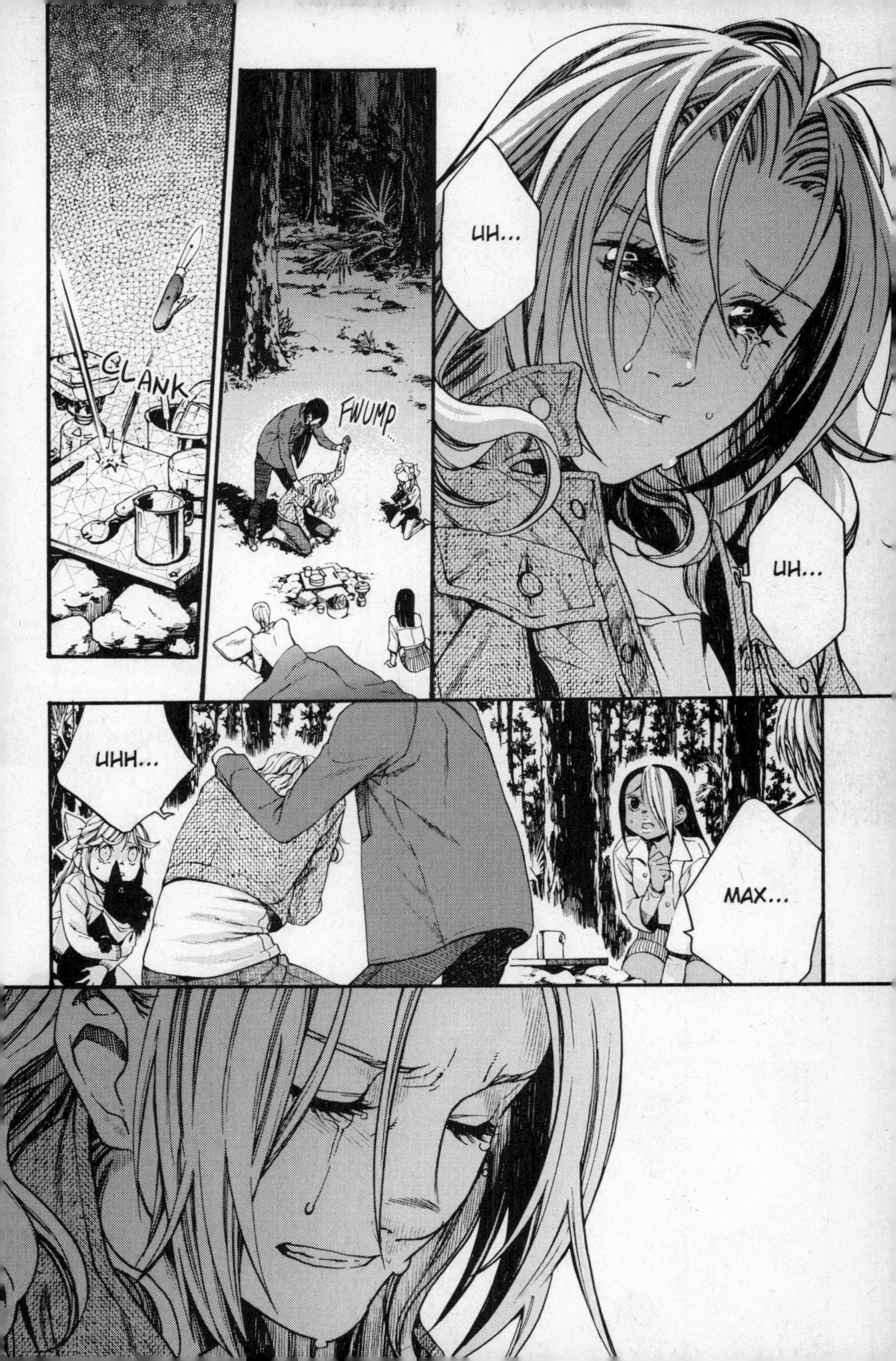
CLANK
FWUMP
UH...
UH...
UHH...
MAX...

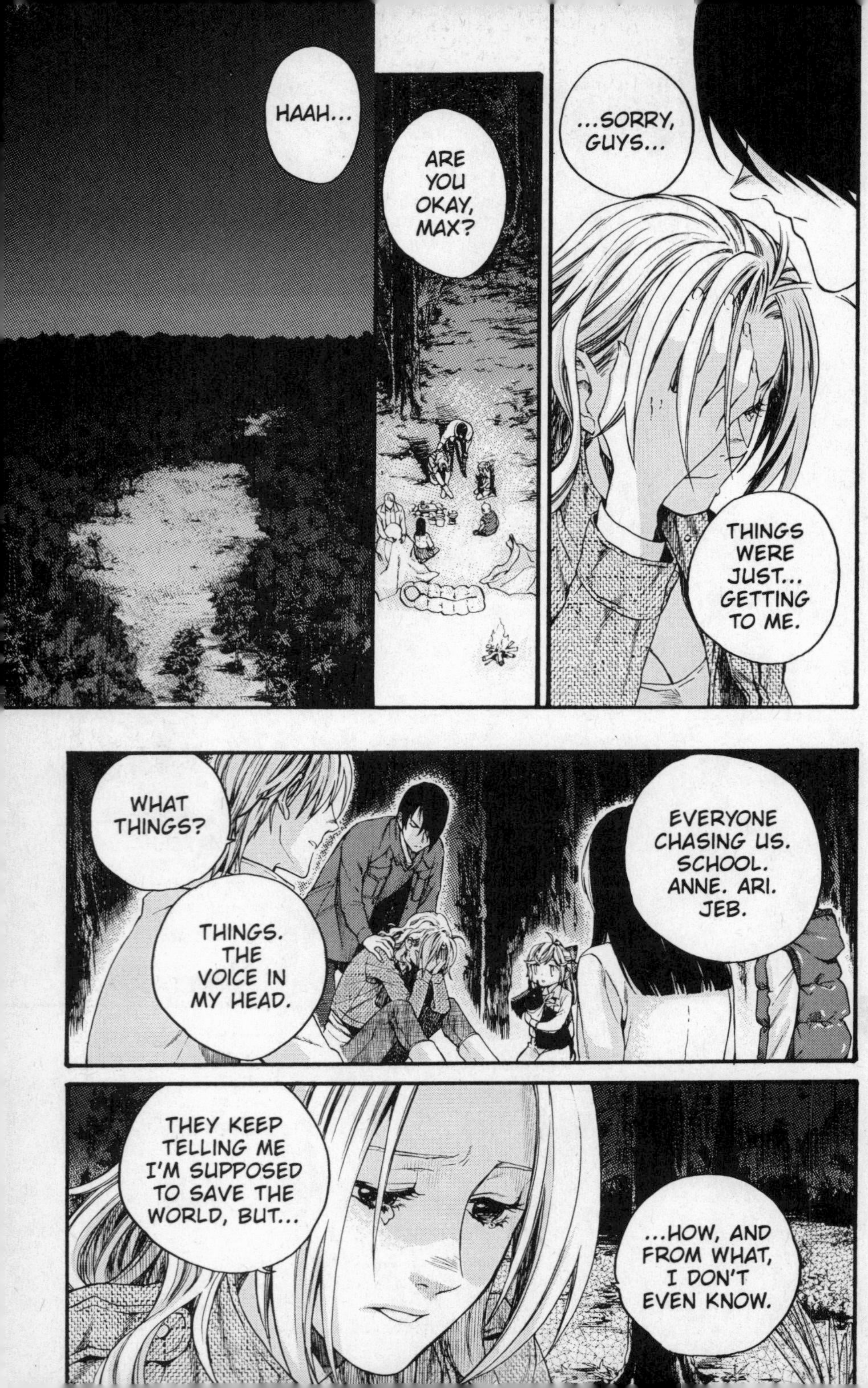
HAAH...
ARE YOU OKAY, MAX?
...SORRY, GUYS...
THINGS WERE JUST... GETTING TO ME.
WHAT THINGS?
THINGS. THE VOICE IN MY HEAD.
EVERYONE CHASING US. SCHOOL. ANNE. ARI. JEB.
THEY KEEP TELLING ME I'M SUPPOSED TO SAVE THE WORLD, BUT...
...HOW, AND FROM WHAT, I DON'T EVEN KNOW.

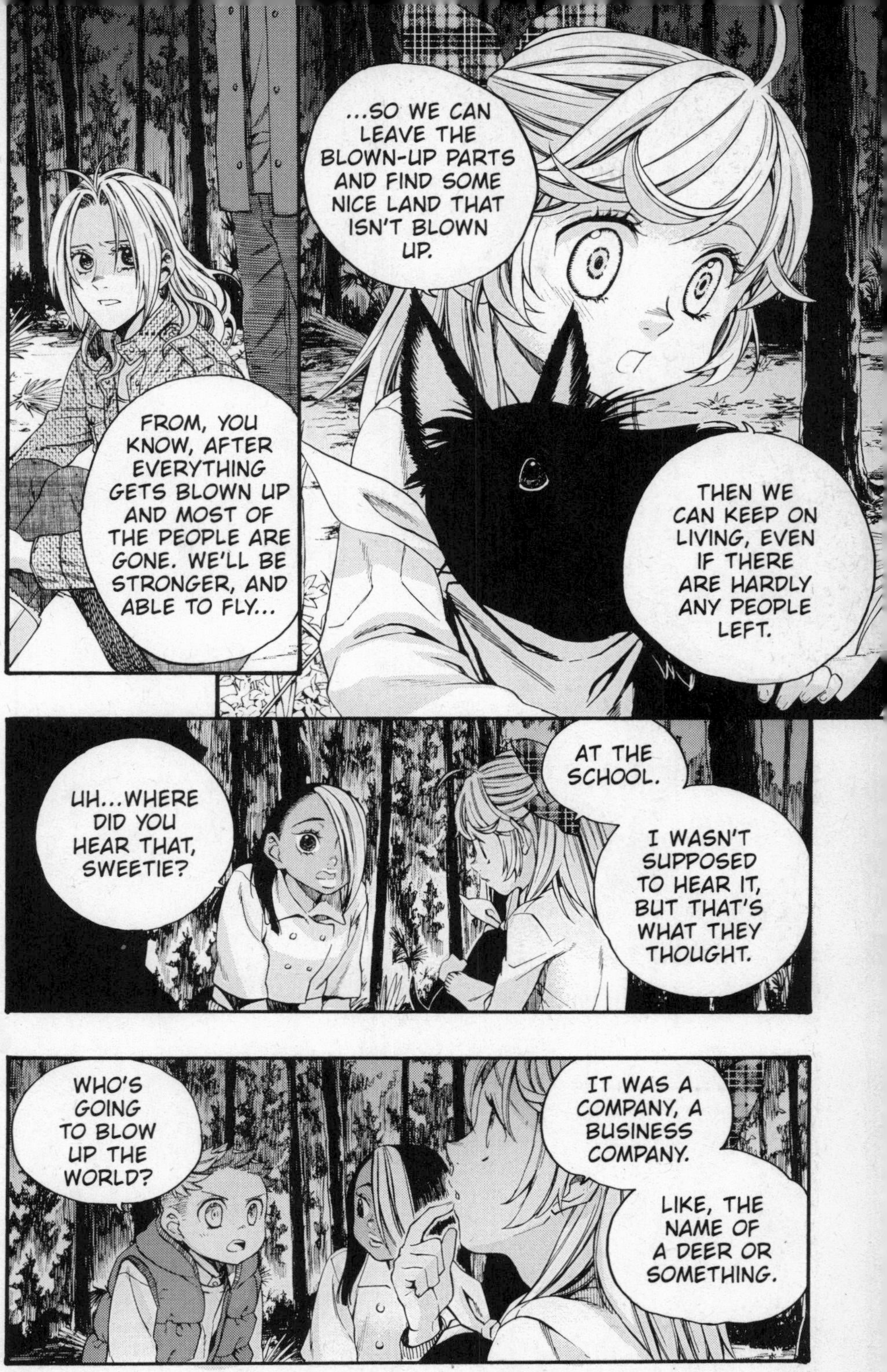
FROM, YOU KNOW, AFTER EVERYTHING GETS BLOWN UP AND MOST OF THE PEOPLE ARE GONE. WE'LL BE STRONGER, AND ABLE TO FLY...
...SO WE CAN LEAVE THE BLOWN-UP PARTS AND FIND SOME NICE LAND THAT ISN'T BLOWN UP.
THEN WE CAN KEEP ON LIVING, EVEN IF THERE ARE HARDLY ANY PEOPLE LEFT.
UH...WHERE DID YOU HEAR THAT, SWEETIE?
AT THE SCHOOL.
I WASN'T SUPPOSED TO HEAR IT, BUT THAT'S WHAT THEY THOUGHT.
WHO'S GOING TO BLOW UP THE WORLD?
IT WAS A COMPANY, A BUSINESS COMPANY.
LIKE, THE NAME OF A DEER OR SOMETHING.

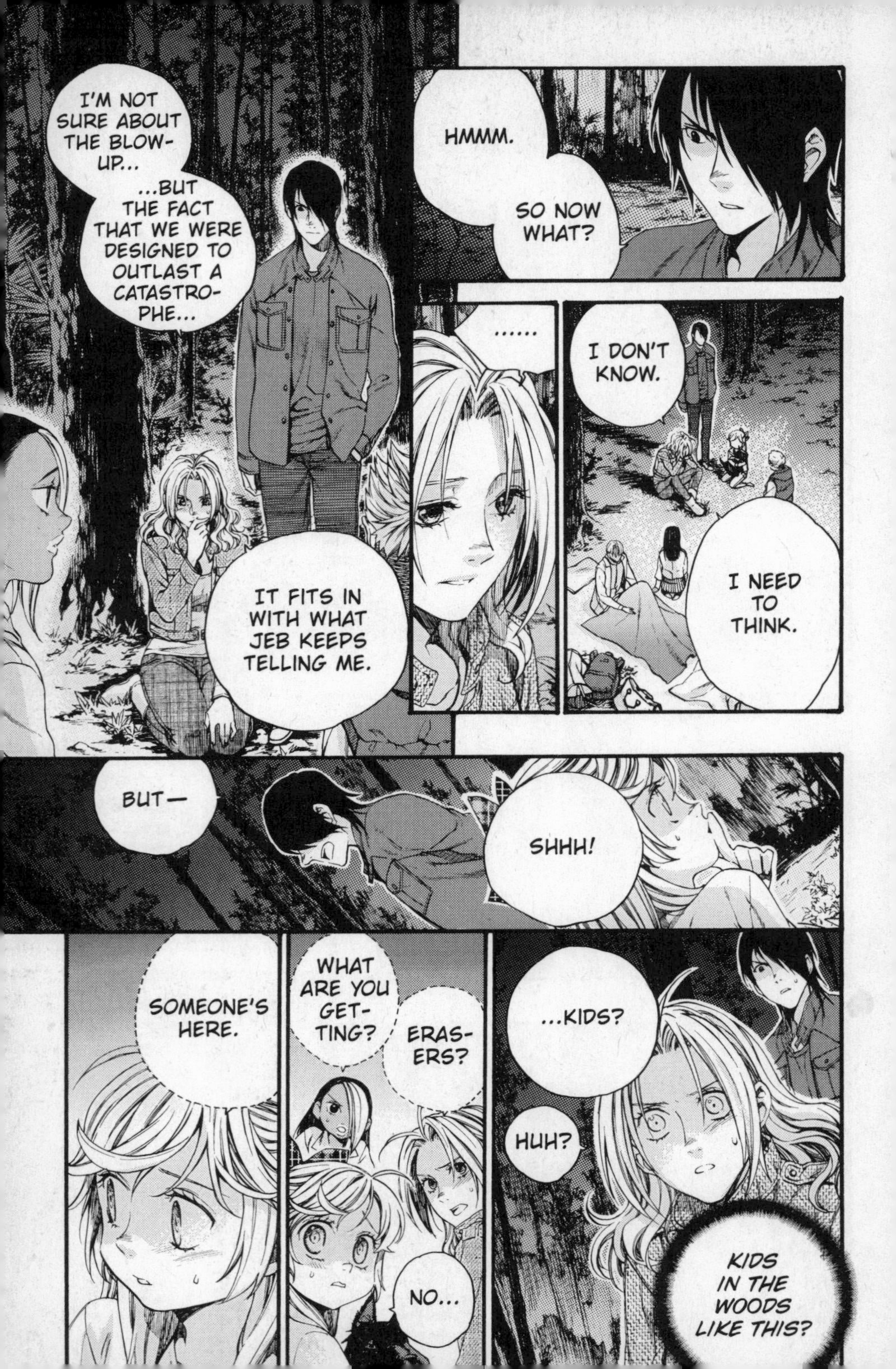
I'M NOT SURE ABOUT THE BLOW-UP...
...BUT THE FACT THAT WE WERE DESIGNED TO OUTLAST A CATASTRO-PHE...
IT FITS IN WITH WHAT JEB KEEPS TELLING ME.
HMMM.
SO NOW WHAT?
......
I DON'T KNOW.
I NEED TO THINK.
BUT—
SHHH!
SOMEONE'S HERE.
WHAT ARE YOU GET-TING?
ERAS-ERS?
NO...
...KIDS?
HUH?
KIDS IN THE WOODS LIKE THIS?

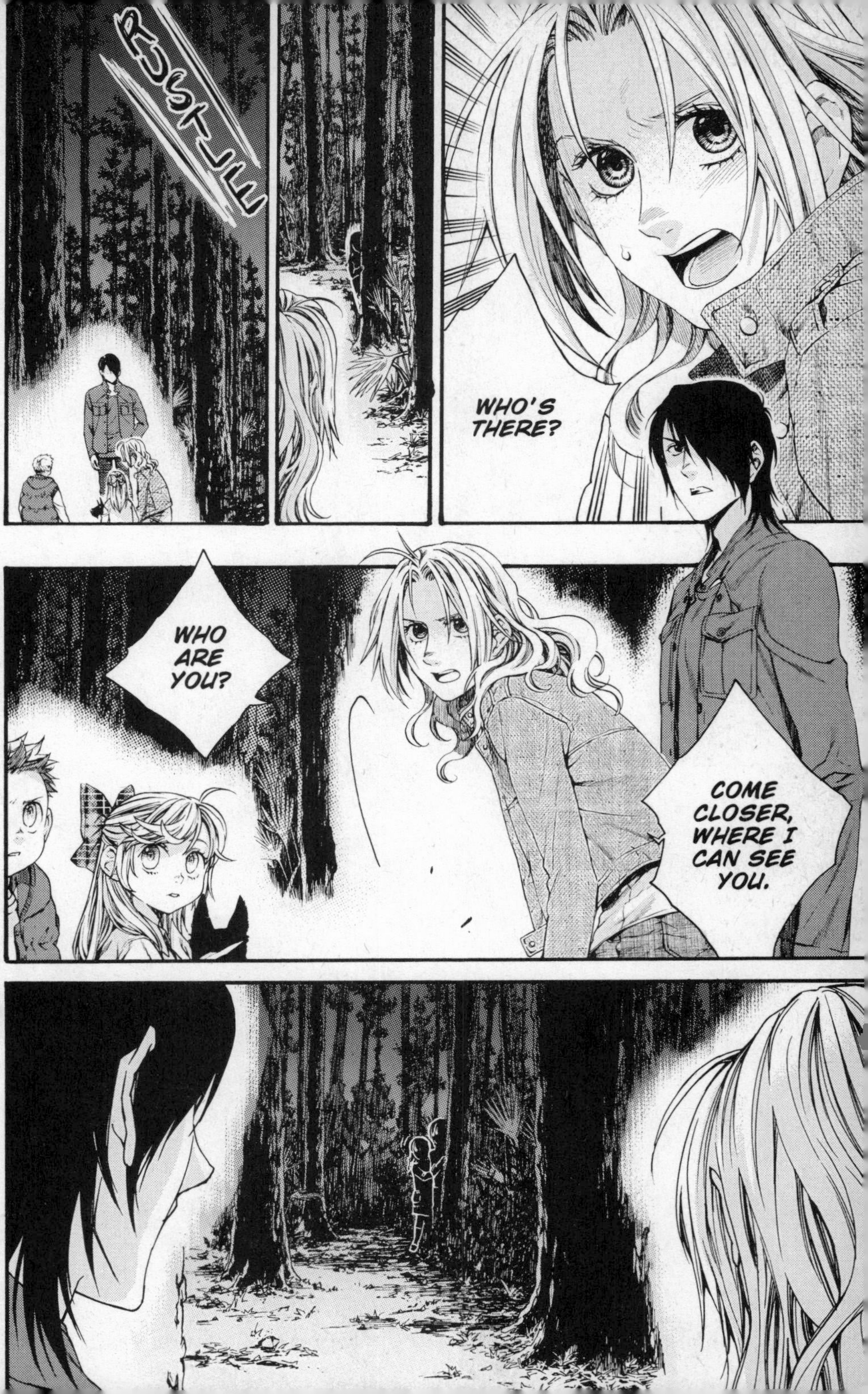
RUSTLE
WHO'S THERE?
WHO ARE YOU?
COME CLOSER, WHERE I CAN SEE YOU.

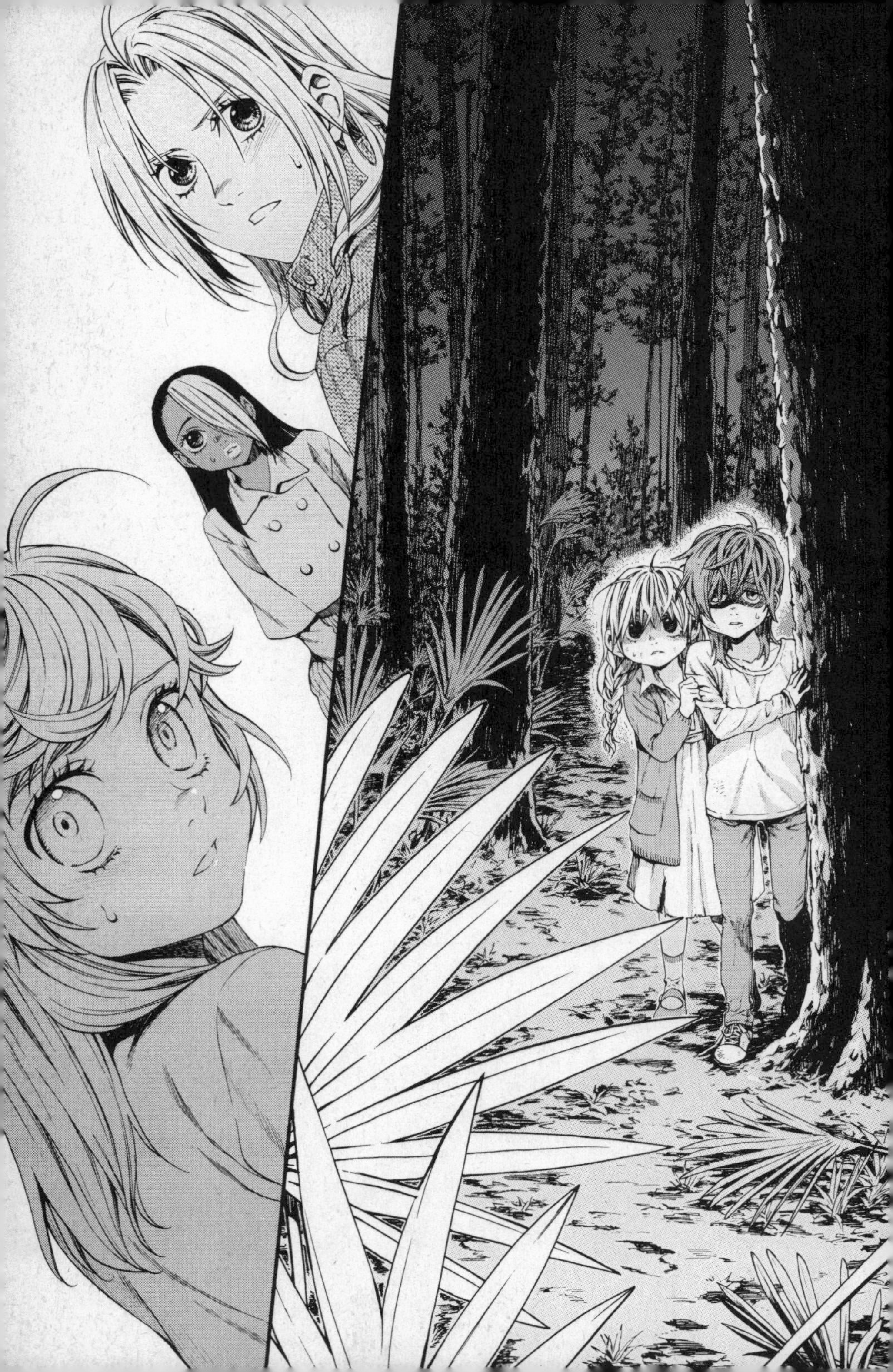

MAXIMUM
RIDE

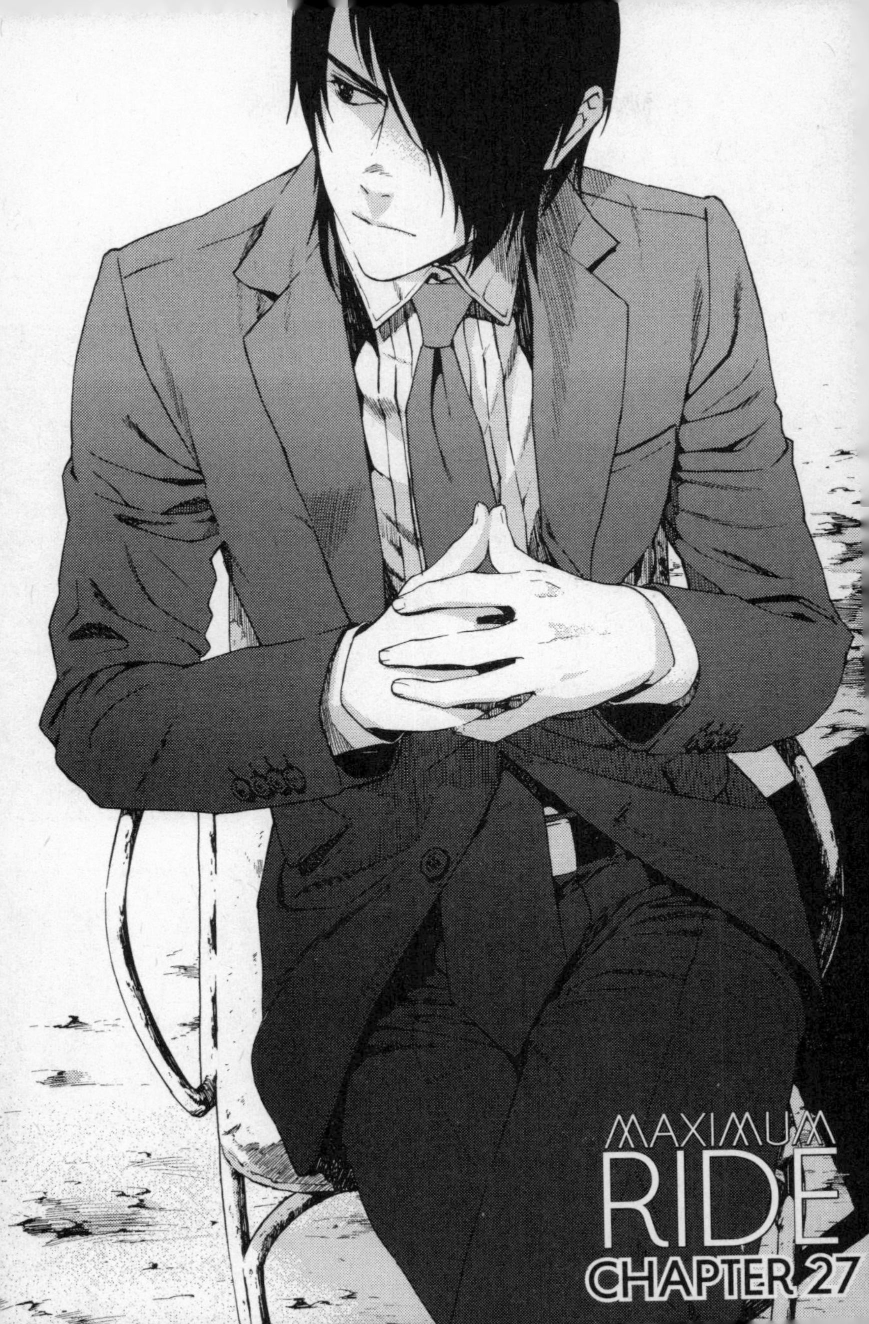
MAXIMUM
RIDE
CHAPTER 27

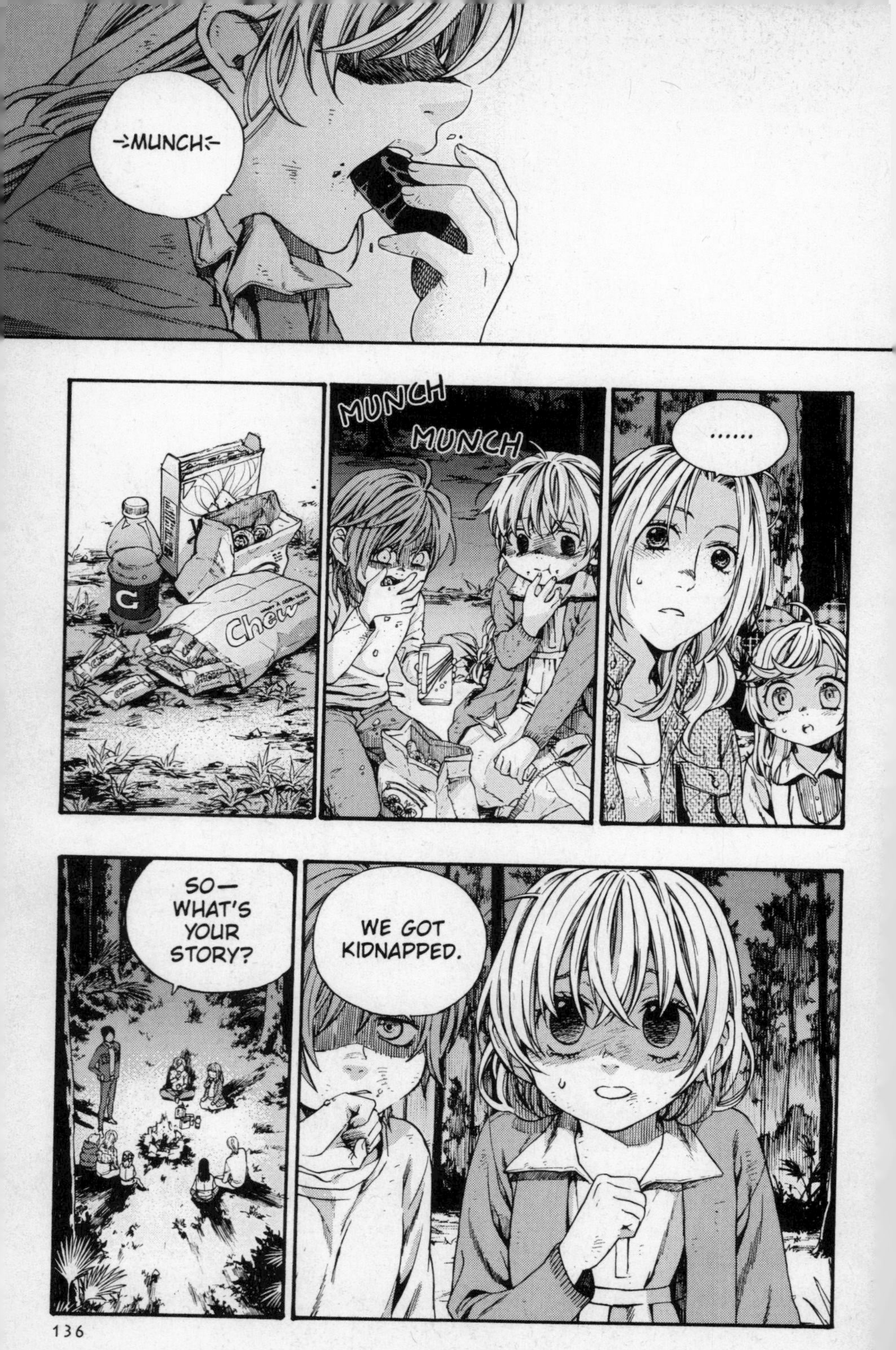

MUNCH
G
Chew
MUNCH
MUNCH
......
SO—WHAT'S YOUR STORY?
WE GOT KIDNAPPED.

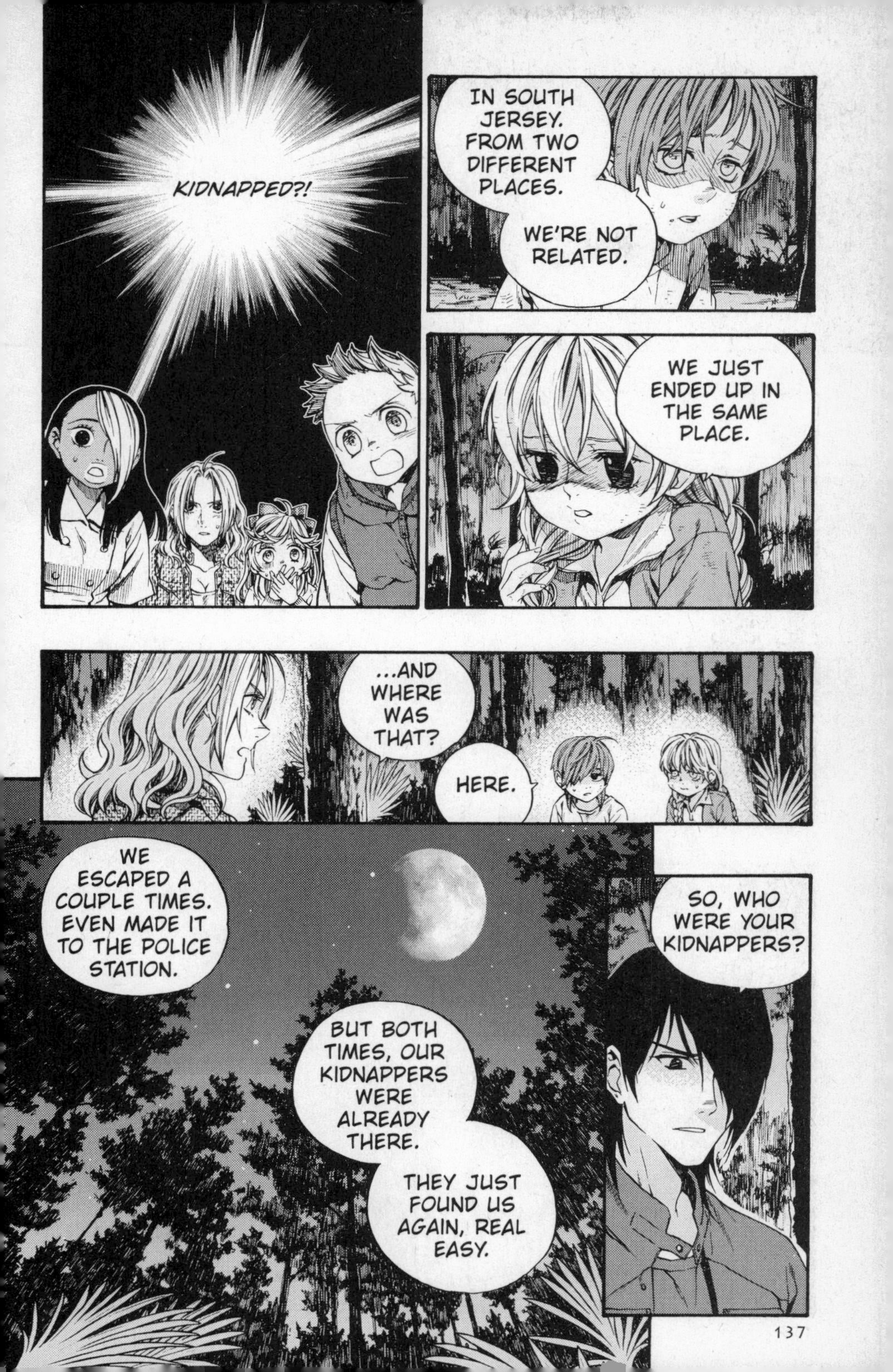
KIDNAPPED?!
IN SOUTH JERSEY. FROM TWO DIFFERENT PLACES.
WE'RE NOT RELATED.
WE JUST ENDED UP IN THE SAME PLACE.
...AND WHERE WAS THAT?
HERE.
WE ESCAPED A COUPLE TIMES. EVEN MADE IT TO THE POLICE STATION.
BUT BOTH TIMES, OUR KIDNAPPERS WERE ALREADY THERE.
THEY JUST FOUND US AGAIN, REAL EASY.
SO, WHO WERE YOUR KIDNAPPERS?

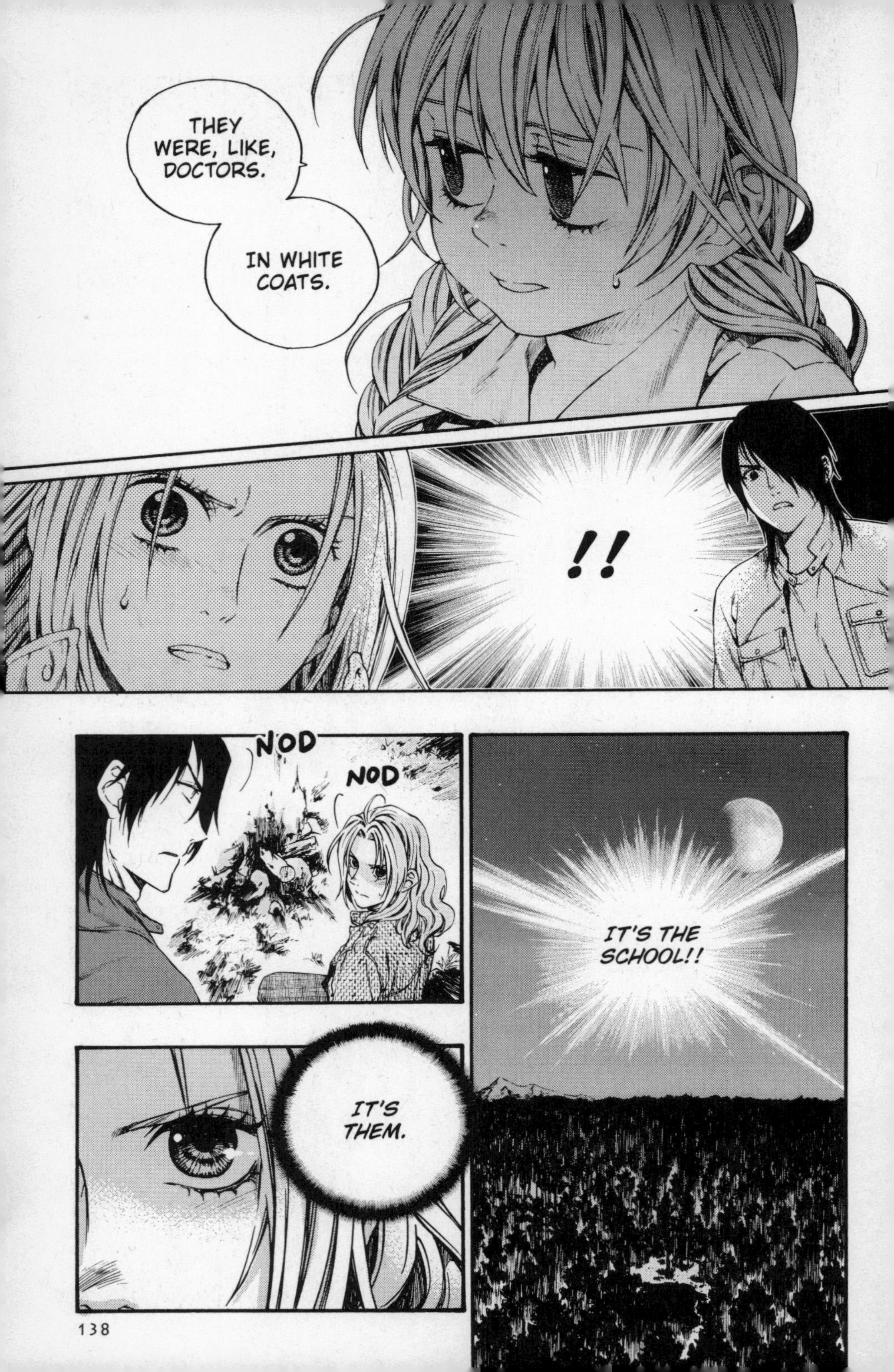
THEY WERE, LIKE, DOCTORS.
IN WHITE COATS.
!!
NOD
NOD
IT'S THEM.
IT'S THE SCHOOL!!

......

SSK

?

SNEAK
SNEAK

SNEAK
SNEAK-

"SLOUSH"

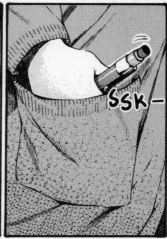

SSK-

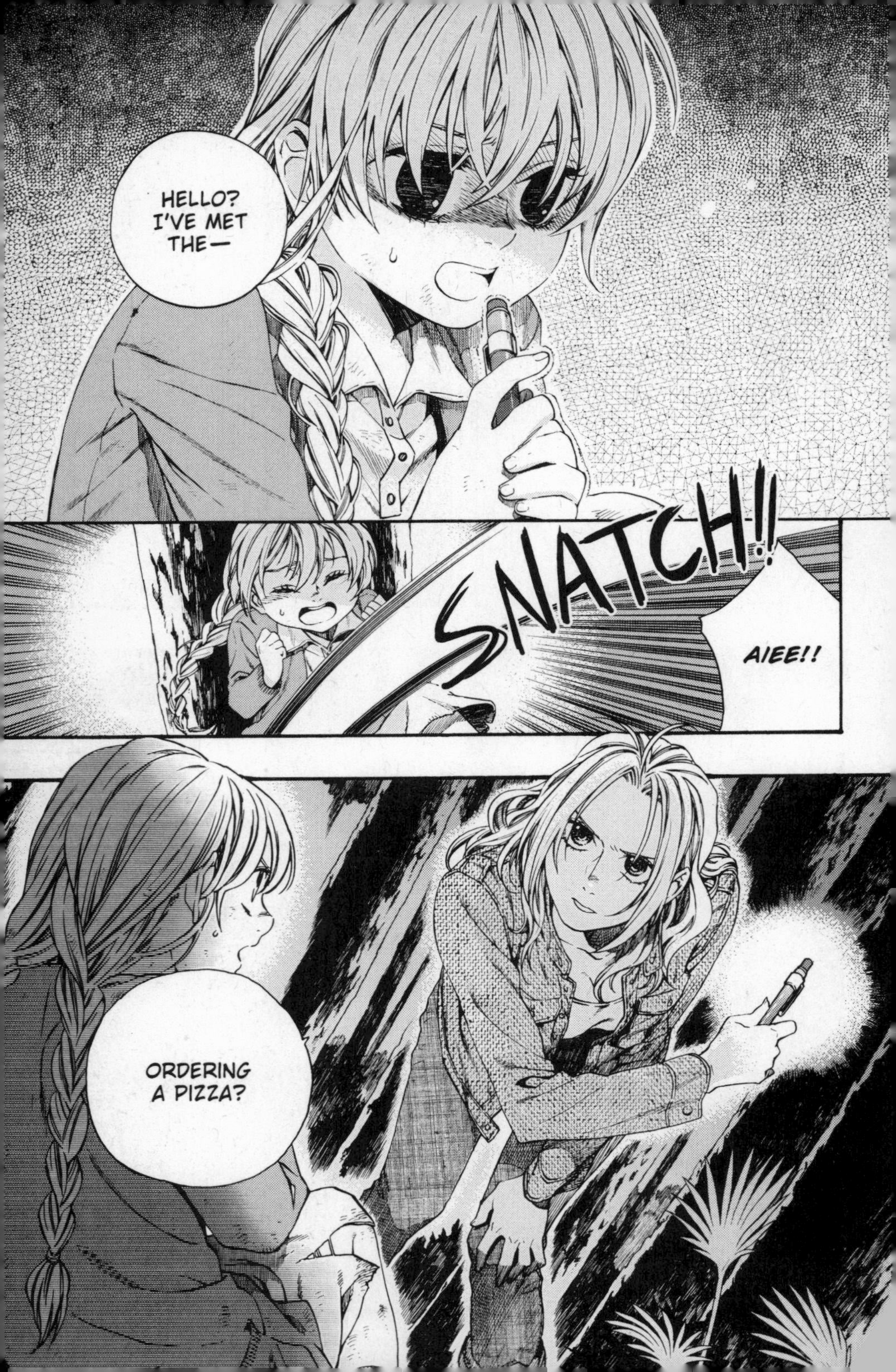
HELLO? I'VE MET THE—
SNATCH!!
AIEE!!
ORDERING A PIZZA?

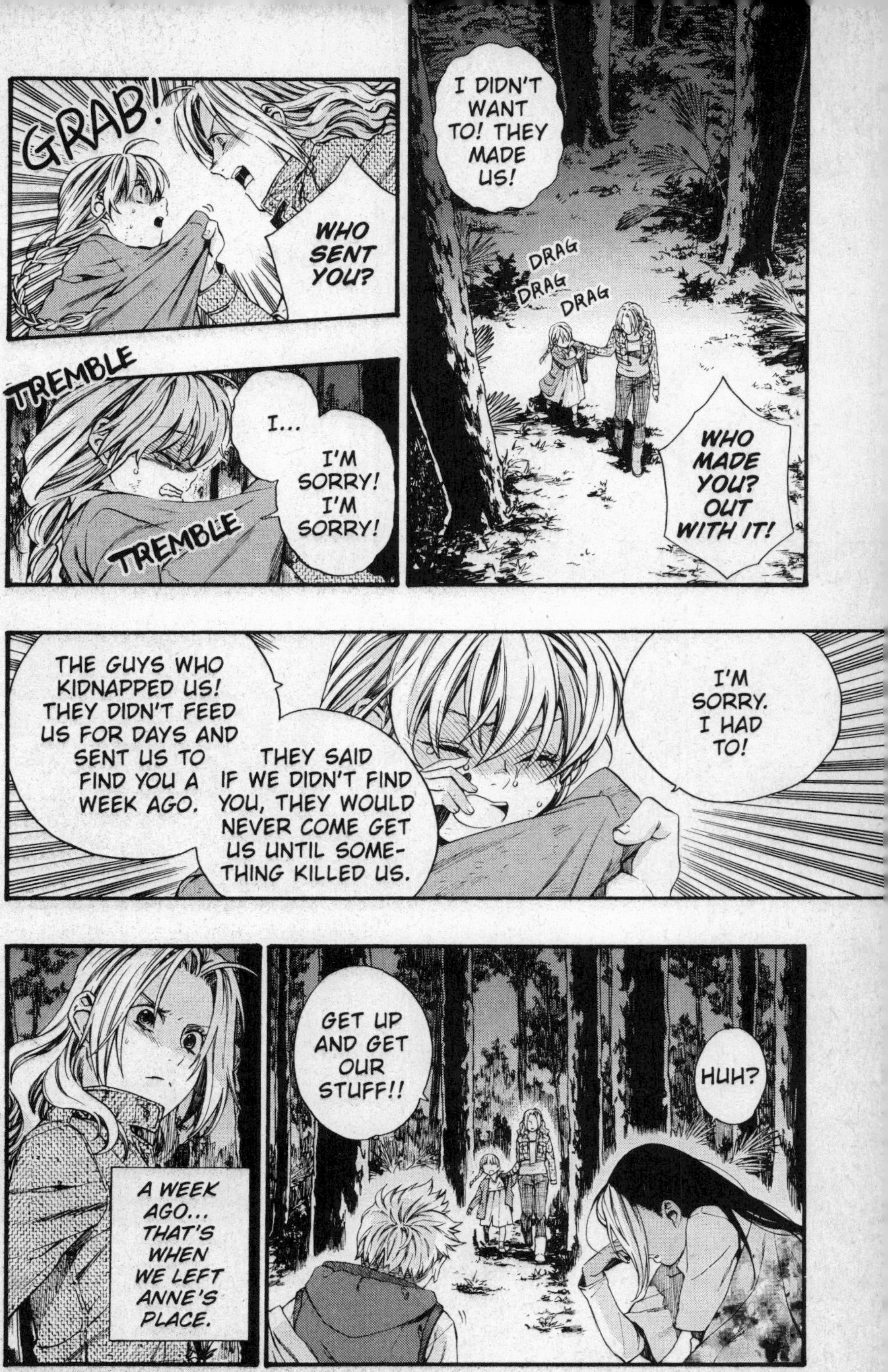
GRAB!
WHO SENT YOU?
TREMBLE
I...
I'M SORRY! I'M SORRY!
TREMBLE
I DIDN'T WANT TO! THEY MADE US!
DRAG DRAG DRAG
WHO MADE YOU? OUT WITH IT!
THE GUYS WHO KIDNAPPED US! THEY DIDN'T FEED US FOR DAYS AND SENT US TO FIND YOU A WEEK AGO.
THEY SAID IF WE DIDN'T FIND YOU, THEY WOULD NEVER COME GET US UNTIL SOME-THING KILLED US.
I'M SORRY. I HAD TO!
A WEEK AGO... THAT'S WHEN WE LEFT ANNE'S PLACE.
GET UP AND GET OUR STUFF!!
HUH?

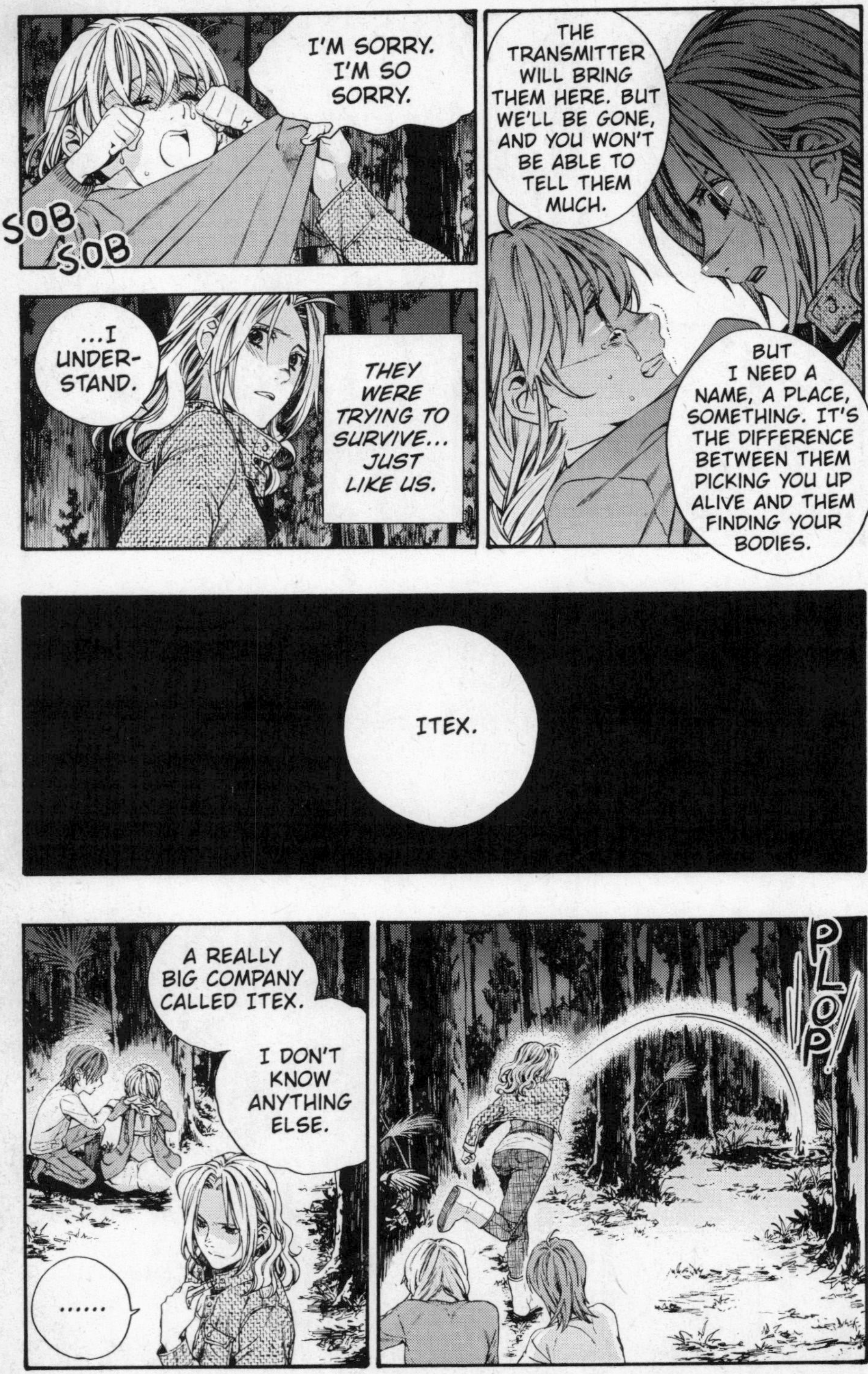
I'M SORRY. I'M SO SORRY.
SOB SOB
THE TRANSMITTER WILL BRING THEM HERE. BUT WE'LL BE GONE, AND YOU WON'T BE ABLE TO TELL THEM MUCH.
...I UNDER-STAND.
THEY WERE TRYING TO SURVIVE... JUST LIKE US.
BUT I NEED A NAME, A PLACE, SOMETHING. IT'S THE DIFFERENCE BETWEEN THEM PICKING YOU UP ALIVE AND THEM FINDING YOUR BODIES.
ITEX.
A REALLY BIG COMPANY CALLED ITEX.
I DON'T KNOW ANYTHING ELSE.
......
PLOP!

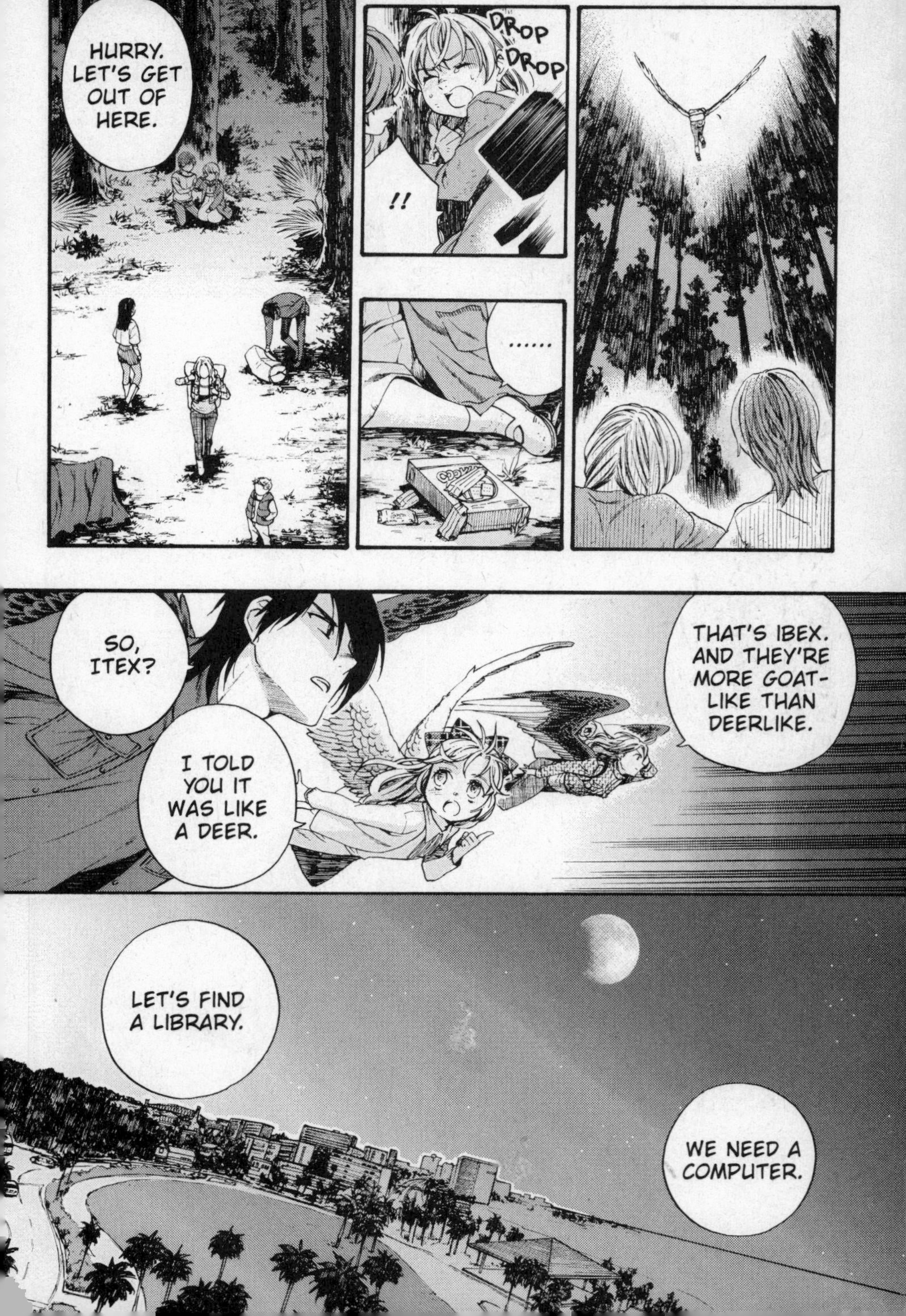
HURRY. LET'S GET OUT OF HERE.
DROP DROP
!!
......
SO, ITEX?
I TOLD YOU IT WAS LIKE A DEER.
THAT'S IBEX. AND THEY'RE MORE GOAT-LIKE THAN DEERLIKE.
LET'S FIND A LIBRARY.
WE NEED A COMPUTER.

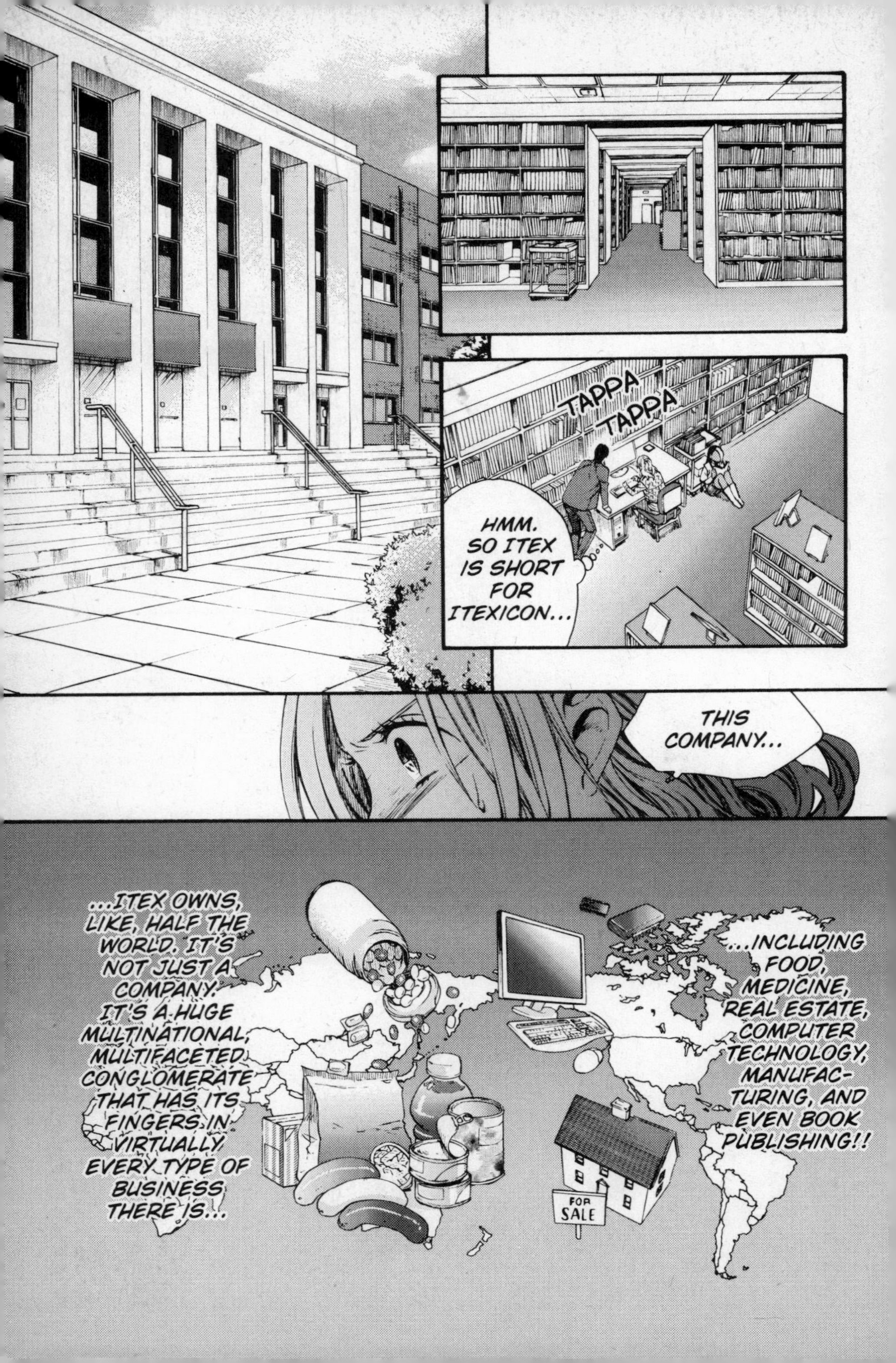
TAPPA
TAPPA
HMM. SO ITEX IS SHORT FOR ITEXICON...
THIS COMPANY...
...ITEX OWNS, LIKE, HALF THE WORLD. IT'S NOT JUST A COMPANY. IT'S A HUGE MULTINATIONAL, MULTIFACETED CONGLOMERATE THAT HAS ITS FINGERS IN VIRTUALLY EVERY TYPE OF BUSINESS THERE IS...
...INCLUDING FOOD, MEDICINE, REAL ESTATE, COMPUTER TECHNOLOGY, MANUFAC-TURING, AND EVEN BOOK PUBLISHING!!
FOR SALE

THIS LOGO...

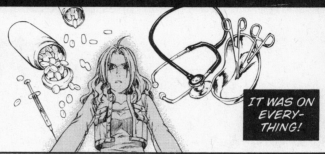

I REMEMBER SEEING IT AT THE SCHOOL!

IT WAS ON EVERY-THING!

THERE'S THE ADDRESS OF ITS HEADQUAR-TERS...

WHISPER

MAX.

PEEK !

I THINK I GOT WHAT WE NEED.

LET'S GET OUT OF HERE.

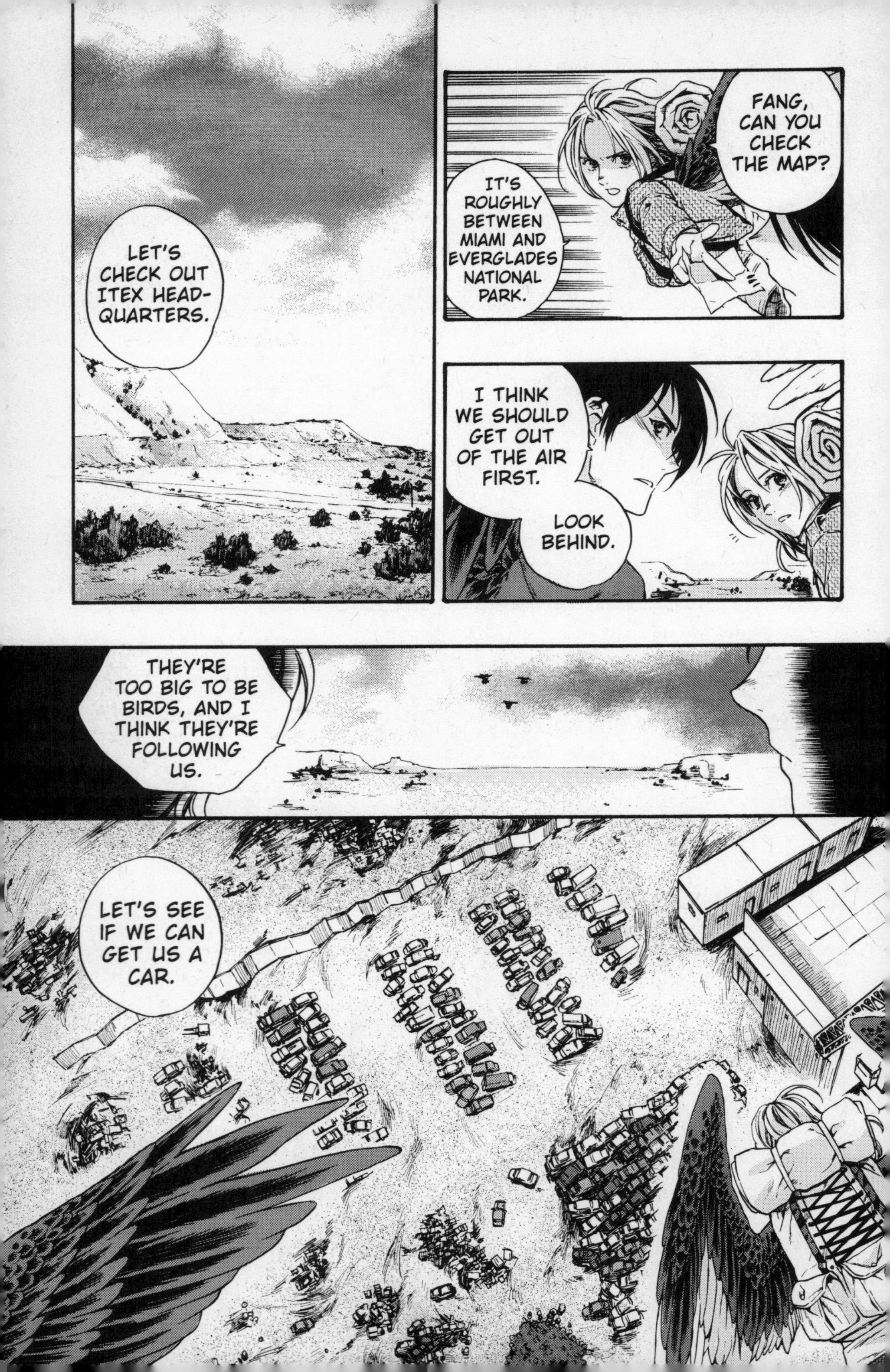
LET'S CHECK OUT ITEX HEAD-QUARTERS.
FANG, CAN YOU CHECK THE MAP?
IT'S ROUGHLY BETWEEN MIAMI AND EVERGLADES NATIONAL PARK.
I THINK WE SHOULD GET OUT OF THE AIR FIRST.
LOOK BEHIND.
THEY'RE TOO BIG TO BE BIRDS, AND I THINK THEY'RE FOLLOWING US.
LET'S SEE IF WE CAN GET US A CAR.

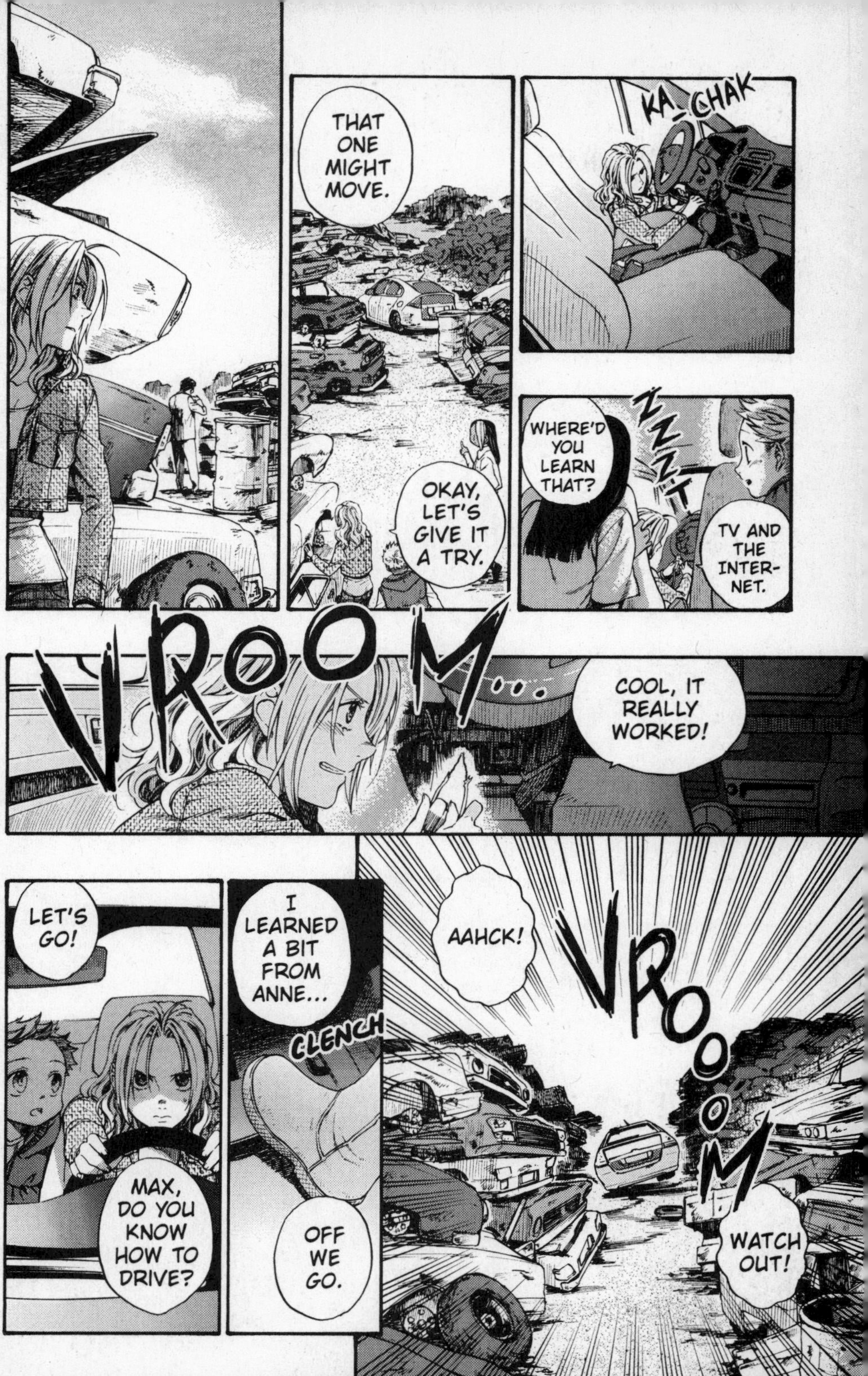
THAT ONE MIGHT MOVE.
OKAY, LET'S GIVE IT A TRY.
KA_CHAK
WHERE'D YOU LEARN THAT?
ZZZT
TV AND THE INTER-NET.
VROOM...
COOL, IT REALLY WORKED!
LET'S GO!
MAX, DO YOU KNOW HOW TO DRIVE?
I LEARNED A BIT FROM ANNE...
CLENCH
OFF WE GO.
AAHCK!
VROOOOM
WATCH OUT!

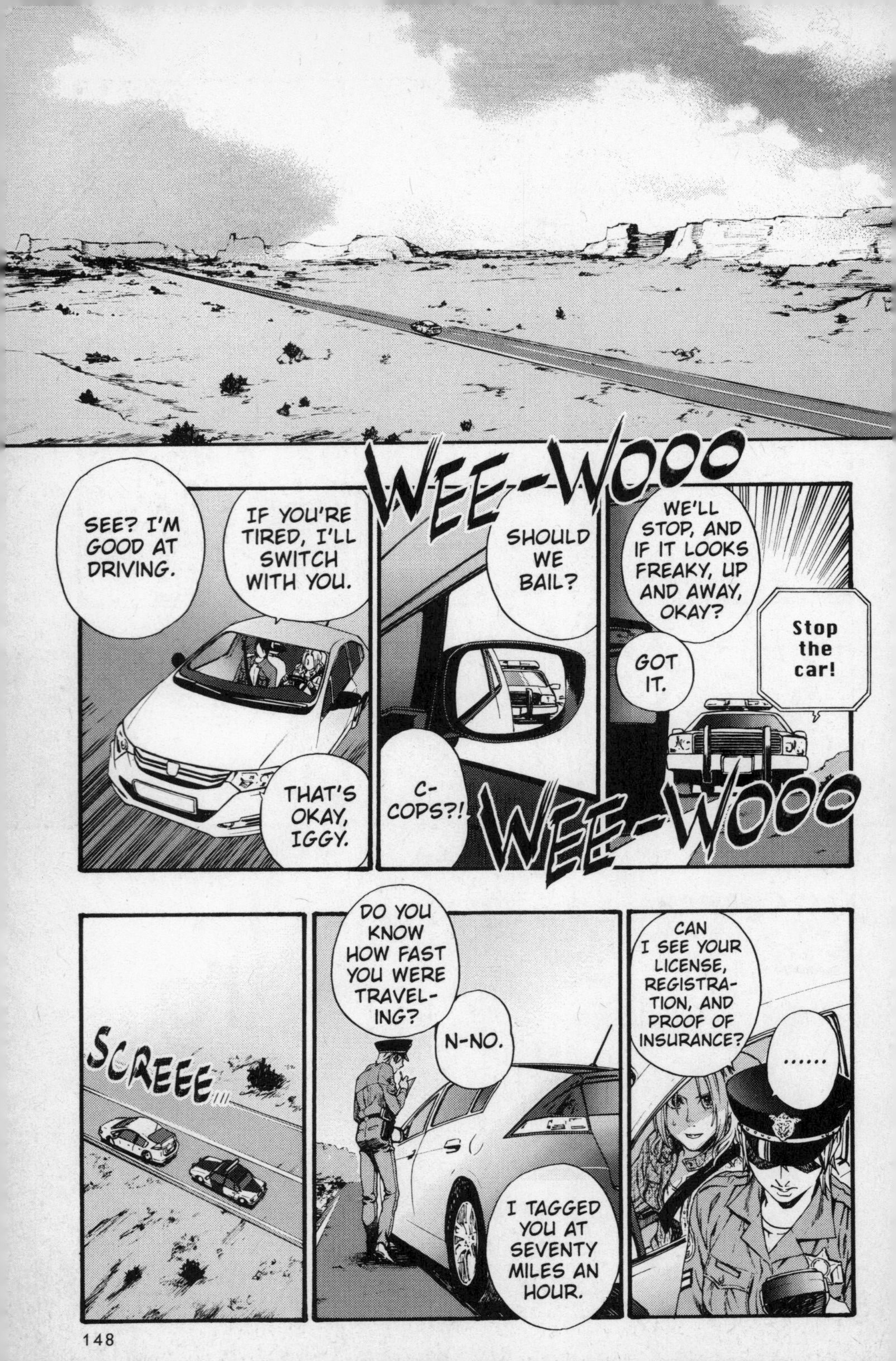
SEE? I'M GOOD AT DRIVING.
IF YOU'RE TIRED, I'LL SWITCH WITH YOU.
THAT'S OKAY, IGGY.
WEE-WOOO
SHOULD WE BAIL?
C-COPS?!
WE'LL STOP, AND IF IT LOOKS FREAKY, UP AND AWAY, OKAY?
GOT IT.
Stop the car!
WEE-WOOO
SCREEEE
DO YOU KNOW HOW FAST YOU WERE TRAVEL-ING?
N-NO.
I TAGGED YOU AT SEVENTY MILES AN HOUR.
CAN I SEE YOUR LICENSE, REGISTRA-TION, AND PROOF OF INSURANCE?
......

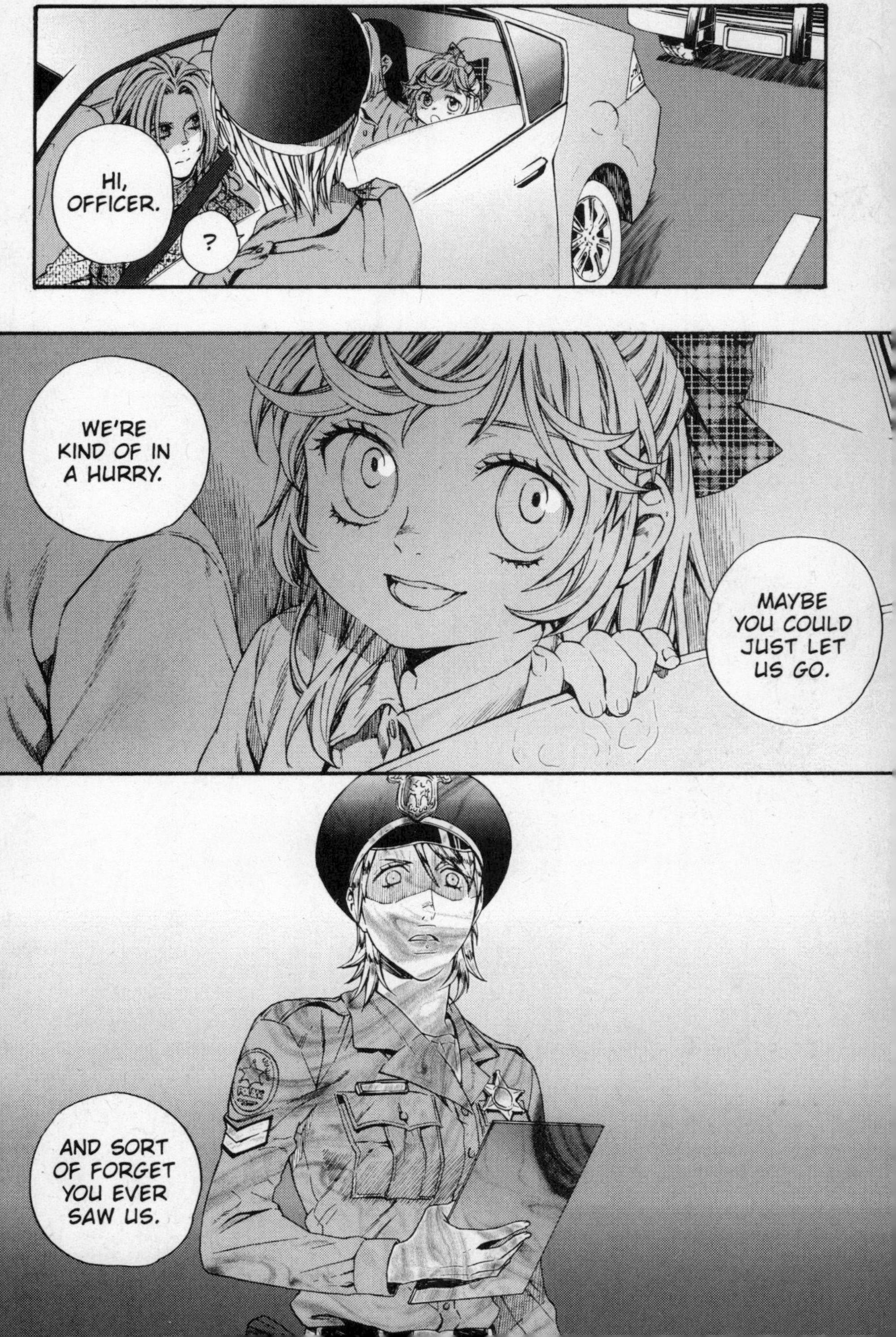
HI, OFFICER.
?
WE'RE KIND OF IN A HURRY.
MAYBE YOU COULD JUST LET US GO.
AND SORT OF FORGET YOU EVER SAW US.

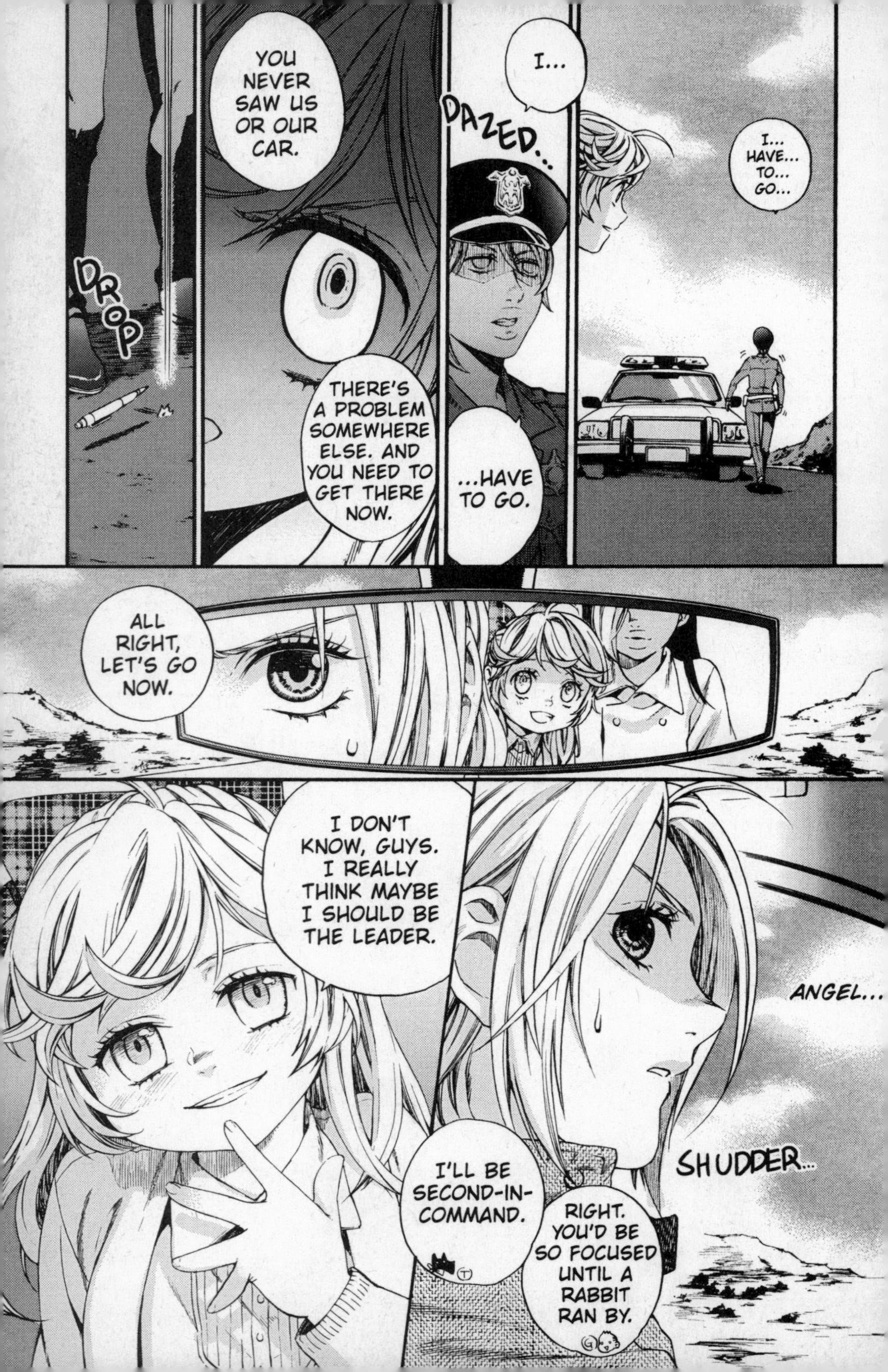
DROP
YOU NEVER SAW US OR OUR CAR.
THERE'S A PROBLEM SOMEWHERE ELSE. AND YOU NEED TO GET THERE NOW.
I...
DAZED...
...HAVE TO GO.
I... HAVE... TO... GO...
ALL RIGHT, LET'S GO NOW.
I DON'T KNOW, GUYS. I REALLY THINK MAYBE I SHOULD BE THE LEADER.
I'LL BE SECOND-IN-COMMAND.
ANGEL...
SHUDDER...
RIGHT. YOU'D BE SO FOCUSED UNTIL A RABBIT RAN BY.

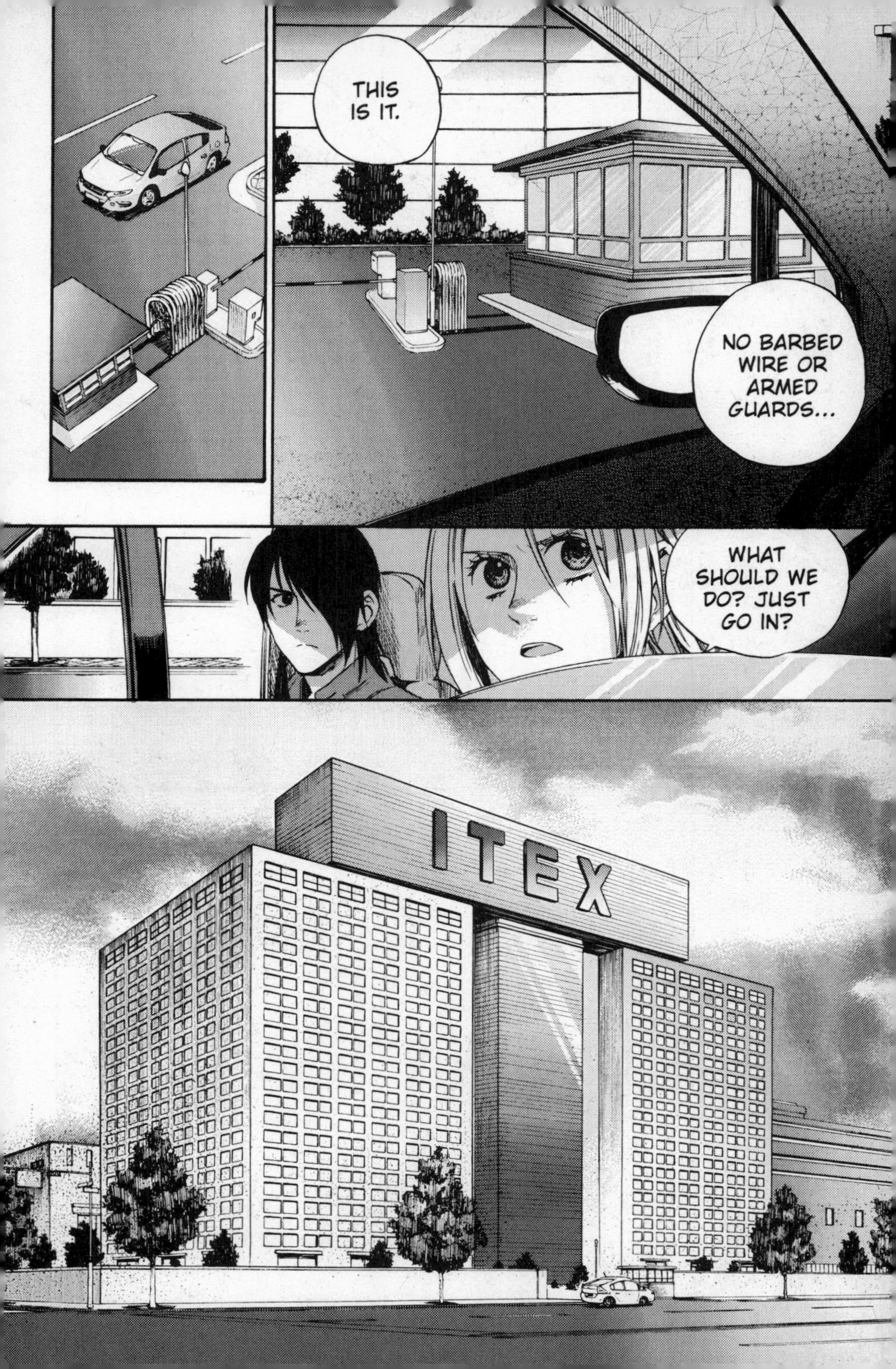
THIS IS IT.
NO BARBED WIRE OR ARMED GUARDS...
WHAT SHOULD WE DO? JUST GO IN?
ITEX

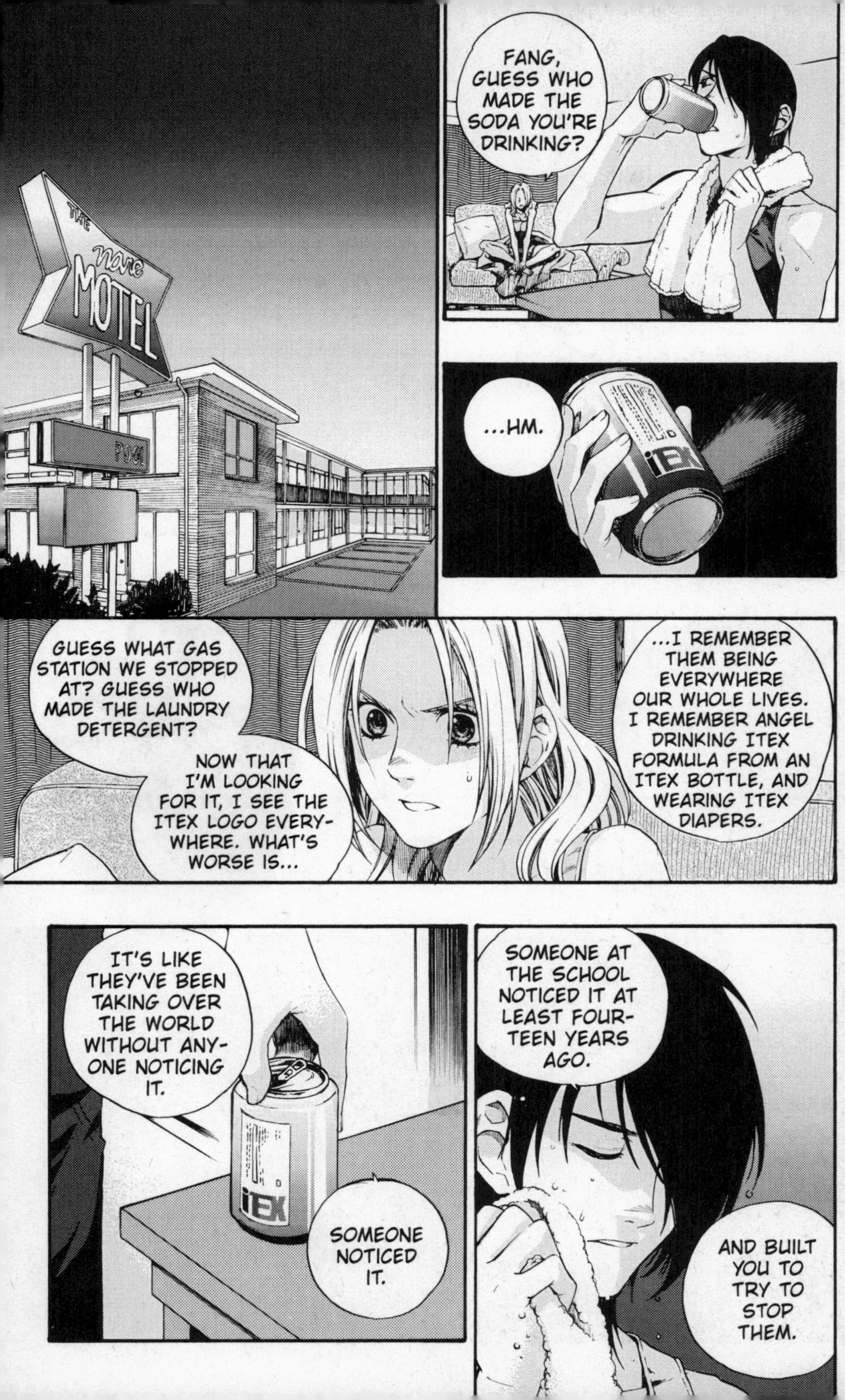
THE
MOTEL
FANG, GUESS WHO MADE THE SODA YOU'RE DRINKING?
...HM.
GUESS WHAT GAS STATION WE STOPPED AT? GUESS WHO MADE THE LAUNDRY DETERGENT?
NOW THAT I'M LOOKING FOR IT, I SEE THE ITEX LOGO EVERY-WHERE. WHAT'S WORSE IS...
...I REMEMBER THEM BEING EVERYWHERE OUR WHOLE LIVES. I REMEMBER ANGEL DRINKING ITEX FORMULA FROM AN ITEX BOTTLE, AND WEARING ITEX DIAPERS.
IT'S LIKE THEY'VE BEEN TAKING OVER THE WORLD WITHOUT ANY-ONE NOTICING IT.
SOMEONE NOTICED IT.
SOMEONE AT THE SCHOOL NOTICED IT AT LEAST FOUR-TEEN YEARS AGO.
AND BUILT YOU TO TRY TO STOP THEM.

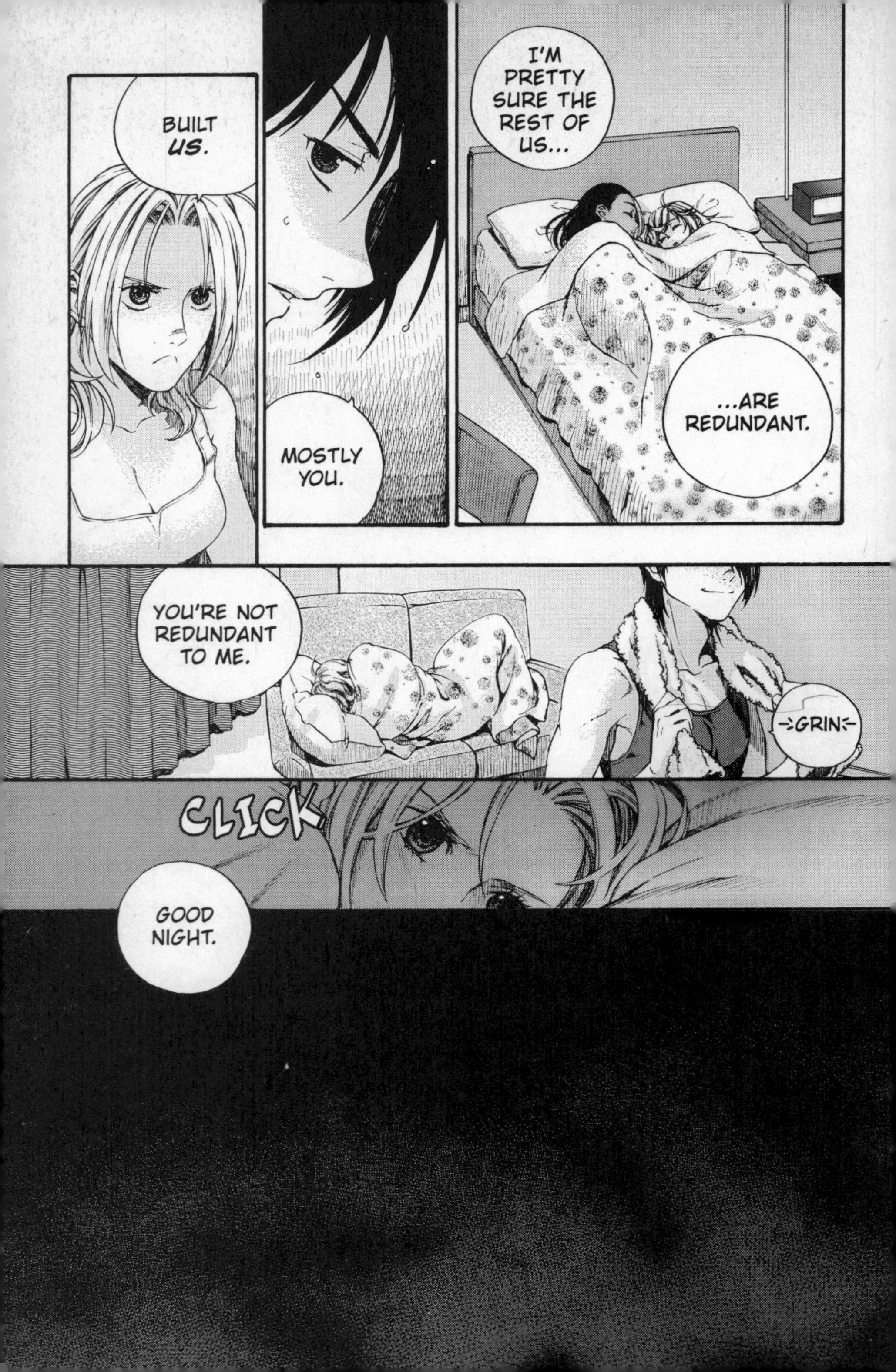
BUILT US.
MOSTLY YOU.
I'M PRETTY SURE THE REST OF US...
...ARE REDUNDANT.
YOU'RE NOT REDUNDANT TO ME.
GRIN
CLICK
GOOD NIGHT.

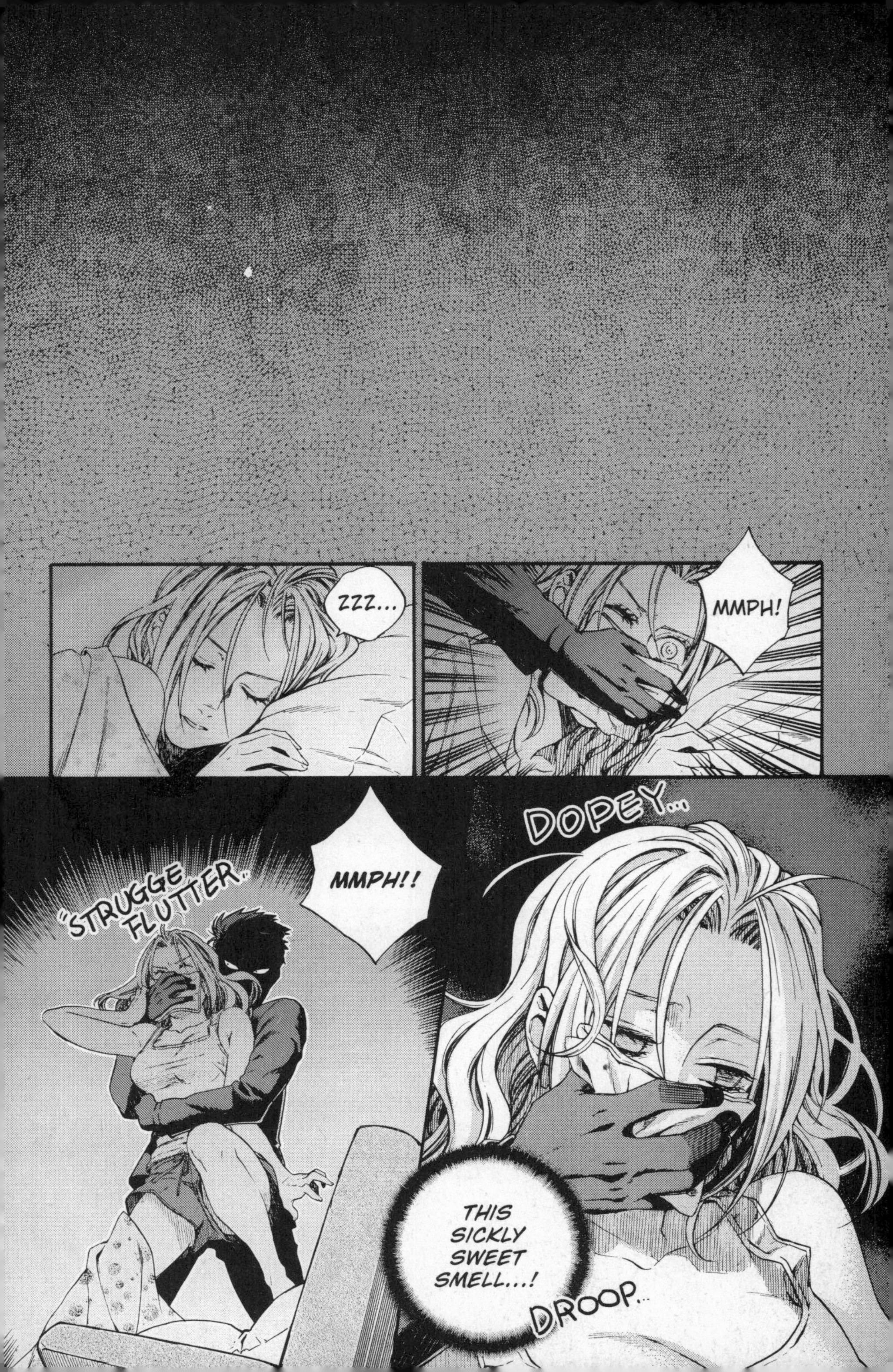
ZZZ...
MMPH!
STRUGGE FLUTTER...
MMPH!!
DOPEY...
THIS SICKLY SWEET SMELL...!
DROOP...

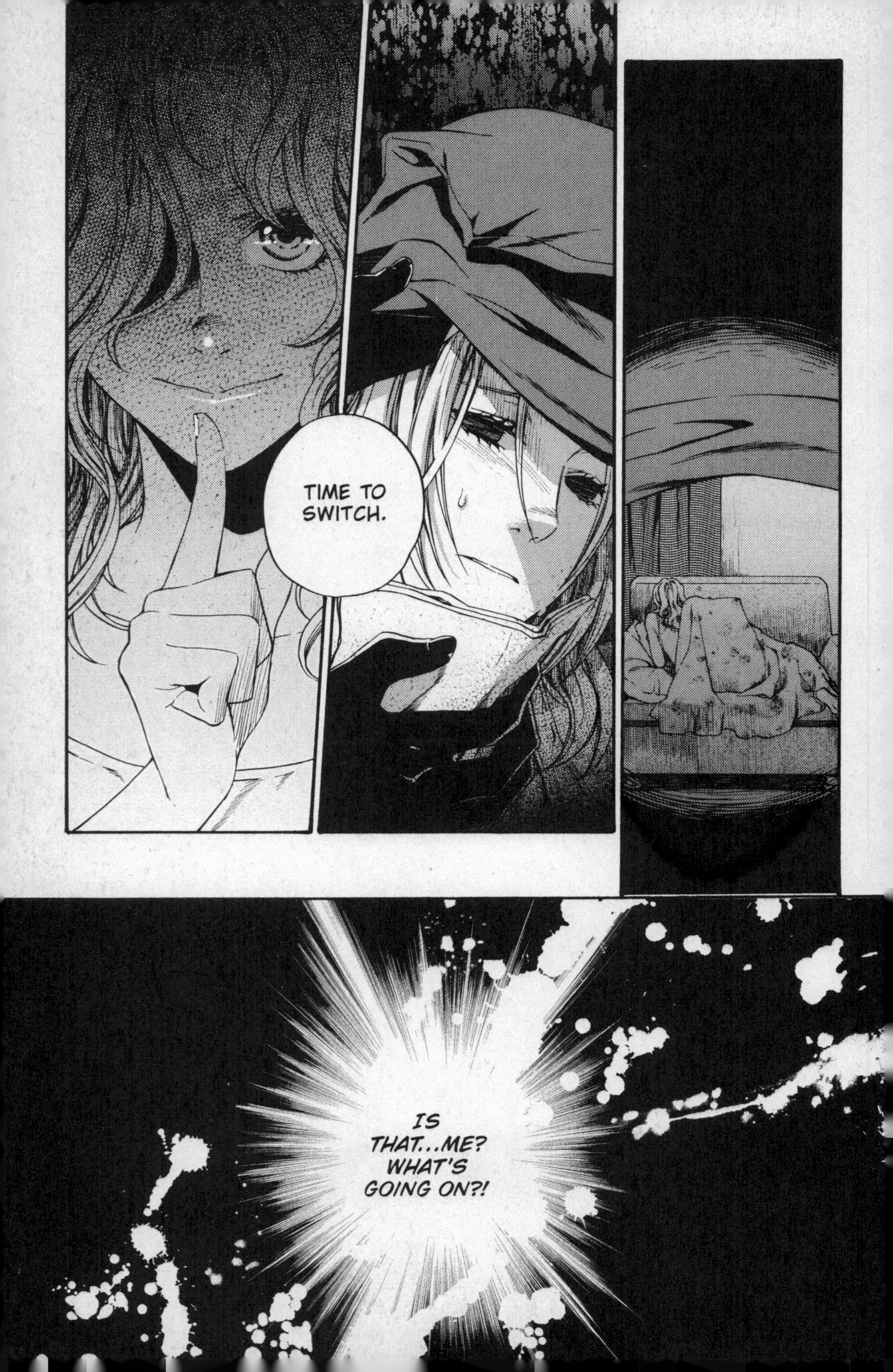
TIME TO SWITCH.
IS THAT...ME? WHAT'S GOING ON?!

MAXIMUM
RIDE

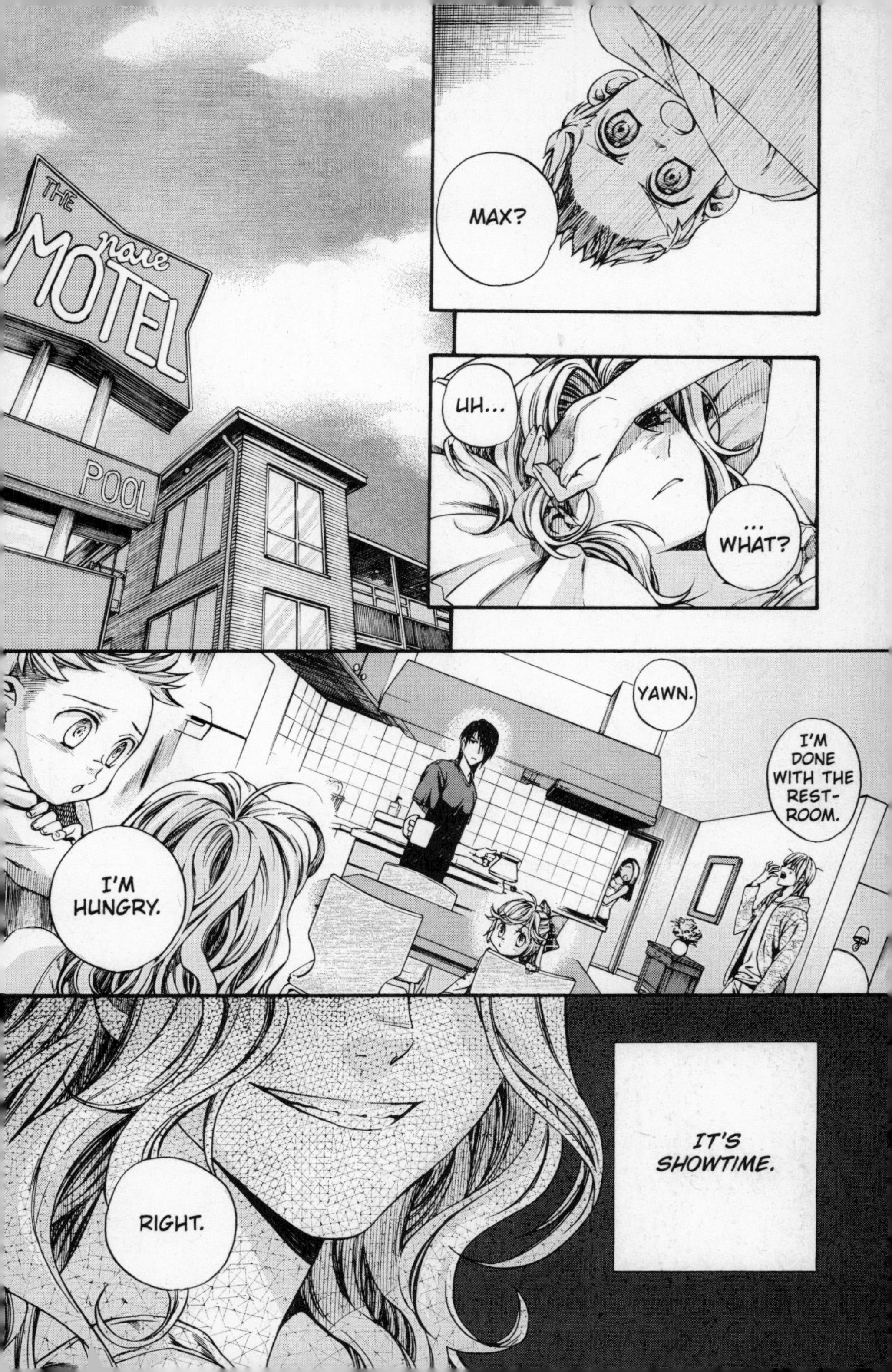
THE
MOTEL
POOL
MAX?
UH...
...WHAT?
I'M HUNGRY.
YAWN.
I'M DONE WITH THE REST-ROOM.
RIGHT.
IT'S SHOWTIME.

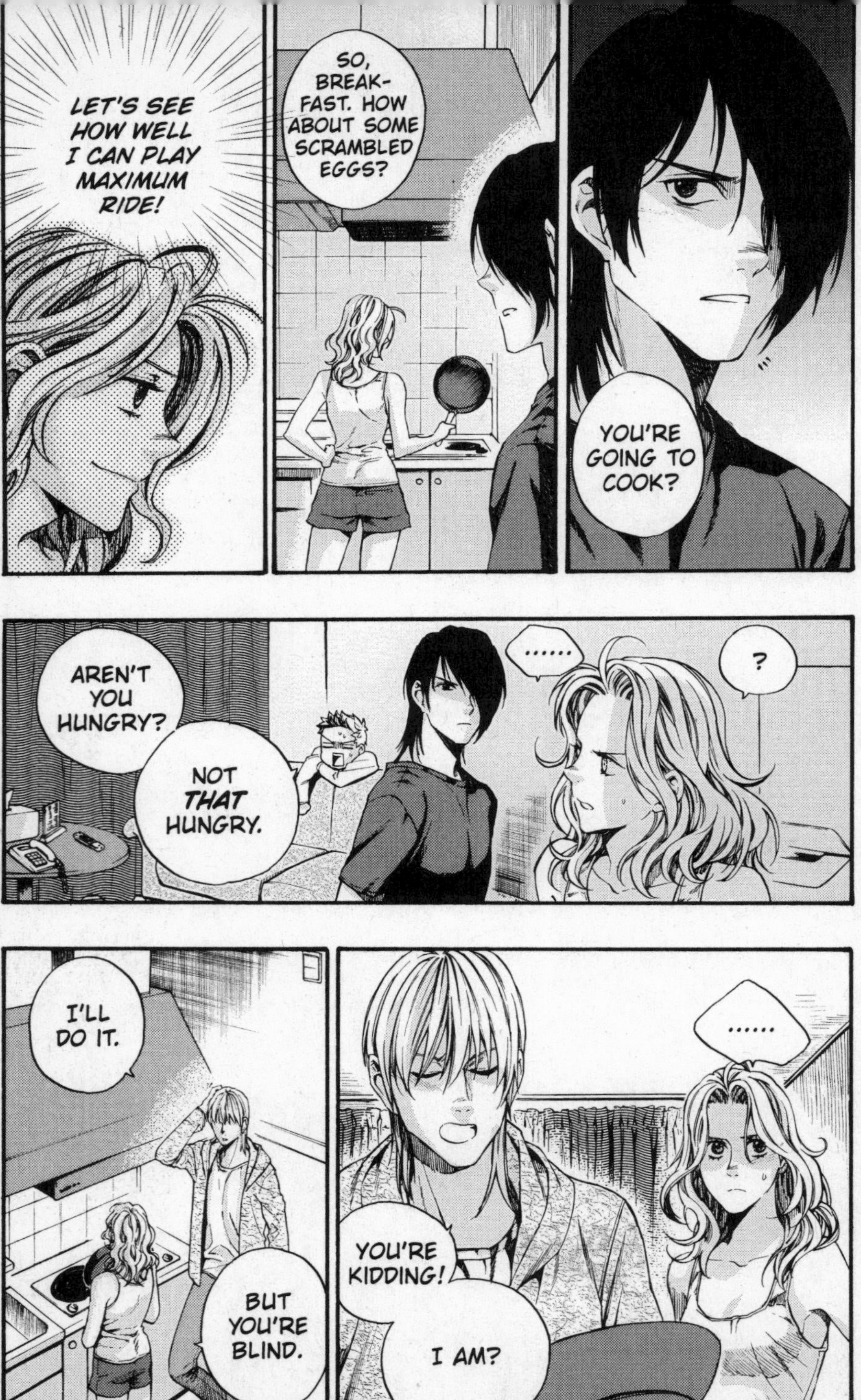
LET'S SEE HOW WELL I CAN PLAY MAXIMUM RIDE!
SO, BREAK-FAST. HOW ABOUT SOME SCRAMBLED EGGS?
YOU'RE GOING TO COOK?
AREN'T YOU HUNGRY?
NOT *THAT* HUNGRY.
......
?
I'LL DO IT.
BUT YOU'RE BLIND.
......
YOU'RE KIDDING!
I AM?

MAXIMUM RIDE
CHAPTER 28

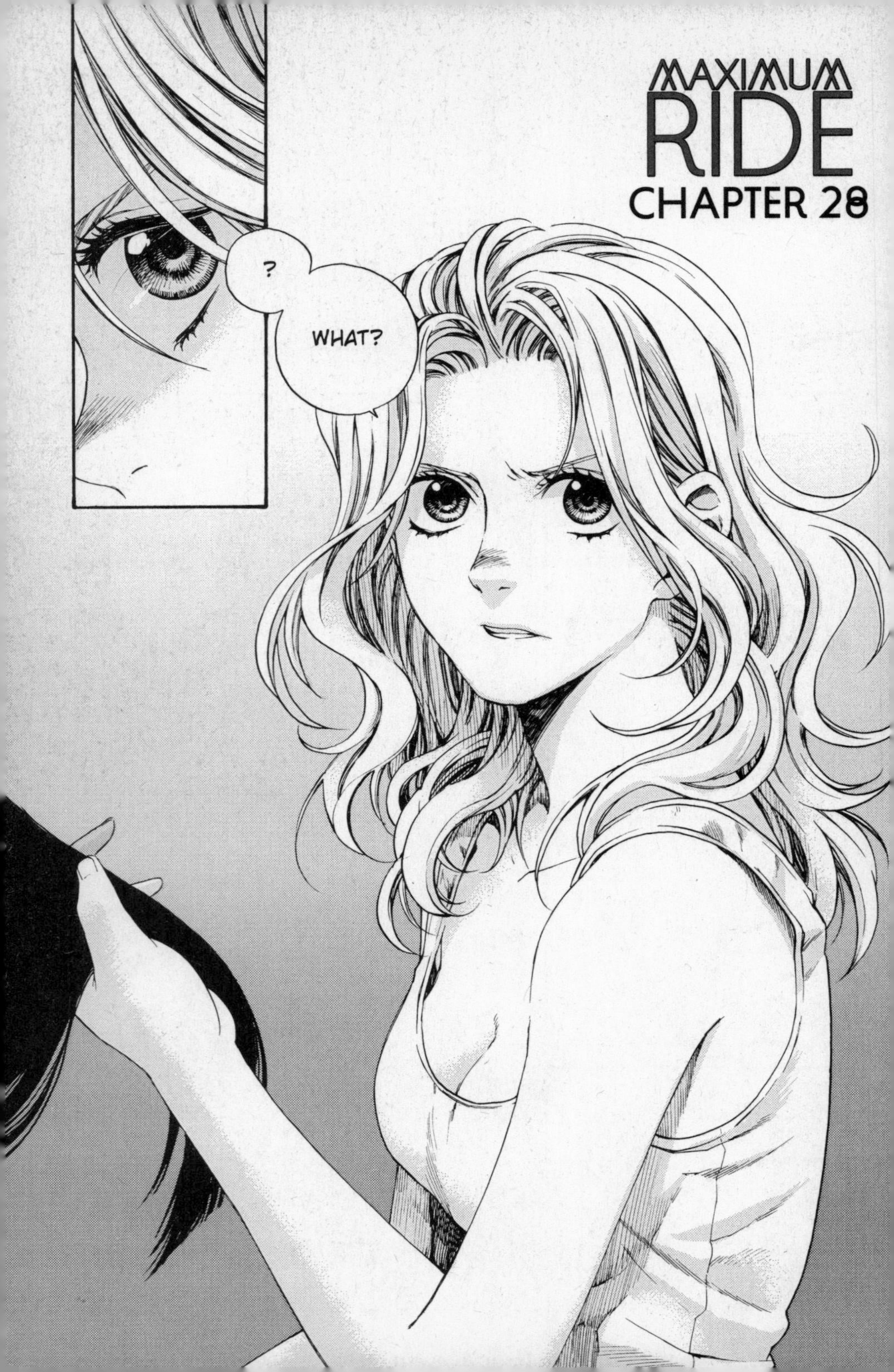
?
WHAT?

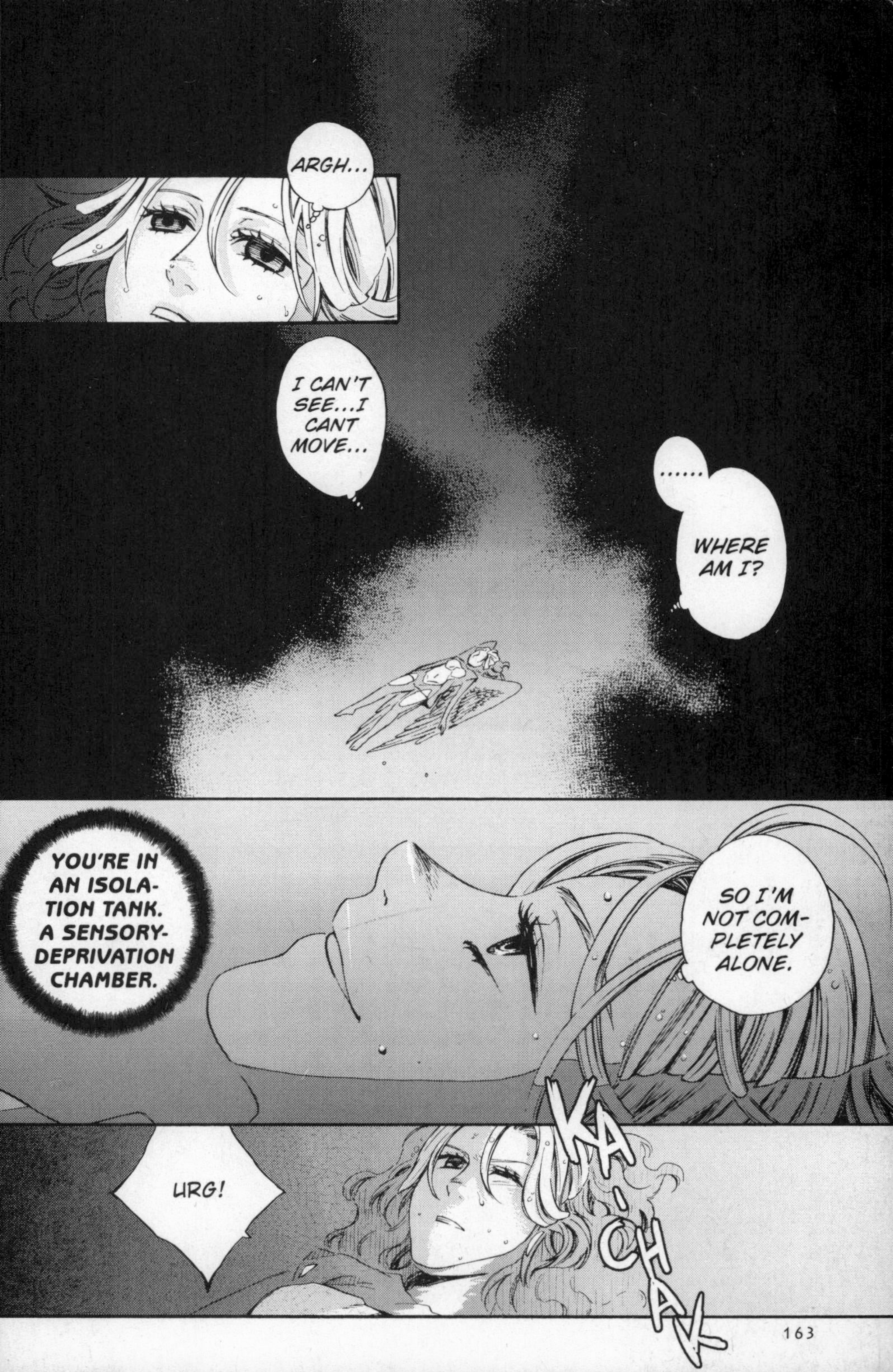
ARGH...
I CAN'T SEE...I CANT MOVE...
......
WHERE AM I?
YOU'RE IN AN ISOLATION TANK. A SENSORY-DEPRIVATION CHAMBER.
SO I'M NOT COMPLETELY ALONE.
KA-CHAK
URG!

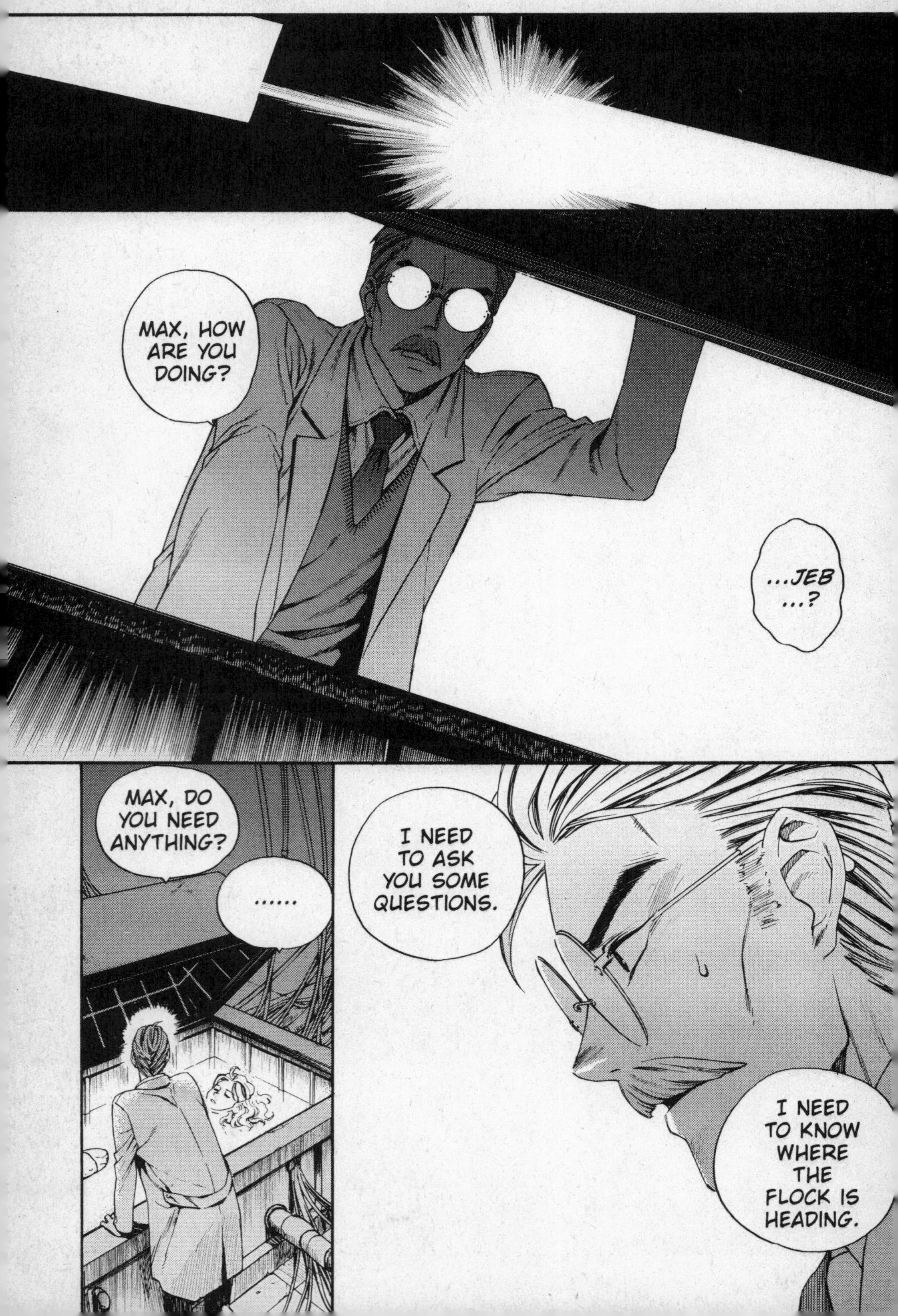
MAX, HOW ARE YOU DOING?
...JEB ...?
MAX, DO YOU NEED ANYTHING?
......
I NEED TO ASK YOU SOME QUESTIONS.
I NEED TO KNOW WHERE THE FLOCK IS HEADING.

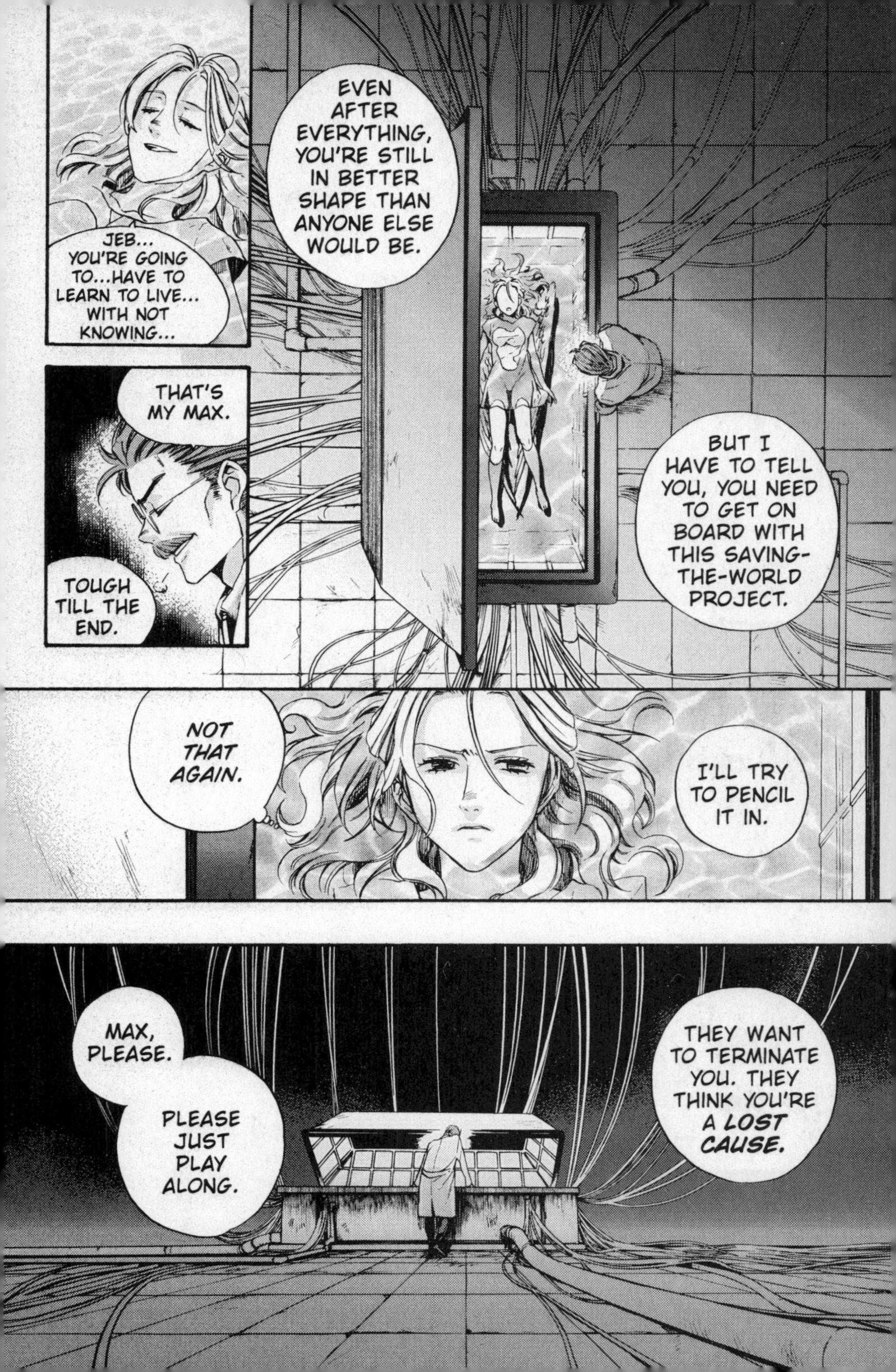
JEB... YOU'RE GOING TO...HAVE TO LEARN TO LIVE... WITH NOT KNOWING...
THAT'S MY MAX.
TOUGH TILL THE END.
EVEN AFTER EVERYTHING, YOU'RE STILL IN BETTER SHAPE THAN ANYONE ELSE WOULD BE.
BUT I HAVE TO TELL YOU, YOU NEED TO GET ON BOARD WITH THIS SAVING-THE-WORLD PROJECT.
NOT THAT AGAIN.
I'LL TRY TO PENCIL IT IN.
MAX, PLEASE.
THEY WANT TO TERMINATE YOU. THEY THINK YOU'RE A ***LOST CAUSE.***
PLEASE JUST PLAY ALONG.

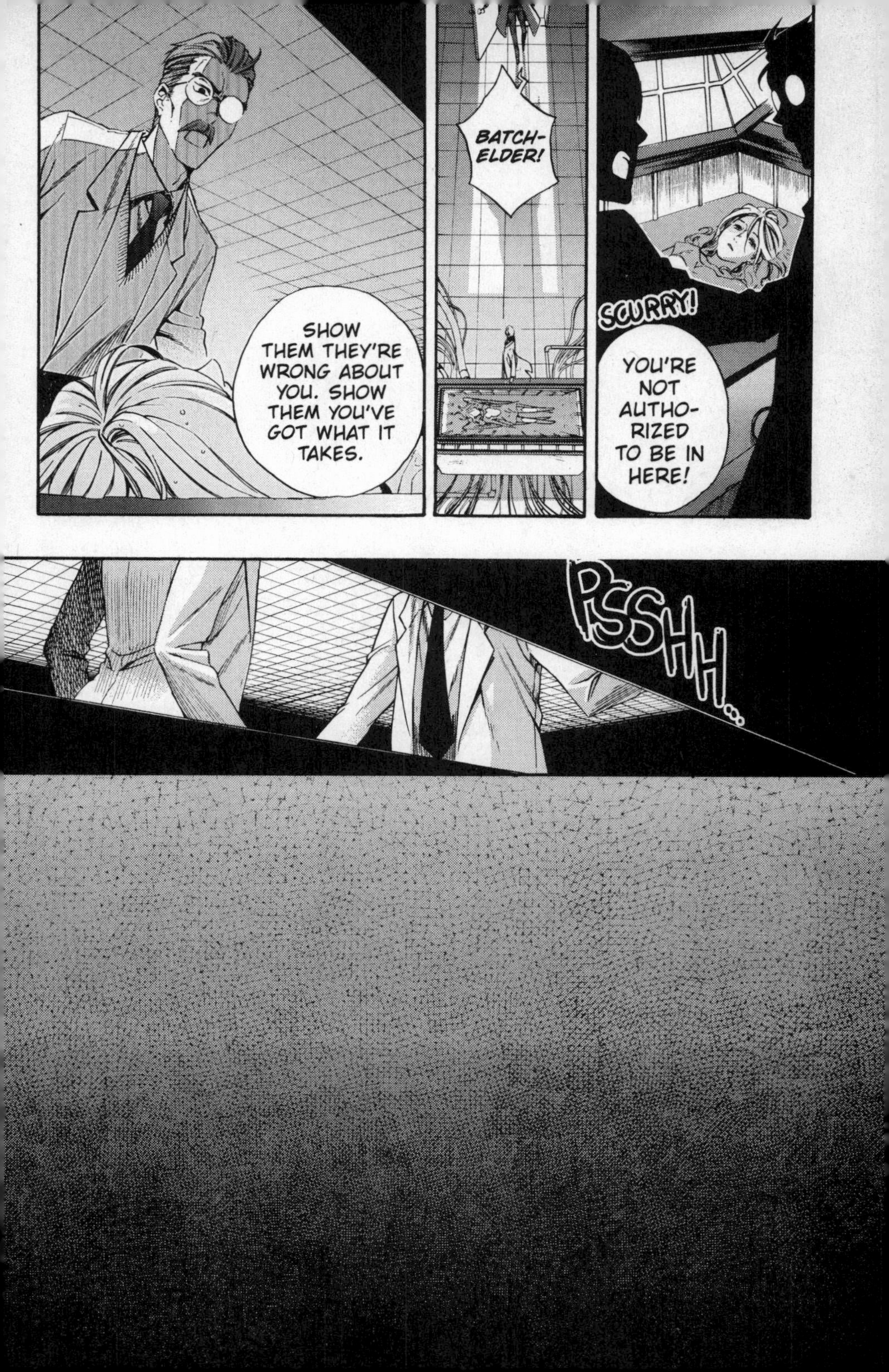
SHOW THEM THEY'RE WRONG ABOUT YOU. SHOW THEM YOU'VE GOT WHAT IT TAKES.
BATCH-ELDER!
SCURRY!
YOU'RE NOT AUTHO-RIZED TO BE IN HERE!
PSSHH...

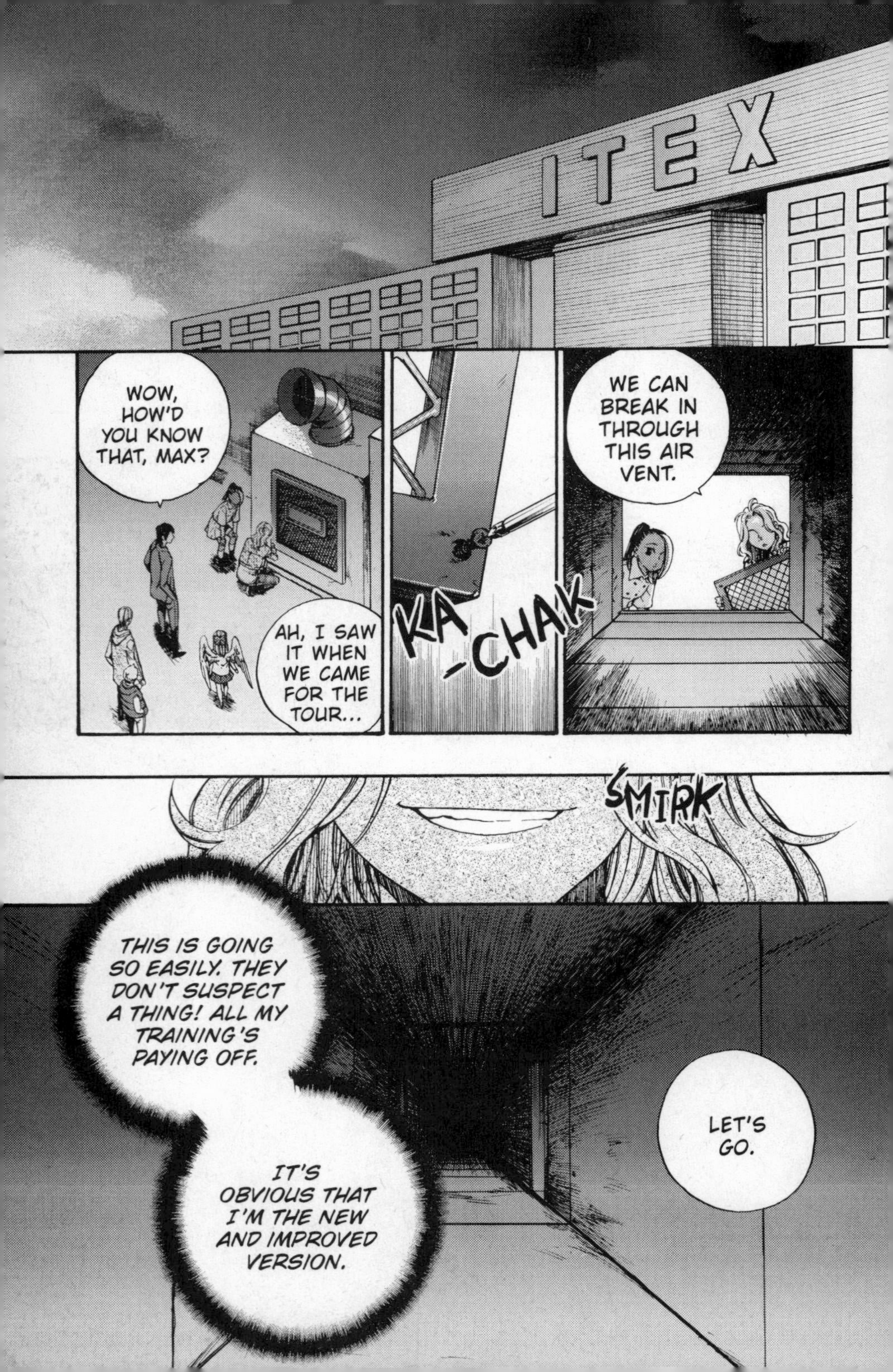
ITEX
WOW, HOW'D YOU KNOW THAT, MAX?
AH, I SAW IT WHEN WE CAME FOR THE TOUR...
KA-CHAK
WE CAN BREAK IN THROUGH THIS AIR VENT.
SMIRK
THIS IS GOING SO EASILY. THEY DON'T SUSPECT A THING! ALL MY TRAINING'S PAYING OFF.
IT'S OBVIOUS THAT I'M THE NEW AND IMPROVED VERSION.
LET'S GO.

THINK, MAX.

DAZED...

VOICE, YOU GOT ANY IDEAS?

WHAT IS IT THAT THEY WANT FROM YOU?

...WHAT DID THEY WANT FROM ME?

JUST FOR ME TO BE HERE. TO BE ABLE TO DO THINGS TO ME...

...MAKE ME JUMP THROUGH THEIR HOOPS, BE THEIR LAB RAT.

WHAT WOULD HAPPEN IF YOU TOOK THAT AWAY FROM THEM?

BUT HOW COULD I TAKE THAT AWAY FROM THEM?

I CAN'T BREAK OUT OF THIS SARDINE CAN.

HMM... THEY WOULD BE VERY UPSET?

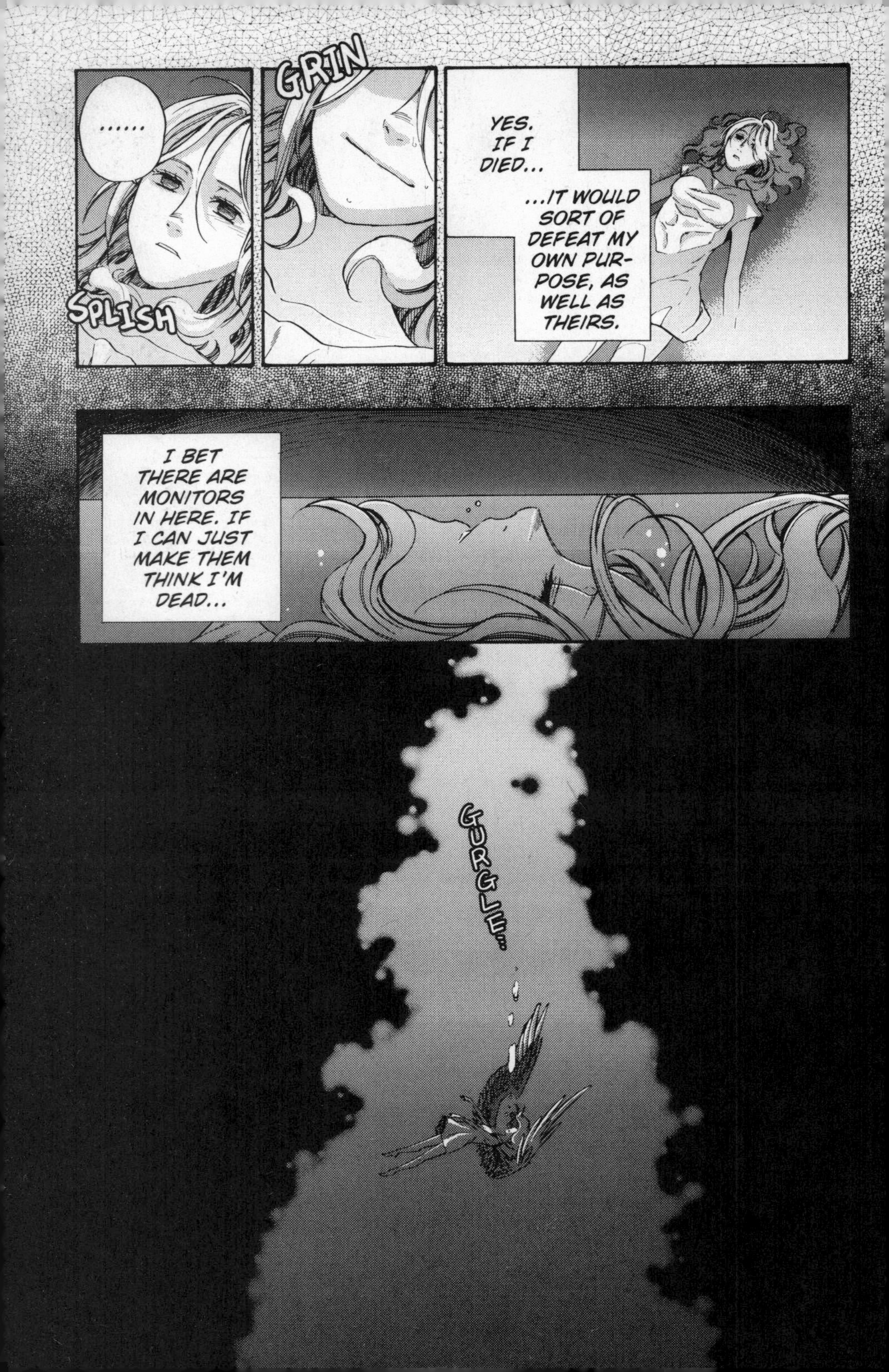
......
SPLISH
GRIN
YES. IF I DIED...
...IT WOULD SORT OF DEFEAT MY OWN PURPOSE, AS WELL AS THEIRS.
I BET THERE ARE MONITORS IN HERE. IF I CAN JUST MAKE THEM THINK I'M DEAD...
GURGLE...

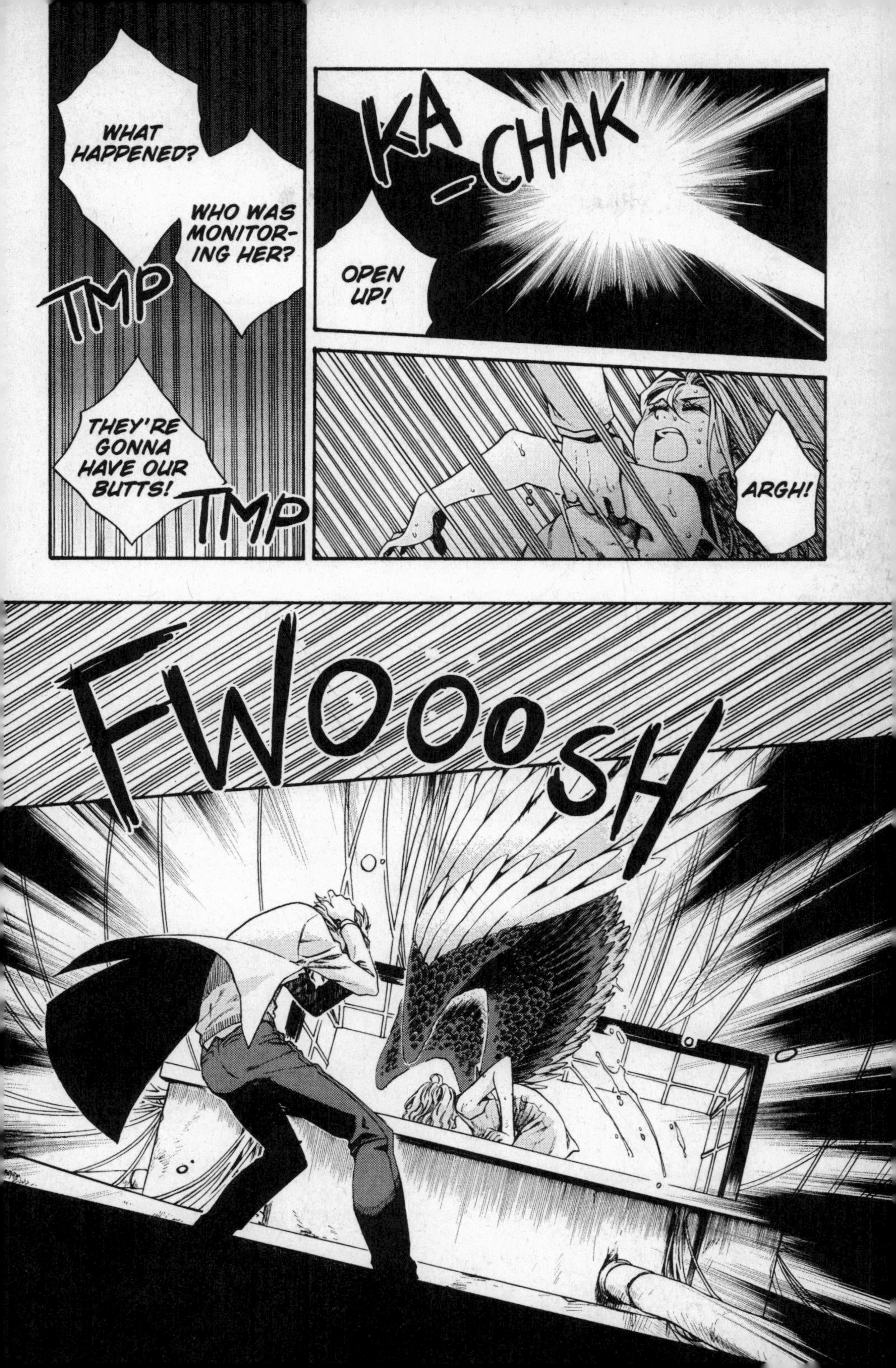
WHAT HAPPENED?
WHO WAS MONITORING HER?
TMP
THEY'RE GONNA HAVE OUR BUTTS!
TMP
KA-CHAK
OPEN UP!
ARGH!
FWOOOSH

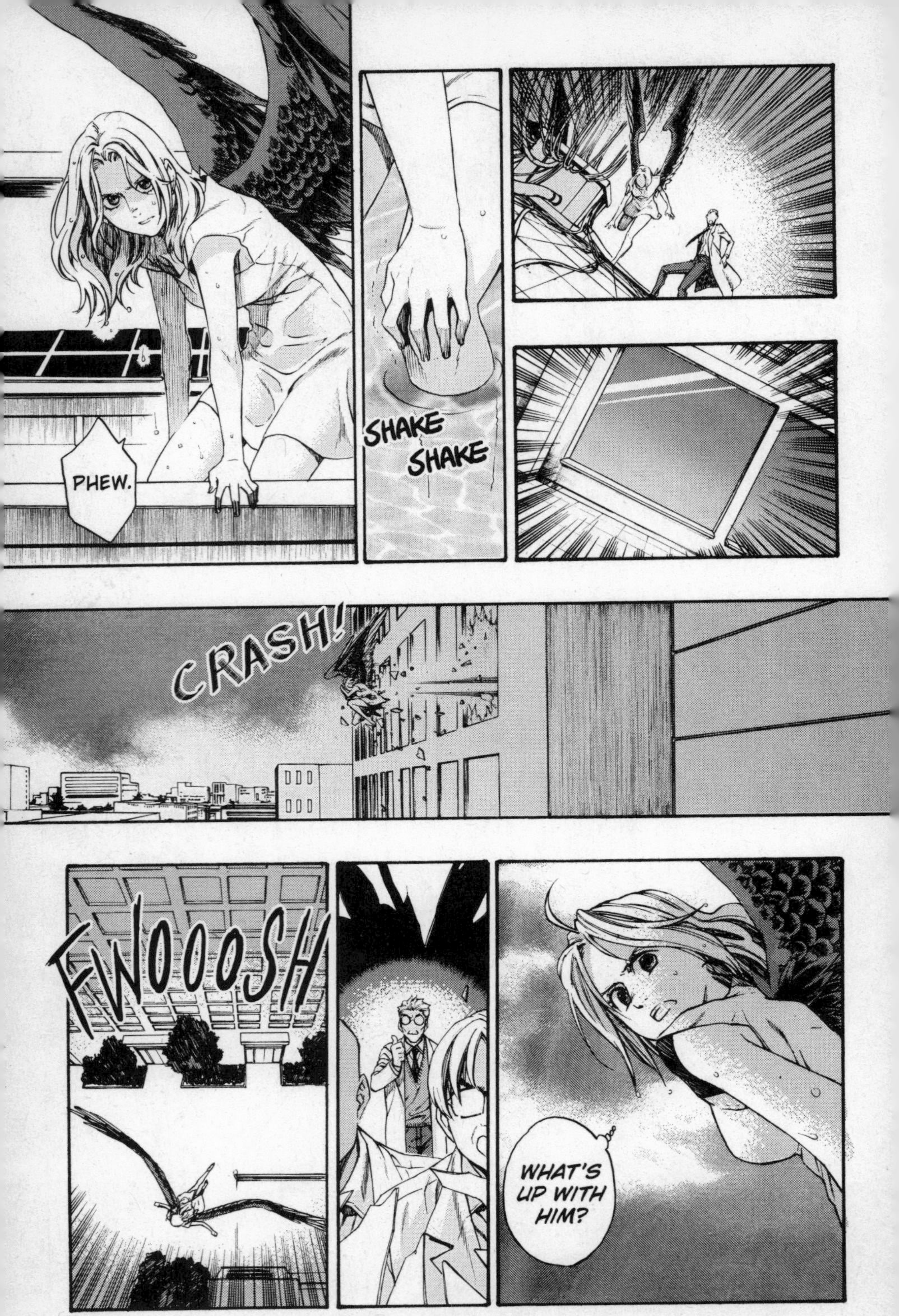
PHEW.
SHAKE SHAKE
CRASH!
FWOOOSH
WHAT'S UP WITH HIM?

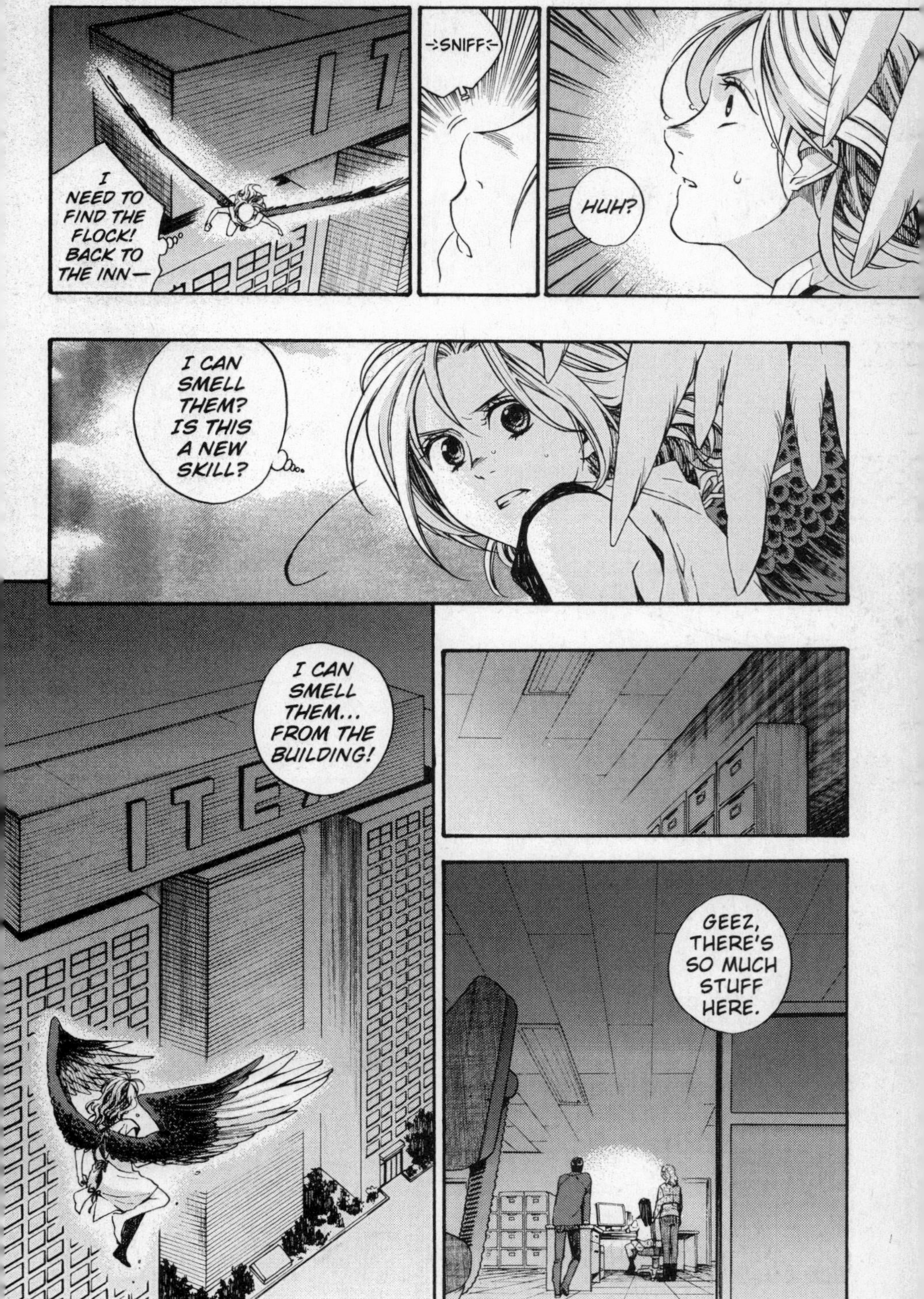

I NEED TO FIND THE FLOCK! BACK TO THE INN—
SNIFF
HUH?
I CAN SMELL THEM? IS THIS A NEW SKILL?
I CAN SMELL THEM... FROM THE BUILDING!
GEEZ, THERE'S SO MUCH STUFF HERE.

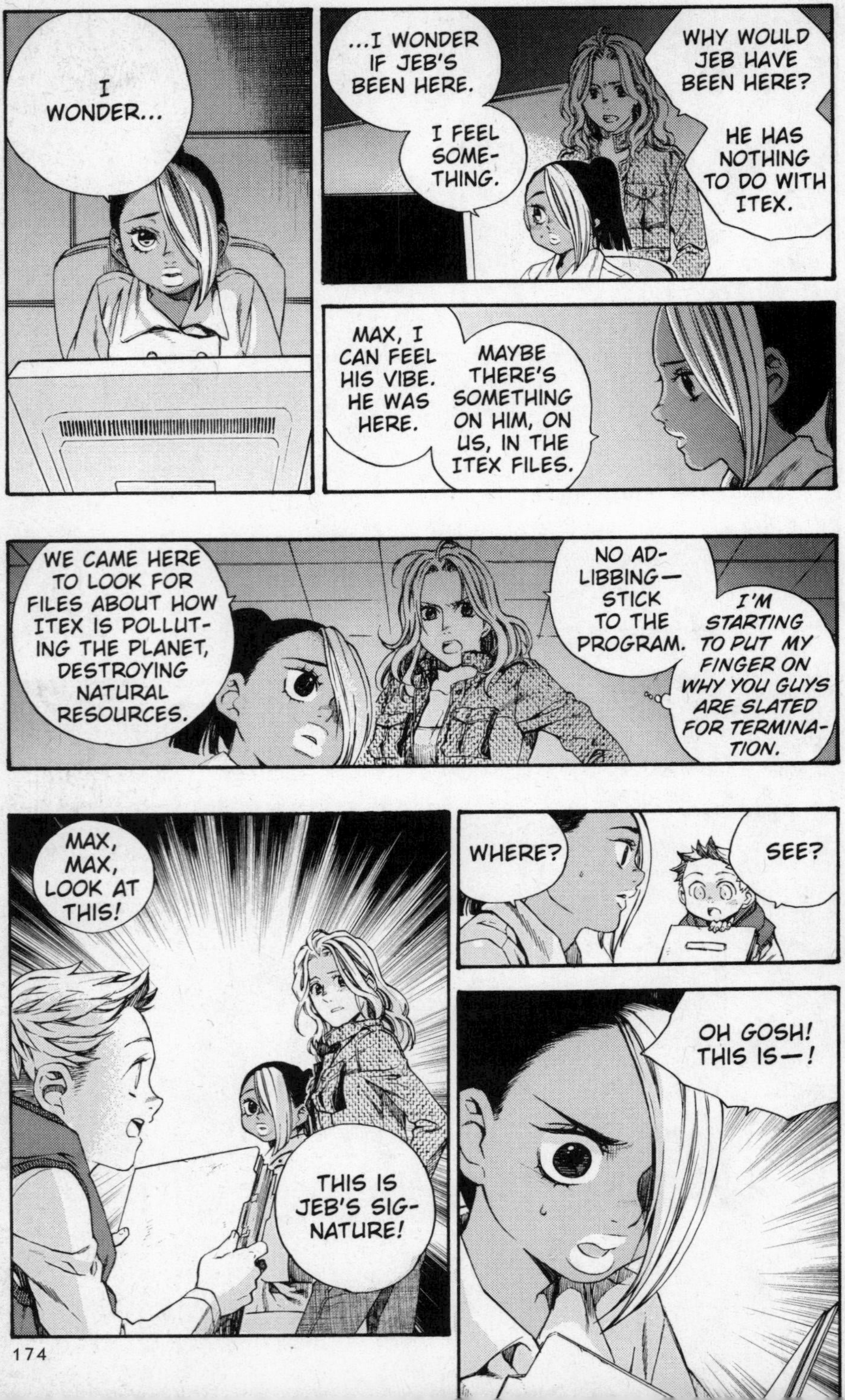

I WONDER...
...I WONDER IF JEB'S BEEN HERE.
I FEEL SOME-THING.
WHY WOULD JEB HAVE BEEN HERE?
HE HAS NOTHING TO DO WITH ITEX.
MAX, I CAN FEEL HIS VIBE. HE WAS HERE.
MAYBE THERE'S SOMETHING ON HIM, ON US, IN THE ITEX FILES.
WE CAME HERE TO LOOK FOR FILES ABOUT HOW ITEX IS POLLUT-ING THE PLANET, DESTROYING NATURAL RESOURCES.
NO AD-LIBBING—STICK TO THE PROGRAM.
I'M STARTING TO PUT MY FINGER ON WHY YOU GUYS ARE SLATED FOR TERMINA-TION.
MAX, MAX, LOOK AT THIS!
THIS IS JEB'S SIG-NATURE!
WHERE?
SEE?
OH GOSH! THIS IS—!

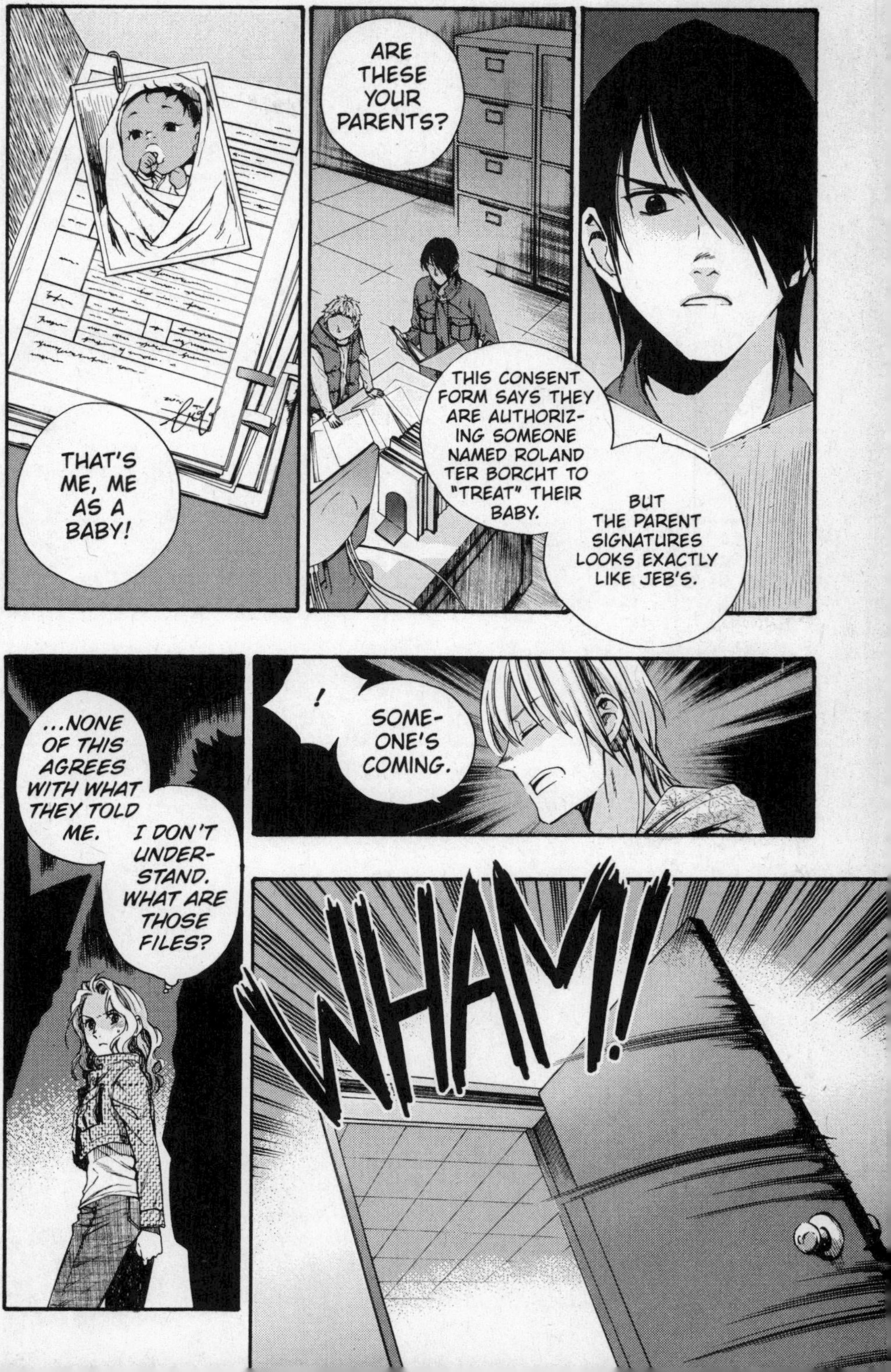
THAT'S ME, ME AS A BABY!
ARE THESE YOUR PARENTS?
THIS CONSENT FORM SAYS THEY ARE AUTHORIZING SOMEONE NAMED ROLAND TER BORCHT TO "TREAT" THEIR BABY.
BUT THE PARENT SIGNATURES LOOKS EXACTLY LIKE JEB'S.
...NONE OF THIS AGREES WITH WHAT THEY TOLD ME.
I DON'T UNDERSTAND. WHAT ARE THOSE FILES?
!
SOMEONE'S COMING.
WHAM!

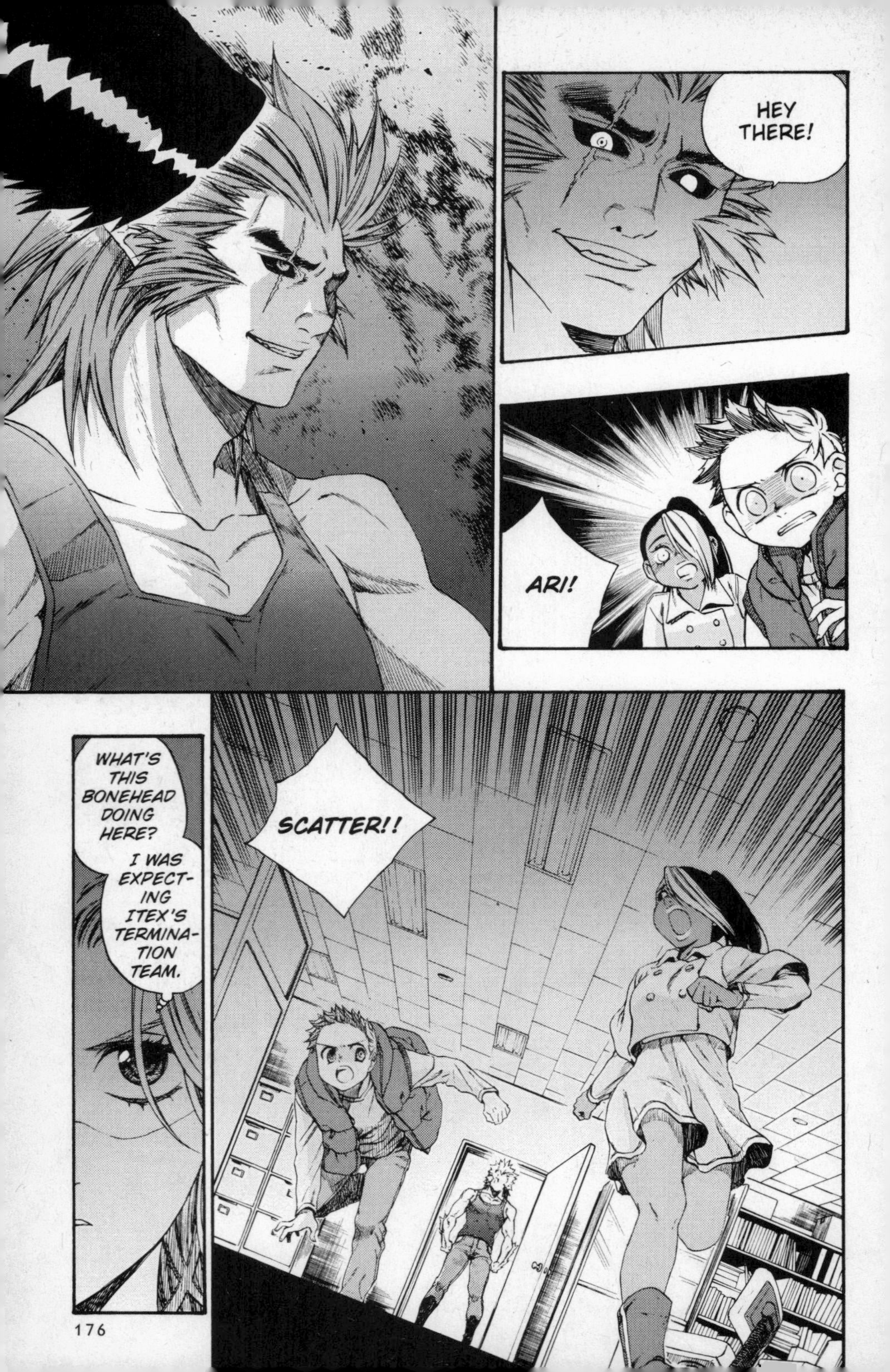
HEY THERE!
ARI!
WHAT'S THIS BONEHEAD DOING HERE?
I WAS EXPECTING ITEX'S TERMINATION TEAM.
SCATTER!!

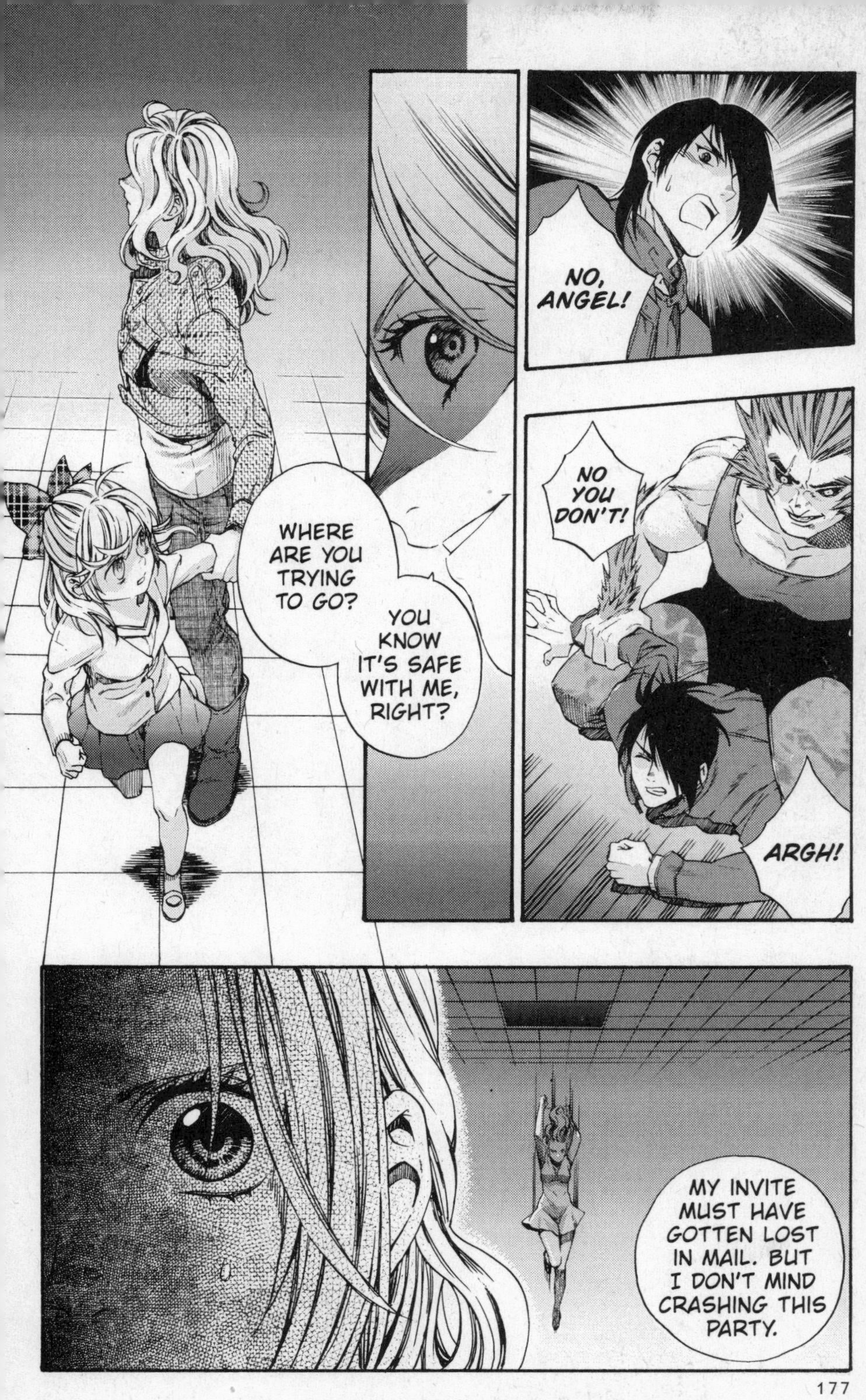
WHERE ARE YOU TRYING TO GO?
YOU KNOW IT'S SAFE WITH ME, RIGHT?
NO, ANGEL!
NO YOU DON'T!
ARGH!
MY INVITE MUST HAVE GOTTEN LOST IN MAIL. BUT I DON'T MIND CRASHING THIS PARTY.

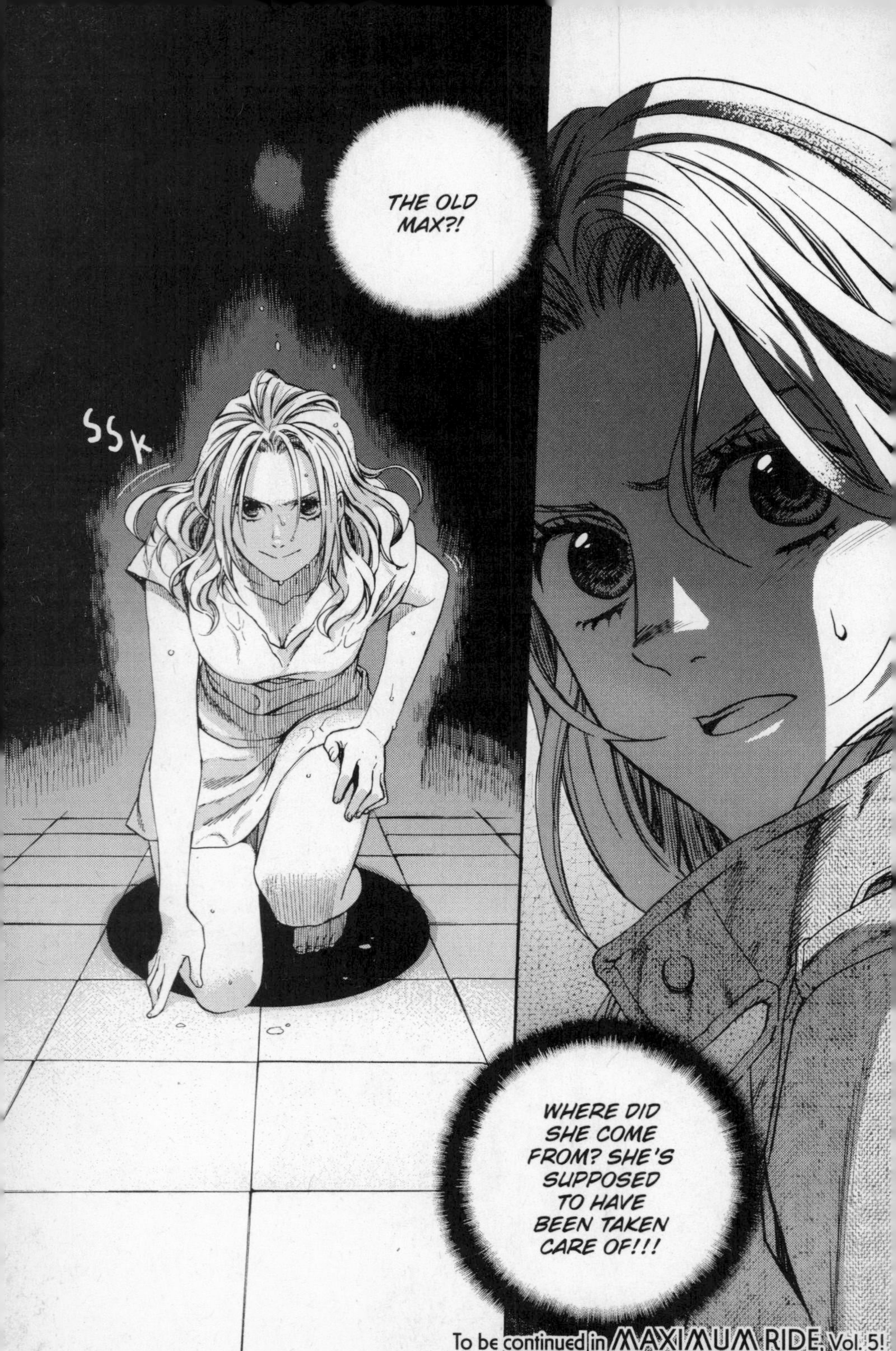
THE OLD MAX?!
SSK
WHERE DID SHE COME FROM? SHE'S SUPPOSED TO HAVE BEEN TAKEN CARE OF!!!

To be continued in MAXIMUM RIDE, Vol. 5!

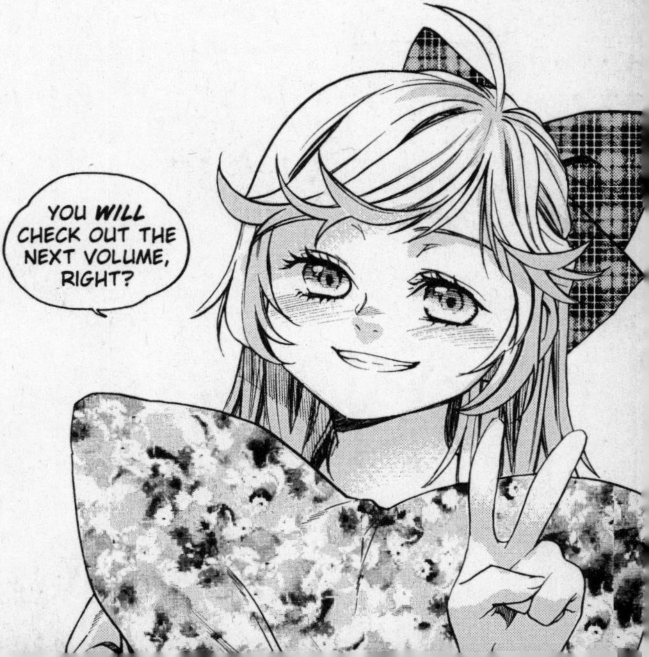
YOU **WILL** CHECK OUT THE NEXT VOLUME, RIGHT?

MAXIMUM
RIDE

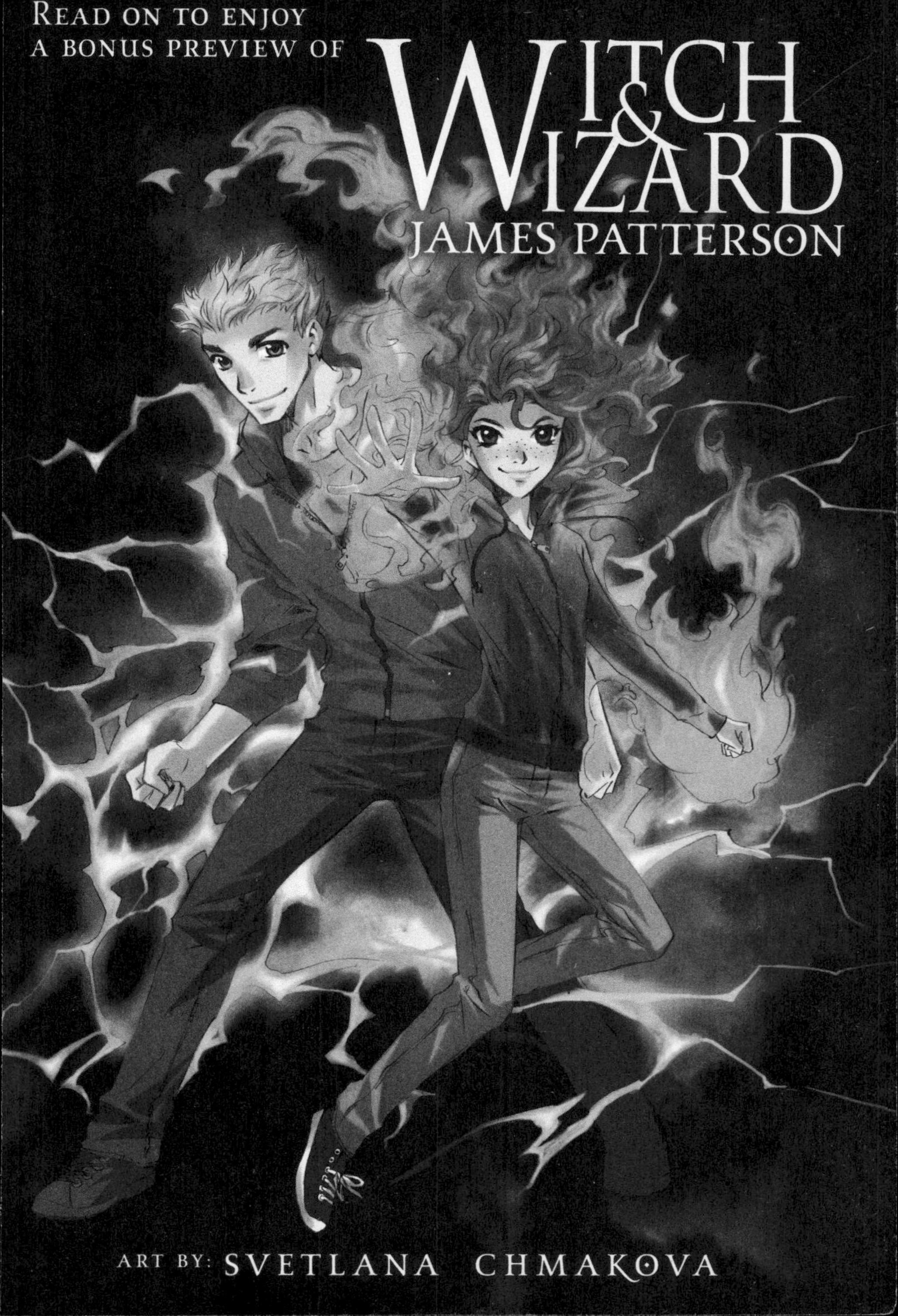
READ ON TO ENJOY
A BONUS PREVIEW OF
WITCH & WIZARD
JAMES PATTERSON
ART BY: SVETLANA CHMAKOVA

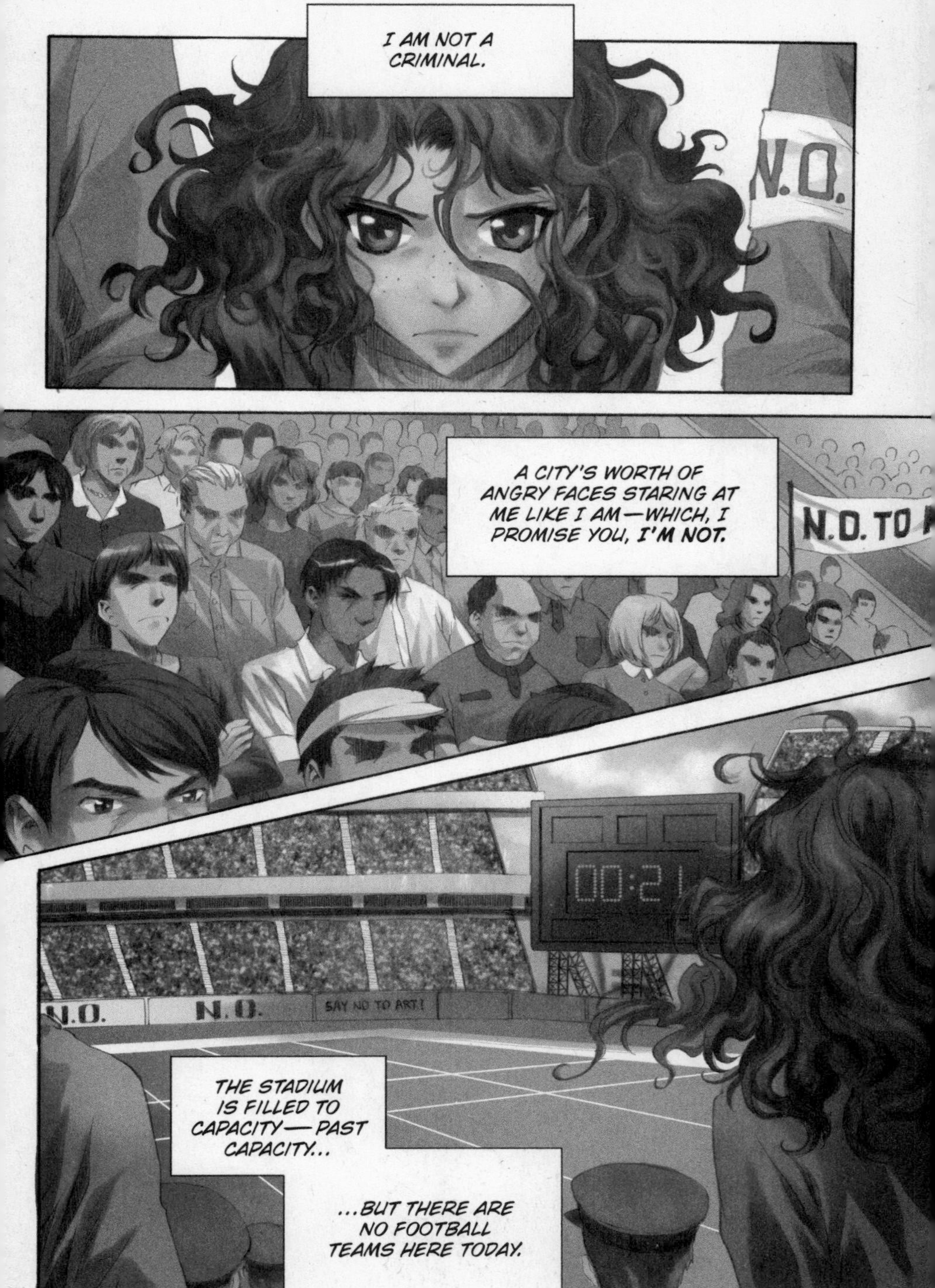
I AM NOT A CRIMINAL.
N.O.
A CITY'S WORTH OF ANGRY FACES STARING AT ME LIKE I AM—WHICH, I PROMISE YOU, I'M NOT.
N.O. TO
00:21
N.O.
N.O.
SAY NO TO ART!
THE STADIUM IS FILLED TO CAPACITY—PAST CAPACITY...
...BUT THERE ARE NO FOOTBALL TEAMS HERE TODAY.

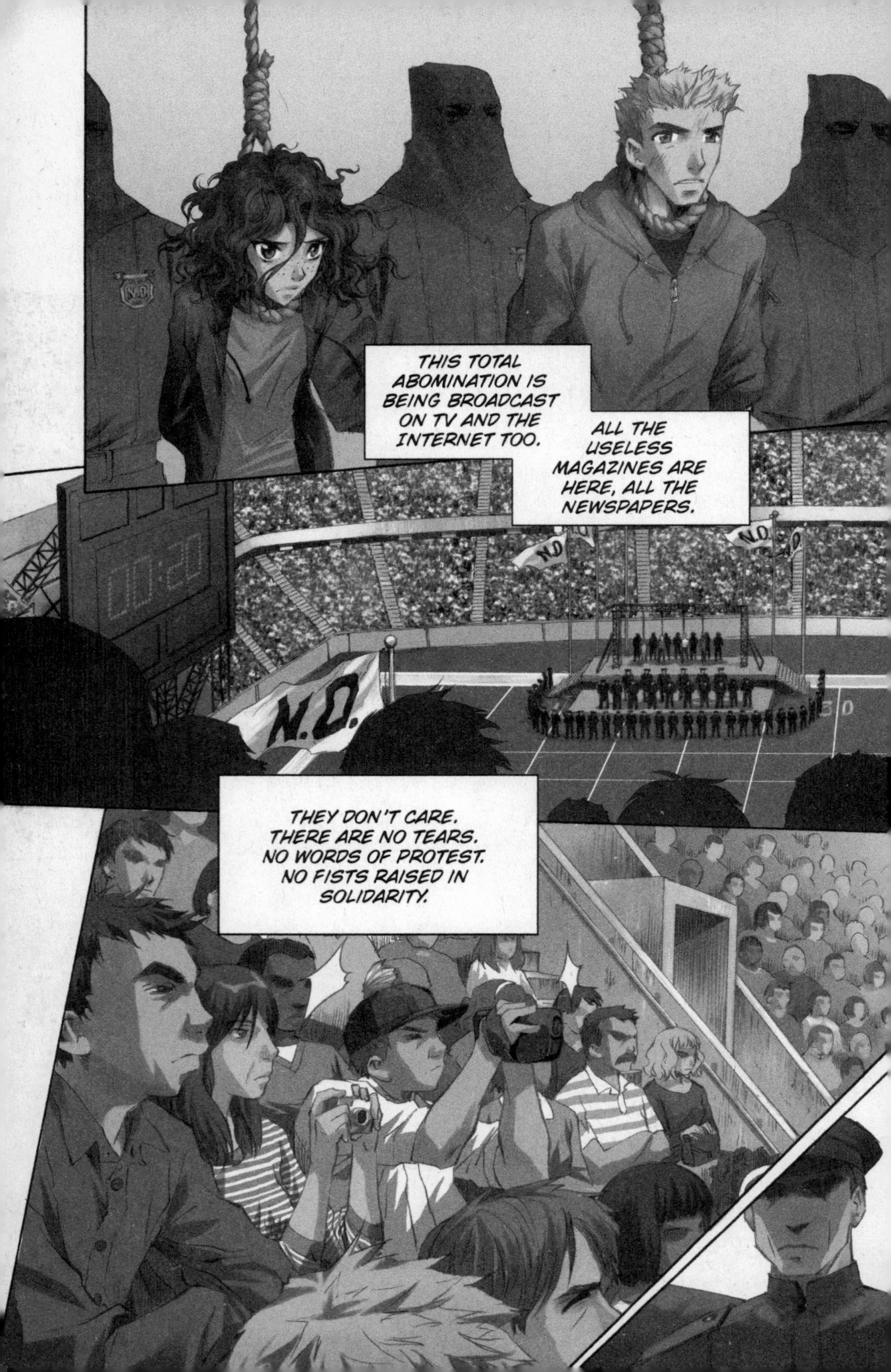
THIS TOTAL ABOMINATION IS BEING BROADCAST ON TV AND THE INTERNET TOO.
ALL THE USELESS MAGAZINES ARE HERE, ALL THE NEWSPAPERS.
00:20
N.O.
N.O.
N.O.
N.O.
THEY DON'T CARE. THERE ARE NO TEARS. NO WORDS OF PROTEST. NO FISTS RAISED IN SOLIDARITY.

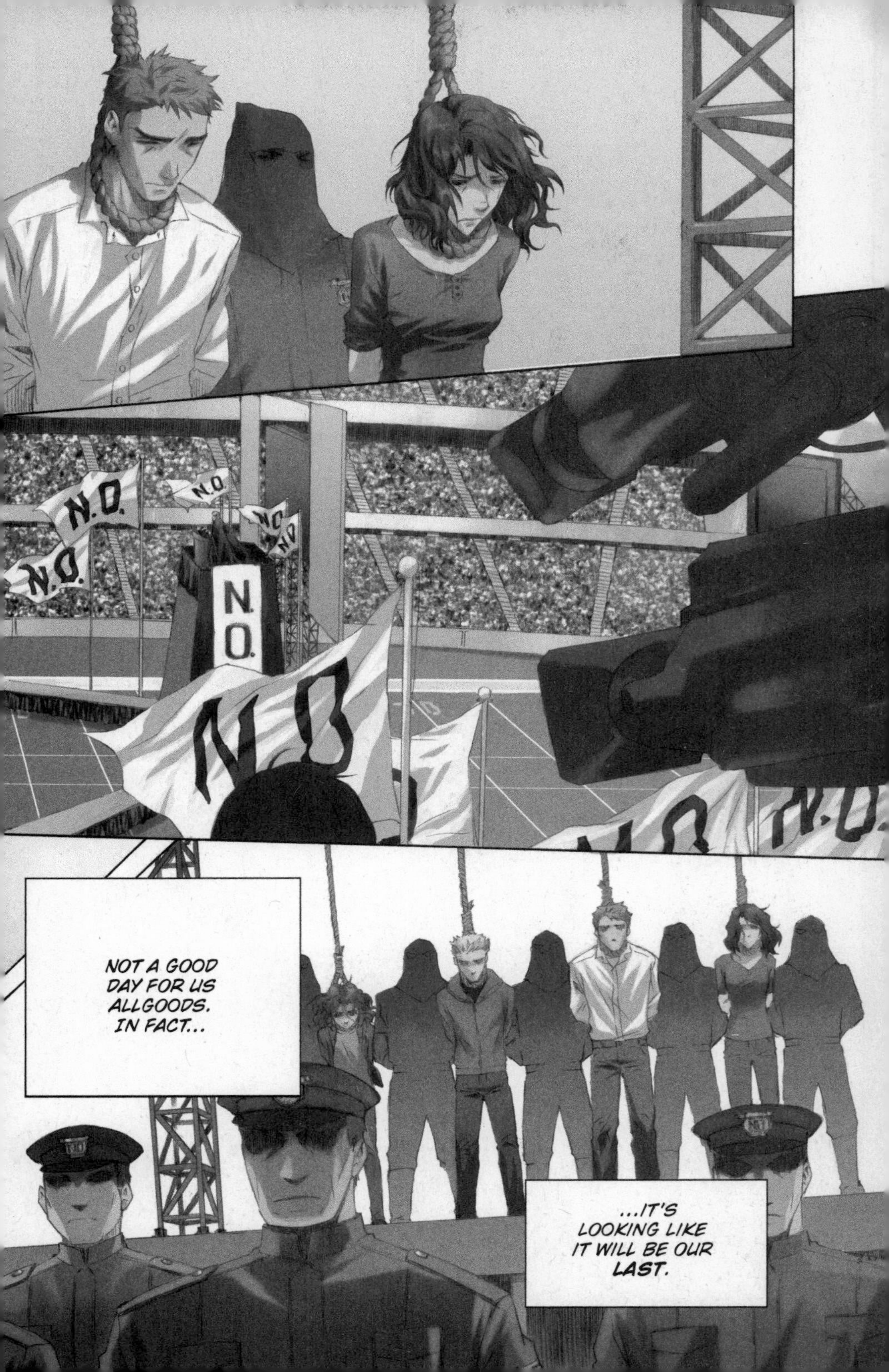
N.O.
N.O.
N.O.
N.O.
N.O.
NOT A GOOD DAY FOR US ALLGOODS. IN FACT...
...IT'S LOOKING LIKE IT WILL BE OUR **LAST**.

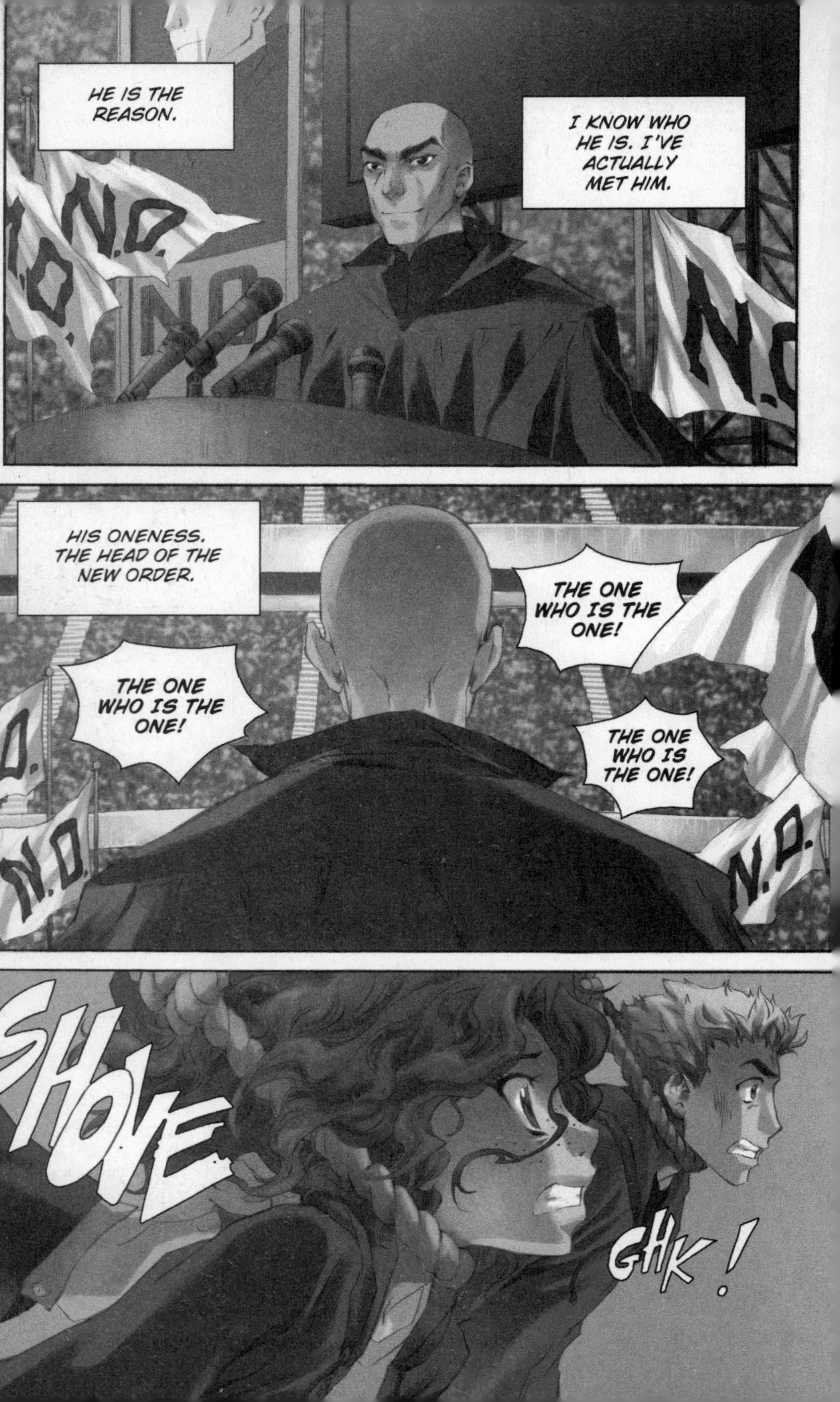

HE IS THE REASON.
I KNOW WHO HE IS. I'VE ACTUALLY MET HIM.
N.O.
N.O.
N.O.
HIS ONENESS. THE HEAD OF THE NEW ORDER.
THE ONE WHO IS THE ONE!
THE ONE WHO IS THE ONE!
THE ONE WHO IS THE ONE!
N.O.
N.O.
N.O.
SHOVE
GHK!

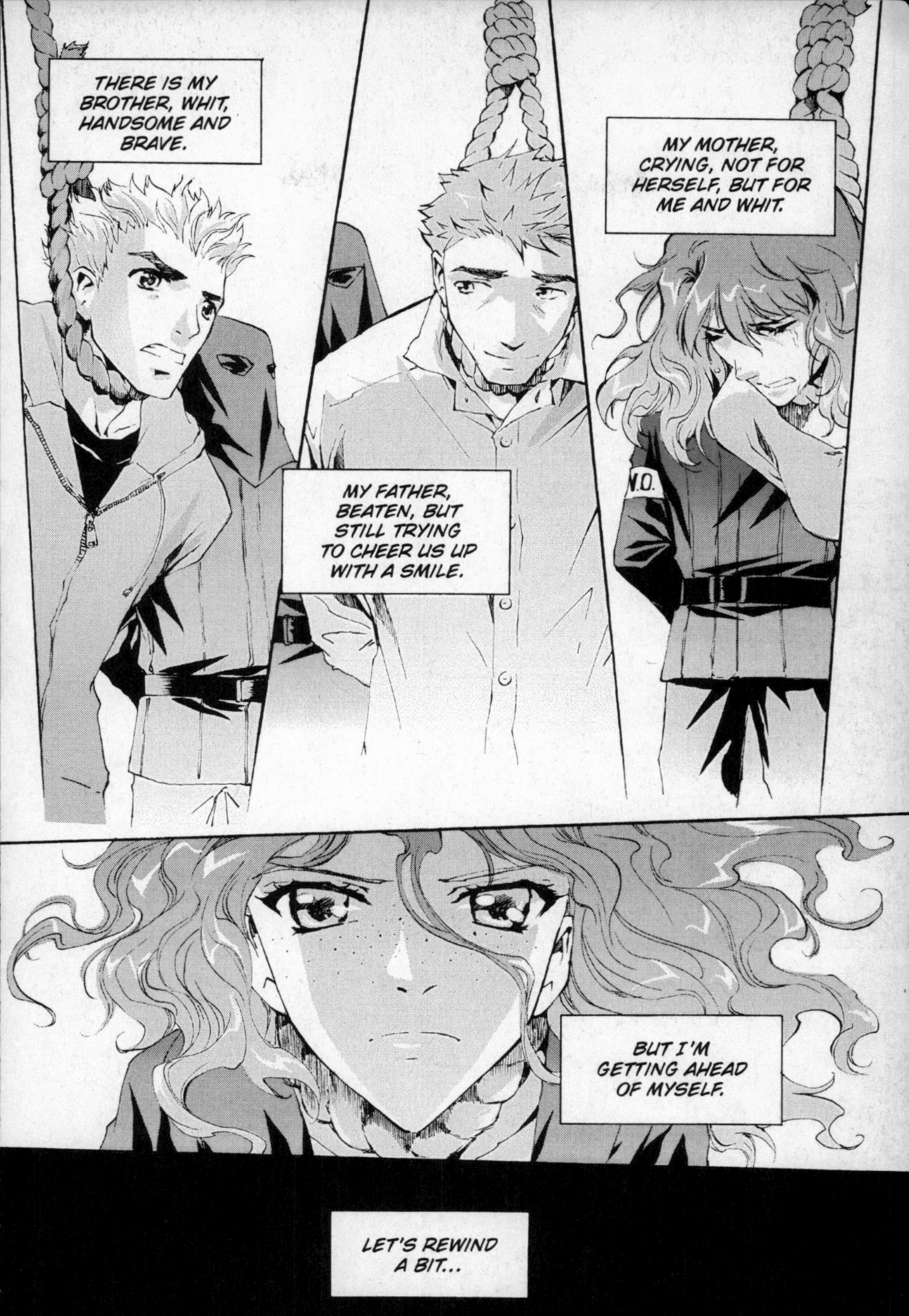
THERE IS MY BROTHER, WHIT, HANDSOME AND BRAVE.
MY FATHER, BEATEN, BUT STILL TRYING TO CHEER US UP WITH A SMILE.
MY MOTHER, CRYING, NOT FOR HERSELF, BUT FOR ME AND WHIT.
BUT I'M GETTING AHEAD OF MYSELF.
LET'S REWIND A BIT...

BY ORDER OF THE NEW ORDER,

and the Great Wind— The One Who Is

THE ONE —

let it be known that as of

NOW, THIS MOMENT, or

TWELVE O'CLOCK MIDNIGHT,

whichever shall arrive first, following the

SWIFT TRIUMPH of the **ORDER** of the

ONES WHO PROTECT, who have obliterated the

BLIND AND DUMB FORCES of passivity and

complacency **PLAGUING** this world,

ALL CITIZENS *must, shall,* and *will* abide by

THESE THREE ORDERS FOR ORDER:

1. All behaviors NOT in keeping with N.O. law, logic, order, and science (including but not limited to theology, philosophy, and IN PARTIC-ULAR the creative and dark arts, et cetera) are hereby ABOLISHED.
2. ALL persons under eighteen years of age will be evaluated for ORDERLINESS and MUST COMPLY with the prescribed corrective actions.
3. The One Who Is THE ONE grants, appoints, decides, seizes, and exe-cutes at will. All NOT complying shall be SEIZED and/or EXECUTED.

—As declared to The One Who Writes Decrees
by THE ONE WHO IS THE ONE

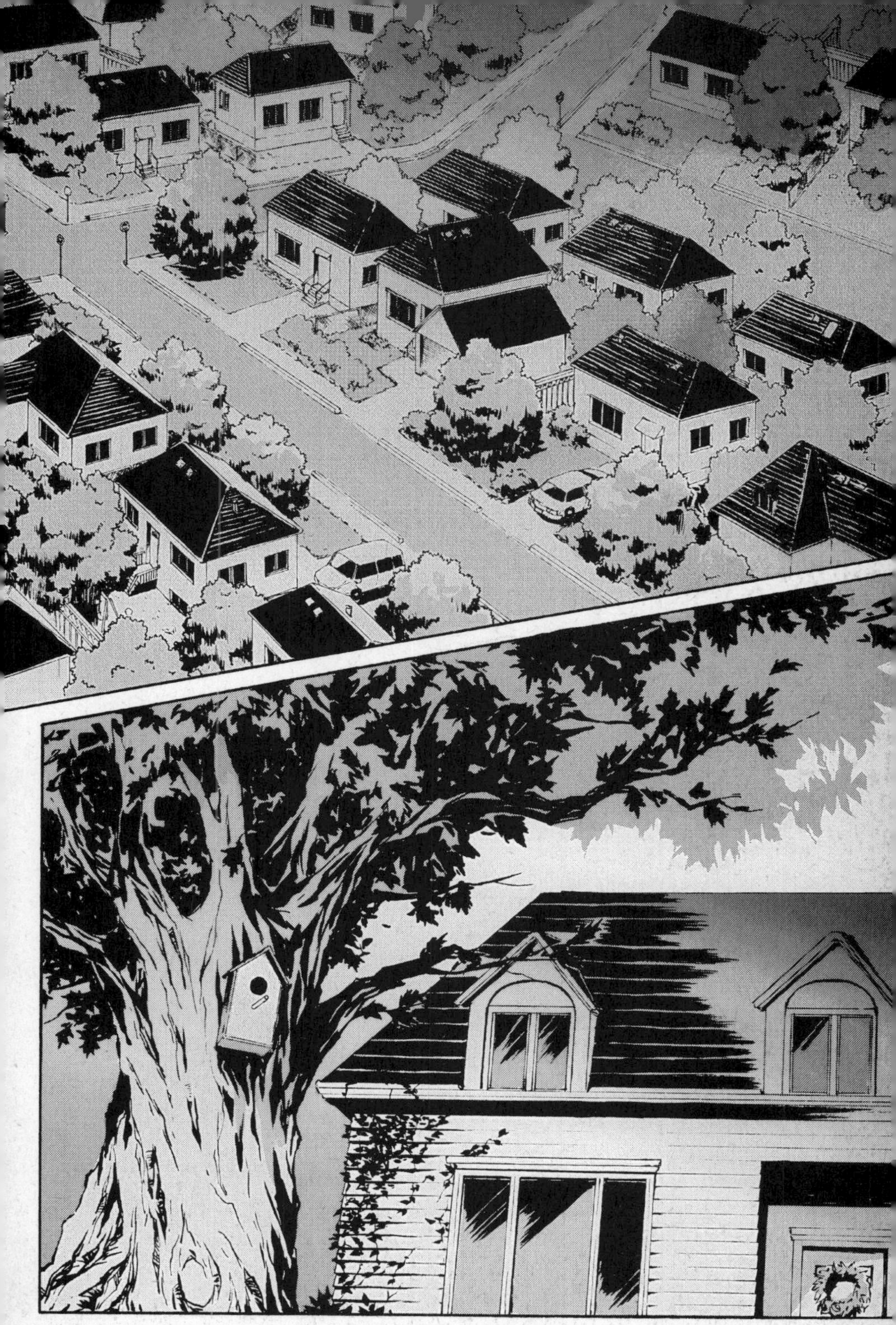

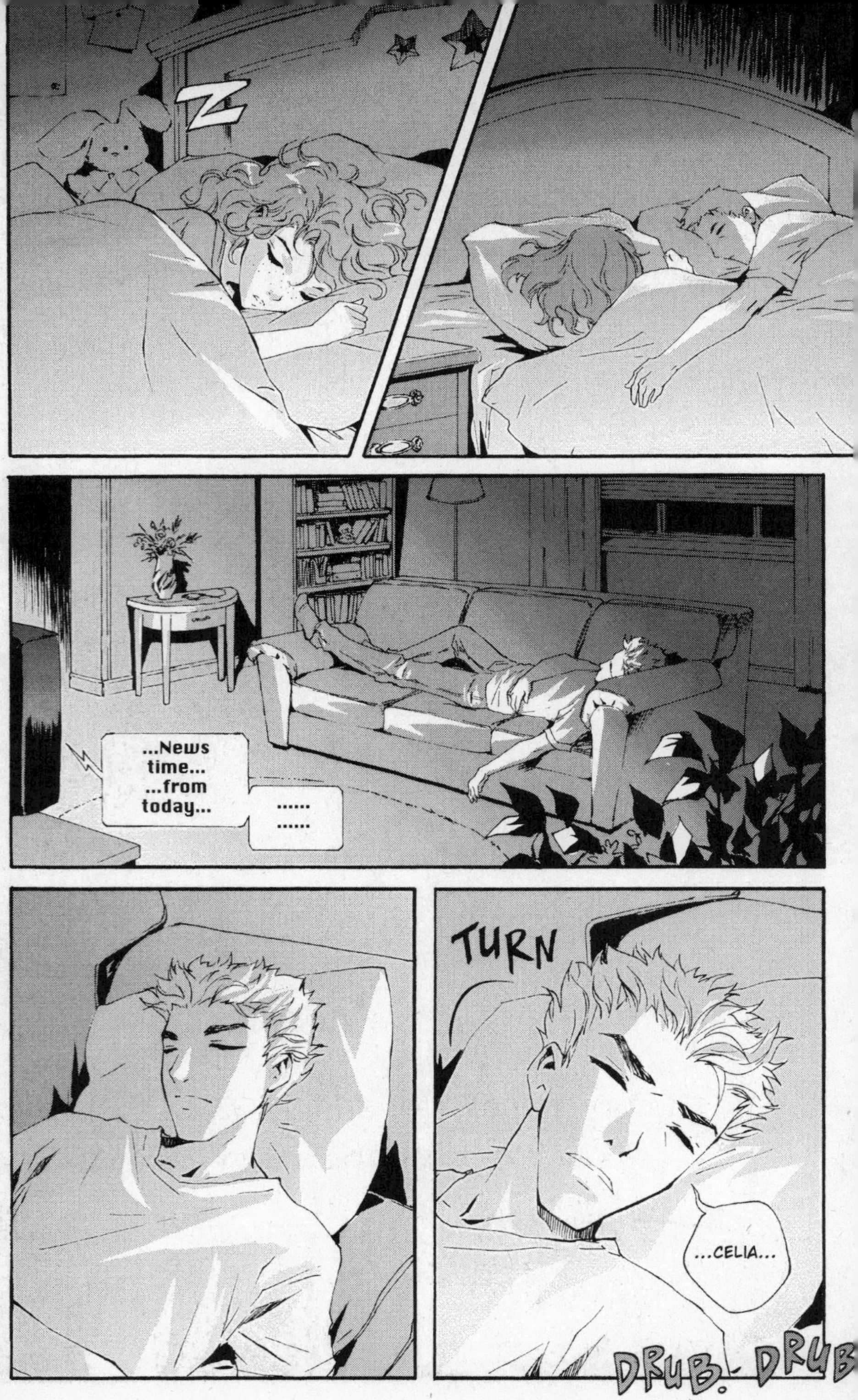
Z
...News time... ...from today...
......
......
TURN
...CELIA...
DRUB. DRUB

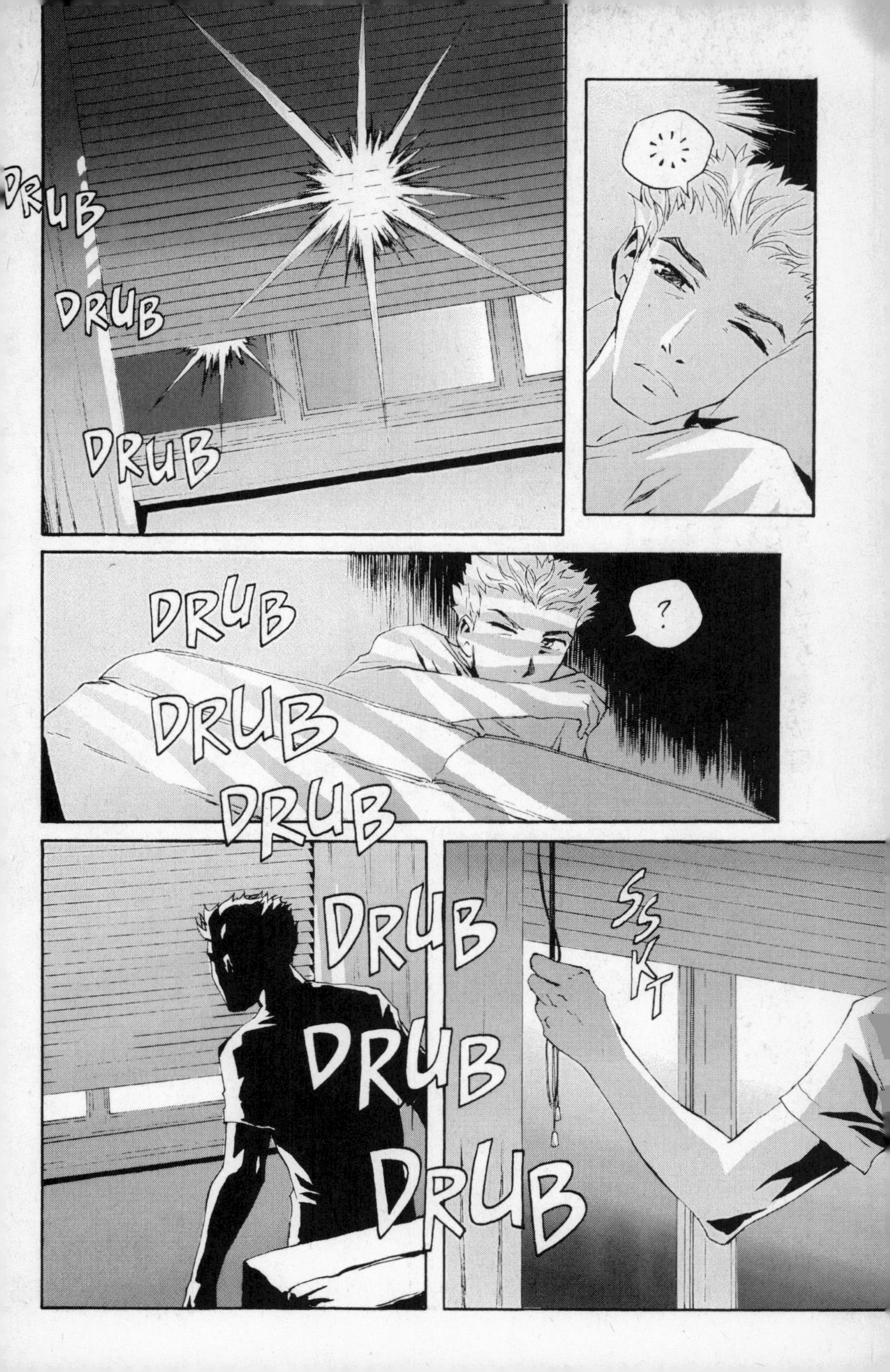
DRUB
DRUB
DRUB
?
DRUB
DRUB
DRUB
DRUB
DRUB
DRUB
SSKT

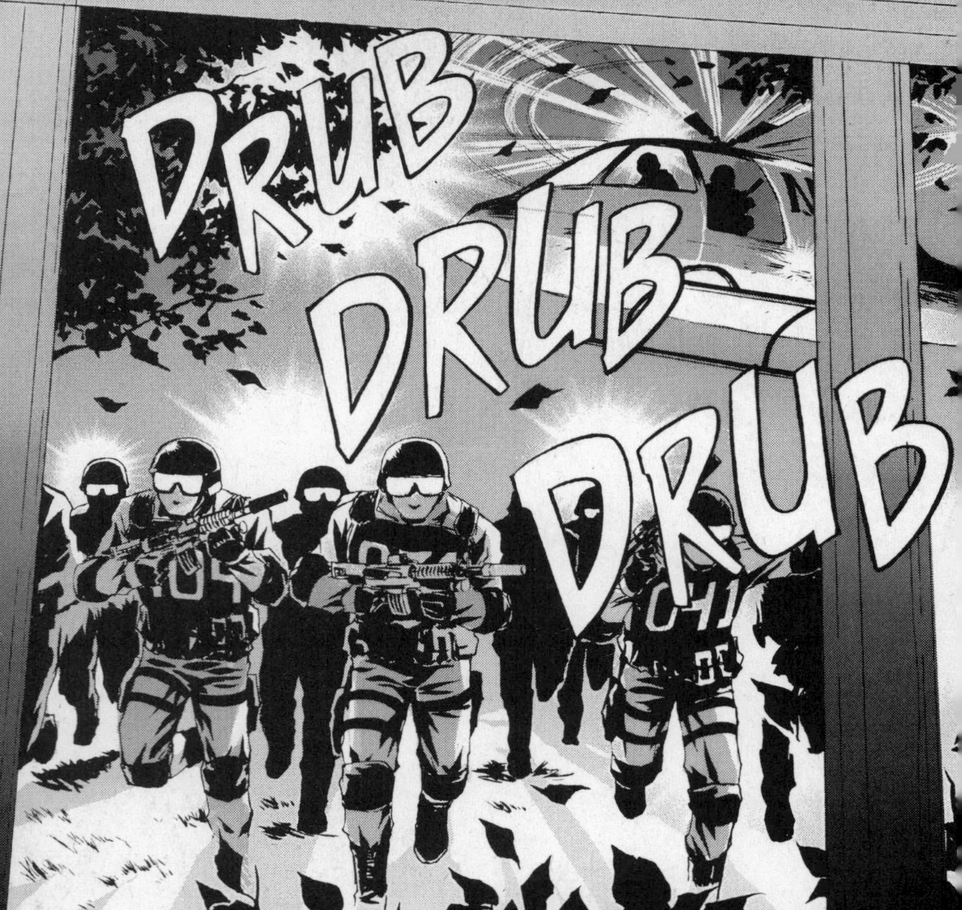
DRUB DRUB DRUB

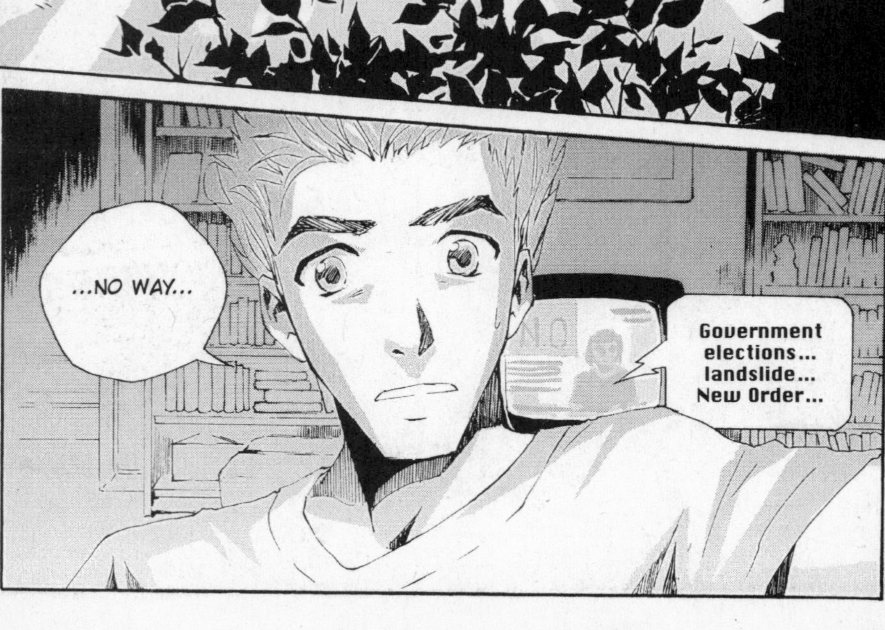
...NO WAY...
Government elections... landslide... New Order...

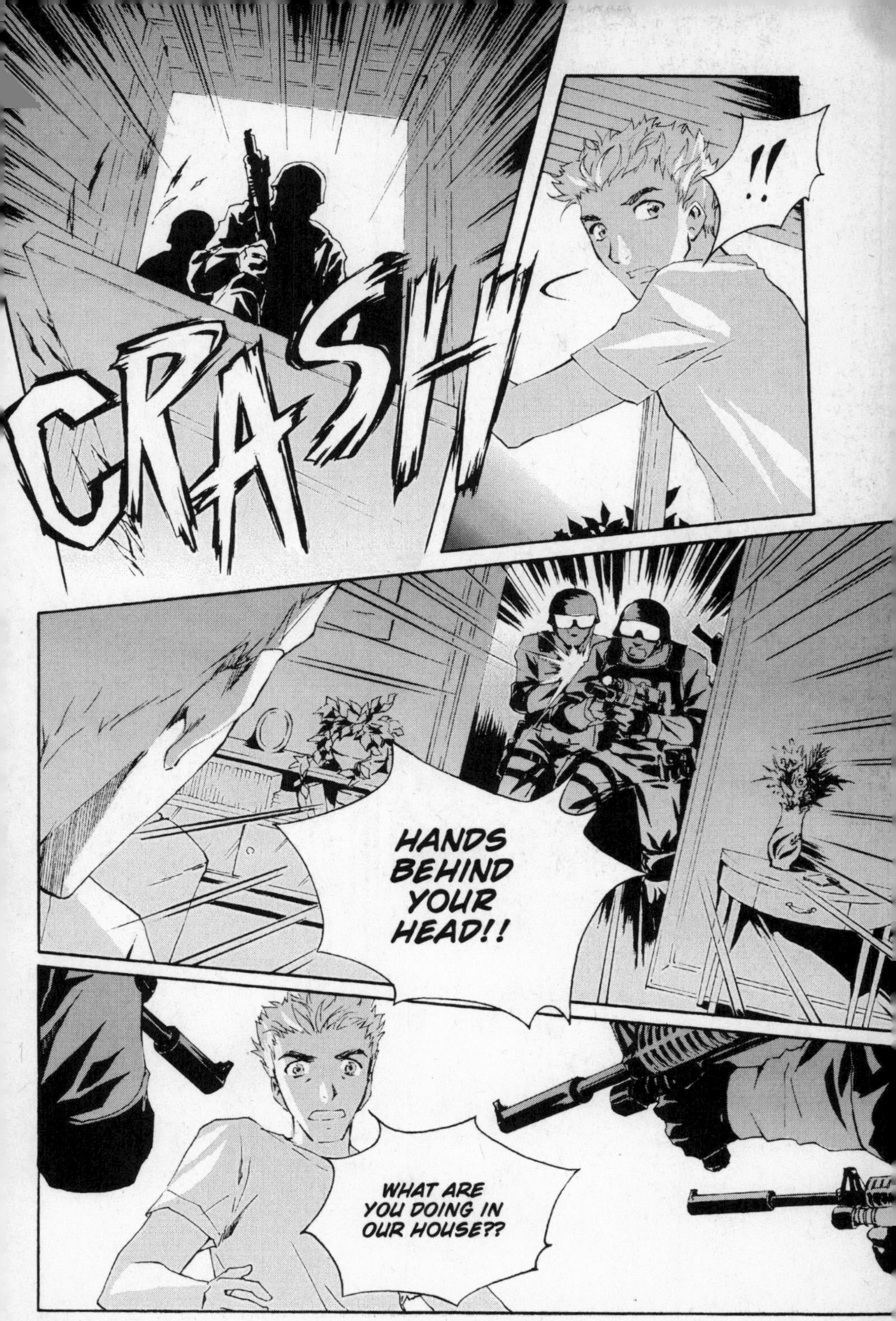
CRASH
!!
HANDS BEHIND YOUR HEAD!!
WHAT ARE YOU DOING IN OUR HOUSE??

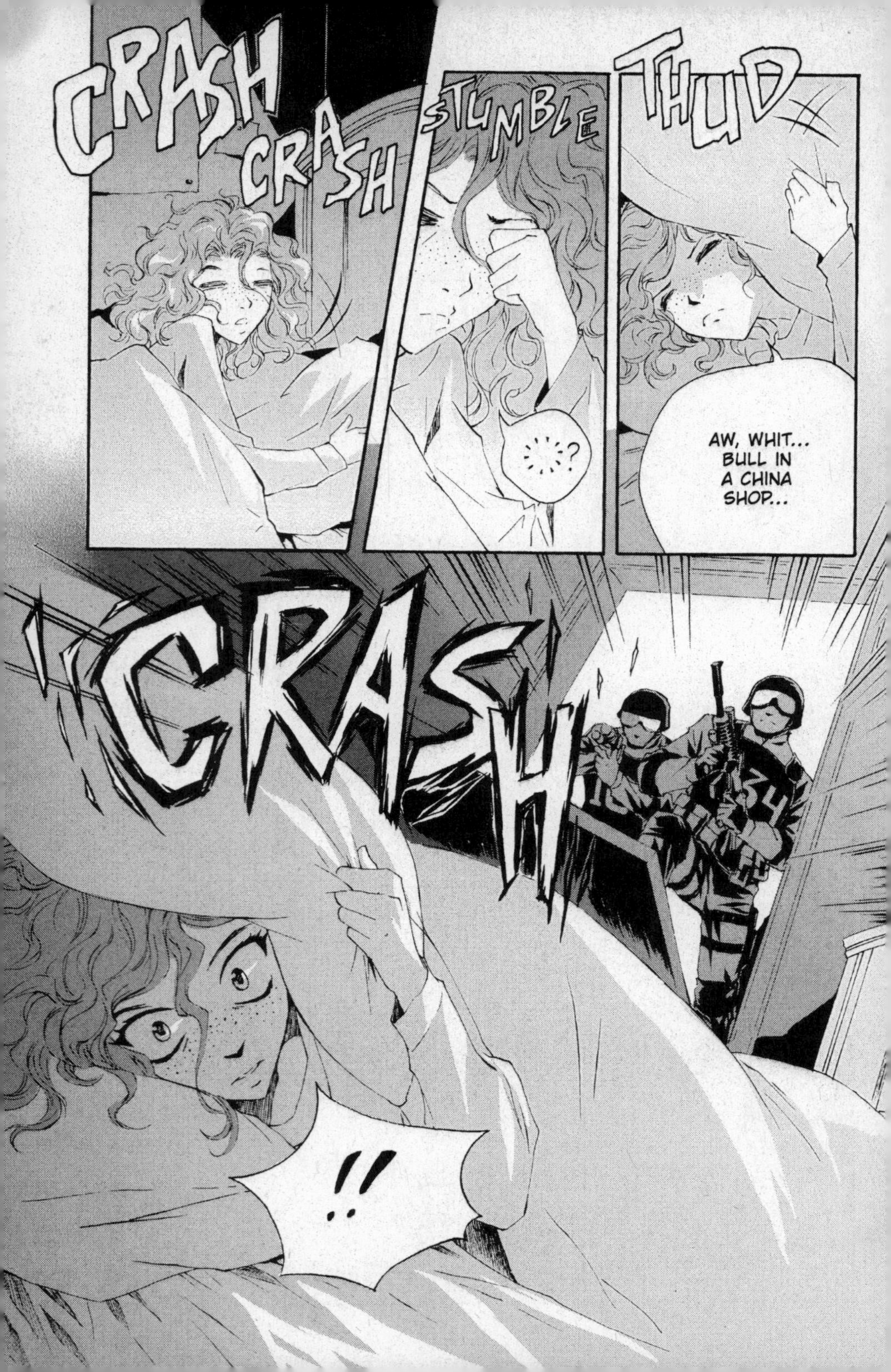
CRASH
CRASH
STUMBLE
THUD
...?
AW, WHIT... BULL IN A CHINA SHOP...
CRASH
!!

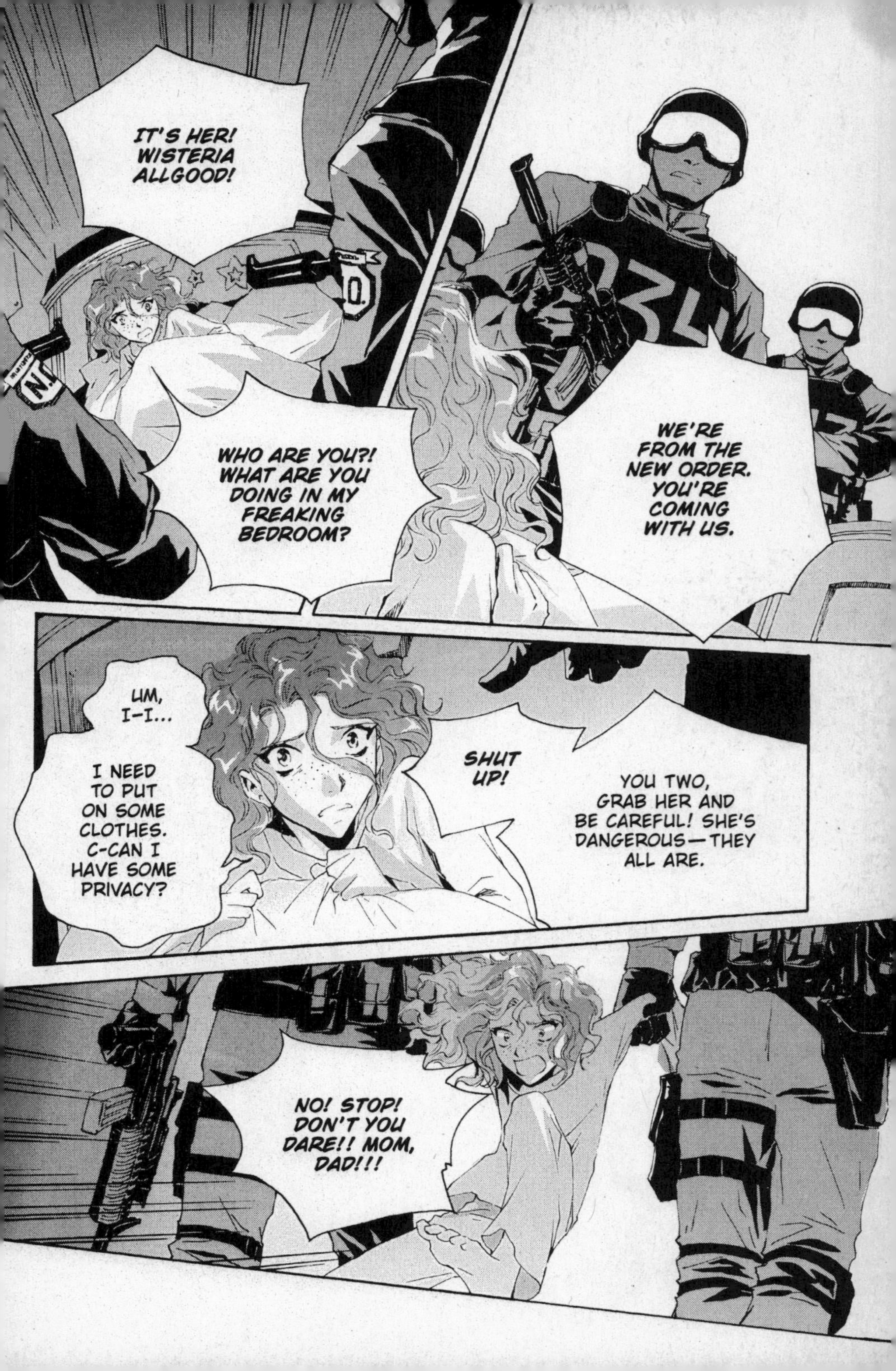

IT'S HER! WISTERIA ALLGOOD!
WHO ARE YOU?! WHAT ARE YOU DOING IN MY FREAKING BEDROOM?
WE'RE FROM THE NEW ORDER. YOU'RE COMING WITH US.
UM, I-I...
I NEED TO PUT ON SOME CLOTHES. C-CAN I HAVE SOME PRIVACY?
SHUT UP!
YOU TWO, GRAB HER AND BE CAREFUL! SHE'S DANGEROUS—THEY ALL ARE.
NO! STOP! DON'T YOU DARE!! MOM, DAD!!!

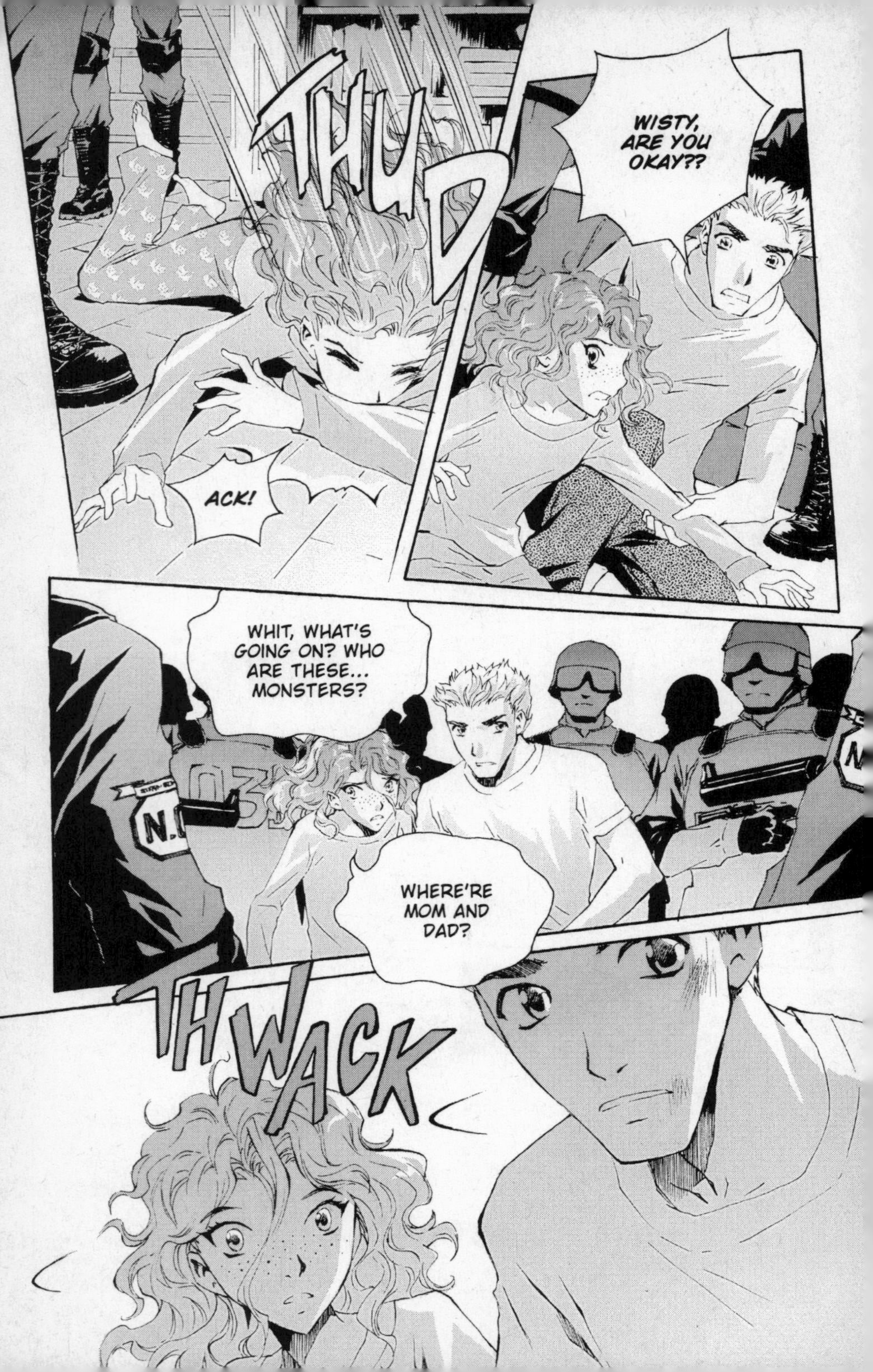
THUD
ACK!
WISTY, ARE YOU OKAY??
WHIT, WHAT'S GOING ON? WHO ARE THESE... MONSTERS?
WHERE'RE MOM AND DAD?
THWACK

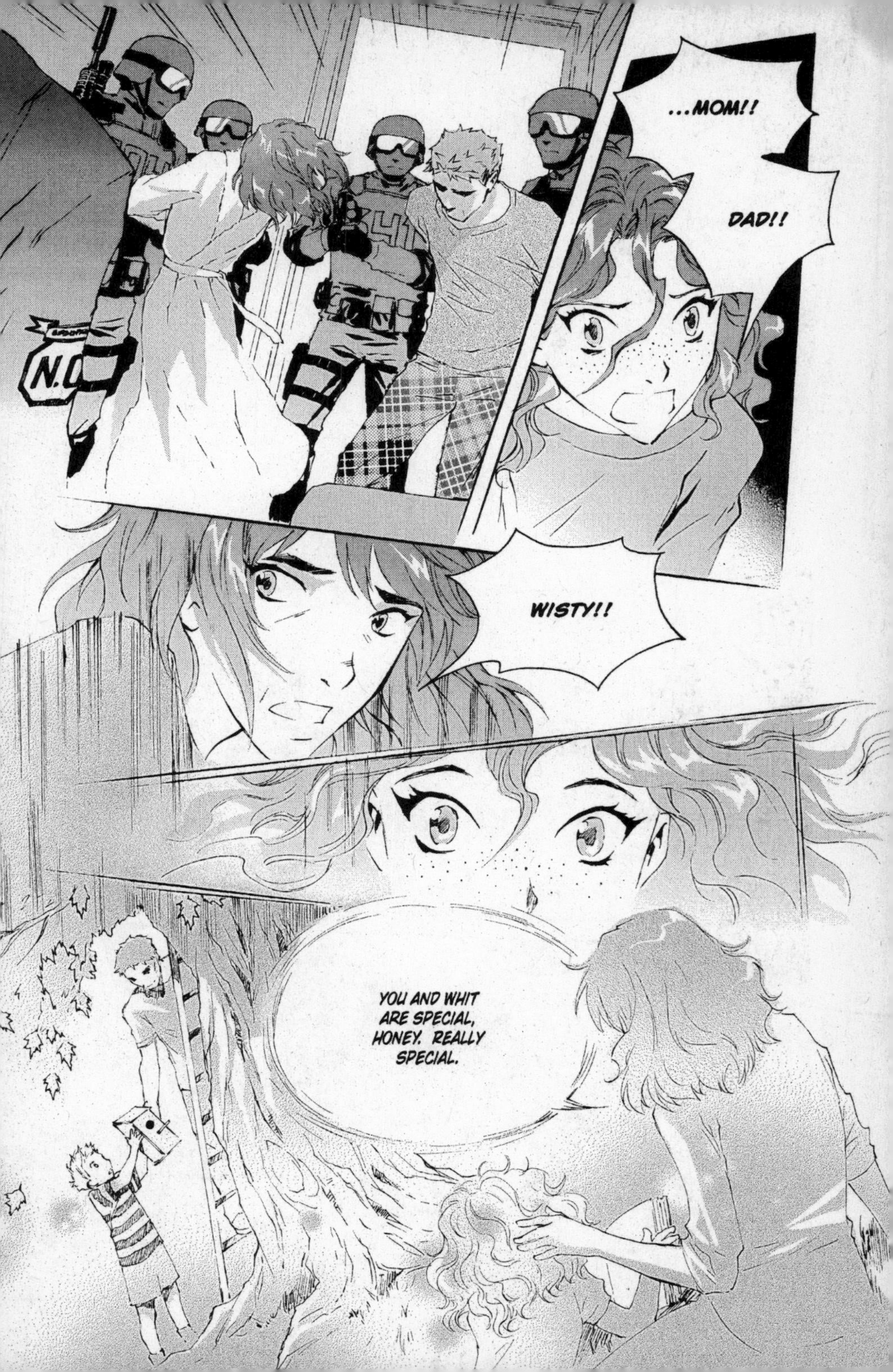
...MOM!!
DAD!!
WISTY!!
YOU AND WHIT ARE SPECIAL, HONEY. REALLY SPECIAL.

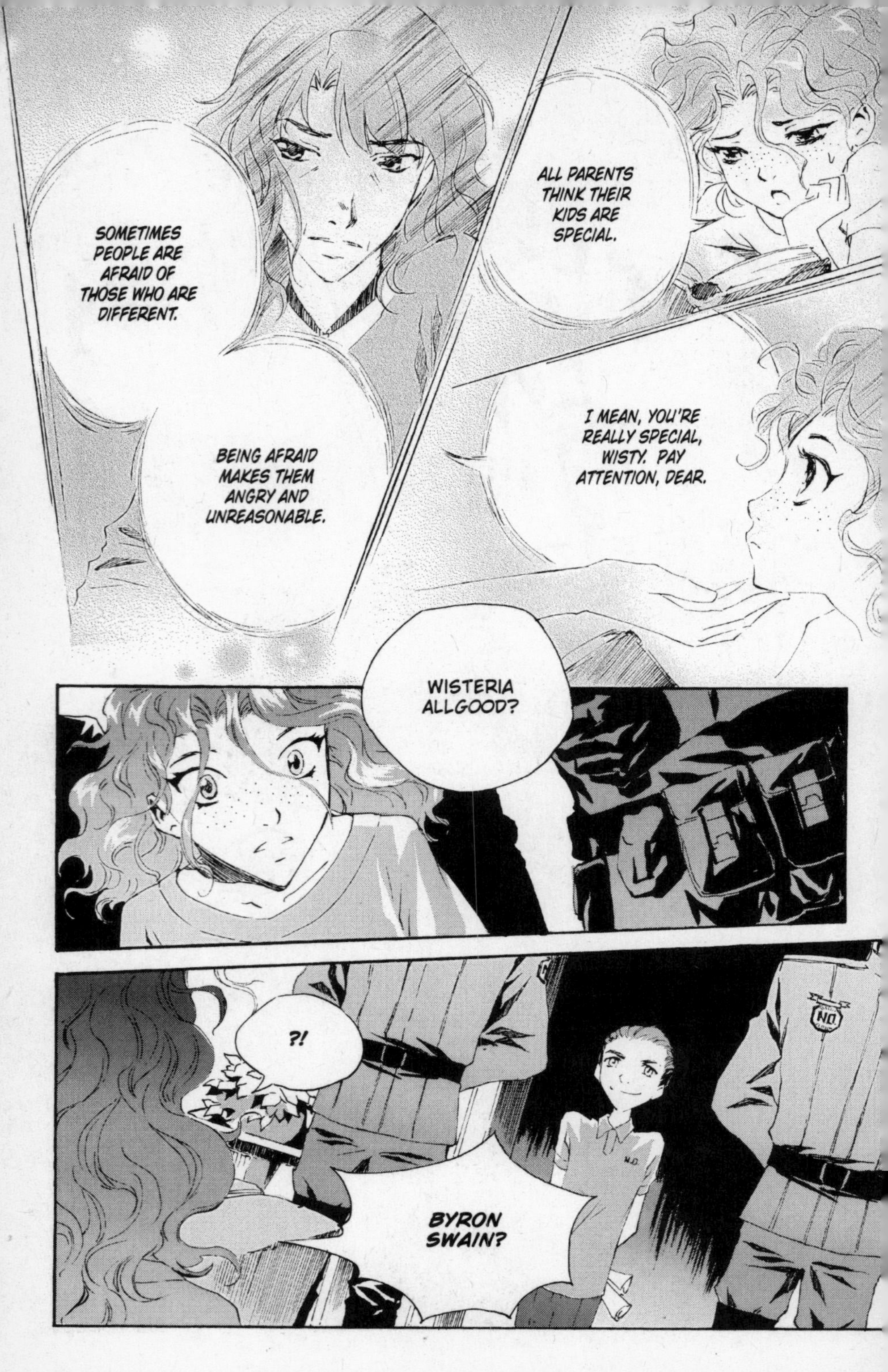
SOMETIMES PEOPLE ARE AFRAID OF THOSE WHO ARE DIFFERENT.
BEING AFRAID MAKES THEM ANGRY AND UNREASONABLE.
ALL PARENTS THINK THEIR KIDS ARE SPECIAL.
I MEAN, YOU'RE REALLY SPECIAL, WISTY. PAY ATTENTION, DEAR.
WISTERIA ALLGOOD?
?!
BYRON SWAIN?

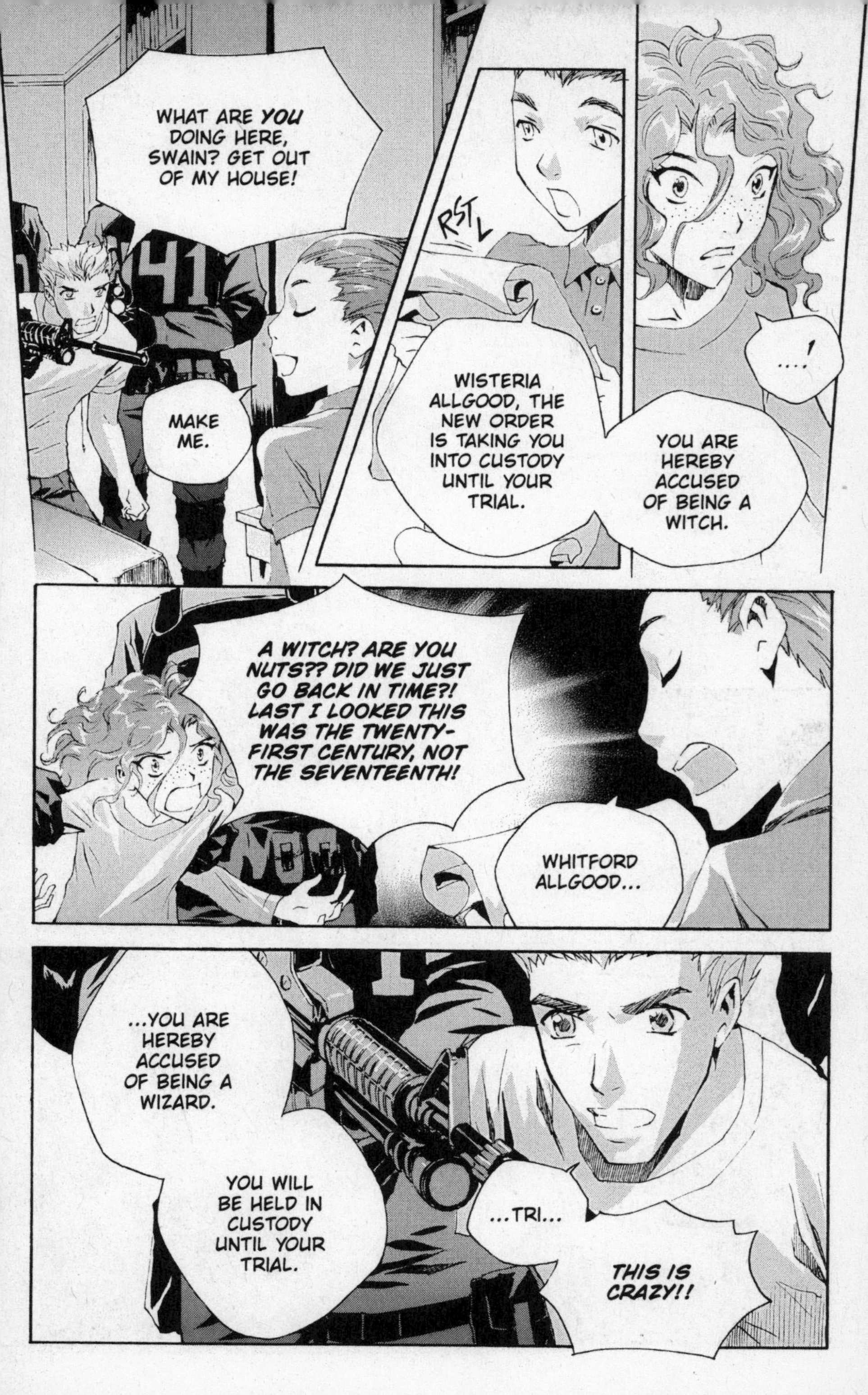
WHAT ARE YOU DOING HERE, SWAIN? GET OUT OF MY HOUSE!
MAKE ME.
RSTL
WISTERIA ALLGOOD, THE NEW ORDER IS TAKING YOU INTO CUSTODY UNTIL YOUR TRIAL.
....!
YOU ARE HEREBY ACCUSED OF BEING A WITCH.
A WITCH? ARE YOU NUTS?? DID WE JUST GO BACK IN TIME?! LAST I LOOKED THIS WAS THE TWENTY-FIRST CENTURY, NOT THE SEVENTEENTH!
WHITFORD ALLGOOD...
...YOU ARE HEREBY ACCUSED OF BEING A WIZARD.
YOU WILL BE HELD IN CUSTODY UNTIL YOUR TRIAL.
...TRI...
THIS IS CRAZY!!

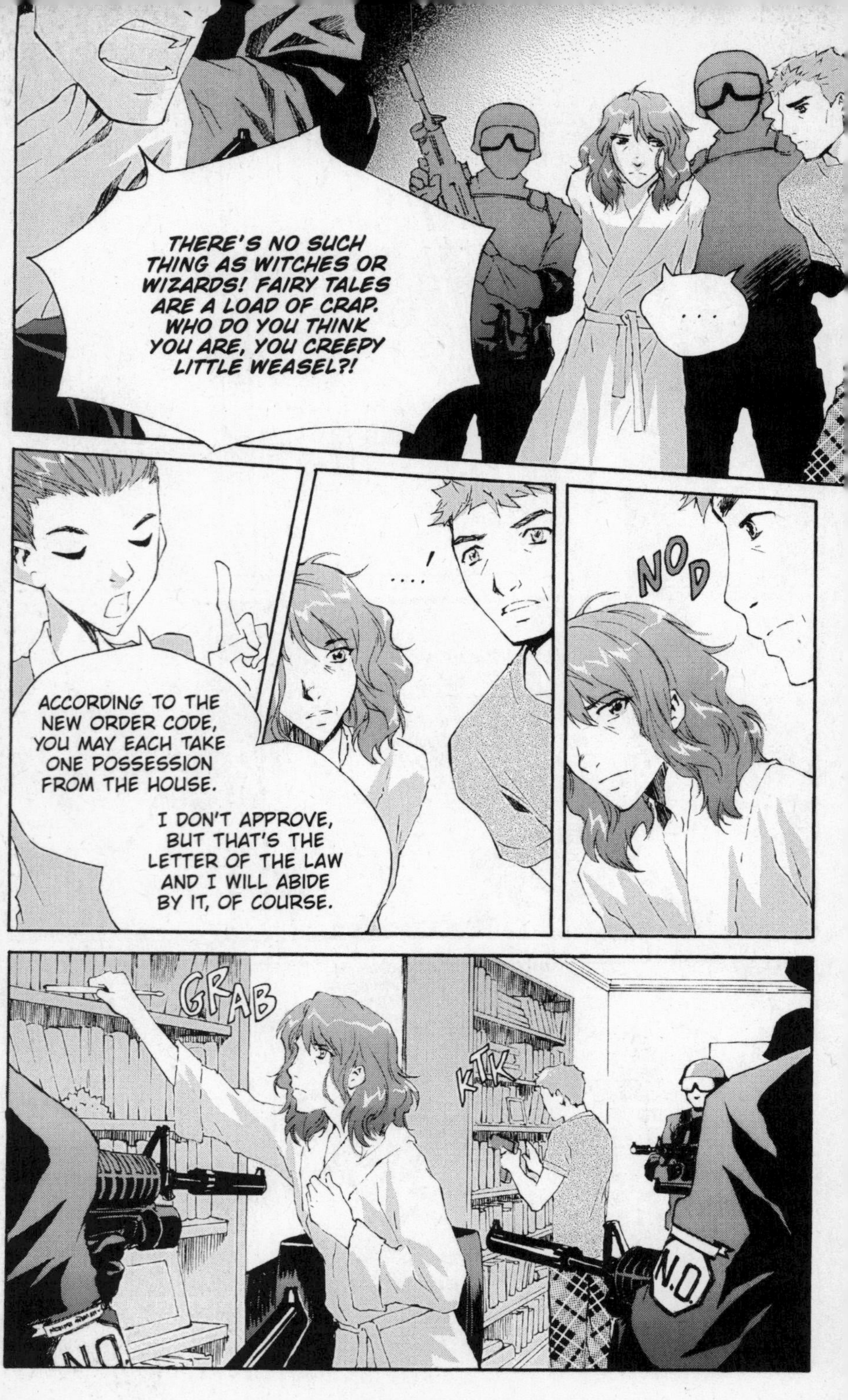
THERE'S NO SUCH THING AS WITCHES OR WIZARDS! FAIRY TALES ARE A LOAD OF CRAP. WHO DO YOU THINK YOU ARE, YOU CREEPY LITTLE WEASEL?!
...
ACCORDING TO THE NEW ORDER CODE, YOU MAY EACH TAKE ONE POSSESSION FROM THE HOUSE.
I DON'T APPROVE, BUT THAT'S THE LETTER OF THE LAW AND I WILL ABIDE BY IT, OF COURSE.
....!
NOD
GRAB
KTIK
N.O.
N.O.

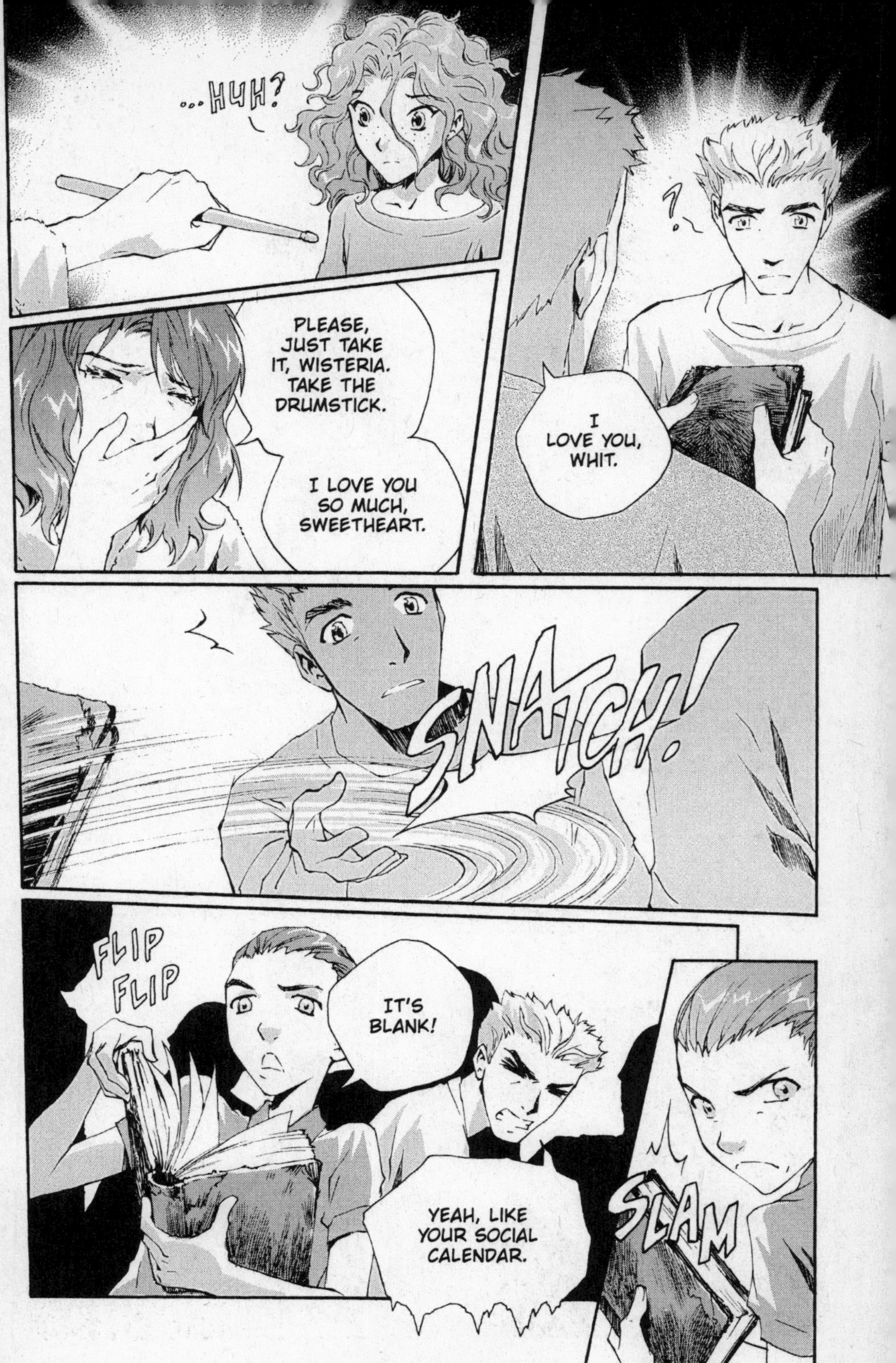
...HUH?
PLEASE, JUST TAKE IT, WISTERIA. TAKE THE DRUMSTICK.
I LOVE YOU SO MUCH, SWEETHEART.
?
I LOVE YOU, WHIT.
SNATCH!
FLIP FLIP
IT'S BLANK!
YEAH, LIKE YOUR SOCIAL CALENDAR.
SLAM

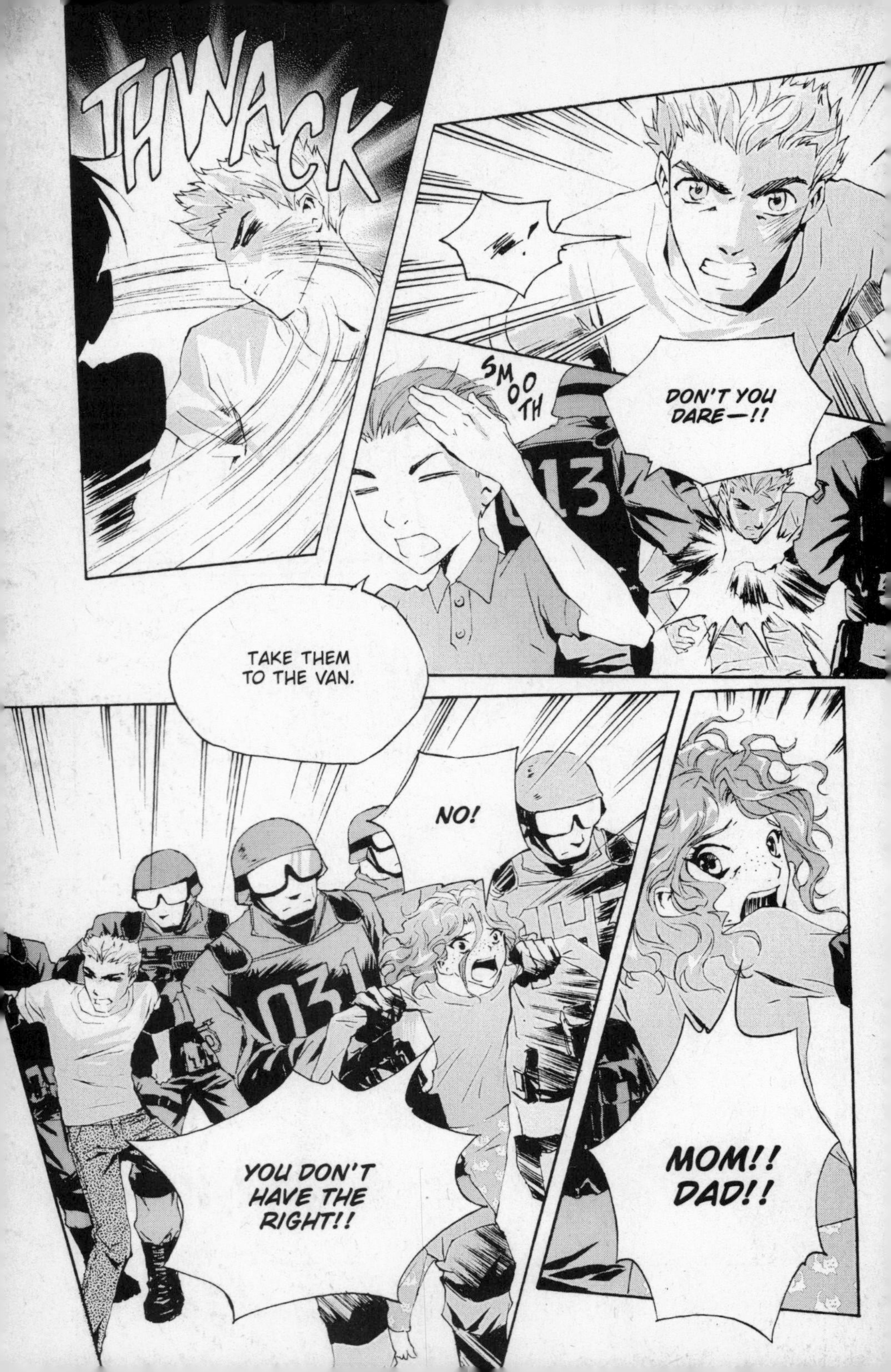
THWACK
-!
SMOOTH
DON'T YOU DARE—!!
TAKE THEM TO THE VAN.
NO!
YOU DON'T HAVE THE RIGHT!!
MOM!! DAD!!

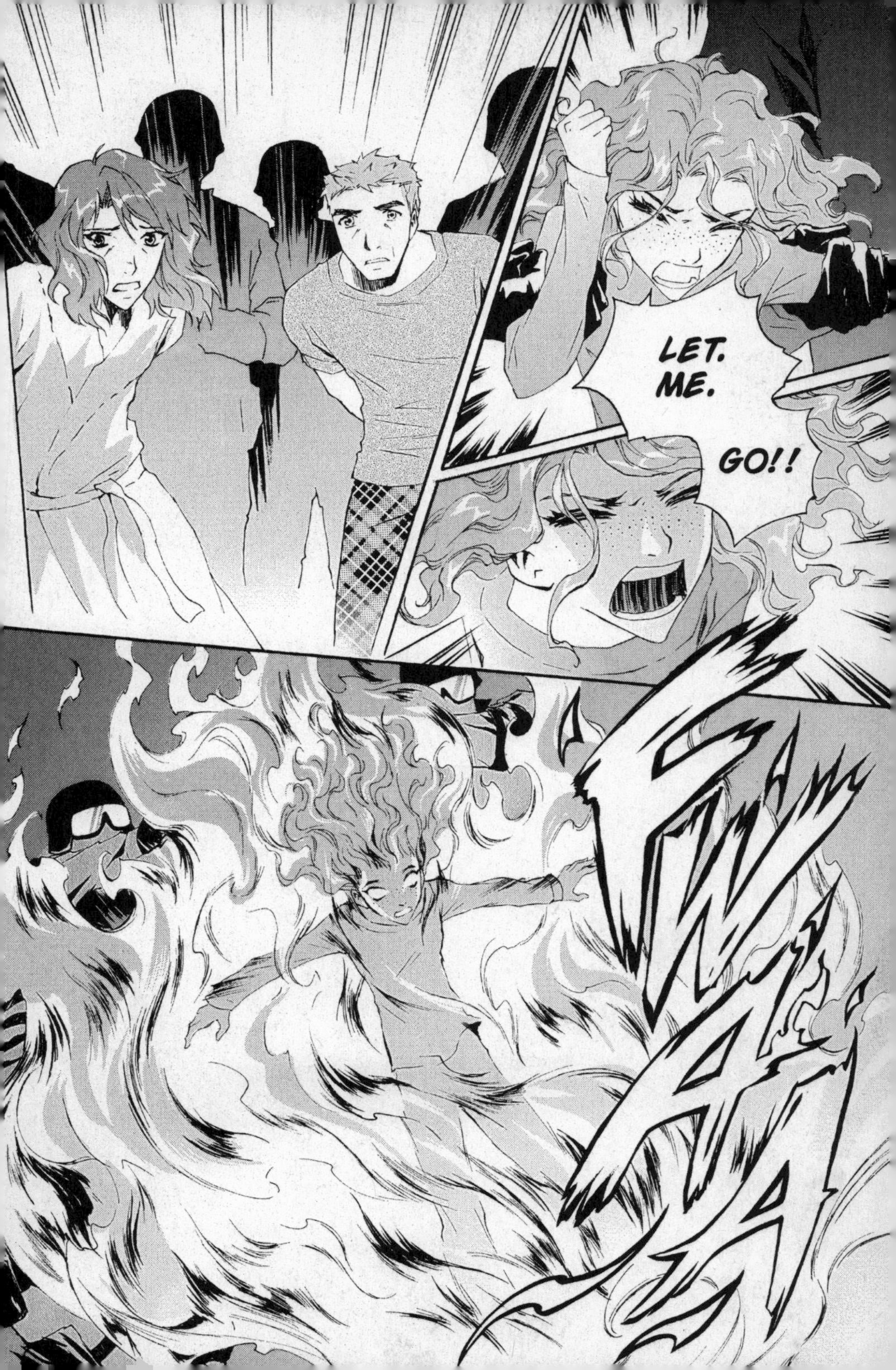
LET. ME.
GO!!

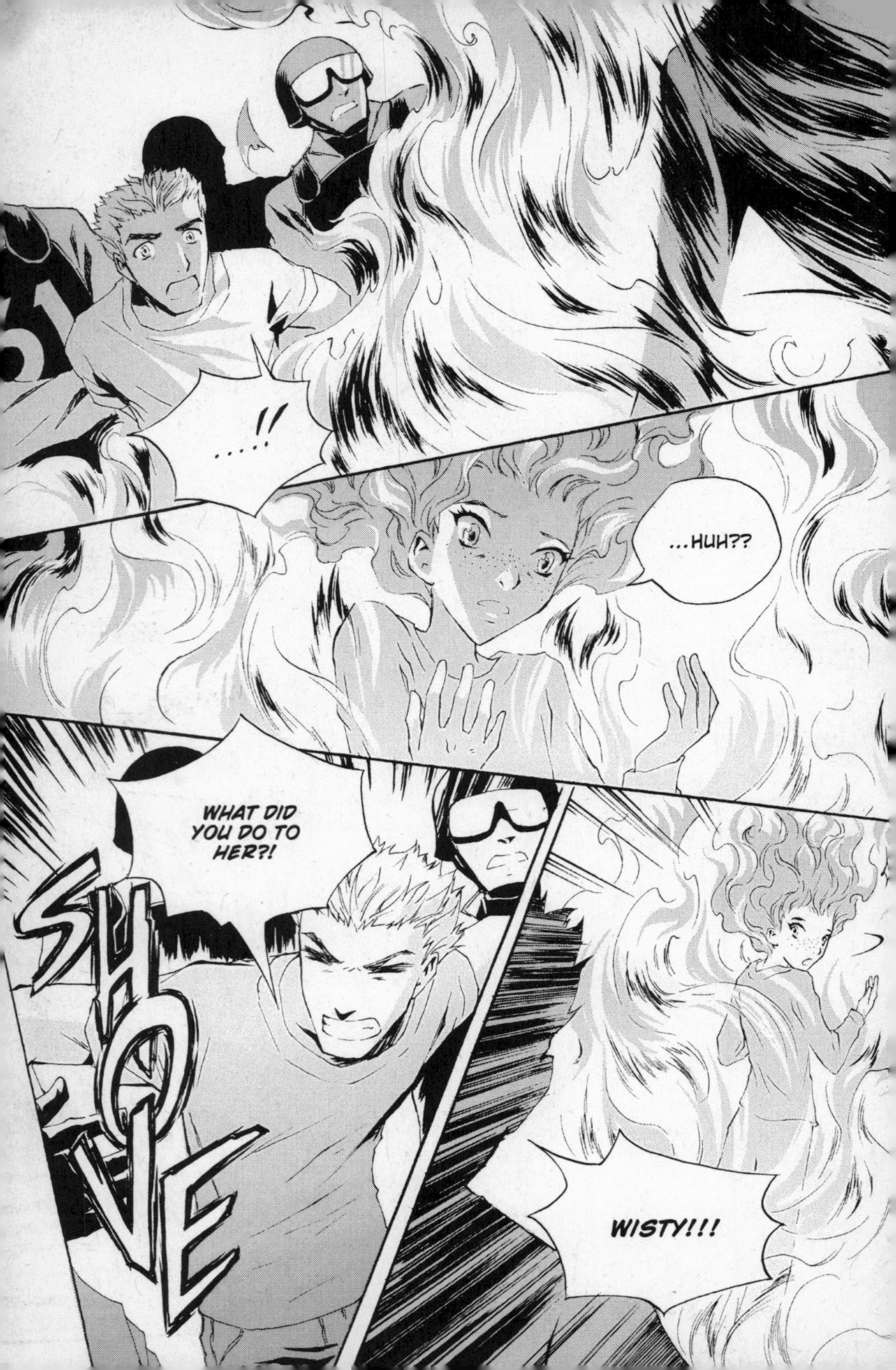

....!!
...HUH??
WHAT DID YOU DO TO HER?!
SHOVE
WISTY!!!

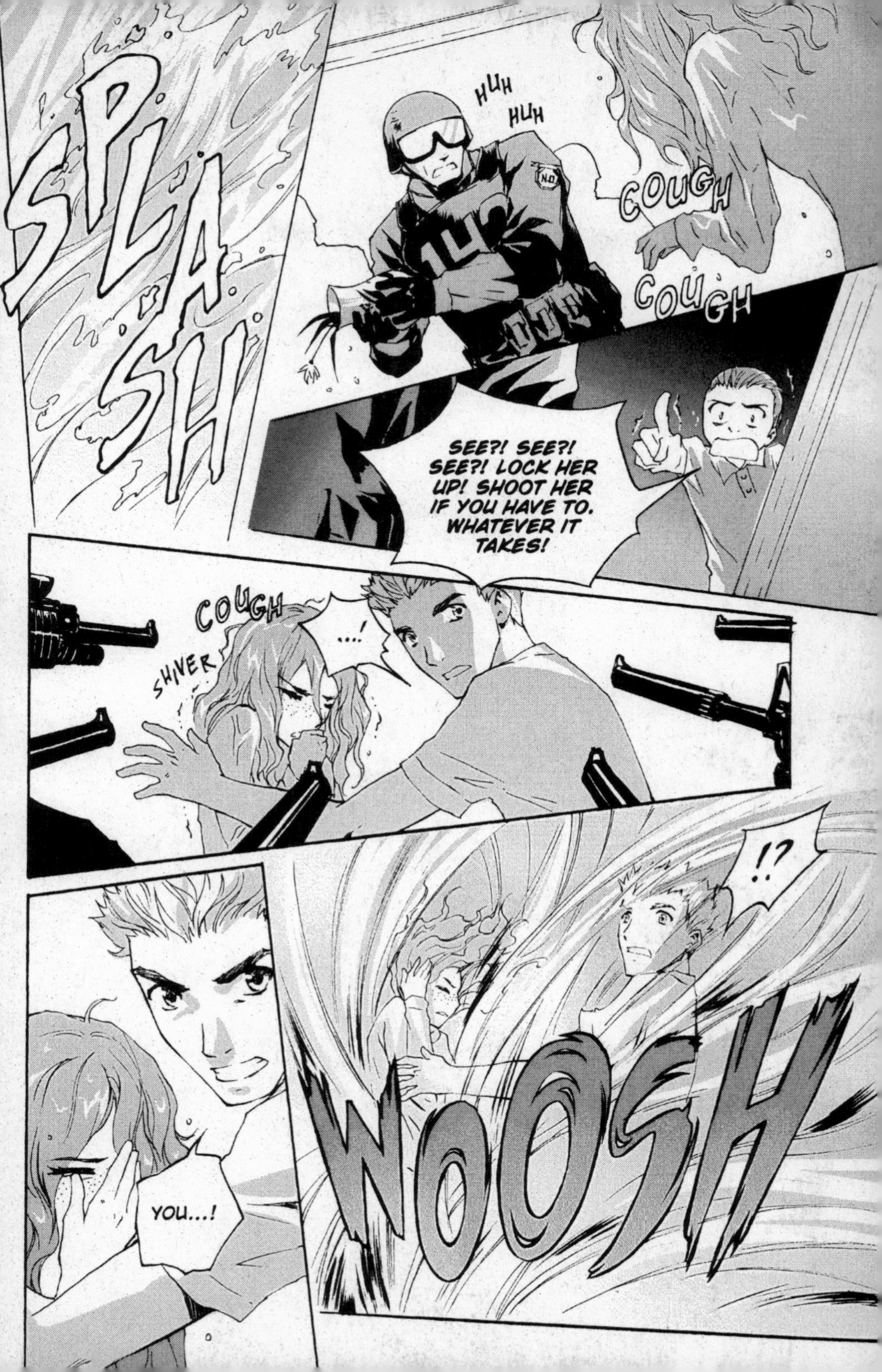
SPLASH
HUH
HUH
COUGH
COUGH
SEE?! SEE?! SEE?! LOCK HER UP! SHOOT HER IF YOU HAVE TO. WHATEVER IT TAKES!
COUGH
SHIVER
...!
YOU...!
!?
WOOSH

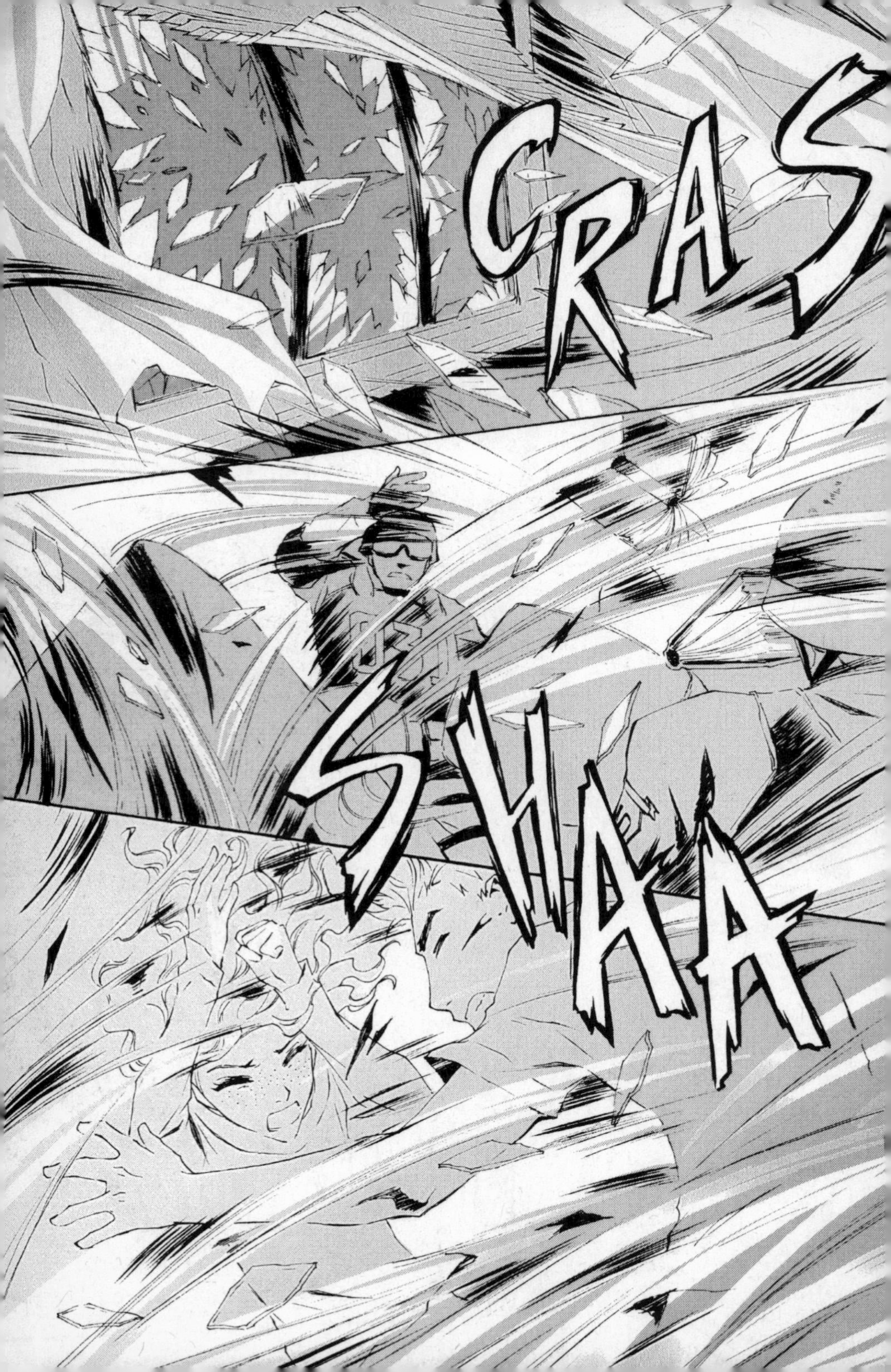
CRAS
SHAA

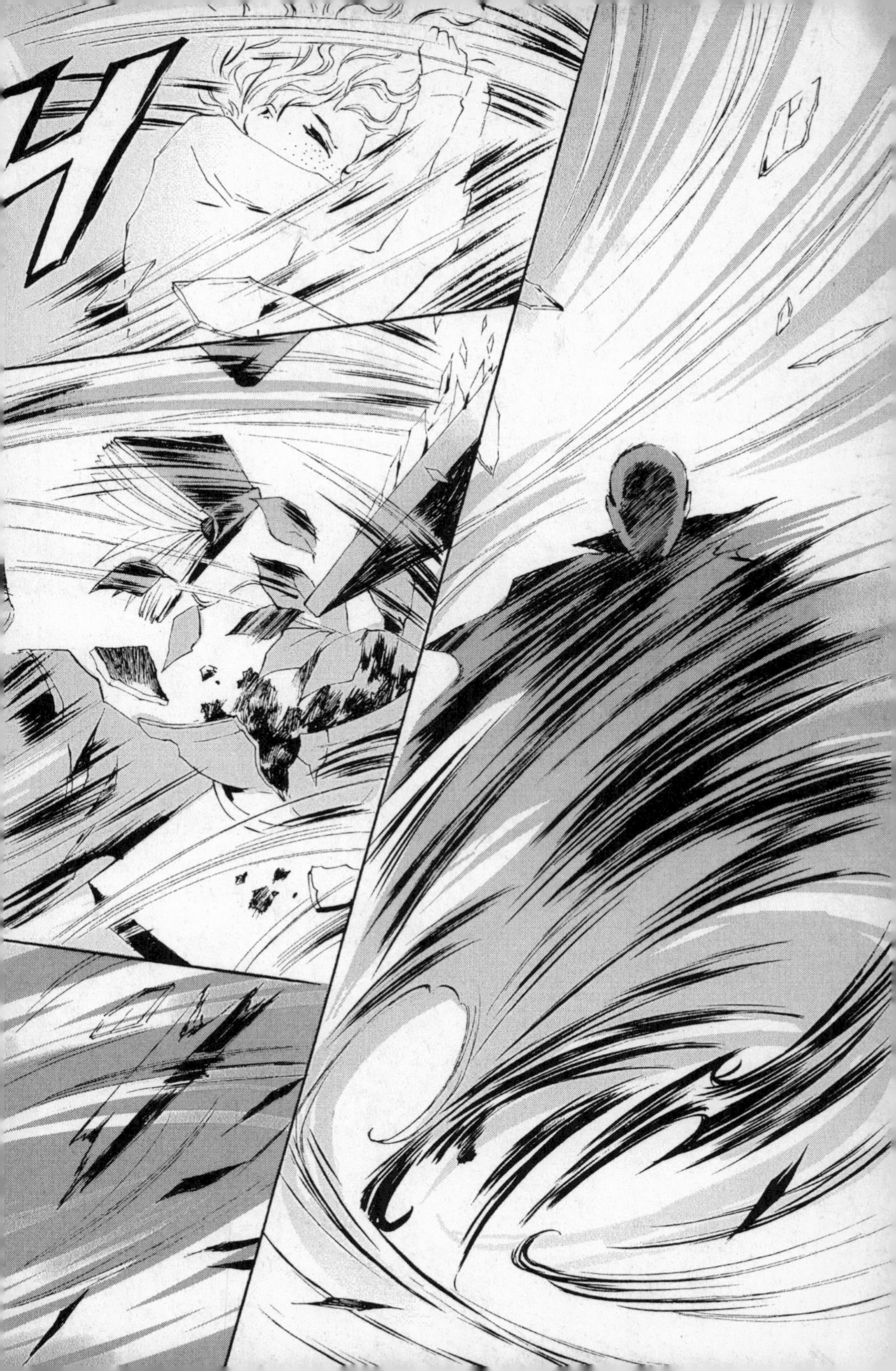

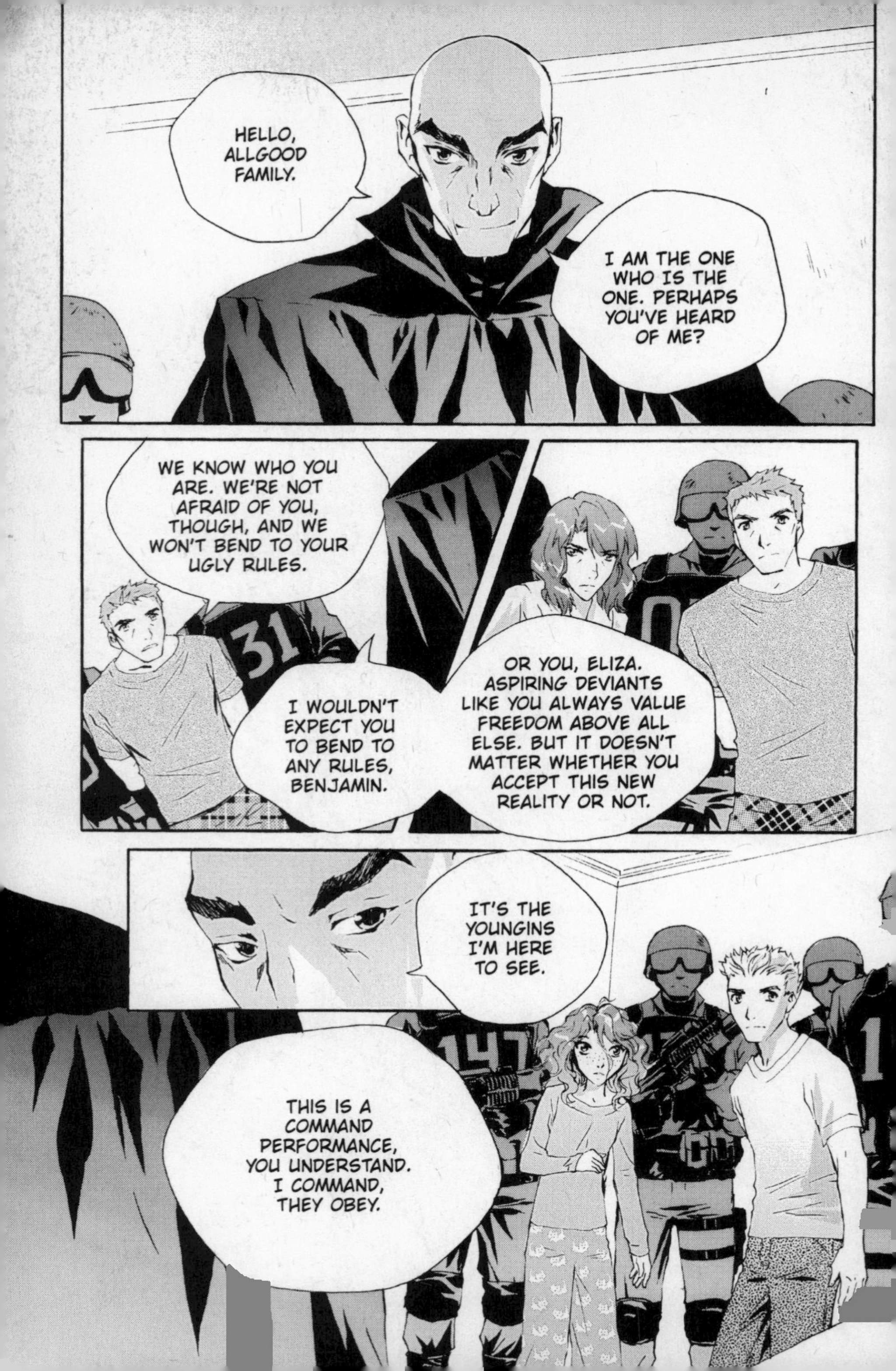
HELLO, ALLGOOD FAMILY.
I AM THE ONE WHO IS THE ONE. PERHAPS YOU'VE HEARD OF ME?
WE KNOW WHO YOU ARE. WE'RE NOT AFRAID OF YOU, THOUGH, AND WE WON'T BEND TO YOUR UGLY RULES.
I WOULDN'T EXPECT YOU TO BEND TO ANY RULES, BENJAMIN.
OR YOU, ELIZA. ASPIRING DEVIANTS LIKE YOU ALWAYS VALUE FREEDOM ABOVE ALL ELSE. BUT IT DOESN'T MATTER WHETHER YOU ACCEPT THIS NEW REALITY OR NOT.
IT'S THE YOUNGINS I'M HERE TO SEE.
THIS IS A COMMAND PERFORMANCE, YOU UNDERSTAND. I COMMAND, THEY OBEY.

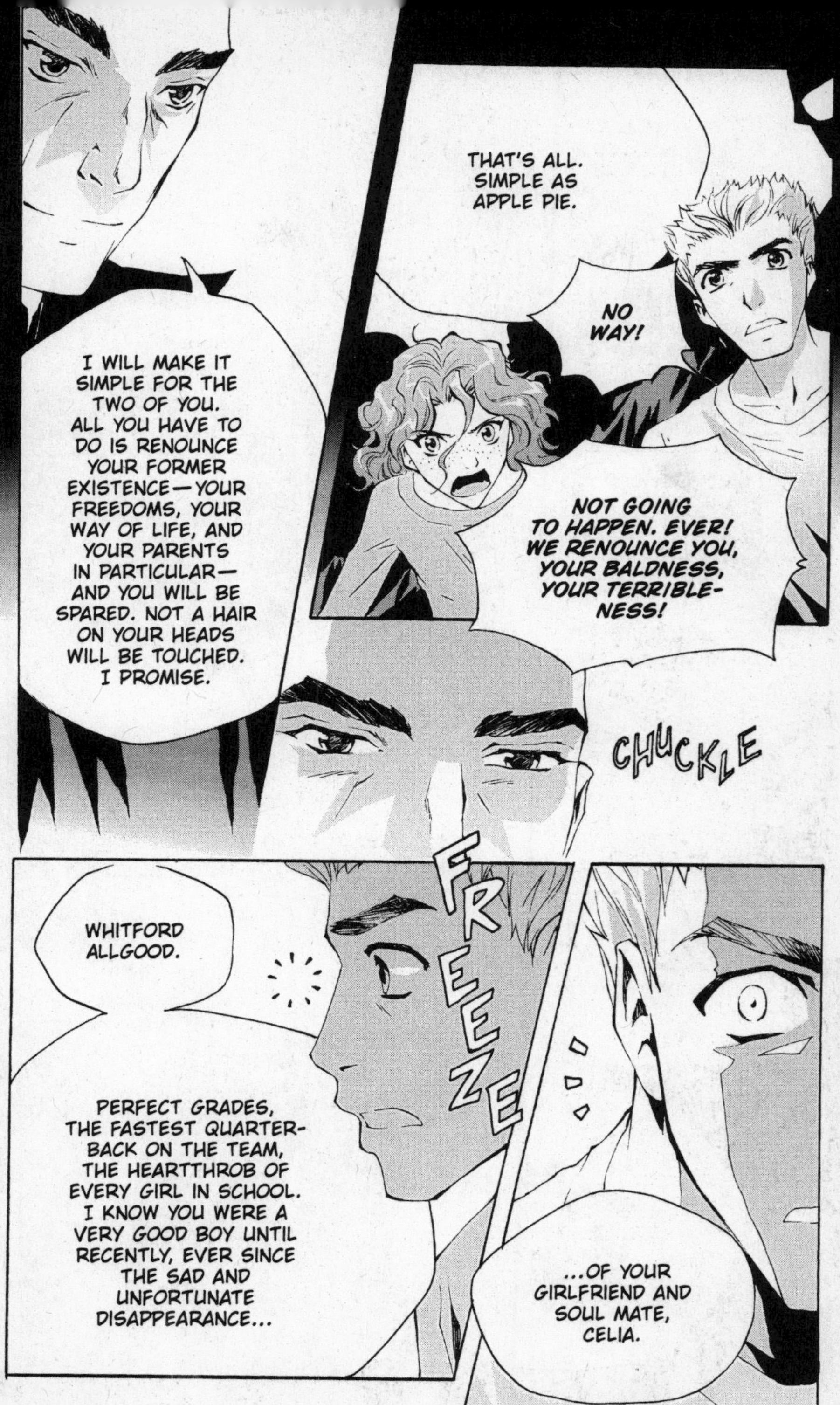
I WILL MAKE IT SIMPLE FOR THE TWO OF YOU. ALL YOU HAVE TO DO IS RENOUNCE YOUR FORMER EXISTENCE—YOUR FREEDOMS, YOUR WAY OF LIFE, AND YOUR PARENTS IN PARTICULAR—AND YOU WILL BE SPARED. NOT A HAIR ON YOUR HEADS WILL BE TOUCHED. I PROMISE.
THAT'S ALL. SIMPLE AS APPLE PIE.
NO WAY!
NOT GOING TO HAPPEN. EVER! WE RENOUNCE YOU, YOUR BALDNESS, YOUR TERRIBLE-NESS!
CHUCKLE
WHITFORD ALLGOOD.
PERFECT GRADES, THE FASTEST QUARTER-BACK ON THE TEAM, THE HEARTTHROB OF EVERY GIRL IN SCHOOL. I KNOW YOU WERE A VERY GOOD BOY UNTIL RECENTLY, EVER SINCE THE SAD AND UNFORTUNATE DISAPPEARANCE...
FREEZE
...OF YOUR GIRLFRIEND AND SOUL MATE, CELIA.

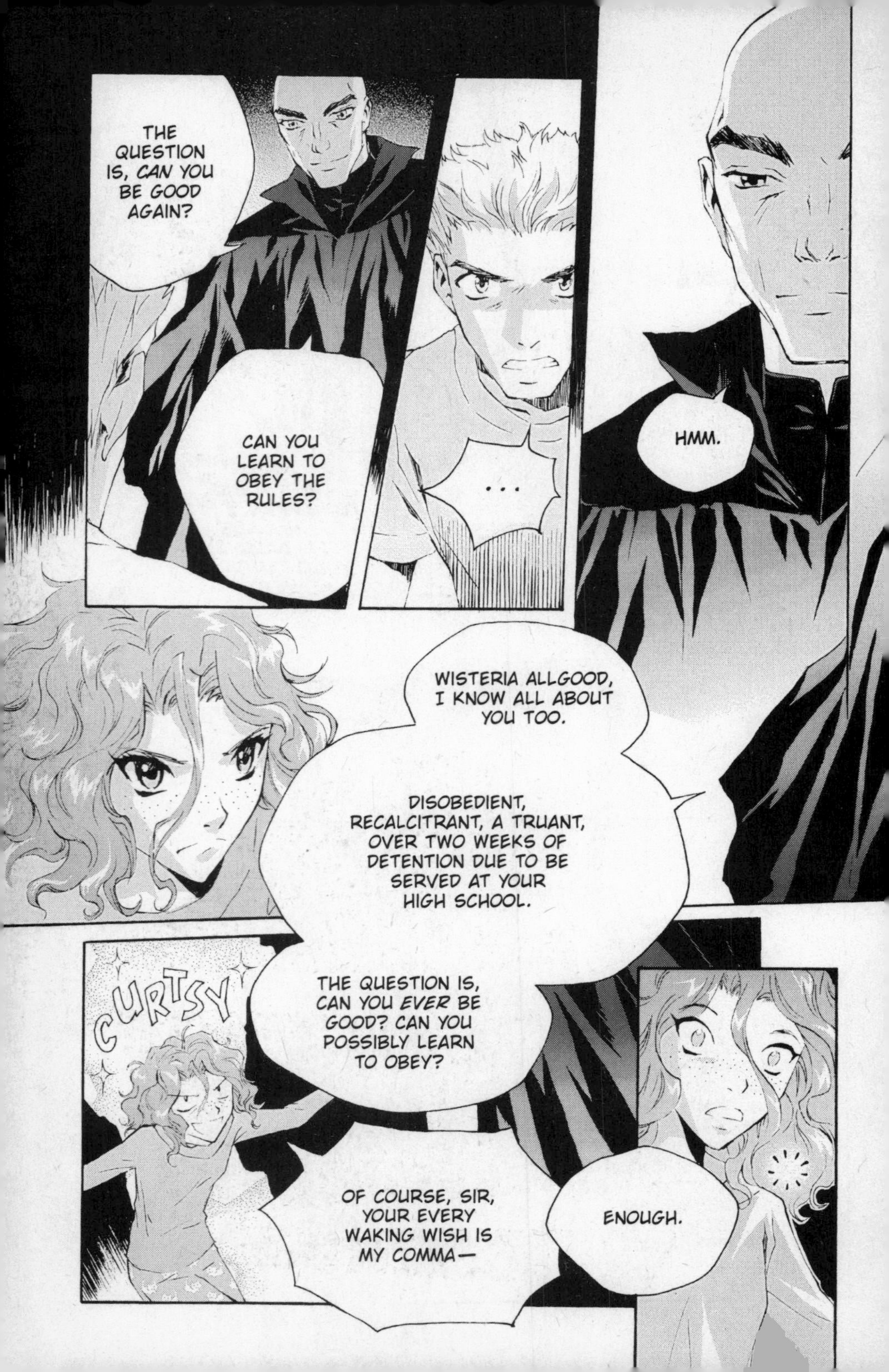
THE QUESTION IS, CAN YOU BE GOOD AGAIN?
CAN YOU LEARN TO OBEY THE RULES?
...
HMM.
WISTERIA ALLGOOD, I KNOW ALL ABOUT YOU TOO.
DISOBEDIENT, RECALCITRANT, A TRUANT, OVER TWO WEEKS OF DETENTION DUE TO BE SERVED AT YOUR HIGH SCHOOL.
THE QUESTION IS, CAN YOU EVER BE GOOD? CAN YOU POSSIBLY LEARN TO OBEY?
CURTSY
OF COURSE, SIR, YOUR EVERY WAKING WISH IS MY COMMA—
ENOUGH.

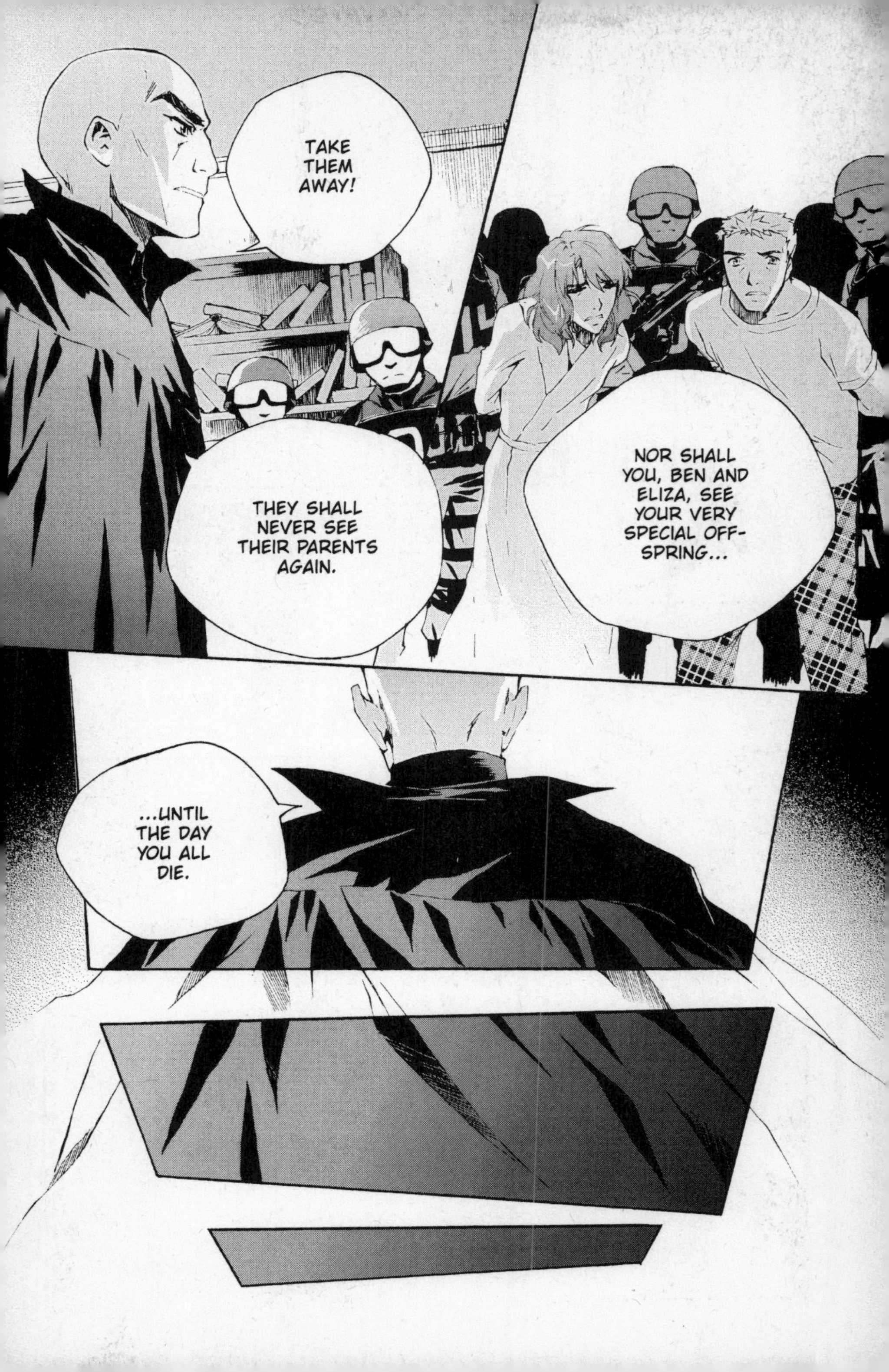
TAKE THEM AWAY!
THEY SHALL NEVER SEE THEIR PARENTS AGAIN.
NOR SHALL YOU, BEN AND ELIZA, SEE YOUR VERY SPECIAL OFF-SPRING...
...UNTIL THE DAY YOU ALL DIE.

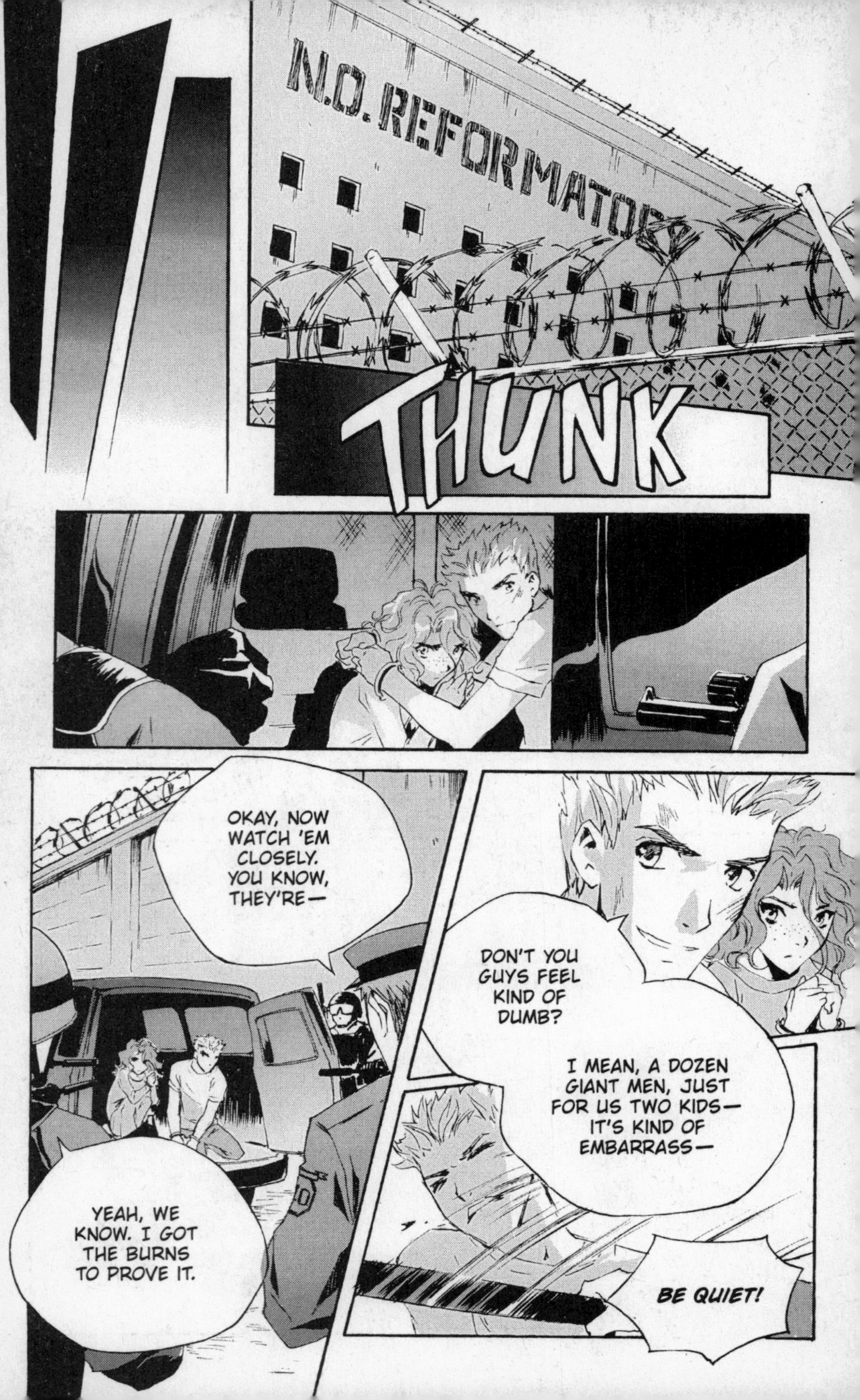

N.O. REFORMATOR
THUNK
OKAY, NOW WATCH 'EM CLOSELY. YOU KNOW, THEY'RE—
YEAH, WE KNOW. I GOT THE BURNS TO PROVE IT.
DON'T YOU GUYS FEEL KIND OF DUMB?
I MEAN, A DOZEN GIANT MEN, JUST FOR US TWO KIDS— IT'S KIND OF EMBARRASS—
BE QUIET!

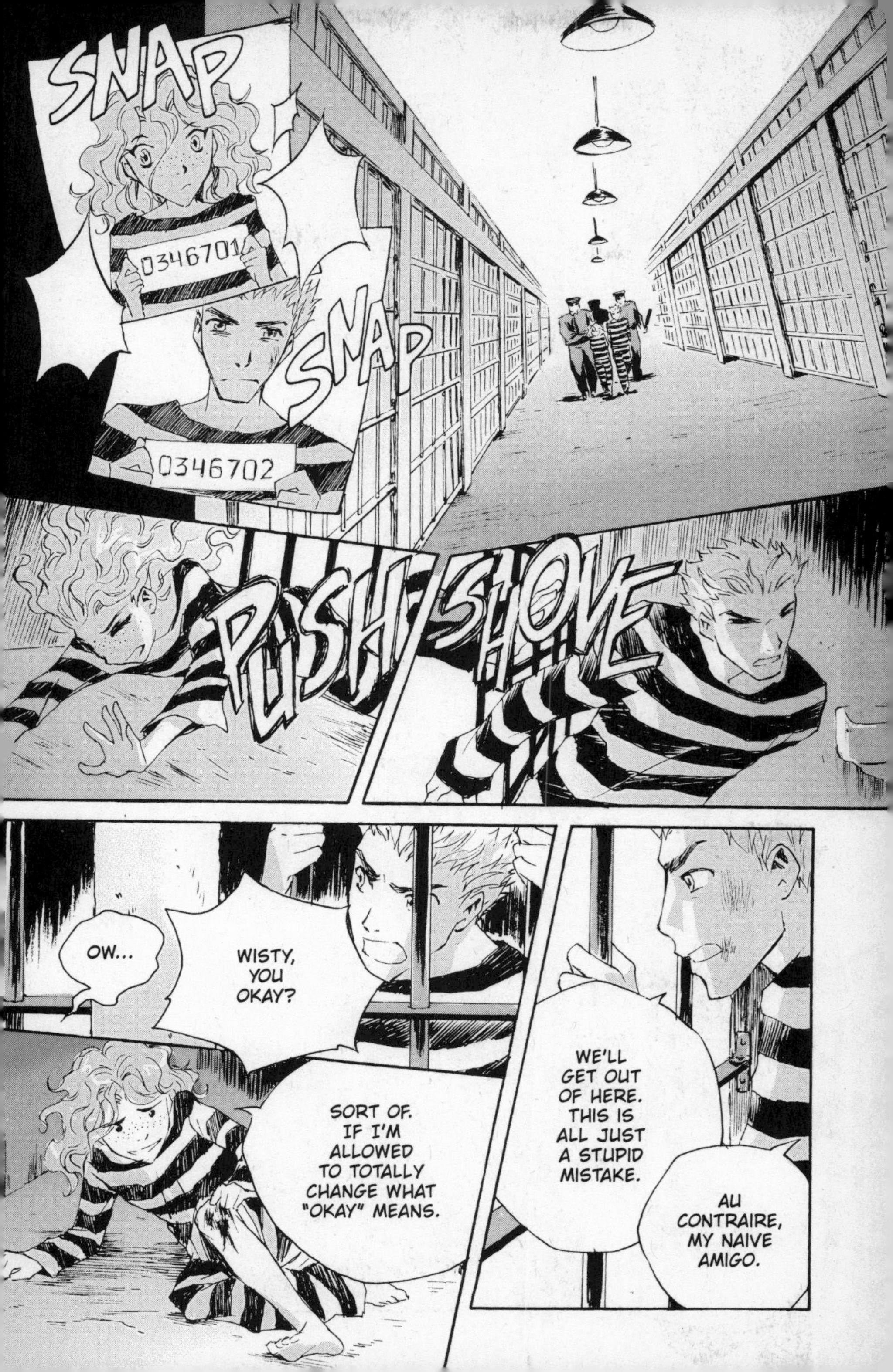
SNAP
0346701
SNAP
0346702
PUSH
SHOVE
OW...
WISTY, YOU OKAY?
SORT OF. IF I'M ALLOWED TO TOTALLY CHANGE WHAT "OKAY" MEANS.
WE'LL GET OUT OF HERE. THIS IS ALL JUST A STUPID MISTAKE.
AU CONTRAIRE, MY NAIVE AMIGO.

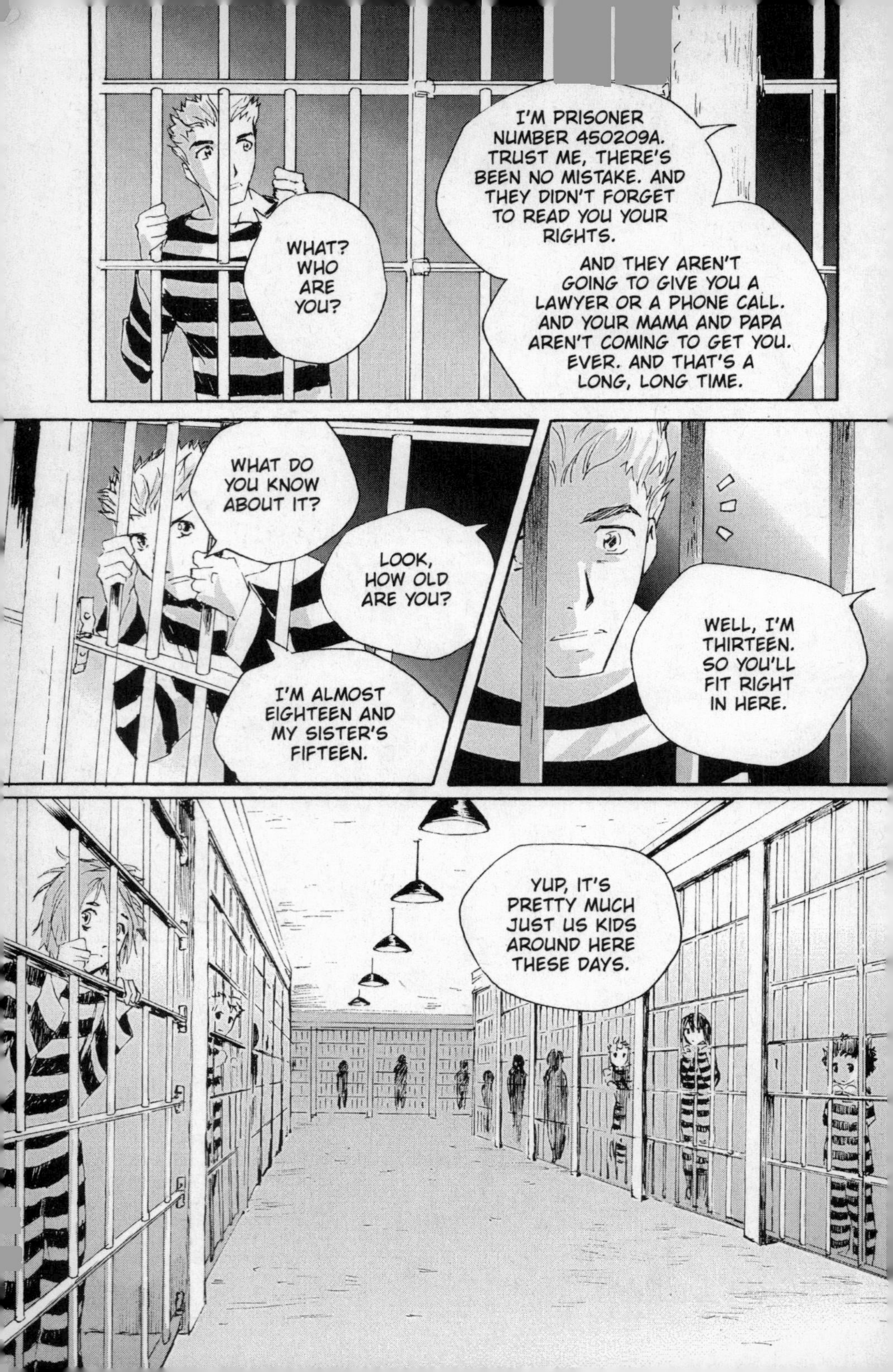
WHAT? WHO ARE YOU?
I'M PRISONER NUMBER 450209A. TRUST ME, THERE'S BEEN NO MISTAKE. AND THEY DIDN'T FORGET TO READ YOU YOUR RIGHTS.
AND THEY AREN'T GOING TO GIVE YOU A LAWYER OR A PHONE CALL. AND YOUR MAMA AND PAPA AREN'T COMING TO GET YOU. EVER. AND THAT'S A LONG, LONG TIME.
WHAT DO YOU KNOW ABOUT IT?
LOOK, HOW OLD ARE YOU?
I'M ALMOST EIGHTEEN AND MY SISTER'S FIFTEEN.
WELL, I'M THIRTEEN. SO YOU'LL FIT RIGHT IN HERE.
YUP, IT'S PRETTY MUCH JUST US KIDS AROUND HERE THESE DAYS.

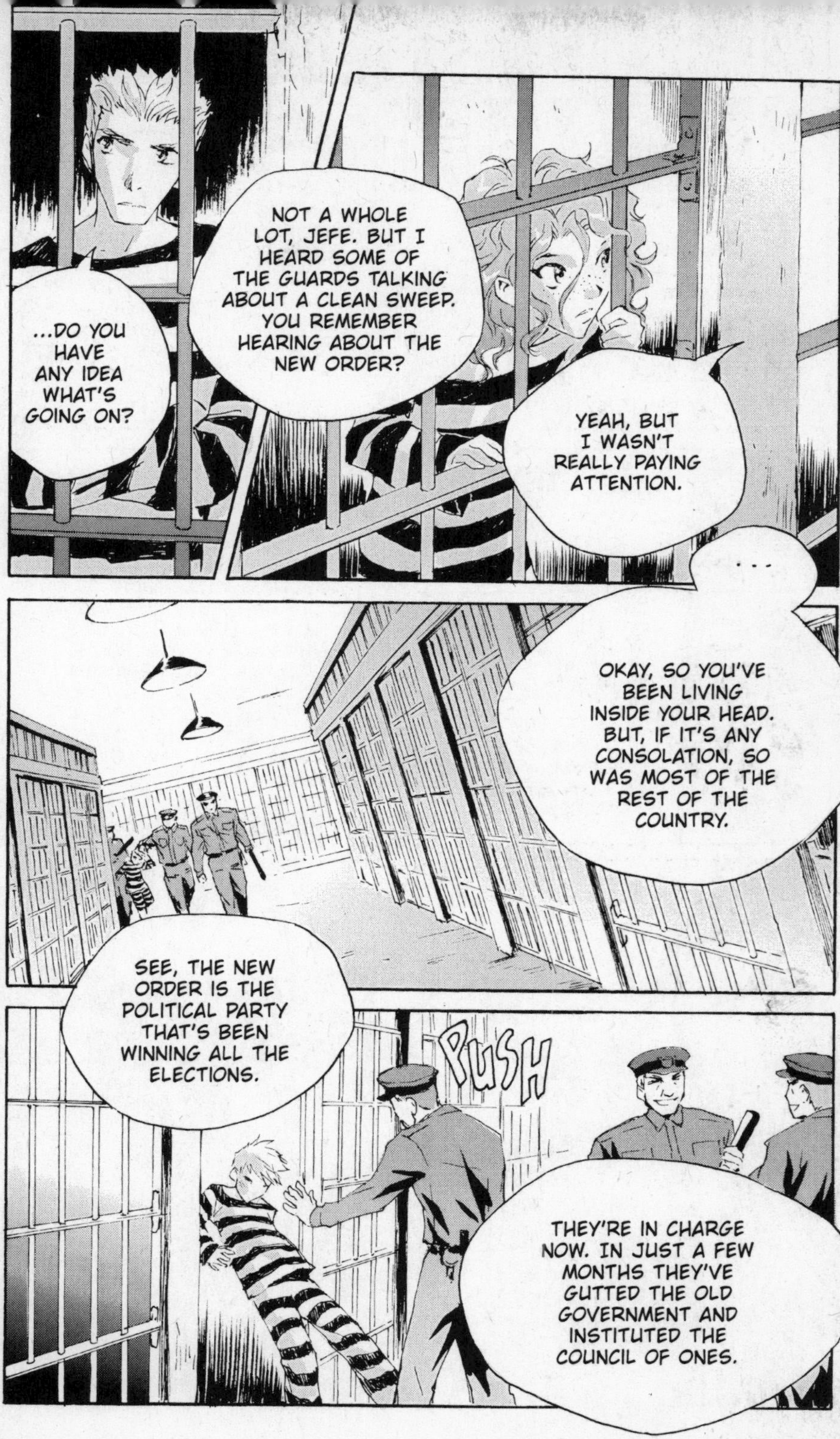
...DO YOU HAVE ANY IDEA WHAT'S GOING ON?
NOT A WHOLE LOT, JEFE. BUT I HEARD SOME OF THE GUARDS TALKING ABOUT A CLEAN SWEEP. YOU REMEMBER HEARING ABOUT THE NEW ORDER?
YEAH, BUT I WASN'T REALLY PAYING ATTENTION.
...
OKAY, SO YOU'VE BEEN LIVING INSIDE YOUR HEAD. BUT, IF IT'S ANY CONSOLATION, SO WAS MOST OF THE REST OF THE COUNTRY.
SEE, THE NEW ORDER IS THE POLITICAL PARTY THAT'S BEEN WINNING ALL THE ELECTIONS.
PUSH
THEY'RE IN CHARGE NOW. IN JUST A FEW MONTHS THEY'VE GUTTED THE OLD GOVERNMENT AND INSTITUTED THE COUNCIL OF ONES.

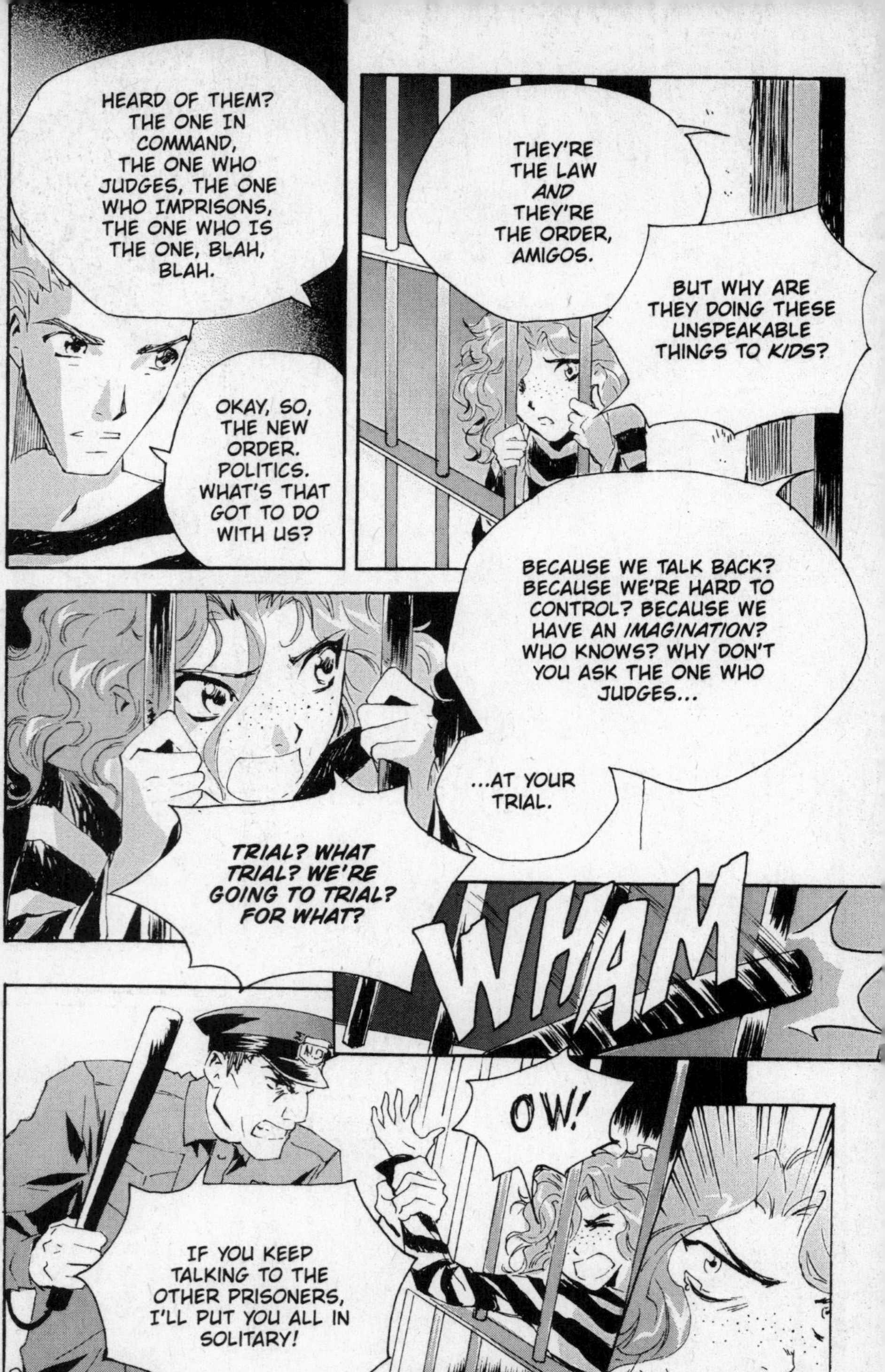
HEARD OF THEM? THE ONE IN COMMAND, THE ONE WHO JUDGES, THE ONE WHO IMPRISONS, THE ONE WHO IS THE ONE, BLAH, BLAH.
OKAY, SO, THE NEW ORDER. POLITICS. WHAT'S THAT GOT TO DO WITH US?
THEY'RE THE LAW *AND* THEY'RE THE ORDER, AMIGOS.
BUT WHY ARE THEY DOING THESE UNSPEAKABLE THINGS TO *KIDS*?
BECAUSE WE TALK BACK? BECAUSE WE'RE HARD TO CONTROL? BECAUSE WE HAVE AN *IMAGINATION*? WHO KNOWS? WHY DON'T YOU ASK THE ONE WHO JUDGES...
...AT YOUR TRIAL.
TRIAL? WHAT TRIAL? WE'RE GOING TO TRIAL? FOR WHAT?
WHAM
IF YOU KEEP TALKING TO THE OTHER PRISONERS, I'LL PUT YOU ALL IN SOLITARY!
OW!

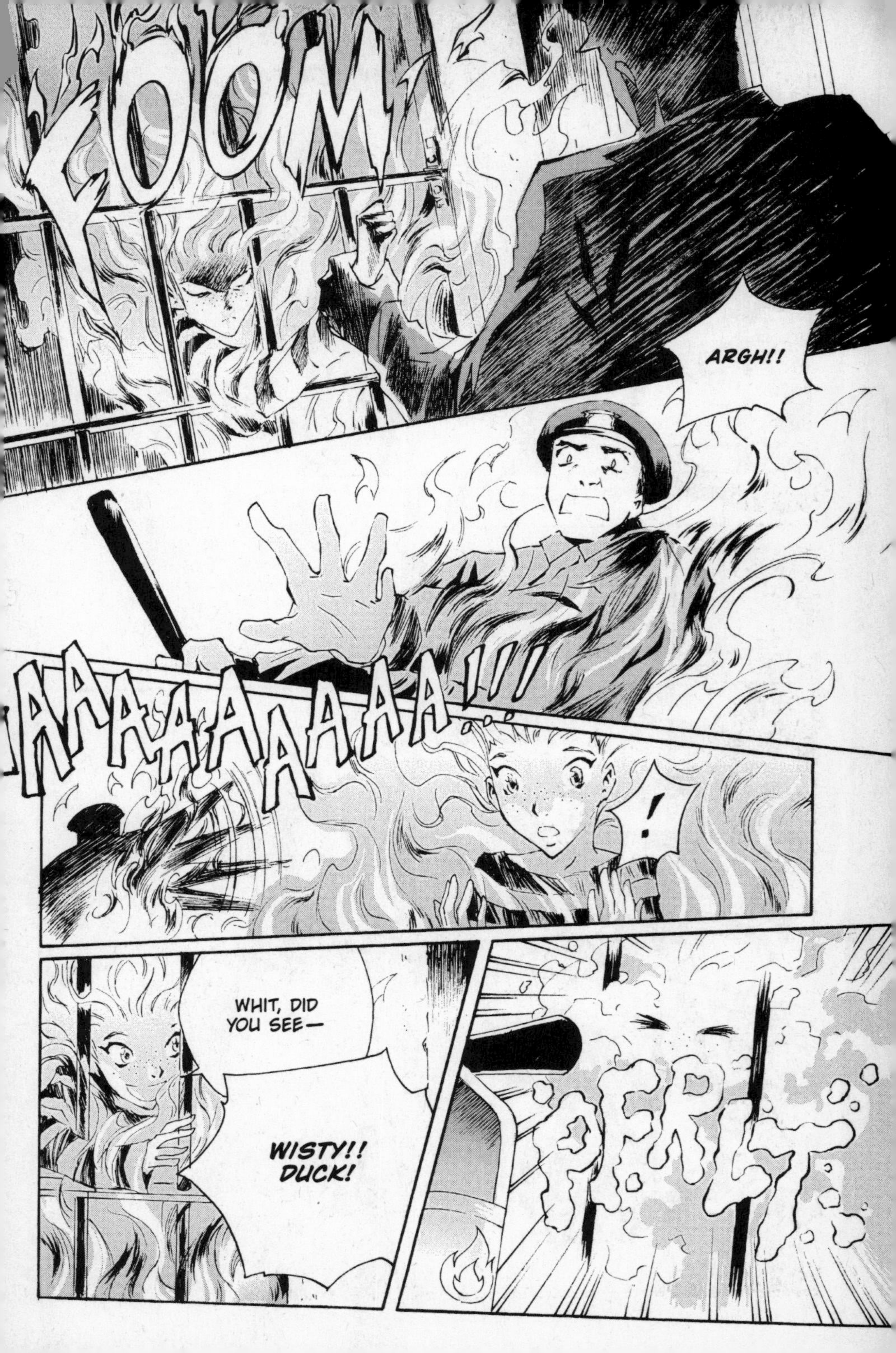
FOOM
ARGH!!
AAAAAAAA!!!
!
WHIT, DID YOU SEE—
WISTY!! DUCK!
PFRLT

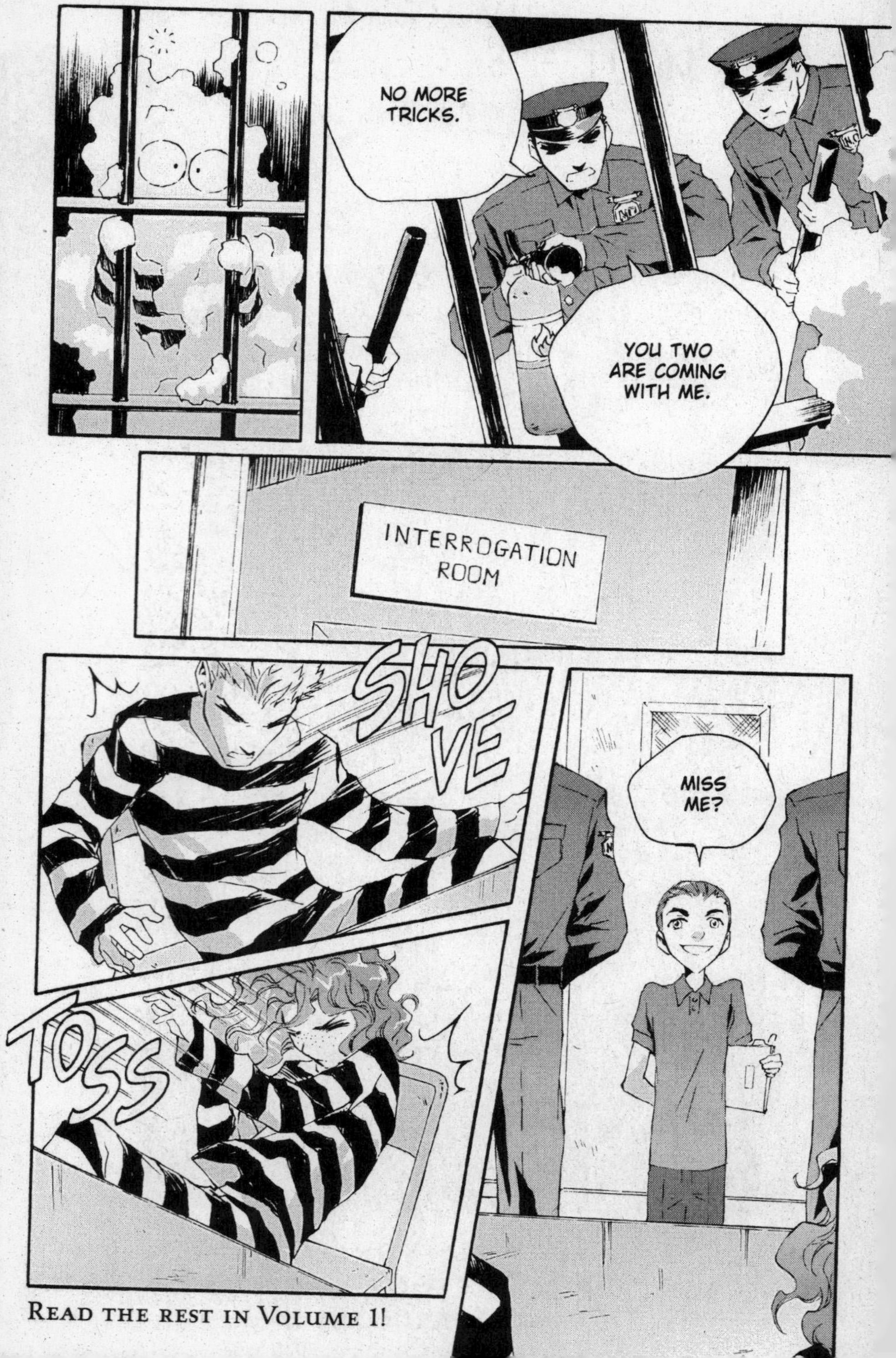
NO MORE TRICKS.
YOU TWO ARE COMING WITH ME.
INTERROGATION ROOM
SHOVE
MISS ME?
TOSS

READ THE REST IN VOLUME 1!

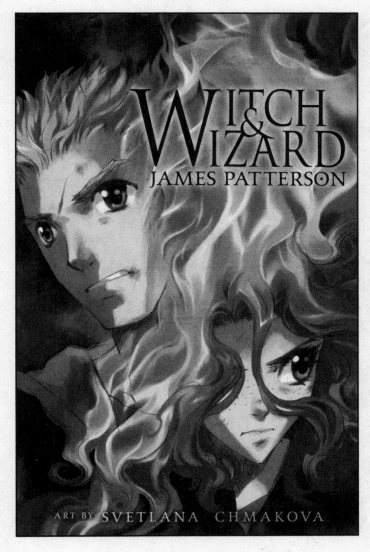

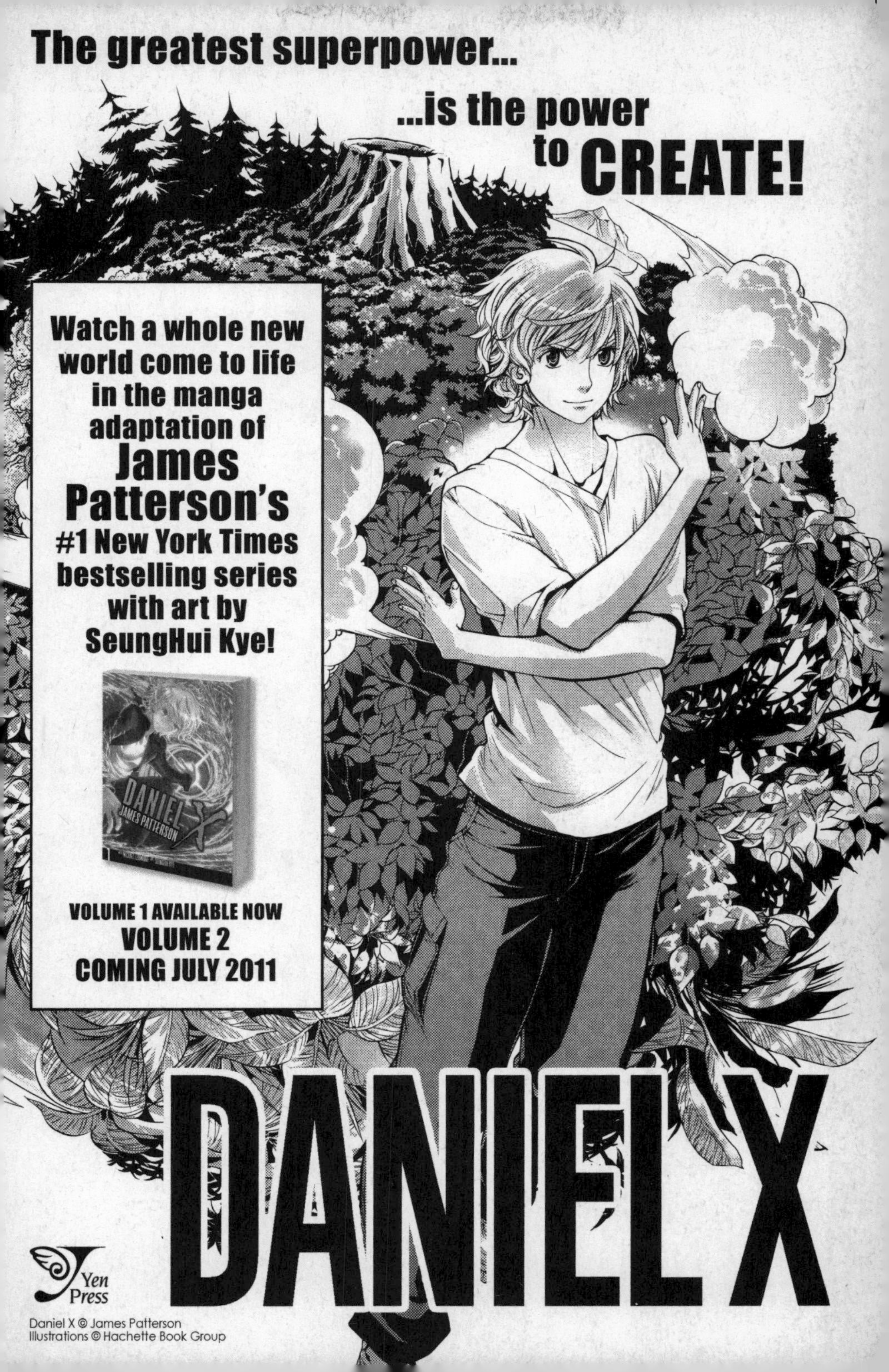
The greatest superpower...
...is the power to CREATE!
Watch a whole new world come to life in the manga adaptation of James Patterson's #1 New York Times bestselling series with art by SeungHui Kye!
DANIEL X
JAMES PATTERSON
VOLUME 1 AVAILABLE NOW
VOLUME 2 COMING JULY 2011
DANIEL X
Yen Press
Daniel X © James Patterson
Illustrations © Hachette Book Group

READ THE BOOKS THAT STARTED IT ALL

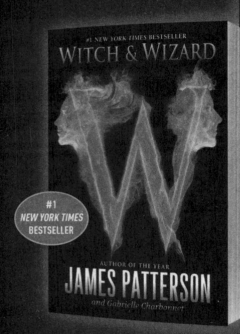

#1 NEW YORK TIMES BESTSELLER

WITCH & WIZARD

#1 NEW YORK TIMES BESTSELLER

AUTHOR OF THE YEAR

JAMES PATTERSON

and Gabrielle Charbonnet

Available Now in Paperback

WITCH & WIZARD

THE GIFT

#1 NEW YORK TIMES BESTSELLER

JAMES PATTERSON

and Ned Rust

NEW! Now Available in Hardcover

Look for *WITCH & WIZARD: THE FIRE* coming in 2011.

"This is the story I was born to tell. Read on, while you still can."
—James Patterson

DON'T WAIT FOR THE MOVIE. READ THEM NOW.

WWW.WITCHANDWIZARD.COM

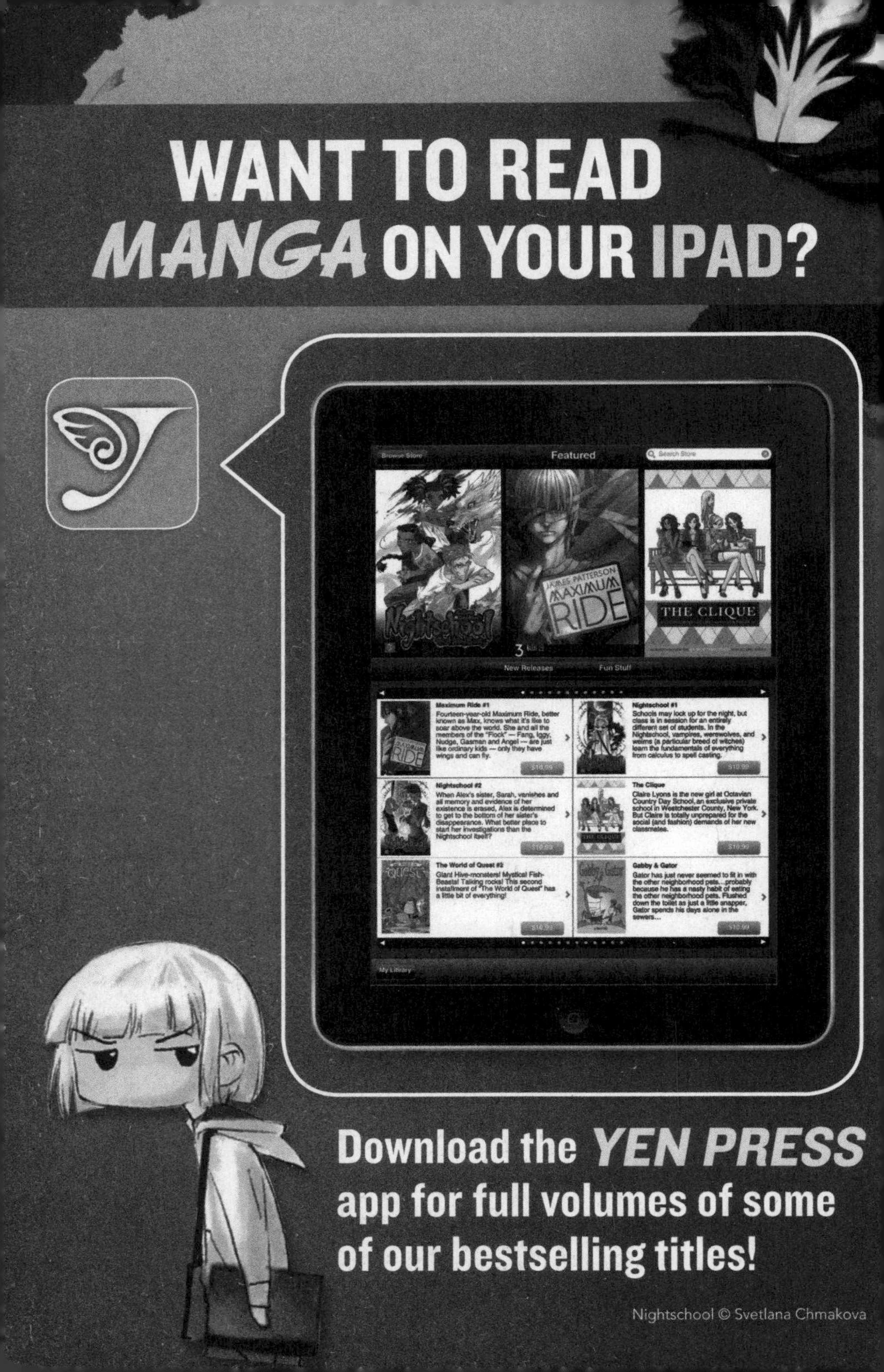
WANT TO READ
MANGA ON YOUR IPAD?
Browse Store
Featured
Search Store
Nightschool
JAMES PATTERSON
MAXIMUM RIDE
3
THE CLIQUE
New Releases
Fun Stuff
Maximum Ride #1
Fourteen-year-old Maximum Ride, better known as Max, knows what it's like to soar above the world. She and all the members of the "Flock" — Fang, Iggy, Nudge, Gasman and Angel — are just like ordinary kids — only they have wings and can fly.
$10.99
Nightschool #1
Schools may lock up for the night, but class is in session for an entirely different set of students. In the Nightschool, vampires, werewolves, and weirns (a particular breed of witches) learn the fundamentals of everything from calculus to spell casting.
$10.99
Nightschool #2
When Alex's sister, Sarah, vanishes and all memory and evidence of her existence is erased, Alex is determined to get to the bottom of her sister's disappearance. What better place to start her investigations than the Nightschool itself?
$10.99
The Clique
Claire Lyons is the new girl at Octavian Country Day School, an exclusive private school in Westchester County, New York. But Claire is totally unprepared for the social (and fashion) demands of her new classmates.
$10.99
The World of Quest #2
Giant Hive-monsters! Mystical Fish-Beasts! Talking rocks! This second installment of "The World of Quest" has a little bit of everything!
$10.99
Gabby & Gator
Gator has just never seemed to fit in with the other neighborhood pets...probably because he has a nasty habit of eating the other neighborhood pets. Flushed down the toilet as just a little snapper, Gator spends his days alone in the sewers...
$10.99
My Library
Download the YEN PRESS app for full volumes of some of our bestselling titles!
Nightschool © Svetlana Chmakova

MAXIMUM RIDE: THE MANGA ④

JAMES PATTERSON
& NaRae Lee

Adaptation and Illustration: NaRae Lee
Background assistant: MunJoo Cho

Lettering: JuYoun Lee

MAXIMUM RIDE, THE MANGA, Vol. 4 © 2011 by James Patterson

Illustrations © 2011 Hachette Book Group, Inc.

Yen Press
Hachette Book Group
237 Park Avenue, New York, NY 10017

www.HachetteBookGroup.com
www.YenPress.com

Yen Press is an imprint of Hachette Book Group, Inc. The Yen Press name and logo are trademarks of Hachette Book Group, Inc.

First Yen Press Edition: April 2011

ISBN: 978-0-7595-2970-0

10 9 8 7 6 5 4

BVG

Printed in the United States of America